Living Ideology in Cuba

Katherine A. Gordy demonstrates how the Cuban state and its people engage in an ongoing negotiation that produces a "living ideology." In contrast to official slogans and fiats, Cuba's living ideology is a decentralized phenomenon, continually adapting, informing, and responding to daily life, without losing sight of the fundamental principles of socioeconomic equality, unified leadership, and inclusive nationalism.

Tracing Cuba's ideological history, Gordy first looks at the ways in which the 19th century wars of independence and the 1959 revolution were used as the basis for both challenging and legitimizing Cuban socialism. Following the embrace of a socialist ideology in the 1960s, state policies of the 1970s became more accommodating of market imperatives, while still framing policies in terms of principles articulated by Che Guevara and Karl Marx. In the 1990s, the Cuban people themselves pushed back against free market economic reforms, reasserting the value of socioeconomic equality. Gordy also examines ideological debates among intellectuals, from the controversy sparked by Fidel Castro's "Words to the Intellectuals" speech to the demand in the 1990s for a separation between academia and the state—not to safeguard academia from politics, but to ensure that academics as such could contribute to the political dialogue.

Katherine A. Gordy is Associate Professor of Political Science at San Francisco State University.

Living Ideology in Cuba

Socialism in Principle and Practice

Katherine A. Gordy

University of Michigan Press
Ann Arbor

Copyright © 2015 by Katherine A. Gordy
All rights reserved

This book may not be reproduced, in whole or in part, including illustrations, in any form (beyond that copying permitted by Sections 107 and 108 of the U.S. Copyright Law and except by reviewers for the public press), without written permission from the publisher.

Published in the United States of America by the
University of Michigan Press
Manufactured in the United States of America
♾ Printed on acid-free paper

2018   2017   2016   2015   4   3   2   1

A CIP catalog record for this book is available from the British Library.

Library of Congress Cataloging-in-Publication Data

Gordy, Katherine A.
    Living ideology in Cuba : socialism in principle and practice / Katherine A. Gordy.
       pages   cm
    Includes bibliographical references and index.
    ISBN 978-0-472-07261-3 (hardcover : alk. paper) — ISBN 978-0-472-05261-5 (pbk. : alk. paper) — ISBN 978-0-472-12102-1 (ebook)
    1. Socialism—Cuba.   2. Political culture—Cuba.   3. Cuba—Social conditions—1959–1990.   4. Cuba—Social conditions—1990–   I. Title.

HX158.5.G67   2015
335.43′47—dc23

2014044830

All photographs by the author.

For Areta Inés

Contents

Acknowledgments ix

List of Abbreviations xi

INTRODUCTION. Spheres and Principles: Theorizing Cuban Socialism 1

1 Whose Revolution? Making Ideology, Making History 27

2 Words and Intellectuals: Cultural Production in Revolutionary Times 61

3 What Would Che Say? Making the Market Socialist 88

4 Political Unity and Spheres of Difference: Social Scientists and Censorship in the 1990s 121

5 "Sales + Economy + Efficiency = Revolution"? 157

CONCLUSION. Another View of Ideology: Cuba and Beyond 192

Notes 213

Bibliography 255

Index 275

Acknowledgments

I write these acknowledgments on the eve of returning to Cuba once again. Each trip is always a chance to learn more and to find confirmation that this book, on which I have worked for so many years, will simply never be complete. Each trip also reminds me of the tremendous gratitude I have for the help of so many people in Cuba, some of whom no longer reside on the island and some of whose names I have since forgotten or never knew. I owe great thanks to many Cuban academics and intellectuals, who gave me their time and insights. They include Aurelio Alonso, Desiderio Navarro, Santiago Benítez, Haroldo Dilla, Mayra Espina, Juan Valdés, Carlos Alzuguray, Rafael Hernández, and Pedro Monreal. I also owe thanks to Jorge Luis Acanda and the Department of Philosophy and History at the University of Havana, where I did an independent study. Sergio and Roma Quimper provided me with housing and conversation for many of my visits to Havana. Ariel Arias and Janet Acosta, whom I first came to know in Havana, were and continue to be honest and true friends as well as sources of much insight and knowledge. Ariel's photo graces the cover of this book. Nilda and Guelo Machado have given me a home in Cuba.

This project, while greatly transformed, began as a PhD dissertation for the Department of Government at Cornell University. I am grateful to Maria Cristina García, Susan Buck-Morss, and Isaac Kramnick for their patience, guidance, and insight through the various stages of what was an eclectic and unconventional project, especially for a political theorist.

At San Francisco State University, where I now teach, I have received invaluable institutional and collegial support. A Presidential Award for Professional Development in the spring of 2011 provided me with much needed time off from teaching to focus on the manuscript. Warm, compassionate, and brilliant colleagues in the Department of Political Science have given me an excellent environment in which to finish the book. Special thanks to Aaron Belkin, Francis Neely, Nicole Watts, Amita Shastri, and Jason McDaniel. I am indebted to my fellow political theorist in the department, James Martel, whose intellectual and emotional support throughout the progress of the manuscript was unflagging.

Outside of SFSU, several colleagues read and commented upon the entire manuscript. They include Keally McBride, Sujatha Fernandes, Antoni Kapcia, and Juliet Hooker. I am particularly grateful to Megan Thomas and James Martel, who read and commented upon multiple manuscript drafts. Others who read and commented on chapters include Mark Anderson, Banu Bargu, Ximena Briceno, Sarah Burgess, Raúl A. Fernández, Deirdre de la Cruz, Marina Gold, Lisa Maya Knauer, Shaianne Osterreich, Jade Larissa Schiff, and Vanita Seth.

My editor, Melody Herr, along with Susan Cronin, Kevin Rennells, and Jillian Downey at the University of Michigan Press, have been wonderful to work with and I am grateful for their work putting this book together. An earlier version of chapter 5 was published in *Public Culture*. I thank Duke University Press and the editors and reviewers of this journal for their feedback.

Many friends deserve acknowledgement: Megan Thomas, Clem Fatovic, Juliet Hooker, and Olena Prokopovych studied with me at Cornell and continue to be wonderful friends and colleagues. I also wish to express my gratitude to Saskia Grooms, Jay D'Ercola, Sarra Brill, Shaianne Osterreich, Matthew Rudolph, and Johanna Westeson. Finally, thanks to my parents, Alice Adams and Bill Gordy, and to Javier Machado. This book is dedicated to our daughter Areta Inés.

Abbreviations

CC	Central Committee
CEA	Center for the Study of America
CMEA	Council for Mutual Economic Assistance
CNA	*Cuadernos de Nuestra América*
FMC	Federation of Cuban Women
JUCEPLAN	Central Planning Board
OPP	Organs of Popular Power
PCC	Cuban Communist Party
PSP	Popular Socialist Party
SDPE	System of Management and Planning of the Economy
UNEAC	Union of Cuban Writers and Artists

Introduction

Spheres and Principles

Theorizing Cuban Socialism

This is a book about how Cubans theorize and live Cuban socialism. It also proposes a new way to study ideologies as living and lived, and as essential, rather than detrimental, to politics. In this sense, Cuba appears as a difficult case because both supporters and critics of Cuban socialism tend to associate its ideology with the Cuban state. Studies of ideology, particularly in socialist or formerly socialist states, frequently treat ideology as a curtain that state power hides behind and that loses its meaning once its mechanism is revealed. However, I argue here, that while not all Cubans espouse socialist ideology and other ideologies compete fiercely with it, Cuban socialism is not, as many think, a static ideology monopolized by the Cuban state or an imitation of other 20th-century socialisms. It is articulated in different idioms and in different spheres of Cuban society, and all these articulations share common principles, such as socioeconomic equality, inclusive nationalism, and political unity, that have roots in 19th-century discourse and practice. Cuban socialist ideology draws upon these principles indigenous to Cuban political culture and organizes them in a manner that brings socialistic elements of the principles to the fore. For instance, the principle of socioeconomic equality, key for many 19th-century independence leaders seeking to unify Cubans against the Spanish, took on a deeper meaning with the 1959 revolution, and came to be an end in and of itself rather than a means to political unity.

Examples and articulations of Cuban socialism can be found not just in the speeches and proclamations of the Cuban leadership, but also in newspapers, academic publications, art, music, and popular expressions. Drawing on written texts supplemented with ethnographic evidence gathered during many extended visits to Cuba between 1996 and 2011, this book traces the interrelations between what I identify as different "spheres" of Cuban political thought—political doctrine (official sphere), political theory (academic sphere), and daily practice (popular sphere).[1] These divisions among different forms of political thought are blurred and complicated by the fact that all three spheres invoke principles of socioeconomic equality, political unity, and inclusive nationalism as evidence of a particular and uniquely Cuban version of socialism. Each sphere has arranged these principles differently at particular historical junctures. These arrangements can be distinguished on the basis of their privileging of certain principles over others. This leads, in turn, to slight differences in the meaning of the individual principles, which, to use the language of political theorist Michael Freeden, "acquire meaning not only through accumulative traditions of discourse . . . but also by means of their particular structural position within a configuration of other political concepts."[2] The Cuban leadership or official sphere, for instance, has often defined political unity as unified leadership and privileged unified leadership over socioeconomic equality, insisting the former is a condition for the latter. Those in the academic and popular spheres have called this equation into question, linking political unity more closely to inclusive nationalism, pointing to the dangerous possibility that socioeconomic equality can be compromised by the leadership's call for political unity. In these various instances, the meanings of individual principles, however, are not limitless, nor are the permutations of the various principles infinite: there is a continuity and coherence to Cuban socialism as a living ideology.

An awareness of how the "parts" of Cuban socialist ideology, or what I call principles, fit together is particularly significant for discussions of contemporary (and a post-Fidel, post–Raúl Castro) Cuba. These discussions are frequently dominated by inaccurate assumptions about the flimsiness of the Cuban system or equally misguided beliefs that dissent comes only from outside of Cuba or the revolutionary tradition. They ignore the resilience of Cuban socialist ideology, which is not inextricably bound up with the fate of Fidel or Raúl Castro. By 2014, it appeared that the future of Cuban socialism was more uncertain than ever, given the government's shift away from many of the elements of its socialist legacy. If Cuba survives as some sort of socialist state, however, it will be because of socialist ideology's constant renegotiation. If it does not survive, a way of thinking and living, and not simply an authoritarian dogma, will be lost. The purpose of this book is to recognize and recuperate this lived socialist ideology and to examine one particularly rich and dense fabric of ideological negotiation as a way to think further about ideology (and the way it can be lived) more generally.

An awareness of the principles of Cuban socialism, then, is also significant for studies of ideology, since the discordant and harmonious relationship of these principles within the various spheres of Cuban society suggests that the boundaries between politics, ideology, and political theorizing are often quite porous, both conceptually and practically. A study of these specific negotiations of socialist ideology provides an occasion to explore ideologies as, in the words of Freeden, "forms of political thought that provide important direct access to comprehending the formation and nature of political theory, its richness, varieties and subtlety."[3] The explicitly ideological nature of public and private discourse in Cuba is not an obstacle to social science research but, rather, is an asset. Ideology gives meaning to lived experiences: it provides the structure, the narrative, and the coherence of Cuban ways of living. At the same time, it is always necessarily insufficient and must always be adjusted in light of past, present, and future history.

It is common for those advocating for an objective assessment of the Cuban Revolution to argue that the country is "neither heaven nor hell." The assumption behind this tidy truism is that only those accounts that push ideology to the side can accurately describe the meaning, processes, failures, and successes of the Cuban Revolution. However, not only is it impossible to push ideology to the side, but a fair assessment of Cuba requires an understanding of how ideology functions both in Cuba and in Cuban studies. This understanding, in turn, teaches us about ideology and politics in their most general senses. Given that political ideologies are necessarily defined by their relationship to political practice, they are best studied vis-à-vis their concrete manifestations.

It is important not to underrate the limitations on freedom of expression, press, and organization in Cuba. It is also important not to lump Cubans into the simplistic categories of active, thinking opponents to the system, fearful citizens of a totalitarian state, or fanatical hardline Communist Party elites. Such categories do not accurately describe the ways in which the various Cuban reactions to their political system reflect a genuine conflict between the goals and measures of the revolution as well as an acute awareness of how politics affects both principles and practices.

The predominance and visibility of *political* ideology in everyday life is often offered as proof that Cuban socialism exists only as dogma. However, because political ideology is intrinsic to Cuban life, even critiques of official policy use principles of Cuban socialism to articulate their grievances. Embattled intellectuals of a Cuban academic think tank disbanded by the Party in 1996 (the subject of chapter 4) defended themselves with terms shared with their Central Committee critics. Not every Cuban complaining on the street or in song about daily living conditions is a convert to neoliberalism (the subject of chapter 5). Their critiques pose a challenge not only to the leadership, which believes itself the only true protector of Cuban socialism, but also to disciplines that reduce these articulations to dogma, repeated by victims of an authoritarian state, or, conversely, untheorized authentic experience, which supposedly speaks for itself against imposed ideologies.

The Cuban government views claims of neutrality or autonomy with suspicion; it measures the value of the mass media, education, academic research, intellectual production, work, and, to some degree, art, according to their contribution to the revolution's ideological struggle. While the Cuban government's insistence that one is either for or against the revolution might seem to stifle discussion, the political situation of Cuba constantly pushes tensions between means and ends, principles and practice, into high relief. Cubans, whether they be government ministers, physics professors, dancers, bakers, mechanics, or athletes, cannot escape from politics and the language of ideology in which such a politics operates. Cubans are always aware of political choices, even if they themselves cannot always make them as they wish. To many, both on and off the island, this is an oppressive curse. But this curse also produces rich material for political theory, because Cuban thinking about the meaning of socialism is not just the practice of politicians or academics. It is an everyday practice. Tensions produced by global capitalism and by state socialism come to the fore empirically and at the level of public and private discourse.

Rather than separating the lived empirical experience of Cuba and the ideology of socialism in Cuba into two separate sources or foci of study, this book focuses on the dynamic relationship between the two. Looking at the interaction between economic-social policy of Cuba and Cuban socialist ideology enriches the larger ideological-political debate on existing socialism. It does not attempt to provide a specific alternative model of economic development for every country in the global South. An examination of the interaction between policy and ideology demonstrates the larger problematic in Marxist theory of how the application of socialist models forces a reinterpretation of Marxist theory itself rather than a resignation to liberalism as the only viable option.

It is a historical fact that many countries and movements found in Marxism both a tool of criticism and a model for an alternative society. To use Marxism was also to transform it. Its application in light of specific contexts and histories showed that the practice of Marxist politics was far from monolithic. These different Marxist politics, in turn, led to theoretical shifts within Marxism itself. Disposing of certain epistemological claims of Marxism, such as historical materialism and class essentialism, need not imply that the experiences of socialist countries and the theorizing by those living in those countries should be discarded. It also should not mean that Marxism's only role in the 21st century is as a critique of capitalism. The widespread belief that socialism has failed should not serve as the occasion to ignore the lessons of these countries, allowing their significant histories to be swallowed up by the larger neoliberal triumphalist narrative. Such a move fails to recognize that the Cuban Revolution itself called into question, in its practice, both Marxist stageism and class essentialism, even if at times, some versions of official discourse and practice espoused them.

The method of this book could be called Marxist in the sense that the concrete case of Cuba does not illustrate political theory, but changes it, augmenting our very understanding of how theory needs to be studied. Rather than beginning with a specific theory and testing its validity using the Cuban case, the method here involves a more dialectical approach whereby initial theories and frameworks are constantly modified in light of the ways that Cuban socialism is articulated and practiced.

Seeing the process of reinterpretation of Marxist theory requires a shift in terms. Thus, the particular socialist model itself must inform the conceptual categories used to investigate the meaning, practice, and study of Cuban socialism. For this reason, my time in Cuba was fundamental to the development of this project.

The Development of the Project

My time in Cuba led me to the conclusion that it was not possible to judge Cuban socialism on the basis of what might be considered its founding texts alone. The theme of this book—how political thought is mobilized in politics—requires a study of how the different principles that constitute an ideology are experienced and lived in different social spheres. The mobilization of political thought is particularly remarkable in times of economic, political, and social transformation, such as those that Cuba went through in the 1990s.

I became interested in Cuban socialist ideology, not by reading the texts of Che Guevara and Fidel Castro, but because I was there at a time of dramatic change, which made me wonder about the Cuban government's ideological justifications of post-Soviet economic policies that challenged Cuba's egalitarian project. I was interested in Cuba not because it was where Fidel Castro was from or the place where Che Guevara first participated in revolution nor because I thought it was the best or worst example of socialism, communism, authoritarianism, or radical participatory democracy. Rather, events in Cuba at a particular historical moment raised very clearly the question of how political thought was mobilized in politics. Had I focused only on the texts considered representative of Cuban socialist ideology, I would not have arrived at this question. The texts themselves might only have fostered an understanding of Cuban socialist ideology as, at best, a utopian program out of step with geopolitical realities, and, at worst, state-imposed dogma constituted primarily by a flimsy anti-imperialist nationalism.

When I first went to Cuba in December 1996, the country was beginning to pull itself out of the economic crisis known as the Special Period in Times of Peace, a phrase introduced by Fidel Castro in 1990 to describe the wartime conditions Cuba found itself in after the loss of Soviet subsidies and trade following the termination of the Soviet trading bloc in 1991.[4] Nevertheless, all the charms of Cuba that I was so prepared to reject as naive romanticism and political tourism made an impression upon me; the old cars, the beautiful colonial and modern architecture of Havana and the city's charm, the music, the enormous old movie palaces, the traces of Soviet influence, the revolutionary slogans that dominated public spaces, and the absence of American-style megastores and megamalls and corporate advertising.

Material conditions in Cuba, however, were harsh and had been even harsher in the earlier 1990s. Havana had crumbling buildings. Public transportation was unreliable and overcrowded. Children begged for chewing gum from tourists. Everyone had a story about the deprivation they suffered during the 1990s. The hustlers who attached themselves to us were on edge and scared of the police. The policy of prohibiting Cubans from entering hotels led not just to tourist apartheid, but to racial profiling as well. Yet, what was striking to me was less the clash between dream and reality (a clash upon which so many accounts of Cuba at that time depend) than that the question of how to distribute economic and political goods was constantly made explicit, both in daily life and at the level of political discourse.

During that first trip, my companions and I met with an economist at the Center for the Study of the Cuban Economy (CEEC) who described Cuba's now well-known economic free fall following the termination of the Soviet trading bloc and the measures taken to pull Cuba out of the crisis. He recounted the near collapse of the economy in 1993 (industry was operating at 15% capacity) and the slow recovery that followed. He explained how Cuba's increased reliance on remittances produced class differences that contradicted its socialist ideology. The state legalized U.S. dollars in 1993, he explained, so as to reduce the contradictions arising from the growth of the tourist sector and a small group of Cuban workers with access to foreign currency through tips. The state developed tourism because it was cheaper than industry, despite grave social repercussions, including a rise in prostitution.

The economist pointed to the tensions produced by the three kinds of property in Cuba—state owned, cooperative, and private—and to the greater effectiveness of the private form. He also said socialism came at a price. It meant that Cuba was left extremely vulnerable when the Soviet Union disappeared. It meant that the country was not eligible for loans from the International Monetary Fund and the World Bank, and that it suffered shortages in basic goods as a result of a decades-old U.S. blockade that impeded trade, not just with the United States, but with other countries as well. However, the economist also said that market liberalization of the sort carried out in Eastern Europe was not the solution to Cuba's economic woes, and he explained the rewards of socialism. Socialism meant that all felt the economic crisis of the 1990s equally. It meant that, unlike other small Caribbean countries in the region, Cuba had struggled to create an industrial infrastructure and an educated workforce. The market alone, he said, could not provide for education, worker security, and a 100% vaccination rate for Cuban children. Socialism with the market was his solution, but he ended with a key question: how much market could Cuban socialism tolerate before it was no longer socialism at all?

His question was one many Cubans, not just officials and academics, were asking at the time. It was a question that I decided I wanted to study. Specifically, I was interested in the following questions: What was Cuban socialist ideology and who defined it? To what extent could Cuban socialist ideology account for or help to make sense of the changes taking place in Cuba? How were people negotiating and making sense of socialist ideology in light of these changes? How far could the ideology itself be stretched before it was no longer socialist? And, finally, how integral was socialism itself, not just in terms of a language the people of Cuba were forced to adopt, but in terms of a shared set of values, conditions, and understandings of the world around them?

During some of my first visits to Cuba, I was often struck by the desire of visitors to find authentic Cuban voices, real Cubans, who could tell them the truth about Cuban socialism. The one time that I was in Cuba with an organized group of North Americans, healthy suspicion of officially organized trips and speakers on the part of the younger members of the group was remedied by a fanatical search to experience a nonsanitized Cuba. This nonofficial Cuba, where poverty, racism, marginalization, and police surveillance were not things of the past, came to stand for all that was authentic Cuba. I found too that individual Cubans themselves sometimes insisted that only Cubans could truly understand anything about Cuba, that they could tell foreigners how Cuba "really was." The situation became no less complicated when discussions centered on the issue of Cuban socialist ideology. Frustration with material scarcity, bureaucratic red tape, political repression, and a sense of powerlessness had become the nonofficial party line, repeated not just as an attempt to give voice to what the official line does not, but to stand in for it.

I heard the official line from many of the functionaries I met during my trips.[5] For them, Fidel Castro was the primary author of Cuban socialist ideology.[6] As a consequence, they advised me to read the official Party newspaper, *Granma,* and the texts of the Communist Party congresses, held every five years since 1975 (and less regularly since the Special Period). During our conversations, they tended to emphasize U.S. aggression toward the island and expressed suspicion toward any complaints voiced on the street and toward studies about Cuba produced abroad. The functionaries were doctrinaire at times, always conscious that they were speaking with a North American interested in studying the meaning of Cuban socialist ideology following the end of the Soviet Union. One functionary insisted that "development" was a far better term than "economic changes" to describe the economic policies of the 1990s, since the former implied a level of control that economic change did not. Yet they were also passionate about their beliefs and seemed genuinely concerned not just with convincing me of their point of view but of showing me that they lived like other Cubans (in the peso economy) and thus lived their ideology. It was impossible to discount what functionaries said entirely, even if they themselves trivialized any concerns about material shortages or political repression voiced by other Cubans.

Social scientists from various academic think tanks in Havana with whom I met were equally concerned with the language used to describe the changes taking place in Cuba.[7] They, however, were less insistent that Cuban socialism could be so easily defined or its sources so easily identified. They did not tell me to ignore Fidel Castro's speeches and other official Party documents, but neither did they suggest that Cuban socialism could be entirely encapsulated by these sources. During my initial visits to Cuba, several of these social scientists suggested that using the term "ideology" might bring problems with the authorities and make future research difficult. Ideology, they explained, was a dangerous term because the leadership was no longer quite sure what the ideology of the revolution was, given the changes it had made to its own economy, and given the global discrediting of socialism in particular and the concept of ideology more generally. As a consequence, I began using the term "principle" in my interviews and informal conversations and I found that the term gave people far greater leeway in expressing their views. It allowed those with whom I spoke, and later myself, to take seriously the ideas and concepts used to make sense of and guide the revolution without apologizing for or accepting all that has been done in the revolution's name.

While I initially adopted the term principle (*principio*) for politically strategic reasons, the term was not simply a euphemism for ideology. I found that it appeared in the writings of 19th-century Cuban political thinkers, in the speeches of Fidel Castro and other government officials, in revolutionary slogans written on walls and signs throughout the country ("We have and we will have our principles" or "Our Principles are not Negotiable"), in the official Party newspapers, in the work of postrevolutionary intellectuals, and in everyday speech (to do something "*por principio*"). The term principle appeared to imply a level of commitment and virtue that ideology did not. Thus, my political maneuvering in response to possible censorship led to greater accuracy, rather than less. It provided me with a vocabulary to examine the interaction of the different views on Cuban socialism that I encountered on the many subsequent trips. It allowed me to see how socialist ideology in Cuba was both living and lived.

Living and Lived Ideology

The title "Living Ideology" refers to Cuban socialist ideology in two senses. First, it refers to an ideology that lives because people use it and think about its meaning, even when its relationship to conspicuous facts seems tenuous. It lives because its meaning matters. Its meaning matters because the principles it defends matter and because it provides a compelling framework through which people understand the world. Second, "living ideology" refers to the actual experience of an ideology, as opposed to its existence as an abstract canon of beliefs. To live an ideology is to live *by* it, in the sense that the world in which one lives and the choices one has and makes are informed by that ideology. One lives an ideology because one lives the consequences as well as the intentions of it. Each of these two related meanings of "living ideology" merits greater elaboration, especially since it is often presumed that in Cuba, while socialist ideology lives—that is, continues to function in the realm of officialdom—it is not actually lived, except as a result of direct coercion by the state.

Cuban socialist ideology is living because it is a robust ideology constituted by a set of interrelated principles that fit together in particular ways and help to make sense of the world and guide people's actions. This definition of ideology is a political one, where the principles, and their relationship to one another, have implications for the distribution of political and economic goods in society. Politics, far from compromising ideology, provides the mechanism by which values and beliefs organize themselves into coherent frameworks known as political ideologies. Once organized as political ideologies, they come not simply to be values or beliefs, but principles. Whereas beliefs represent a faith in the way the world is or should be, and values are norms we hold dear, principles combine beliefs and values, requiring that we demonstrate commitment to them by living by them and actualizing them in the world.

One ideology is distinct from another, not just because it is constituted by a particular set of principles, but also because of the way in which those principles are organized and placed together. Thus, for instance, inclusive nationalism could be understood as a definition of what it means to be a member of the Cuban nation that is based on inclusion, rather than exclusion. *Cubanía* (Cubanness) is defined by what people have in common, rather than what distinguishes them from others. Placing inclusive nationalism together with socioeconomic equality also points to the importance of creating the conditions that facilitate a common sense of identity, so that being Cuban is not about abstract equality (we are equal because we are all Cuban) but on actual equality (we are Cuban because everyone is equal, because our lives are materially lived in a similar way, and because we share common experiences). Socioeconomic equality might be understood in relation to inclusive nationalism as a basic principle of guaranteeing all citizens health care, housing, food, and education, or it might be understood as equal opportunity. Both these meanings of socioeconomic equality have functioned in Cuba, with one dominating at different times, and in different spheres. Thus, while the principles ground ideology as it negotiates particular historical and political contexts, their meaning takes on different connotations depending on how they are placed together. Their meaning, however, is deep enough that they cannot be simply applied to any situation, nor can they be put back together as a random laundry list. The relationship between the principles is not fixed, but it is also not infinitely elastic because the principles take on different meanings depending on how they are placed together.

What makes an ideology more than a list of disparate values and thus successful, as Antonio Gramsci argued, is its ability to make sense of lived conditions. A critique of a particular ideology, therefore, must show that its categories and the way that they are linked together exclude other forms of thought that would expose other elements of that same social reality; not that the ideology is false in the sense of failing to correspond directly to concrete conditions. For instance, to draw on Marxist theory, bourgeois political economy is not a set of lies.[8] Rather, it is a framework that allows us to see one level of economic activity (the level of exchange and the market that is already more easily grasped because it is public and visible), while occluding another (the level of production, hidden behind factory walls or today, in other countries). A commodity has exchange value because it *can* be exchanged for another object that is qualitatively different, but this exchange functions simultaneously to occlude the fact that this same object is on the market in the first place because of labor. To see the level of production, however, requires not the (false) abandonment of ideology, but rather the adoption of a different ideology that allows us to see what was previously excluded. In this sense, ideology is a framework expressed through language that serves to shed light on the world and the possibilities and considerations it presents. It proposes alternatives, and forecloses others. It makes visible one set of facts, while occluding or silencing others. Without ideology, one cannot make any political judgments. In this sense, Cuba is no different than anyplace else.

An ideology lives because it is constituted by a shared set of principles and functions to make sense of and give meaning to past, present, and future.[9] Just as history is produced by selecting and emphasizing certain facts from the past in order to construct a coherent narrative, so too does ideology gain meaning by selecting from past events, which in turn function to legitimate that ideology and the history out of which the ideology is constructed. The ideology that is constructed out of past events serves to explain that same past, and specifically the extent to which the goals of that ideology were realized, what dilemmas the group attempting to achieve the goals confronted, and why these goals were and were not realized. Ideology also functions to guide present and future actions, not just in terms of what the goals of those espousing that ideology should be, but in terms of means as well. The goals of a particular ideology cannot be separated, practically or theoretically, from the means by which they are realized.

In Cuba, the life of socialist ideology depends not solely on the Cuban state's espousal of it as its official ideology, or even on the fact that the state's version of this ideology is disseminated and dominates in officially sanctioned public discourse (particularly in the mass media) and in the ideological state apparatuses. Its life has depended as much on those who have refused to allow the state to monopolize the meaning of Cuban socialism, either by directly challenging the state's interpretation or by rearticulating the ideology in ways that appear on the surface to be nonpolitical. This does not mean that the state's version of Cuban socialism has been static or always necessarily opposed to these other versions. The Cuban leadership is itself made up of a variety of currents or competing discourses, and each current has had to justify and explain past, present, and future policies in light of what is an overarching shared ideology and in light of changing internal and external conditions. All those within the leadership, however, have had to negotiate and articulate this ideology under a different set of circumstances than other Cuban citizens, whose negotiations are influenced by the conditions and spheres in which they operate. The same Cuban individual may travel between these different spheres, articulating socialist ideology in an idiom specific to that sphere. In this sense, the concept of *doble-moral* (double morality), used to describe the situation of Cubans who say one thing and do another, does not do justice to the various ideological modes in which those in Cuba operate because it ignores the ways behavior is determined not only by direct censorship but by the material and social requirements of specific spheres.

This brings us to the second meaning of "living ideology," as the lived experience of socialism. Cubans live Cuban socialism because it is a one-party state ruled by the Communist Party, the economy is centrally planned, and government policies have often, but not always, been guided by socialist principles, and because the state has a monopoly on the means of communication. They live it because it has become hegemonic.[10] Yet there is also another way in which Cubans live socialism. Any living ideology must be lived, but not in the sense that those living that ideology simply adopt or reject it, conforming to its strictures or resisting them. Rather, ideology emerges out of material practices, which give the ideology meaning and substance, and in turn guide those same practices. Ideology produces its subjects and is produced by them. In this dynamic, both are changed. The stark opposition between theory and practice does not capture this meaning of "living ideology." No ideology could survive such a rigorous demand to conform entirely to the facts or to behavior at all times. The more counterhegemonic an ideology is, the harder it will be for it to conform to, or explain, all practices, if only because those practices are determined by the counterhegemonic ideology. Even if socialist ideology is hegemonic at the national level in Cuba, it continues to be counterhegemonic at the international level. Living ideology is thus not simply a question of behaving in accordance with ideological commandments imposed either from some higher authority or from a worldview adopted wholesale. Rather, living ideology involves both believing in the fundamental value of the core principles that constitute that ideology and using that ideology as a way to navigate sets of circumstance that may or may not lend themselves to the actualization of the central principles of that ideology. One always sees the world through the lens of a particular ideology, but this makes one aware that the world does not conform entirely to the blueprint proposed by that ideology. To live an ideology is both to negotiate a world where choices are not entirely determined by that ideology, and also to reconceptualize that ideology as one encounters particular sets of conditions.

The Value of "Ideology"

This book asks readers to suspend conventional understandings of the ideology/truth relationship. It asks positivists, who juxtapose ideology to the truth, and poststructuralists, who see ideology and truth as two sides of the same positivist coin, to rethink the meaning of ideology. While the term "ideology" enjoys a long history in political theory, contemporary political theory, from poststructuralism to post-Marxism, has tended to discard ideology along with economic determinism, class reductionism, and other essentialisms that are seen to have led to the totalitarianism of existing socialisms. Much of this suspicion of the term ideology takes its cue from Michel Foucault, who argued that the problem with the notion of ideology was threefold: it presumed a truth against which an ideology could be measured; it presumed a subject who adopted or rejected an ideology, and it presumed an object that determined an ideology.[11] Ideology, in short, was plagued by Marxist positivism and crude materialism. In place of ideology, Foucault called for the term "discourse," whose study involved not assessing its truth or falsity, but rather its effects. The advantage of this emphasis on discursive practices is that it challenges the boundaries of what constitutes the political. This is useful in the context of Cuba, where politics is not necessarily expressed through elections, opinion polls, or public protest. The risk of this expansive view, however, is that everything can be reduced to a political expression or veiled dissent. For instance, while the common refrain "no es fácil" (it isn't easy) often refers to the difficulties of daily life, it is not always necessarily a political statement in Cuba. Moreover, Foucault's framework can be so totalizing that it precludes the possibility of talking about alternative, or perhaps desirable, sets of principles used to organize one's life. The notion of a political preference has little place in his political theory. In the case of Cuba, a totalizing view like that of Foucault facilitates equating Cuban socialism either with totalitarianism or with a worldview that the Cuban (colonial) subject is not aware of espousing or rejecting—even as one resists, one is incorporated in. Foucault's analysis, which emerged from careful attention to historical shifts and to the conditions that made certain ways of thinking possible (epistemes), can be easily put to ideological ends to illustrate the total absence of agency in nonliberal systems. This would be a disservice to Foucault's own work, which questioned the myth of the timeless, natural, and free individual under liberal and nonliberal systems alike. Using Foucault to show that agency disappears due to the totalitarianism of the Cuban state implies incorrectly that total agency exists outside of "totalitarianism" in liberal democracies.

Abandoning the term ideology has not released us from the dogmatism or stifling universalism with which it is currently associated. Instead, it leaves us without the method of ideological critique. Ideology critiques can serve constructive as well as deconstructive purposes. They have long served as correctives to any totalizing narrative, and have done well at questioning capitalist and socialist triumphalism and exposing the assumptions upon which it is based. The term ideology, particularly in the context of nonliberal states, gives us a way to move beyond facile stories of repression or liberation, just as Foucault's work did.[12]

Ideology may be a far more Foucauldian term than Foucault and his followers acknowledge. Far from presuming the truth, an ideology can be understood as a kind of episteme, in that it is self-contained and historically contingent. Ideologies are related to material conditions in that they make them intelligible, but are not wholly determined by them. Like discourses, they produce subjectivities, which then interact with these same ideologies. Louis Althusser famously describes the process of interpellation as the ideological formation of subjectivity. For Althusser, "the category of the subject is only constitutive of all ideology insofar as all ideology has the function (which defines it) of 'constituting' concrete individuals as subjects."[13] There is no such thing, for Althusser, as a preexisting subject who creates, adopts, and acts upon ideologies. Rather, ideologies could be said to actualize or concretize the abstract category of the subject who then perpetuates that ideology via a variety of social practices.

The work of Marxists like Antonio Gramsci and José Carlos Mariátegui, however, suggests that the system is not quite so closed. Ideology, they argue, evolves through political action and acquires legitimacy because it helps people to make sense of their lived (and not simply their material) conditions. Unlike the terms "episteme" or "discourse," however, ideology is a more explicitly political term that is directly related to the distribution of political and economic goods and power. As Terry Eagleton notes, to exchange ideology for discourse "may be to relinquish too quickly a useful distinction between those power struggles that are somehow central to a whole form of social life, and those that are not."[14]

Ideology is also a useful term for those wishing to ground the study of political theory in political practice, rather than isolating political theory to an enclave concerned only with textual analysis and certain themes and questions. Recent work in political theory has increasingly blurred the boundaries between area-based research in comparative politics and the study of political theory, particularly on topics such as sovereignty, multiculturalism, postcolonial studies, social movements, and the meaning of democracy and civil society in non-Western and/or nonliberal democratic contexts.[15] This interdisciplinary approach, which I, with others, call comparative political theory, does not represent an abandonment of political theory as a field concerned with examining and challenging ideological and epistemological assumptions, and proposing new conceptual formulations and frameworks with which to reveal what may not be immediately apparent. Rather, it represents a desire to bring theory back into political science, not as formal modeling or as a theory to be tested, but rather as a tradition that resists the division between theory as the realm of ideas and science as the realm of facts. The field of comparative political theory has placed front and center the problem of how to avoid privileging the questions, themes, and mediums of Western political thought, such that only those non-Western expression of political theory that speak to the West are considered.[16]

The concept of ideology is one way to approach this problem, since it allows us to look for political thought, not just in texts that conform to the dictates of the canon of Western political theory, but in newspapers, government speeches, art, music, and other forms of popular expression. In this respect, this book responds to Michael Freeden's call to study ideologies as forms of political theory. Freeden argues that the division between ideology and political philosophy is not as clear as political philosophers would like to believe since "both are, as a form of political thinking, shaped from political concepts and their interrelationships."[17] The approach to studying ideology here draws on Freeden's morphological method. However, the book also argues that the methodological framework for studying a particular situated ideology should emerge from the context in which the ideology operates. As I argued earlier, fieldwork was essential to the development of the framework of spheres and principles that I then used to study Cuban socialist ideology. The book, then, also reminds those who see ideology as an important facet of political life to consider the ways in which the opposition between ideology and truth can reassert itself via other types of analytic categories and oppositions such as those between principle and opportunism, coercion and consent, idealism and pragmatism, or, most recently, between state and civil society. Such oppositions unravel on the ground.

Civil Society and Fetishizing Opposition

Recent work focusing on how ideology is negotiated in Cuba has tended to do so through the lens of civil society and culture. There is much disagreement as to whether civil society exists in Cuba and, if so, who or what constitutes it. The Cuban government has long maintained that Cuban civil society is made of up the mass organizations established in the 1960s as a way of mobilizing Cuban workers, students, women, farmers, and Cubans in general. These mass organizations were appealing to many Cubans who were sick of the corruption of the pre-1959 political system and eager to participate in the social and economic development projects, such as the literacy campaign, that the newly triumphant revolution was embarking upon.[18] While providing important services to the Cuban population, however, these organizations also slowly turned into mechanisms of state control.[19] In spite of their inclusive nature and power to mobilize large portions of the population, mass organizations tended to serve as conveyor belts for policy dictated by the leadership, while discussions within mass organizations rarely influenced government policies.[20]

Academic studies tend to be more critical of the Cuban government's definition, although there is diversity within this literature. In keeping with the classical view of civil society, from social contract theory to the Hegelian/Marxist tradition, some studies of Cuban civil society view it as dependent upon or related to the state.[21] In this view, both legal and illegal nongovernmental organizations in Cuba—from think tanks to dissident organizations—constitute civil society. Other studies, influenced by the literature on countries that transitioned from centrally planned economies and one-party states to liberal democracies and free market economies, equate the growth of civil society with the establishment of market institutions and the expansion of economic and political activities carried out independently of the state, and often in opposition to it.[22] Often those individuals or organizations with left ideologies are not included in the discussion. Civil society, within this framework, exists in Cuba in spite of, rather than because of, the state. When these studies recognize civil society as a political sphere, they see it as (inappropriately, unjustly, and tyrannically) politicized as socialist, and therefore not true civil society, or they see a civil society not permitting politics, understood as opposition to socialism, and therefore not true civil society. In this way, the term "civil society," like the term "ideology," is used ideologically, in the sense that it is often defined by its content and according to the political system in which it exists. Civil society is valorized because of what it opposes (socialism), rather than because civil society is understood *always* as a site of political participation that makes demands upon and challenges the state.

This is a problem analytically. Once opposition is fetishized in this way, the degree to which groups opposed to the state exist and operate is the measure of civil society, rather than the diversity of actors within political society and the degree to which groups represent the concerns of people within Cuban society and work to achieve certain goals. As Bert Hoffman notes:

> A concept of civil society, which *a priori* defines it as political opposition to the system remains analytically unconvincing. Politically, it hardly promotes the domestic pluralization of Cuban society. On the contrary, it promotes a hardening of the existing political polarities, which has proven to be an efficient instrument for preventing a process of gradual socio-political reform.[23]

The fetishizing of opposition can take more subtle forms than the outright privileging of dissidence. Many studies produced about and during the first years of the Special Period that examined the impact of ideology outside the official sphere tended to equate behavior within civil society with nonideological cultural traits and customs. They presumed that any illegal activities (usually economic or consumer related) and/or disagreements with the Cuban government were necessarily rejections of Cuban socialist ideology, as opposed to rejections of government paternalism or of specific policies. Participation in the unofficial economy received particular attention as a way in which Cubans passively expressed their discontent with the Cuban state.[24] The behavior of Cubans in everyday life, including daily acts of resistance, and the survival of traditional cultural practices were cited as evidence in the 1990s of the failure of attempts to create a new revolutionary culture or of the "exhaustion of ideology" in Cuba.[25] At the same time, it pointed to the growth of a Cuban "civil society" that was purportedly oriented toward liberal capitalism, a development assumed by the antinomies by which Cuban socialism has traditionally been understood by mainstream outside scholars. This model drew largely on the experiences of the former Soviet Union and Eastern Europe, where, unlike in Cuba, Communist governments "were installed on the points of Soviet bayonets."[26] The popular nature of the 1959 Cuban Revolution made comparisons to Eastern Europe of limited use.

Other accounts attributed the absence of great upheaval in Cuba, in spite of material scarcity and high levels of dissatisfaction, to these same improvised economic activities and to cultural and social bonds that were distinguished from socialist ideology and practice.[27] While such accounts rightly acknowledged the complex factors explaining the survival of the Cuban government—fear of an unknown future, repression, shared experiences of crisis, the informal economy, resourcefulness, to name a few—they tended to presume that these actors were without any ideology, or, conversely, that certain behaviors had clear ideological implications that were not in need of interrogation. Without fieldwork analyzing the ways that participants in these activities actually understand them, however, daily acts of resistance can hardly be presumed to be unqualified rejections of Cuban socialist ideology.

Particularly since 2000, when it was clear that predictions of systemic collapse were premature, studies have taken a more micro-level approach, often relying upon extensive fieldwork to examine the specific ideological negotiations of Cubans outside the leadership. In these studies, civil society or any sphere outside the state becomes a way to approach ideology in a supposedly "nonideological" way. The impetus for these studies was not just the survival of the Cuban government, but also often the growth of NGOs in Cuba in the 1990s.[28]

In 1985, the Cuban government created a Cuban version of NGOs.[29] The law regulating them was hard to use and few people knew about it. The 1993 New Association Act, however, while still excluding organizations whose goals were deemed in violation of the Cuban constitution, had a greater impact, permitting greater numbers and types of organizations and giving legal recognition to some organizations already in existence.[30] Those already in existence included academic think tanks, such as the Center for the Study of America (treated in chapter 4), and traditional institutions such as the Catholic Church, the Masonic Lodge, and Afro-Cuban religious organizations.[31] International NGOs also arrived to the island, some with more or less acceptance from the Cuban government. Dissident NGOs, although in existence since the 1970s, also grew in the 1990s, often banding together into larger umbrella organizations such as the Concilio Cubano and Todos Unidos.[32]

As with studies of Cuban civil society, studies of Cuban NGOs tend to focus on the degree of autonomy they have from the state.[33] This focus often precludes analyzing their ideological agendas. This has been an issue for the Cuban government as well, which since the 1990s has at times adopted the U.S. government's definition of civil society as a sphere necessarily occupied by those engaged in antirevolutionary, antistate, and/or oppositional activities. Using this same definition, the U.S. government declares civil society positive and largely absent from Cuba, whereas the Cuban government declares it negative, and its existence the result of foreign intervention and a direct threat to Cuban sovereignty. Lost in this battle of labels are the contents of the ideologies of those who make up civil society, including dissident organizations, which frequently find their specific political platforms silenced by the war of words between Cuba and the United States.[34] While the Cuban government declares them all mercenaries and counterrevolutionaries and ignores the content of their platforms, the U.S. government paints them as a homogeneous group and generally gives more press coverage, support, and attention to those with political and economic agendas more in keeping with the United States' interests.

Alongside the Cuban government's either entirely negative or narrow definition of civil society as either antirevolutionary or only made up of mass organizations, the 1990s saw a vigorous discussion among Cuban intellectuals, like Jorge Acanda, Haroldo Dilla, Desiderio Navarro, Rafael Hernández, and others, attempting to rescue civil society from its liberal and neoliberal connotations and conceptualize a specifically socialist one in closer keeping to the empirical reality of Cuba.[35] They tended to view civil society not necessarily in oppositional terms or as only safe under the direct guidance of the state, but rather as a way of describing "a project of pluralist renewal of socialism."[36] These intellectuals often used the work of political theorists like Rousseau, Hegel, and Gramsci to show that civil society had long been considered both part of the state and a sphere of the political (as opposed to a sphere that was political only insofar as it was opposed to the state and/or a sphere of market-oriented activities).[37] At the same time, the state was increasingly caught between the demands of global capital and the legacy of the socialist revolution, so much so that some of these authors suggested that civil society was not just pushing back against the socialist Cuban state, but also against a Cuban state increasingly allied with market forces.[38]

Out of this situation emerged a number of studies published within the last ten years that have focused on the specific ideological negotiations of Cubans who make up a civil society not necessarily in direct opposition to the Cuban state, but at times in tension with it. Sujatha Fernandes examines how revolutionary ideology was negotiated and rearticulated in what she calls artistic public spheres. She shows how the Cuban state harnessed what it viewed to be the more traditional or palatable revolutionary elements of these public spheres, but also how it had to respond to their demands and concerns. The transnational links of these spheres, she argues, blocked their total reincorporation back into state institutions. For Fernandes, hegemony and the idea of partial reincorporation are the most apt terms for understanding these ideological negotiations.[39] Robin Moore too explores the Cuban Revolution through the lens of culture, focusing specifically on how musicians and musical genres have interacted with state cultural institutions, finding both support and censorship from them.[40] Adriana Hernandez-Reguant has written on how the Cuban state increasingly turned to the arts and culture as a source of foreign currency and ideological legitimacy, but still sought "to preserve the socialist hierarchy of power and knowledge by granting privileges to certain cultural producers while policing any attempts to profit on the part of individual intermediaries."[41] Adrian Hearne's work looks at how Afro-Cuban religious groups struggled to maintain their focus on Afro-Cuban religion and spirituality and race-based solidarity, while participating in state-directed projects.[42] P. Sean Brotherton looks at how Cubans in 1990s made sense of and responded to the changes in Cuba's health care system, which had long been a source of state legitimacy. He argues that Cubans' disappointment with the failures of the health care system in the 1990s and the informal strategies they adopted to compensate for these failures were not clear-cut rejections of or challenges to the state and instead illustrate the degree to which the state has successfully produced "medicalized subjectivities."[43] All these studies make a valuable contribution to understanding both how the state deals with ideological challenges to its authority and the degree to which nonstate actors and institutions are disciplined by it. Brotherton's ethnography, in particular, complicates a simple story of co-option or dissent by showing how even informal activities can be evidence of the success of state-run programs and at times help to sustain that same state.

My interest in this book is with the extent to which these other spheres refused the state a monopoly on socialist ideology specifically. In other words, I am interested in the ways that other spheres of Cuban society theorize Cuban socialism, not instrumentally as a way of achieving other goals (often understood to be their true interests), but rather because they had an alternative conceptualization of socialism per se and/or were concerned that the state's policies and understandings of socialism were harmful for the overall socialist project. At the same time, my work does not necessarily privilege as more authentic these alternative articulations of Cuban socialist ideology, partially in recognition of the fact that the state that must negotiate ideology differently than other spheres. The Cuban state's size and strength relative to other spheres and its distinct geopolitical position present it with particular challenges, but these challenges make visible issues of sovereignty that are constitutive of all states, liberal or not. Indeed, alternative conceptualizations of Cuban socialism and critiques of the Cuban state have often been critiques of state sovereignty more generally and thus do not necessarily lend themselves easily to vindicating liberal ideology.[44]

The risk of focusing on the opposition between state and civil society is that the issues of sovereignty and ideology fall by the wayside in the name of accessing which side of the state civil society relationship wins out. Rather than focusing on the state versus civil society opposition, the framework of this book emphasizes relations between a variety of different spheres of Cuban society, all of which have public and private aspects to them and which at times overlap and at times are distinct. The overlap can be due to a variety of factors. Some actors occupy more than one sphere. Academics and some officials, especially lower-level officials, also operate in the popular sphere. Those in the popular sphere must also negotiate state institutions, including bureaucracies and schools. How everybody talks about Cuban socialism among their neighbors is different from how they speak in academic or government settings. This distinction, however, cannot be reduced simply to opportunism or fear, but also to the different demands of these different spheres.[45] No one sphere can be said to be more political than the others. Rather, it is that different kinds of politics operate in each, none more opportunistic or principled than the other.

While the literature on civil society focuses on these particular ideological negotiations, it tends to either fetishize opposition or presume that civil society is the only place of honest ideological negotiations. What it ignores is how ideology is always situated, in the sense that it is created and re-created in light of specific political problems posed within different spheres that escape the state/civil society categorization. In Cuba, while the state has often had the last word in the form of laws, it has not always had the first. While the state disciplines, and this is most clearly seen in the case of dissidents on the island, it is also a participant in a larger discussion.

Some articulations of Cuban socialism within other spheres of Cuban society escape state control, but this does not mean that these other articulations represent the true version of socialism in opposition to the state. In other words, one misses much of the story of the negotiation of Cuban socialism in Cuba if one frames this discussion always in terms of state control versus freely expressed ideas. This book, instead, shows that ideology is always present, in various permutations, sometimes in thinner versions than others. Certain basic socialist principles are widely held by the population and even when the state is being its most repressive, there are negotiations and struggles that serve to demarcate how those principles remain in effect.

A Tour of the Spheres and Principles

Seeing these negotiations and struggles requires that we take seriously the existence of a distinct Cuban socialist ideology. Chapter 1 looks at how two revolutionary periods in Cuban history—the wars of the independence of the 19th century, and the years immediately before and after the revolution of 1959—serve as a basis for contesting or legitimating Cuban socialist ideology. A discussion of this literature, some of which has now largely been dismissed as Cold War propaganda, provides an occasion to consider the nature and sources of ideology and explore some of the traps that continue to obscure investigations of Cuban socialist ideology and how those traps might be avoided. I argue in this chapter that we must think about ideology in a way that is not limited to questions of instrumentalization and oppression, and that we cannot understand an ideology independent of the particular conditions with which it is confronted. The instrumental use of history is not exceptional, but part of all ideological negotiations. However, the failure of ideologies to explain historical examples exposes their own fundamentally local and contingent nature.

Chapter 2 argues that the institutions created by the revolution were not simply transmission belts for centralized Cuban authority, but also provided a space for debate and engagement. Most accounts of Cuban revolutionary history tend to frame this history in terms of political opening and closing. Normally, this model suggests that during periods of closing, there is no option but compliance and compromising of one's principles. I argue, on the contrary, that even under conditions of "closing," debate does not end but rather focuses on understanding how to respond and adapt to the revolutionary context. To make this argument, I treat debates of the 1960s and show some of the ways that Cuban artists and intellectuals responded to, and theorized, Fidel Castro's famous "Words to the Intellectuals." While normally this speech is read as eliminating artistic freedom, I argue that the problem that some Cuban intellectuals had with it was its inability to appropriately theorize what it would mean to be both an intellectual and a revolutionary at the same time. Rather than understanding these debates as necessarily between dogmatic hardliners and liberals, I show that they are better understood as between hardliners and those wishing to participate in the revolution as intellectuals and not merely as political subjects.

Chapter 3 treats the economic policies of the 1970s and early 1980s that are usually thought of as purely "pragmatic" and shows this period to be riven with ideological debate and negotiation. In 1976 the Cuban government adopted the System of Management and Planning of the Economy (SDPE), in a move generally characterized as abandoning the idealism of the 1960s. This chapter shows instead that the Cuban press attempted to link the supposedly "pragmatic" shift to the model of economic calculus, including material incentives, firm autonomy, and parallel markets, with both the ideas of Che Guevara and the work of Karl Marx. While Guevara's ideas are generally associated with moral incentives rather than market mechanisms, journalists and the head of the economic planning commission sought to show that the new economic model of the 1970s was neither more nor less idealist than Guevara's own principles of socialist political economy (known as the budgetary finance system). They also drew upon Marx's argument, as found in his "Critique of the Gotha Program," that minimal material incentives were necessary during the initial stages of socialism, but that they were offset by other methods of decommodifying labor. This account of official explanations of the SDPE shows that this period of pragmatic accommodation to market imperatives demanded an even greater attention to its relationship to socialist principles than during a period when those principles seemed more clearly embodied in practice.

Chapter 4 shows how in the 1990s intellectuals responded to accusations from the state that they had abandoned the revolutionary project. In 1996, the Cuban government disbanded the Havana research institute of the Center for the Study of America, a social science center that had been important not just for the Cuban government, but also for many sympathizers to the Cuban Revolution, and which had becoming increasingly recognized both in Cuba and internationally. The closing of the center therefore become emblematic of the argument that even those who show loyalty to the revolution are ultimately subject to the whims of the Cuban state. This chapter argues that, as in the case of the repression of intellectuals in the 1960s, examined in chapter 2, here again, intellectuals took the occasion of the censoring of this center to articulate an alternative vision of intellectual production that could not be captured by either the liberal antistatist or dogmatic statist paradigm.

Specifically, they argued that it was important to distinguish between the academic sphere and the state, not in order to protect academia from politics, but rather to ensure that academics could make political contributions to the revolution as academics. The academic sphere, they insisted, was not immune to the ideological struggle of the revolution, but it had to participate in the creation and renegotiation of the hegemonic ideology and not simply be disciplined by it.

Chapter 5 situates the negotiation of Cuban socialist ideology in the space of a Cuban shopping mall in Havana in the late 1990s/early 2000s. The texts and consumption activities within the mall could easily be read as indicative of the decline of Cuban socialism, its existence only as a set of empty slogans, and used as evidence of a new market subjectivity of the Cuban people. I argue that while the Cuban government's attempts to bring the revolutionary message to the mall itself (via the slogan "sales + economy + efficiency = revolution") was a failure, popular responses to the economic reforms that led to this mall's existence continue to insist upon the primacy of Cuban socialist principles. Here, it was not the state at all, but the Cuban population, that successfully negotiated the principles of Cuban socialism, albeit under very different constraints and conditions. While the state hid behind the assumption of revolutionary progress, the Cuban population (especially in the form of popular culture) engaged with real threats posed by the arrival of market principles. Popular criticisms of government policy in the 1990s were not an embrace of liberal style consumerism but rather constituted both a criticism of the state for failing to live up to socialist principles of socioeconomic equality and also evidence for the need for the state to relinquish its control over socialist ideology itself.

The conclusion returns to the same Havana shopping mall in the 21st century in order to show the Cuban government's increasing abandonment of attempts to relate marketization to Cuban socialist ideology. This inability to contain marketization both as an ideology and as a practice can be seen in the proliferation of state sanctioned small-scale private business throughout Havana (and Cuba more generally). The government's attempt to monopolize ideology, combined with its silence about marketization, has led to the creation of an officially sanctioned civil society that looks much like the liberal version that the government formally opposes. Even so, while the public realm appears more and more to be occupied by market principles, there remains a space in which socialist principles are still seriously debated. Ironically then, through its political repression, the Cuban government ends up promoting a de facto liberal form of civil society constituted by marketizing practices, and the opposition, even though often espousing liberal ideology, ends up promoting a more socialist understanding of civil society as a space of political participation and debate. Here, then, we see the resilience of Cuban socialist principles even in a context where both the state and the population are read as abandoning the revolution. Such an understanding helps us to think further about the nature and resilience of ideology more generally, including in contexts such as in the United States, where we do not necessarily consider ourselves under the sway of any particular one.

The book's illumination of political dynamics and forms of political thinking specific to Cuba also makes Cuba seem less exceptional. It thus opens up new ways of seeing how ideology, understood as a set of principles and practices informed by the historical moments and spheres in which they operate, functions elsewhere.

One

Whose Revolution?

Making Ideology, Making History

In Cuba, apparently ideological statements can be seen everywhere. Revolutionary slogans cover virtually every public space from billboards on highways and town plazas to school and factory walls (see figures 1, 2, and 3). Ideology does not just manifest itself in material culture and in the Cuban landscape. Throughout the 1960s, 1970s, and 1980s, the term "ideology" itself appeared frequently in official discourse, in the press, on television, and on the radio, suggesting a kind of self-consciousness about the use and nature of the term. The role and meaning of ideology in the revolution has also been a central preoccupation of Cuban intellectuals. It is surprising then that relatively little has been written about ideology by scholars inside or outside Cuba, especially after the 1960s, when the revolution was institutionalized.[1]

The paucity of studies is understandable when one considers the theoretical and methodological difficulties of studying ideology generally and in Cuba specifically. One of the most significant challenges is that there is a fundamental tension between the concept and the practices of ideology. On the one hand, as a set of abstract propositions about the world, ideologies have a timeless quality. On the other hand, to identify a specific ideology is to pin down its historically contingent content and meaning, to distinguish it from others, and to be able to hold elites and citizens accountable for what is done in its name. Political ideologies must be responsive in order to remain compelling. They must confront the harsh demands of politics, where time and incomplete information are constants, and where one must always navigate between means and ends. Questions of expediency, collaboration, effectiveness, compromise, and strict adherence to principles always arise. The problem of effective means becomes even more difficult for revolutionaries

Fig. 1. "Nuestro Deber es Vencer! Viva [*sic*] Fidel y Raúl" (Our duty is to overcome! Long live Fidel and Raúl). (The second part of the slogan is grammatically incorrect but suggests the degree to which the brothers are seen as unified, at least symbolically, as representatives of the revolution.) Slogan appearing on a water tank in Holguín Province, 2011.

who wish to overthrow an existing system and establish an alternative to the prevailing order. They must worry that the failure of their actions to produce intended results invalidates not only those intentions but the entire political ideology underlying them as well. Even once they seize political power, revolutionaries must confront these demands, especially if their ideology remains marginal globally.

In sum, there is no purely ideational perspective from which to examine ideologies; they remain constant only in hindsight. The challenge, then, for studying Cuban socialist ideology is to acknowledge its changing nature, while at the same time holding its adherents accountable for the decisions that are made and positions that are taken in its name. It is to track the development of a distinct revolutionary ideology in Cuba, recognizing its relationship to material and social conditions without reducing that connection to a moment of opportunism (whether opportunism is either a criticism

Fig. 2. "Socialismo es Soberanía e Independencia" (Socialism is sovereignty and independence). Slogan appearing on a wall in Central Havana, 2011.

Fig. 3. "52 Años de Luchas y Victorias" (52 years of struggles and victories). Sign on a highway with the image of Fidel and Camilo Cienfuegos, Havana Province, 2011.

or a defense of Cuban socialism) or a tool of oppression. This requires us to distinguish between instrumental deployments of ideology and principled expressions of ideology that respond to and emerge out of particular historical conditions.

The problem with this analytical distinction, however, is that ideologies do not fit so neatly into such clear categories precisely because both instrumental and principled forms emerge out of history *and* help to shape and understand it. Ideologies, in other words, are always both instrumental and principled. One sees this problem particularly clearly in the literature dealing with two revolutionary periods in Cuban history—the second half of the 19th century and the years leading up to and following the 1959 revolution—which have served as a basis for contesting or legitimating Cuban socialist ideology. While critics argue that socialism was a betrayal of Cuban revolutionary history, defenders of the 1959 revolution use this same history to give socialism legitimacy as an indigenous ideology (rather than a form of Marxism/Leninism imported from abroad). The "revolution betrayed" argument of critics lost popular support as the years wore on, but there remains in later literature an analytically weak understanding of ideology as either static and unchanging or, conversely, instrumental and subject to the whims of the political leadership. Contemporary treatments of Cuban socialist ideology also argue that the Cuban leadership uses Cuban history to give the socialist project a legitimacy it would not otherwise have. This criticism has some validity when looking at how the Cuban leadership relied upon 19th-century history in order to depict itself as carrying on a revolution that began with the wars of independence (what one might call "the revolution realized" thesis). Yet this instrumental use of history is not exceptional: all ideology to some extent involves a selective and instrumental approach to history. Rather than understanding Cuban socialism as having superseded the thought of 19th-century Cuban nationalist and proto-nationalist thinkers, we should understand that it has inherited many of the same problems and dilemmas that they confronted.

Similarly, one might understand the apparently dramatic ideological shifts following 1959 neither as a betrayal of the principles of the popular struggle against Fulgencio Batista nor as the conscious acknowledgment of an ideology already in operation before 1959. Instead, we should see these shifts as particular configurations of principles that responded to historically contingent political, social, and economic demands. These configurations then contributed to a new ideological arsenal from which to draw to confront new developments following the conquest of the state.

To make these kind of arguments is to reject the teleology presumed by both the "revolution betrayed" thesis and what one might call "the revolution realized" thesis and instead focuses on the specific ways that ideologies are localized, responding to and emerging out of particular historical conditions, which also limit the degree to which they can be stretched and instrumentalized. Comparing the two literatures dealing with these periods side by side allows us to see that in both cases, there is a negotiation between desired state interests and the kinds of principles that emerge out of the revolutionary experience of all involved. Advocates of the revolution betrayed thesis must contend with the memories, histories, and experiences of participants in both the 19th-century wars of independence and the 1959 revolution, which complicate a story of repression and betrayal of a popular, but not socialist, movement. By the same token, the Cuban state can't simply subsume every aspect of Cuban history into a teleological narrative that culminates in whatever the state deems revolutionary. This is because the state too must contend with the principles and experiences that have evolved out of these historical moments. In this way, living ideology doesn't just refer to the present, but also to a set of historical constellations that connect past, present, and future via shared political problems and experiences.

Ideology Everywhere and Nowhere

Ideology is extremely difficult to study because the concept itself is so slippery. The term is subject to much manipulation and is often deployed opportunistically, and applied inconsistently, depending on the political context. In many cases, critics of a specific ideology will mark a view as "ideological" to suggest that it is dogmatic, fanatical, and blind to the facts, as opposed to their own principled, reasonable, or empirically grounded position. In other cases, critics will deny that a position they reject deserves/has any ideological status whatsoever, dismissing it as merely opinion, impulse, self-interest, or opportunism.

The common presumption of many studies of (principled and opportunistic) ideology is that important facts are being hidden and that lifting the curtain of ideology will reveal the power sustaining it, enabling us to see the world as it truly is.[2] Thus, to say that ideology is everywhere in Cuba is not to say that there are always many ideologies floating around, each equally valid or at least freely chosen by their believers, as there supposedly are in liberal democracies. Instead, it is to say that one ideology dominates all aspects and spheres of people's lives. In this version, ideology is everywhere and everything because a one-party state imposes its ideology universally. The world is as those in power say it is. Ideology is everywhere hiding the facts. To say that all is ideological in this case implies also that nothing is, since ideology gets in the way of seeing the world as it "really is." All decisions are made without recourse to facts and in accordance with a utopian blueprint. Often, however, the argument is not simply that the leadership has strategically chosen a particular ideology and, because it has power, can impose it on everyone else. It is that those who are "being ideological" are actually cloaking their base self-interest *in* ideology. They claim to be ideological, but they are in fact guided by cold facts (namely the imperatives of power), which point them in the same direction as the ideology does. In the case of Cuba, there is no legitimate ideology and once ideology is stripped away and exposed, everything ultimately is about power and opportunism.[3]

The suspicion of ideology as all-pervasive and blinding has influenced contemporary studies of Cuba for decades, many of which reflect a wariness of ideology. This wariness reflects both the view of ideology as unscientific (from a social science perspective), and of the way that Cuban studies as a discipline has historically been implicated in larger geopolitical battles. In the field of Cuban studies, "ideology" has long been a weapon used to discount any study with which one disagrees. Scholars of Cuba, living on the island and off, especially in the 1960s and 1970s but today as well, find themselves constantly criticized for their ideological position, which is frequently presumed on the basis of their place of residence. U.S. State Department officials, for instance, dismiss Cuban academics as mouthpieces of the Cuban state, incapable of independent and critical thought.[4] Cuba-based officials and academics have criticized scholars of Cuba who do not reside on the island (and particularly those of Cuban descent) for ideological biases against the revolution that preclude accurate representations of the Cuban reality.[5] At the same time, if scholars off the island do not condemn the Cuban system wholesale and support less punitive policies toward the island, others off the island suspect their scholarship.[6] This has led many scholars to include in their work a prophylactic and ritualistic recognition of the difficulty of avoiding ideological bias, but also a promise to minimize this bias as much as possible. In this view, ideology can be kept at bay, though never conquered, by the continual search for truth and collection of raw data and by making political preferences and values explicit at the outset of a study.[7] Such attempts to avoid ideological bias, or the charge of it, have often meant, then, that the concept of ideology itself is insufficiently theorized or avoided entirely.

The study of Cuban socialist ideology is often linked to questions of the revolution's origins and survival as popular and socialist. One set of literature, produced largely but not exclusively in the 1960s, focuses on the years right before and after the 1959 revolution. These studies often reflected a suspicion of ideology as always partial, obscuring, and constraining and/or of Marxism-Leninism in particular as necessarily authoritarian and dogmatic. Both critical accounts of the revolution, which emphasized betrayal, and sympathetic accounts, which emphasized originality, lack of dogma, and process, ultimately reduced ideology to opportunism. Whereas those emphasizing betrayal left no room for ideological transformation and engagement with the real world, those praising ideological flexibility placed ideology entirely at the whim of the changing tides of history and made the actual content of that ideological transformation irrelevant. In both accounts, accountability on the part of those acting in the name of that ideology was irrelevant either because the standards were impossibly high or because there was nothing to be accountable for.

Rather than tackle the challenges of studying ideology that the above studies of ideologies raised, but did not necessarily address, later literature avoided the pitfalls associated with studying ideology by largely avoiding the term. Since the 1960s, studies of Cuba have generally tried to avoid global criticism or praise of the Cuban Revolution.[8] They tend to avoid contending with ideology, as a distinct concept, and instead examine Cuban socialism through the lenses of history or civil society. Works taking a historical perspective focus on the origins of Cuban socialism in the late 19th century during Cuba's Wars for Independence. These works tend either to argue that the Cuban leadership uses history instrumentally (and inaccurately) to legitimate an otherwise illegitimate socialism, or they describe Cuban socialism as the inevitable outcome of radical nationalism (or alternatively as a deviation from Cuba's republican destiny). In either case, teleology removes politics and ideological negotiation from consideration. Moreover, these later approaches often maintained many of the common themes or tendencies found in studies in the 1960s: One tendency is to locate Cuban socialist ideology either solely in the figure of Fidel Castro or in the Cuban government. Another is to presume that socialist ideology gained meaning only by piggybacking on an authentic and truly Cuban nationalism (as opposed both to the purely negative and anti-American understanding of nationalism to which Fidel Castro appealed, and to a foreign socialism). Another tendency is to either ignore the question of Cubans' reception of ideology or treat Cubans outside the government sphere as passive consumers or victims of socialist ideology, rather than active, critical, and engaged producers of it.

Careful reflection on this literature, including the literature that now is largely dismissed as Cold War propaganda, provides an occasion to consider the nature and sources of ideology, to uncover some of the traps that continue to obscure investigations into socialist ideology, and to consider how we might avoid some of these traps. More specifically, it helps to show how to move beyond the opposition between ideology and opportunism. At the same time, it is worth returning to some of this literature, especially from the 1960s, because it raises important questions about the relationship between ideology and political action that are less apparent in later, less polemical, accounts of Cuban socialist ideology that also tend to reduce ideology to opportunism.

Opportunism Everywhere: Revolution Betrayed

Many studies of the Cuban Revolution, particularly those from the 1960s, linked the issue of ideology to understanding and explaining the relationship and apparent rupture between the officially nonsocialist ideology of the 26th of July Movement that overthrew Fulgencio Batista and the socialist ideology of the Cuban government after Batista was overthrown.[9] These studies tried to make sense of a number of events. One was that the revolutionary movement that came to power in 1959 was a broad based, multiclass, popular movement, whose leadership and many (though not all) of whose members disavowed Communism. Another was the revolution's subsequent radicalization, made explicit by its open avowal of socialism in 1961 and later, Castro's declaration that he was a Marxist-Leninist in 1962.[10] Scholars disagreed about when and why Castro became a Communist and what the relationship between Castroism and Communism was, but all ultimately reduced ideology to opportunism. All roads, no matter what the political inclination of the author, led to this same conclusion.

Some scholars identified the ideology of Cuban socialism with Soviet Marxism-Leninism and thus with something foreign and imposed that had little to do with Cuban history and Cuban desires. Fidel Castro, these arguments went, hid his ideological commitments to Marxism-Leninism and distanced himself from the prerevolutionary Communist Party (Partido Popular Socialista or PSP) in Cuba for strategic reasons: he needed middle-class support in order to overthrow Batista. One author attributed Castro's triumph to his ability to hide socialism inside the Trojan horse of nationalism.[11] Yet while they argued that Castro had long been an agent of Soviet Communism and that the United States foolishly failed to realize this before it was too late, they also argued that Fidel Castro was too much of an opportunist to have genuinely believed even in his hidden beliefs.[12] Opportunism marked his hidden espousal of Marxism-Leninism (for which he supposedly received power and money from the Soviets), his decision to hide this espousal (so as to not alienate a Cuban population prejudiced against it), and his decision to adopt Marxism-Leninism (to better consolidate his power by pleasing the Soviets and imposing a one-party state).

Cuba scholars at the time as well as participants in the revolutionary struggle dismissed this work as sensationalist Cold War hysteria that lacked hard evidence, relied upon questionable sources, and pointed to later events to prove the factual accuracy of suspicions about the past.[13] However, they did not reject the logic of opportunism entirely. They argued, explicitly or implicitly, that Castro's turn to socialism represented a betrayal of the 26th of July Movement that he headed and with whose support he came to power. In these accounts, ideologies associated with the Cuban Revolution after 1959 served as its post facto justifications, with no inherent appeal for the Cuban people and no explanatory value. Castro adopted Communism because it was the most convenient road to power. If he was not an opportunistic Communist before, he became one afterward. These works reduced Cuban revolutionary ideology to Castro's words and deeds (Castroism). Castroism, in turn, was reduced to opportunism either by defining ideology as an inflexible set of beliefs that would inevitably be compromised by the need to act, or by refusing to give ideology in Cuba any substance whatsoever.[14] Either way, ideology was ultimately at the service of power. As Theodore Draper put it, Castro "won power with one ideology and held it with another."[15] In such accounts, evidence for Castro's betrayal of the 26th of July Movement included the existence of diverse and contradictory political currents within the movement, especially after 1957, when it had come to include not just student radicals and others committed to deep economic and social change but also businessmen, professionals, and others simply wishing to restore the 1940 constitution.[16] To hold it all together, Draper argued, Castro "voiced little more than the traditional aspirations of the socially conscious, democratic-minded Cuban middle and working classes."[17] Castro's subsequent adoption of Communism had little to do with the principles of egalitarianism or with faith in Marx's theory of history, Draper argued, but rather with the centralizing and homogenizing elements of Marxism that enabled him to consolidate power. Had another ideology suited these ends, he would have adopted it just as easily.[18] The only ideology that interested Castro was one that helped him consolidate power.

Other scholars argue that the constant shifts in ideology illustrated not the instrumental use of ideology, but its absence.[19] According to these scholars, Castroism referred not to any set of abstract principles but to Castro's personal charismatic qualities and did "not possess a single ideologist familiar with 'European communist tradition.'"[20] According to this logic, if the Soviet Union did not consider Cuba a socialist country throughout the 1960s, this was evidence not of ideological differences with the Soviet Union, but rather of the absence of Marxist-Leninist principles and therefore of any coherent socialist ideology.[21] This view simply ignored the discussions and disagreements between members of Cuban's prerevolutionary Communist Party (PSP), who tended to follow the orthodox Soviet line, and the more radical members of the former 26th of July Movement, who tended to push for a more dramatic departure from capitalism.[22]

In both the "hidden communist" argument and the "revolution betrayed" argument, ideological shifts are either proof that there really wasn't any (socialist) ideology at all, or else they "are reduced to individual thirst for power rather than being connected in any direct manner to changing social situations or to different sociopolitical alliances at given periods in time."[23] In politics, where questions of expediency always arise, one had to relinquish any true ideological commitment. In their obsession with political accountability and betrayal, these authors ignored the actual content of Cuban socialism. For them, it was sufficient to know that it had changed. Their analyses precluded any understanding of how Cuban socialist ideology developed of its own accord, at times challenging the Soviet interpretation of socialism and adopting far more radical stances toward revolutionary transformation.[24] These positions were motivated by both principled *and* practical considerations that could not always be distinguished easily from ideology.[25] For instance, Guevara's emphasis on moral incentives in a 1962 speech to a group of workers was a principled argument, but also one that recognized—given Cuba's semicolonial conditions, capital flight following the turn to socialism, and the country's dependence upon raw materials from abroad—that the country's greatest resource was its labor. Cuba could not rely upon material incentives to increase productivity, but this rejection of material incentives also coincided with a longer-term goal of adopting an entirely different attitude toward work.[26] These accounts highlighted the various ideological shifts, but failed to realize that ideology *always* develops in response to specific concrete concerns rather than being created in a vacuum and then exposed to the realities of the world to sink or swim.

Ideology as Process: Opportunism Sneaks Back In

As I suggested earlier, older studies of Cuban socialism focused primarily on Castro, which gave scholars a limited view of ideological transformation because Castro appeared inconsistent in his explanations of his own ideological shifts and in his discussions of the role of ideology in the revolutionary movement. However, this appearance of inconsistency disappears if we rethink ideology, not as a constellation of fixed and logically related ideas, but as a process. This process view of ideology opens up questions of the relationship between ideological narratives and political and social history, the problem of political accountability and the process of subject formation. For instance, in a 1959 speech, Castro explained:

> There cannot be a priori absolute positions, there cannot be unchangeable positions, there cannot be dogmatic thought when we deal with society; thought has to be in close contact with reality . . . it must be adjusted to social realities, to the nature of the people. . . . That is how we conceived of ideology.[27]

Similarly, in a 1965 interview with journalist Lee Lockwood, in which Fidel Castro was asked whether he was already a Marxist-Leninist when he came to power, Castro responded in Hegelian fashion: "Things cannot be understood unless they are analyzed as a process. Nobody can say that he reaches political conclusions except through a process."[28] Castro described his evolution from a questioning university student interested in the relationship between material progress and social welfare to a "kind of utopian socialist" and then later, after reading *The Communist Manifesto*, to someone who found "an extraordinary superiority in the Marxist point of view."[29] Even at this point he was "still not a Marxist," "still very much influenced by the habits and ideas of [his] *petit bourgeois* education" and did not consider himself a Communist.[30] "This encounter with revolutionary ideas helped me to orient myself politically," he explained. "But there is a big difference between having a theoretical knowledge and considering oneself a Marxist revolutionary."[31] His identification as a Marxist would come as his own consciousness evolved alongside that of the people's. What was possible at a given moment set the boundaries of one's consciousness at the same moment. Castro explained:

> At the same time that we were learning, the people were also learning. Through the same process that we, the leaders, became more revolutionary, the people became more revolutionary also. . . . Nobody is born a revolutionary. A revolutionary is formed through a process. It is possible that there was some moment when I appeared less radical than I really was. It is possible too that I was more radical than I myself knew. Ultimately, a revolutionary struggle is like a military war.

You have to set yourself only those goals that are attainable at a given moment. The fight depends on the correlation of forces, on a series of circumstances, and every revolutionary must propose for himself all the objectives that are possible within the correlation of forces and within the circumstances in which he acts.[32]

Thus, for him, and in response to those accusing him of betrayal, promises appropriate to 1953 (the year of the attack on the Moncada Barracks) were not necessarily appropriate for 1959.

In Cuban historiography, that attack often marks the beginning of the revolution. It was carried out on July 26, 1953, by Fidel Castro and others in the traditionally rebellious Oriente Province. Despite its ultimate military failure, the attack marked the beginning of the revolution by drawing attention to the movement and the atrocities of which Batista was capable. Castro used his own trial as an opportunity to place Batista on trial and expound his own revolutionary plans. In his "History Will Absolve Me" speech, he condemned the Batista regime, citing human rights abuses, corruption, and poor conditions throughout the country. He also proposed his own "Revolutionary Laws," including the restoration of the liberal 1940 constitution, and (until elections) the investiture of all legislative, executive, and judicial powers in the hands of the revolutionary movement; major land redistribution of nonmortgageable and nontransferable property; profit sharing among workers and employers of all sugar mills and other large nonagricultural concerns; establishment of quotas guaranteeing materials and a percentage of total production to the sugar *colonos* (independent farmers) who had been established for three years or more; and confiscation of all illegally or fraudulently obtained land, goods, and money and the distribution of half that confiscated to retired workers and the other half to hospitals, asylums, and charity houses.[33]

After the revolution Castro would view elements of this platform as part of a program for the times, but one that was nonbinding. "Every revolutionary movement in every historical epoch proposes the greatest number of achievements possible."[34] What was for some evidence that Castro had betrayed the 26th of July Movement was for Castro simply a list of goals achievable at a given time. At the same time, he argued, the "History Will Absolve Me" speech was "the seed of all the things that were done later on" and while a "true Marxist" may not have said it was Marxist, he believed that the speech represented "an advanced revolutionary program" that "could be called Marxist if you wish."[35]

Castro's discussion of his own ideological development highlights a more general aspect of ideology, that it becomes a constant only retroactively. In reality, ideologies are always adjusting to circumstances, not just for mercenary reasons but instead to reflect the context in which an ideology operates at a particular time, and also to reflect popular experiences and the principles that arise from them (this would apply to Castro himself). The danger of his conceptualization, however, is that Marxism simply becomes a floating signifier that the leadership can attach to whatever past activities they wish to legitimate. It is Marxist because the sovereign says so. Castro's arguments here use the same logic as those accusing him of hiding his Communism, whereby later events give credence to past speculations, or give greater or lesser weight to facts of the past. The journalist Carlos Franqui, who was a member of the 26th of July Movement, editor of its official paper *Revolución* after 1959, and would later leave Cuba and break with the Cuban government, observed in his account of his experiences with the Cuban Revolution:

> At the trial of the Moncada group, one of Lenin's books appeared among the evidence. It's curious how history changes with time. At the trial, the allegations of Batista's prosecutor about communist influences were denied. Years later, the same book would be the badge of honor—the first appearance of Lenin in the context of the Cuban Revolution.[36]

Fidel Castro did promise to carry out a program different from what he actually delivered. He did vehemently deny any charges of Communism and then later claim that his platform contained the seeds of socialism. As he himself explained, in the Sierra Maestra he decided not to openly espouse a radical program because to do so would have "resulted in aligning against the Revolution all the most reactionary forces, which were then divided" and presenting Communism to a Cuban people who were prejudiced against Communism and still lacking a strong "revolutionary consciousness."[37]

Foreign observers also emphasized the evolutionary character of Cuban socialism. They recognized that the revolution began as one kind of movement and transformed into another. Like Castro, they characterized the flexibility of Cuban socialism as a virtue, as evidence of the originality of Cuban revolutionary ideology, its autonomy from Soviet Communism and its link to the Cuban people.[38] Little was done to reconcile past political platforms with postrevolutionary measures, nor was Castro the sole focus of attention. These accounts emphasized the transformative effects of the revolution and the flexibility and creativity that its amorphous ideology allowed. For Jean-Paul

Sartre, the initially putschist 26th of July Movement "saw its objectives disappear one after another, each time discovering new objectives, more popular and more profound; in a word, more revolutionary."[39] The originality of the revolutionary ideology was that it was constantly in tune with the needs of the people and the moment.

Like Sartre, Richard Fagen praised Cuban socialism for its capacity to draw in large numbers of otherwise unconnected and apathetic people. He, too, looked beyond Fidel Castro to the campaigns and policies of the revolutionary government:

> If ideology is taken to mean a symbolic system linking particular actions and mundane practices with a wider set of meanings, then the revolution has a well developed, flexible and seemingly successful ideology. It is successful precisely because it is personalistic, adaptive and artful.[40]

According to Fagen, the brilliance of the 1961 campaign against illiteracy was that it involved a huge number of people of all sexes, ages, occupations, education, social classes, and places of residence.[41] Unlike agrarian reform and the nationalization of industries, the campaign was little criticized even by enemies of the revolution.[42] Even if the campaign was not an overwhelming triumph at the scholastic level, the mass organizations' facilitation of direct involvement meant "tens of thousands of those Cubans who otherwise might have remained aloof were swept into the effort."[43] The revolution created its own protagonists who might otherwise not have supported some of its more radical measures, but who came to do so by virtue of their initial participation in campaigns like the one for literacy. As with Castro himself, these individuals were swept up by events and developed their political ideology not according to a preconceived plan but contingently according to their own experiences.[44]

The history of Fidel Castro's words and actions is one of apparent contradictions, tensions, and opportunism. As Louis Pérez Jr. has noted, "With the proper patience, one could no doubt attribute to the *jefe maximo* some statement at some point to support virtually any reasonable contention."[45] However, this alone is insufficient to dismiss the existence of a coherent socialist ideology in Cuba. Even if we rely upon what Castro and others say and assume their words to be genuine, it is difficult to gauge their authenticity if the consequences of beliefs never come to fruition. But do we then say that those whose beliefs come to fruition were more honest than those whose beliefs did not, or conversely, do we say that those, such as Fidel Castro, whose beliefs came to fruition in a very different form are less honest or moral? If political actors are judged on the basis of results alone, beliefs can always be modified according to results. We cannot help judging political actors by their beliefs, and we cannot help judging them by the results of their decisions, yet there is a persistent tension between one's subjective intentions and the objective consequences of carrying out those intentions.

Some people who fought alongside Castro to topple Batista felt betrayed by the revolution's socialist turn.[46] However, not everyone felt betrayed for the same reasons and at the same time. Agrarian reform scared some, but not all. Leftist supporters of the revolution were less troubled by the revolution's redistributive efforts than by its exclusion of those who played an active role in the struggle against Batista and in the labor movement prior to 1959. Anarchists and Liberals alike grew concerned at the closing, not of the conservative *Diario de la Marina*, but of the papers expressing views they believed in keeping with the revolution's progressive agenda.[47] To those who did not feel betrayed, Castro was able to articulate his ever-changing program by appealing to an already circulating set of principles rooted in Cuban history and political culture rather than creating new ones. Some of those principles came to the forefront at different times, while others receded. Just as the revolution produced the betrayed, so too did it produce protagonists (who might later have joined the betrayed, or vice versa).

This conceptualization is different than the presumption of a fixed and already given subject who gave or denied support to the revolution by referring to preestablished and immutable political preferences, often determined directly by class position.[48] Maria del Pilar Díaz Castañon, among others, finds Antonio Gramsci's work useful for avoiding this assumption, since Gramsci thinks about revolution not in terms of taking and keeping political power but "as a process of social subversion whose essence disappears if the transformation of its protagonist is not achieved *before, during and after* the revolution."[49]

This Gramscian emphasis on the production of subjects is key to seeing how ideology is not simply something adopted or discarded, but is in itself productive. Revolution is not about the triumph of one political program over another, but rather about the extent to which a group is drawn to an ideology as it circulates through various historical moments, being transformed by, and transforming, its adherents. The Cuban Revolution produced subjects who found themselves increasingly committed to the revolutionary project and to the principles upon which it was based. From this perspective we might think neither that Castro hid his Communism (the "revolution betrayed" thesis) nor that he was unaware of how radical he actually was (Castro's own version), but as someone who was himself radicalized during the revolutionary war and then after taking power. That is, Castro's articulation of revolutionary principles and his own experiences led him to his own ideological convictions, rather than just sharpening and clarifying them.

Ideology and Revolution: Modes of Theorizing

We might thus interpret the role of ideology in the revolution in several ways. Nelson Valdés proposes a Gramscian understanding of ideology to distinguish between revolutionary theory as articulated by the leadership (Castro, Guevara, and others) and as a political ideology that has functioned as "a new type or level of civilization."[50] While this theory/ideology distinction helps us see that Cuban socialism has different valences that can and should be distinguished from one another, it may also perpetuate the problems it is attempting to remedy. It reduces ideology to something like political culture, which lacks the intentionality of ideological formation and its principled aspects. Calling the leadership's version "theory" implies that it has greater rigor and tactical significance and so privileges it. I would thus suggest several modifications.

First, in keeping with Gramsci, we should understand theory more broadly as the negotiation of a specific ideology, as the shuffling and organization of the principles that constitute that ideology in order to respond to a particular political problem. All political theories are produced within a particular ideological context, although not all theory is marked as ideological in the same way.[51] Rather than distinguish theory from ideology, then, we ought to concentrate on the sites of ideological negotiation where theory is deployed. If we do, we see that the Cuban leadership is not the only source of revolutionary theory. It simply theorizes ideology in different ways and under different conditions than Cubans in other spheres.

Second, also in keeping with Gramsci, we should recognize the varied contexts in which philosophy is practiced. If everyone is a philosopher in the sense of having a conception of the world, not everyone articulates this conception of the world with the same degree of abstraction or consistency.[52] These different philosophical modes are due less to variation in intellectual capabilities than to their development under different sets of conditions and constraints. Members of the Cuban leadership, operating within the official sphere and responsible for publicly articulating Cuban socialist ideology in light of specific policies, are held to a higher standard of consistency than ordinary Cubans, even as they are less likely to be directly challenged by ordinary Cubans. Official articulations, in turn, cannot be held to the same standard of logic as academic articulations, given officials' need to consider an infinite number of factors beyond the control of any individual or government and given that officials must constantly rearticulate that ideology in light of concrete conditions. Academics and ordinary Cubans must consider concrete historical conditions as well, but they are not as accountable as those in the official sphere for unforeseen events and to large numbers of people.

The development of Cuban socialism may not have been as harmonious and reciprocal as Castro and others have characterized it, partly because it was based upon the embrace of unrealized principles and not simply a rejection of the old order. Moreover, the interrelationship of various principles of Cuban socialism has limited the degree to which they can be instrumentalized. The content of Cuban nationalism, for instance, is informed by its relationship to socialism. Rather than sneaking in through the Trojan horse of nationalism, socialism might instead give nationalism a different and (for believers) fuller meaning. Unity might involve rallying not around an abstract nation, but around principles of socioeconomic equality. Nationalism could serve a similar function for socialism, uniting people not simply on the basis of their labor power, but on the basis of a shared history and cultural identity that has political implications. An examination of the history of these principles, however, should be tempered by a reminder that where in history we identify their sources and when we stop to take stock of their progress through history, are decisions that change the story itself.

Historical Appropriation and the Return of Opportunism

The argument that Cuba's turn to socialism could be attributed to Castro's ability to cloak it in the language of nationalism continued to influence studies of Cuba past the 1960s and 1970s.[53] Perhaps its most sophisticated form can be found in Tzvi Medin's 1990 *The Shaping of Revolutionary Consciousness*, which examines how the revolutionary message was disseminated throughout the country via schools, cinema, literature, poetry, popular music, theater, the military, mass organizations, and the vanguard party.[54] A new revolutionary consciousness was not created out of thin air, but instead, he argued, had to be grafted onto old ways of thinking by establishing "conceptual, axiological, emotional, and lexical worlds and establishing certain basic principles and equivalences."[55] This approach was necessary because, according to Medin, before the revolution Marxism-Leninism was foreign to Cubans' "conceptual and emotional world," which shared more in common with the American way of life.[56] As a consequence, "Cuban revolutionary leaders introduced Marxism-Leninism into the Cuban revolutionary message by grafting it onto the images, symbols, values and concepts of Cuban nationalism" and anti-imperialism, in part by drawing (weak or false) parallels between important national heroes such as Maceo and Martí, on the one hand, and Marx, Engels, and Lenin, on the other.[57] According to this argument, Marxism-Leninism, then, served not to influence, inspire, or give meaning to events, but rather to legitimate radical measures that had already been done in the name of other principles or a general predisposition toward radicalism or because it was simply what needed to be done for a variety of pragmatic reasons. Declaring the revolution socialist was simply an afterthought.[58] According to this account, socialism was a foreign ideology that was only accepted by cloaking it in the garb of Cuban nationalism. In this argument, the ingredients of Cuban nationalism are presumed to be entirely distinct from those of socialism, and the appeal to historical figures necessarily more questionable when done by Communists. The question then becomes one of who is using the ideas of historical figures like Martí instrumentally and who is being faithful to his ideas, when really neither possibility accurately describes how ideologies and historical narratives are created and re-created. Ideologies and histories always draw selectively from the past and suggest that a particular outcome was the only one possible. Cuban socialism is no different. As Michel-Rolph Trouillot has noted in his work on the Haitian Revolution and historical production, the past and present constitute one another. There is no objective standard by which we can measure the amount of historical weight (how often an event, source, or fact is recalled and for what purposes) a past occurrence should have. Instead, these standards are created during particular historical moments.[59] Power, Trouillot argues, works alongside history not just at the moment of its retrieval but at the moment of its creation as well. This is why opposing sides often compete over the same set of historical facts, attempting to harness them for their own political agendas.

For example, the revolutionary slogan "Fieles a Nuestra Historia" (Loyal to Our History) appears throughout the island. Yet the Cuban leadership is not alone in expressing loyalty to Cuban history. Those wishing to see an end to the Cuban revolutionary project and those wishing it had taken and would take another course do, as well. Both the Cuban leadership and these other groups refer to the wars of independence and the ideas and actions of key political figures from the 19th century to show that their cause is heir to these political traditions and struggles. If the Cuban leadership portrays the revolution as the logical end of Cuba's foiled attempts at independence in the 19th and 20th centuries, exiles, for instance, see it as a betrayal of Cuba's republican aspirations. Cuban history textbooks and official speeches recall a variety of 19th-century figures: priest and independence advocate Félix Varela, his student and ally José Antonio Saco, and the later revolutionary war heroes Carlos Manuel de Céspedes, Ignacio Agramonte, Máximo Gómez, Antonio Maceo, and José Martí, among others. Their political thought is available in bookstores and libraries all over Cuba. Schools, airports, and libraries in Cuba bear their names. All of these names, with the exception of Saco, are also used by dissident organizations on the island.[60]

Perhaps the most contested and appropriated figure has been José Martí, the poet, intellectual, political organizer, fighter for independence, and apostle of the Cuban nation. Born in Havana in 1853, Martí spent much of his youth in exile, first in Spain and then in the United States. He founded the Partido Revolucionario Cubano (PRC) (Cuban Revolutionary Party) and died in battle in 1895 at the start of Cuba's third war for independence. The cult of Martí, with its attendant distortions of his political thought, began almost immediately after his death in 1895. By his 100th birthday in 1953, "Martí had 'arrived' as a national hero, with a standard, albeit debatable, 'profile' being widely presented of him."[61] This struggle continued after 1959, with both supporters and opponents of the Cuban Revolution laying claim to Martí's name and legacy. As one historian has put it:

> That Martí represents the highest example of patriotic virtue and political morality is not disputed. Rather, the debate turns on the ideological meaning of virtue and morality, and who most in the present fully exemplifies the ideals of Martí: defenders of the revolution or detractors.[62]

For instance, in 1983 President Ronald Reagan established Radio Martí, a U.S.-government-funded radio station located in Miami that was dedicated to transmitting antirevolutionary and anticommunist broadcasts to Cuba in the hopes of inciting rebellion. In a speech entitled "Martí es nuestro" (Martí is ours), Fidel Castro called the use of Martí's name "utterly absurd, paradoxical and indecent," given that the United States had done so much to "hinder [Martí's] patriotic struggle."[63] Exiles in turn argued that Castro cited Martí only to gain popular support without being a true follower of his beliefs.[64] While Castro himself has stated explicitly that Martí was not a Marxist, he presented a Martí filtered through his own interpretations, arguing, for instance, that Martí would have been a Marxist if confronted with the same historical conditions as he was.[65]

Cuban intellectuals had made similar arguments in the early 1960s. Roberto Fernández Retamar, for instance, wrote in a 1963 piece in the journal *Cuba Socialista* (founded in 1961 with the primary objective of grooming new revolutionary cadres) that while it was true that Martí did not espouse Marxism, it was wrong to see him as just a reformer or a moderate. Martí was, rather, "the most radical that the historical process permitted him to be" and during the historical period "in which Martí happened to live there was not—and could not have been—another position more radical than his."[66] Fidel Castro's declaration of Marxism-Leninism was not an abandonment of his *Martiano* convictions, stated in his 1953 "History Will Absolve Me" speech, but instead represented the best way to be true to Martí's ideas at that particular historical juncture.[67]

> [If] Leninism is the Marxism of the epoch of imperialism and proletarian revolution, [then] *fidelismo* is the *Martiano* position of the period of absolute decolonization, of the step from political liberation to economic liberation, of the definite rejection of imperialism and the triumph of socialism in an underdeveloped country. That is to say, Martí was surpassed in the sense of having been incorporated and assimilated into a new consciousness.[68]

Similarly, Carlos Rafael Rodríguez, one of the few members of Cuba's prerevolutionary, Soviet-affiliated Communist Party (PSP) to hold a position in the postrevolutionary Communist Party (PCC), argued in a speech at UNEAC, published in the Communist Party paper *Hoy* in 1963, that Martí taught us that "a man of culture is not truly one if his creation does not relate directly and completely with the tragedy of other men, and with the hopes of his own people."[69] Martí was radical because he went to the root of things, criticizing both capitalism and imperialism, and noting and valorizing the rise of the working class.[70] Yet, argued Rodríguez, "between Martí, the radical revolutionary and Martí, the socialist, was a historical distance that Martí himself could not overcome."[71] "The revolution of Martí," he wrote, "would have to wait more than half a century to be realized."

According to John Kirk, by the early 1970s in Cuba a more "balanced view" of Martí had won out over both the pre-revolution tendency to view Martí in almost mystical and apolitical terms, and the initial revolutionary tendency to draw tenuous "comparisons between the aspirations of Martí and those of the *fidelista* government."[72] As the same Carlos Rafael Rodríguez put it in 1972:

> We have now a Martí equipped with all the ingredients for today's battle. We do not have, however, (and it is good to repeat it) a socialist Martí. On some occasions, in a desire to take Martí further than he himself could reach, mention has been made of the socialist nature in Martí. But really what we find is Martí's respect for socialism. . . . All of that seems part of the admirable nature of Karl Marx, but he does not reach the same conclusions in regard to the class struggle or the revolutionary forces of the class struggle.[73]

What would it mean to have a Martí "equipped with all the ingredients for today's battle"? How might it be possible to suggest, as a billboard near the Plaza de la Revolución in Havana does, that Antonio Maceo and Che Guevara are part of the same struggle and tradition? (See figure 4.) How might Martí, Maceo, Céspedes, Agramonte, Varela, or Saco be an ingredient? How might they speak to Cuban socialism? Is it possible to locate certain principles in their thought without suggesting that Cuban socialism is the logical historical outcome of 19th-century struggles and political thought? Is it possible to link the political thought of Martí and others to the Cuban revolution without drawing selectively from these author's works, often ignoring or trivializing the racism and classism of their ideas, or reducing Cuban socialism to a nationalism defined purely in terms of faith in the nation-state in whatever form? Finally, if ideologies are always historically contingent, is it even possible for them to have a history?

The term "principle" helps make sense of these questions, since it allows us to avoid two types of ahistoricism—one that fails to recognize how ideologies always come in contact with temporal developments that force choices, and one that fails to recognize that ideologies take on meaning because they speak not just to the present, but also to the past and future. A principle can neither be reduced entirely to its own historical moment, nor retain its meaning unchanged over time. The history of the 19th century does not provide a direct line to contemporary Cuban socialism, but it does show that principles such as unity, leadership, equality, and social justice were key to discussions about independence and the meaning of *Cubania*. It provides, not a history of those principles, but rather examples of how these principles were negotiated in light of historical conditions. What emerges is not a continuous

Fig. 4. "Hombres de Todos los Tiempos" (Men of all times). Image of Antonio Maceo and Ernesto "Che" Guevara on a billboard near the Plaza of the Revolution in Havana, 2011.

picture of socialism, but a continuity of fundamental political dilemmas, and thus the continued importance of certain principles. Varela, Saco, Céspedes, Agramonte, Maceo, and Martí were not socialists or Marxists. Cuban history books and Cuban revolutionary rhetoric generally applaud them for their support of and contributions to Cuban independence, understood as a political, economic, social, military, and intellectual project. Carlos Rafael Rodríguez, for instance, argued in 1982 that Céspedes, Agramonte, and above all Martí provide examples of "combative" intellectuals after which his contemporaries should model themselves.[74]

For many of these 19th-century intellectuals, concerns with independence and opposition to slavery did not necessarily translate into concerns with socioeconomic and racial equality; and those who were concerned with socioeconomic or racial equality did not necessarily challenge the underlying structures that sustained racial and economic privilege. However, a brief examination of these thinkers' political thought—and particularly the thought deemed important by Cuban revolutionary historiography—and an examination of the historical context in which they wrote show how the principles of unity, nationalism, and leadership, on the hand, and racial, social, and economic equality, on the other, clashed and aligned in the search for solutions in keeping with the Cuban experience.

What Price Unity? Historicizing a Dilemma

The principle of unity was at the heart of 19th-century debates over slavery and the possible annexation of Cuba. As the following section will show, thinkers struggled with its meaning in the context of foreign threats and internal divisions. One person important in these debates was Father Félix Varela y Morales. Born in Havana in 1788, Varela was a Catholic priest and professor of philosophy at a seminary there. In 1823, the Spanish Crown condemned him to death after he called for Cuban self-rule and an end to slavery, forcing him to flee to the United States, where he would remain for the rest of his life. His student, José Antonio Saco, born in Bayamo in 1797, taught philosophy at the same seminary. The Spanish Crown banished him from the island for his liberal principles, including his opposition to slavery and annexation. Like his mentor, Saco died in exile. Cuban historiography considers Varela the first theorist of Cuban independence and recognizes Saco for his sophisticated arguments against annexation.[75]

In their writing, Varela and Saco were responding to a context in the first half of the 19th century, when some Cuban elites were entertaining a U.S. proposal to annex Cuba. Varela and Saco opposed annexation and supported the gradual abolition of slavery. However, they directed their arguments to wealthy Creole planters who wished to challenge Spanish military, political, and economic dominance without weakening their own privileged socioeconomic position within the island's hierarchy and without losing Spanish military protection.[76] Both were aware that Creole opposition to annexation and support of independence were often tempered by their reliance upon slavery and fear of slave rebellion, a fear fueled by the 1789 Haitian Revolution.[77] Creoles blamed debates about slavery in the Spanish Cortes for the failed slave rebellion in 1812 devised by José Antonio Aponte Ulabarra, a free Creole artist of Yoruba descent.[78] Their fears were also driven by slave uprisings in Cuba in 1826, 1837, and 1843 and by the fact that by 1841 the white population of Cuba was the minority.[79] Events such as the call in 1854 for the implementation of treaties banning the slave trade by Spain's recently appointed captain-general to Cuba, the Marqués de la Pezuela, drew many Cuban planters to the annexationist cause.[80] In short, Creole planters were frustrated by the social gap between them and the Spanish born (*Peninsu-*

lares) but annexation, rather than independence, seemed to provide the best solution since it would preserve slavery and open up markets for sugar. An alliance with the United States, argued proponents of annexation, would remove Spanish obstacles to Creole industriousness and facilitate the kind of gradual reform within the confines of existing socioeconomic relations that full independence would destroy.

Both Varela and Saco believed that successful Cuban independence depended upon the support of Creole planters, whom they saw as sources of wealth, but they also linked independence to social change and the emergence of enlightened ideas. They wanted to convince Creole planters that independence and the gradual abolition of slavery would bring about the same benefits Creoles sought from annexation—especially the security of their wealth. In the pages of his pro-independence magazine *El Habanero*, first published in Philadelphia in 1824, Varela advocated freeing Cuba without foreign aid or interference. He believed that people would support change on the island on the basis of economic interest, rather than political interests or principles.[81] Varela's support for revolution was not based on a desire to break radically with the past. Rather, he saw revolution as a way to avoid dramatic upheaval on the island and damage to the possessions of Creole planters that might come about if Spain went to war with either the United States or England and was unable to defend Cuba.[82]

Saco's arguments against slavery and annexation were also directed to wealthy Creole planters. He argued against slavery in the name of economic efficiency and of maintaining and augmenting the white population. Wage labor, he argued, was cheaper than slave labor since it avoided the cost of taking care of the young, the old and the infirm. Stopping the slave trade would reduce the threat of slave rebellions, while gradually abolishing slavery would give Cubans time both to educate and subdue their black slaves and augment the white population in anticipation of the eventual abolition of slavery. Saco supported Cuban independence, but rejected outright insurrection, which he thought would destroy Cuban property and precipitate slave rebellion. This was the danger also of forced annexation, which would shatter the peaceful state in which white Cubans lived, inciting "Africans" to act "by the force of their instincts."[83]

In arguing for Cuban independence, Saco recognized the temptations of annexation to the United States with its "immense liberty and . . . extraordinary and rapid growth" and its sanctioning of slavery.[84] However, he warned, annexation—whether forced or peaceful—came at too high an economic and cultural price. Forced annexation, he argued, "would produce a disastrous war between the Republic of Washington and Spain, Britain and France."[85] While it was most likely that the United States would triumph over the other three, much life and property would be lost in the process and the United States, while preferable to other colonial powers, would privilege its own economic and territorial concerns over those of the Cuban people. While no colonial status for Cuba was desirable for Saco, of all possible foreign powers to control Cuba, the United States was the most desirable.[86] However, even in the unlikely event that annexation occurred peacefully and Spain gave or sold Cuba to the United States, Saco expressed reservations. In 1848, he wrote: "In spite of the fact that I recognize the advantages that Cuba would attain forming part of those States, a secret sorrow would remain in the bottom of my heart for the loss of Cuban nationality."[87] Saco worried that Anglo-Saxons, who were different from Cubans in their language, religion, and customs, would impose their will on the island through the ballot box and through political and economic power, which would result not in the annexation of Cuba but in its total "absorption" into the United States.[88] Saco wished that the island "was not only wealthy, enlightened, moral and powerful, but that also that it was Cuban and not Anglo American."[89] Saco ended the same paragraph in which he expressed his attachment to Cuban nationalism with a promise that "if peaceful annexation could take place today [he] would suppress the feelings in his heart and vote for annexation."[90]

We thus see Varela and Saco struggling with a variety of concerns: how to gain Cuban independence from the United States and Spain while recognizing the dependence of Cuban wealth upon them; how to unify Cubans in support of independence in the face of their diverse interests and needs; and what a shared Cuban identity might look like. These general concerns did not go away even when annexation became an increasingly less viable option throughout the second half of the 19th century.

Annexation became a less urgent cause when Spain replaced Captain General Pezuela in 1854, thereby ending his attack on the slave trade in Cuba and eliminating one of the main reasons why defenders of slavery supported annexation.[91] When the South was defeated in the Civil War in 1865, one of the main advantages of annexation for Creole planters—namely the preservation of slavery—also disappeared. Creole planters began looking for other ways to secure their interests on the island, such as seeking to benefit from constitutional reforms taking place in Spain and looking for non-African sources of cheap labor in anticipation of a ban on the slave trade or the abolition of slavery entirely.[92]

Not all planters, particularly in the poorer, less slave-intensive and more isolated eastern part of the island, were content with the piecemeal change allowed by Spain. In October 1868, eastern planter Carlos Manuel de Céspedes freed his slaves and in the "Grito de Yara" called for rebellion, sparking Cuba's first attempt at independence, known as the Ten Years' War, which lasted from 1868 to 1878. On the one hand, Carlos Manuel de Céspedes lends himself much more easily to the rhetoric of revolution than figures like Saco, since he actively called for and participated in rebellion. On the other hand, he too was concerned with protecting the interests of Creole landowners in the eastern part of the island.[93] The content of his ideology reflected the privilege that liberalism accorded rights, particularly property rights. In his speech declaring independence he demanded universal suffrage, the gradual abolition of slavery, free exchange with other free nations, national representation in decisions pertaining to taxes and general laws, and the "religious observance of the unalienable rights of man" to all members of an independent Cuba, and he insisted that property rights, including those of peaceful Spanish residents of the island, be respected. Independence from Spain was a prerequisite for these rights of man, said Céspedes. Under Spain, Cubans would never be able to enjoy them.[94] Since Spain refused to relinquish control of the island, rebels had "unanimously agreed to name a single leader to direct operations to the fullest of his capabilities."[95] This single leader (Céspedes) would also be authorized to name those below him in the chain of command as long as the war lasted. Céspedes thus saw strong and unified leadership as the condition for the rebellion's other goals. Equality and freedom could not come without independence, and independence could not come without strong leadership. Independence could also not come without the abolition of slavery. In his 1868 Decree on Slavery, he declared:

> A Free Cuba is incompatible with a slaveholding Cuba; and the abolition of Spanish institutions must include, and include by necessity and for reasons of the highest justice, slavery as the most wicked of all [Spanish institutions]. As such, abolition is found among the proclaimed principles in the first manifesto of the revolution.[96]

While condemning slavery as "the most wicked" of Spanish institutions, however, he was cautious about ending it too quickly and proposed that a number of conditions be in place before emancipation proceeded.[97] He was also not advocating racial equality. Indeed, Céspedes, like many white Cuban abolitionists and supporters of independence, saw slaves as the recipients of white generosity rather than individuals whose freedom and equality was a given and who had every right to demand and take their freedom, as someone like Aponte attempted to do when he organized what came to be known as the Aponte conspiracy of 1812. Condescension rather than full respect characterized the attitude of many white independence fighters toward their black and mulatto comrades, and official revolutionary history has yet to include, at least with any consistency, someone like Aponte as part of the revolution's genealogy.[98] In spite of Céspedes's own limitations, his call for all Cubans to rise up against Spanish tyranny created the space for a more radical and egalitarian struggle than he himself had anticipated. His emphasis on the importance of unified leadership as a prerequisite for other principles such as independence, whether political or economic, and equality, whether economic or racial, reflects a tension that also exists within Cuban socialism.

At the time, this privileging of strong leadership did not go uncontested by his contemporaries within the revolutionary movement. For instance, Céspedes's contemporary and another important national hero in Cuban revolutionary history, Ignacio Agramonte y Loynaz, backed the cause of independence and the abolition of slavery, but he was critical of what he believed were the authoritarian tendencies of other military leaders like Céspedes.[99] The ideas of the legalistically and constitutionally minded Agramonte are less easily incorporated into the teleology of socialist revolution. His writing is consistently critical of communism in particular because, he argued, it tends to concentrate power. In one of his most well-known speeches, "Patria y Mujer" (Homeland and Wife), he writes, against Hobbes and Rousseau, that living in society is not the result of a social contract, but is man's "natural state" and is an "indispensable condition for the development of his physical, intellectual and moral faculties."[100] Natural "individual rights" are "unalienable and indispensable" and cannot be renounced under any condition.[101] He praises the freedom to think and express oneself, freedom of the press, and freedom of contract and work.[102] Too much uniformity, he argues, squelches progress. Centralization impedes freedom, takes people away from industry, and is just one step away from communism, where people are converted into machines executing or passing along the demands of others.[103] It is not surprising, then, that this speech would *not* be included in a two-volume set of Cuban political thought published in Cuba in 2002 and edited by an orthodox Cuban Marxist academic, Isabel Monal. The volume, instead, includes several shorter speeches by Agramonte criticizing Spanish tyranny, celebrating the abolition of slavery, and praising Cuban bravery and unity.[104] Yet, even among the selections in this volume, one might find fodder for a critique of Cuban socialism and the Cuban government in particular. For instance, in his

1869 letter to the revolutionary junta in Havana, speaking for the revolutionary junta in Camagüey, he wrote:

> We love the tight union of all Cubans, and without it, we cannot conceive of the good of Cuba, but that union cannot have any other base than that of democratic institutions, and we cannot, nor should we, cement [those democratic institutions] on the capriciousness and will of one man, because to do so would be to validate the regime that we condemn in the oppressors of Cuba and which launched us into the revolution.[105]

Someone might easily use this passage to critique the political system of post-1959 Cuba, Fidel Castro's dominant role for forty-five years, and specifically the ways that the Cuban government's call for unity can function to silence dissent. Yet, if Agramonte is understood as part of a larger tradition of revolution, his anticommunism hardly matters, just as it hardly matters that Fidel Castro was not a Communist prior to the triumph of the 1959 revolution. Given the multiple uses to which the ideas of these 19th-century thinkers can be put, what a history of these thinkers ideas points to is less a clear socialist heritage than a set of political *dilemmas* and questions that Cuban socialist ideology has also had to negotiate. These thinkers struggled with the question of what an independent Cuba would look like and what kind of unity it would entail. All asked what the relationship was between that unity, on the one hand, and equality and hierarchy, on the other. As the 19th century wore on, figures who would later become key in official Cuban revolutionary historiography increasingly saw unity intricately connected to socioeconomic and racial equality (not simply to the antislavery position). This shift can be seen in the political thought of General Antonio Maceo and José Martí, both of whom were marked by their experiences during the Ten Years' War.

For Maceo, Martí, and others, the Ten Years' War enforced the importance, not just of unity, understood in military terms, but of broader structural equality among Cuba's races and classes. Divisions based on region, race, class, and military strategy within the Cuban revolutionary ranks during the Ten Years' War had weakened the revolutionary cause and made it difficult for Cubans to take advantage of the Spanish troops' lack of familiarity with the eastern terrain and the guerrilla warfare that was used there.[106] Céspedes and Agramonte were both killed in 1874, opening the way for more radical military leaders like Máximo Gómez and Maceo to take prominent roles. A former Spanish officer and exile from his native Dominican Republic following its 1866 civil war, Máximo Gómez y Báez was moved by the disparity between rich and poor to join the rebel army and was considered a master of guerrilla warfare.[107] Antonio Maceo Y Grajales, born in the Oriente Province of Cuba to free black parents in 1845, was a critic of slavery and Spanish domination from a young age. His entrance into a Masonic Lodge in 1864 brought him into "the inner revolutionary circle," and he eagerly joined the rebel army at the start of the Ten Years' War.[108] He too rose within the ranks to become lieutenant general and shared with Gómez a belief in the importance of guerrilla warfare and bringing the struggle to the western part of the island.[109] Their military contributions and the decrease in those sympathetic to annexation, however, could not make up for the cessation of financial support from rich exiles in New York. Spain took advantage of existing divisions, gaining loyalty or acquiescence among the Cuban ranks by promising reform and amnesty. On February 11, 1878, a majority of insurgent generals signed the Pact of Zanjon.[110] The peace treaty gave Cuba the same political and administrative laws enjoyed by Puerto Rico, amnesty for the insurgents and freedom for those slaves and Asians among them.[111] Missing from the pact were two of the revolution's key demands: Cuban independence and emancipation of all slaves.[112] As a consequence, Maceo refused to comply with the treaty, arguing that there could be no peace without independence and no independence unless it was granted to all.[113]

Despite the disappointing end to the Ten Years' War, the experience served as a lesson in the importance of Cuban unity in the face of foreign aggression and signaled the development of a clear Cuban national identity. The collective identity that began to emerge in the beginning of the 19th century was now strengthened by common outrage against Spanish brutality and a common history of heroism from the Ten Years' War, in which blacks and whites fought together against Spain.[114] Spanish failure to live up to the treaty provided Cubans with yet more evidence of the need for Cuban unity. It showed that compromising was no guarantee that even that on which they compromised would be guaranteed.[115] Taking their lessons from the war into exile in New York City, veteran rebels planned a new mass rebellion to take place simultaneously throughout the island in order to avoid the kind of drawn-out conflict that characterized the Ten Years' War.[116]

There remained tensions based on race and class among the Cuban rebel leadership, both in Cuba and in exile, which Spanish spies among their ranks in New York City were able to exploit. Maceo had to constantly quell the fears of white Cuban elites, which were stoked by rumors spread by Spanish spies that Maceo hoped to establish a black republic in Cuba.[117] Unlike Saco and Céspedes, he did so while insisting upon the importance of racial equality. When the rebellion or what is now known as La Guerra Chiquita (The Little War), which Maceo was supposed to have led, broke out earlier than planned in Santiago de Cuba, Maceo (still in Jamaica) issued a proclamation directed to free Cubans, to Spaniards, to immigrant Cubans, and to slaves, and provided each group with its own specific reasons to champion the cause of independence. He reminded slaves, specifically, that those who had won their freedom in the Ten Years' War had won it because the Cuban flag, "the flag of all Cubans," had been "covering them."[118] Thus Maceo linked Cuban independence not just to the abolition of slavery but to racial equality. Unlike Varela, Saco, and Céspedes, he did not support the abolition of slavery because it was expedient for independence. Rather, he saw independence at the service of racial equality. Independence was the means of emancipation for black Cubans, slave and free, and Maceo directed speeches specifically to that audience.[119] Moreover, he did not shun relations with other predominantly black Caribbean nations and sought exile, aid, and counsel from Haiti and Jamaica.[120] Maceo, who was unwilling to delink Cuban independence from the issue of race, was faced with the tension between political unity and the principle of racial equality, and chose to support the former in the hopes that it would facilitate the latter.

Martí and Inclusive Nationalism: An Evolving Principle

By the early 1890s, a new, more radical and inclusive view of Cuban unity was emerging and could be seen most clearly in the political thought of José Martí. This more radical view was not socialist, nor did it lead necessarily to it. It did, however, reflect a more inclusive vision of Cuban nationalism that would come to inform Cuban socialist ideology. Moreover, it emerged out of conditions that were historically specific, but also not entirely alien to the Cuban political terrain more than fifty years later.

Martí's vision reflected the lessons of the Ten Years' War and a new set of geopolitical considerations. Spain abolished slavery in Cuba in 1886. The island had come to depend far more on U.S. markets than Spanish ones. The liberal Autonomist Party, which had sought Cuban autonomy through peaceful means, had lost much of its support.[121] Cubans were also losing patience with Spanish promises of reform. Many Cubans were now exiled in the United States. The task of organizing them fell to Martí, who founded the Partido Revolucionario Cubano (Cuban Revolutionary Party) in January 1892 and was elected its leader. The position gave Martí the opportunity to organize the Cuban exile community in the same way that he wished all Cubans to be united.[122] Martí also founded La Liga, a society for the advancement of black Cuban exiles in New York City that helped to address some of the racial tensions within the independence movement and put into action his call in the party platform for unity among the Cuban people regardless of race, class, and even place of residence. Article 3 of the "Bases del Partido Revolucionario Cubano" (Fundamentals of the Cuban Revolutionary Party) stated:

> The Revolutionary Party will reunite the existing revolutionary elements and gather together, without immoral compromises with any people or individual, as many new elements as it can, with the end of founding in Cuba through a spirited war and republican methods, a nation capable of ensuring the lasting happiness of its children and of carrying out the difficult duties that its geographical situation assigns it.[123]

Martí had spent much of his life in in New York and Florida, working to gain support for Cuban independence among Cuban émigrés of all socioeconomic backgrounds.[124] While wealthy Cuban exiles were hesitant to support the cause of Cuban independence, Cuban cigar workers in Tampa and Key West became the independence movement's primary constituents in the United States. Many had fled during the Ten Years' War, but they remained committed to the cause of Cuban independence, which they supported financially and politically.[125] The community was, for Martí, "living proof . . . that Cubans had the qualities needed to build a new society and a new state."[126] The lessons of the Ten Years' War, but also the demands of this community, meant Martí had to take the nationalist ideology in a more radical direction than his predecessors.

By 1886, the community was still pro-independence, but deeply disillusioned with the progress on the island. As historian Gerald Poyo argues, beyond independence, the liberal nationalist ideology "had no special attraction for most workers" in Florida.[127] When these workers turned to local problems and labor issues in particular, they found that they could not count on the nationalist independence movement for support.[128] Black Cuban émigrés, who had formed their own communities in Florida with their own associations and agendas, were also skeptical of the independence movement, given the racism of its leadership and the way that slavery had been dealt with during the Ten Years' War.[129] The political thought of Saco and Varela was for them clear evidence of the Cuban revolutionary leadership's privileging of the concerns of white planters over those of black and darker-skinned Cubans.

Martí took on the difficult task of uniting the diverse émigré population behind the independence movement. Even after founding the Cuban Revolutionary Party, he was "consumed by the task of keeping together the various financial, military and political factions of the party."[130] His writings often deal with the need for unity, not just among Cubans, but among all Latin Americans, in light of both Spanish colonialism and an ever-growing North American imperial presence in the region. In his now canonical essay "Our America," Martí emphasized the importance of finding a Latin American identity based on common historical experiences and a commitment to nation-building, while rejecting all those divisions (such as racial ones) that Spain used to divide or weaken the independence movement.[131] His writings consistently emphasized the importance of harmony over conflict. Indeed, his "Tributes to Karl Marx, Who has Died" refers not to the dangers of communism's centralizing logic (Agramonte's concern) but of a political movement driven by hatred. Martí applauds Marx for his ability to get to the roots of problems and for standing up for the downtrodden, but he criticizes the antagonistic path he believes Marx's followers (Europe's working classes) promote.[132] Martí believed that love of one's homeland and fellow Latin Americans, rather than hatred of the oppressor, would spark radical (even violent, revolutionary) change. His rejection of the traditional Marxist emphasis on class antagonism was accompanied by an emphasis on unity, but understood in a much more radical sense than earlier Cuban thinkers. Martí saw unity not, for instance, in terms of common Creole interests or as independence from Spain without any changes in the national political, economic, and racial hierarchies. He believed common experiences and history rooted in the Americas, rather than Europe, would provide knowledge upon which to build not just the Cuban nation, but Latin American nations in general.[133] Latin Americans could not govern effectively if they relied upon European thought and models of governance.[134] Rather than relying on "false erudition," Latin Americans needed to create institutions based on knowledge of themselves, of their character, their customs, and their histories.[135] Solidarity could not be presumed, but instead had to be built, via the search for collective self-understanding and independence.[136] The common project of creating, building, and sustaining a new nation was the true source of Cuban unity. Any divisions that interfered with that project were to be avoided.[137]

Martí's view of national unity as color-blind had more and less radical implications. His argument in "Our America," and his argument about race in particular, would be put to different uses throughout the 20th century. Cuban elites used Martí's works to dismiss racism and racial inequality as a legacy of the past that had supposedly been resolved by abolition, independence, or socialism; and they blamed inequality on individual failings, while accusing those concerned with racial inequality or who dared to express racial pride of insufficient patriotism and racism. A popular form of Martí's view of national unity, however, was used to make demands on the Cuban state and contrast continued inequality with Martí's ideal of a truly racially egalitarian republic.[138]

The same could be said of Martí's political thought more generally. On the one hand, it represented a more radical, progressive view of *Cubania*, of Cuban independence, than his predecessors and one with radical potential political, but, on the other hand, it did not necessarily lead directly (teleologically) to socialism. Looking at the history of Cuban socialism in terms of dilemmas and problems avoids viewing Cuban socialist ideology either as the direct and necessary heir of radical nationalism or as a betrayal of the political thought of the historical figures who articulated this radical nationalism. It also presents not just the linear transformation of an ideology, but its horizontal negotiation, understood both temporally and spatially.

What Cubans call *Cubania* or "the teleological belief in cubanidad" predates and is irreducible to nationalism or even proto-nationalism.[139] Antoni Kapcia traces the historical roots of *Cubania* as a "minority (white) intellectual concern" and its transformation first into an ideology of dissent (what Kapcia calls "*cubania rebelde*") that informed Cuban radicalism of various forms during the late 19th century up to the 1950s, and then, after the 1959 revolution, into "*cubania revolucionaria*," a new hegemonic ideology of dissent that has been fundamental in guiding the revolutionary process" ever since.[140] Specifically, Kapcia shows how certain "value-beliefs," such as agrarianism, collectivism, moralism, activism, culturalism, statism, and revolution, evolved over time into codes that stabilize the meaning of these value-beliefs so that they are comprehensible to those who share that ideology. These codes both extol certain values and respond to particular political problems.[141] Codes that took on such significance as to stand in for the whole ideology, rather than being only a facet of it, became myths.[142] Thus, Kapcia locates the roots of Cuban socialism in earlier political thought, understood both as an intellectual project and a set of popular beliefs, without collapsing, for instance, 19th-century political thought into post-1959 socialist thought.

Kapcia argues that since 1959, *cubania revolucionaria* has operated at two levels: the popular-empirical, which is closer to political culture and is customizable and flexible, and the intellectual-theoretical, which is constituted by a "coherent system of theoretical propositions." The two levels, however, depend upon one another. The second helps codify the first, whereas the first provides an environment in which the second can take root.[143] Moreover, within each level of the new ideology of *cubania revolucionaria*, there have existed competing discourses.[144] As an example, Kapcia points to the Great Debate of the 1962–65 period, when two general positions emerged about the best way to build socialism in Cuba. One represented the more orthodox view that socialism needed to rely on the tools of capitalism, such as profits, material incentives, and pricing, in order to establish a solid economic foundation; the other represented a more "Latin American Marxist" position, which gave greater credence to voluntarism and to the specific conditions and histories of the country in which socialism was to be built. There have been many such discourses throughout Cuban revolutionary history.

While Cuban socialism has a historical trajectory, it is interrupted by moments of ideological negotiation and variation. Those moments of negotiation and variation should be understood, however, not as correct or incorrect appropriations of history, as either faithful or instrumental uses of history, but rather as different ways of combining principles whose significances are historically rooted, but which are combined in different ways to make sense of and respond to particular historical conditions. As Karl Mannheim argues, it is only by studying an ideology as it is articulated by a variety of political actors operating within a shared social and historical context, and then comparing these perspectives, that one can begin to grasp the meaning of that same ideology.[145] Thus, the question is no longer whether ideology is opportunistic, but rather what form does an ideology take at a particular moment (how does it combine key principles inherited from history) and how effectively does that particular combination illuminate and guide people at a particular historical juncture. Ultimately, the answer is found within the ideology itself, but there is also a political answer that escapes analytic categorization.

Two

Words and Intellectuals

Cultural Production in Revolutionary Times

———

In a speech at the opening session of the First Congress of Latin American Youth on July 28, 1960, Che Guevara told his audience that he was aware that many people wanted to know what the ideology of the Cuban Revolution was. "In the case that it is Marxist—and listen well that I say Marxist—it would be because it also discovered, by its methods, the changes that Marx pointed to."[1] Fidel Castro would not declare the revolution socialist until 1961 and himself a Marxist-Leninist until 1962. Che, here and elsewhere, still used conditional grammar when discussing Marxism in relation to the Cuban Revolution.[2] However, even by 1960, as Che said in his speech, "The Cuban Revolution of today, while carrying on, is not the revolution of yesterday, even after its victory."[3]

In this chapter I explore debates in the 1960s about the meaning and future of Cuban socialism to demonstrate the living character of Cuban socialist ideology. The ideology of the Cuban Revolution was not taken for granted or fixed, although some argued that it should be. Many intellectuals invested in the revolution understood the ideology of the revolution as a "living ideology." They believed revolutionary ideology developed out of an active engagement with the project of constructing socialism, rather than being a direct reflection of a particular class position or resulting from the adoption of the proper attitude or point of view for all times and situations. The latter formulations, they argued, were ahistorical and idealist and represented a betrayal of Marxism rather than a loyalty to it.

After the seizure of political power, the primary question was no longer whether one had been for or against Batista, but rather what a new Cuba would look like: who would lead in this new stage, and how. Many firsthand

and secondary accounts of the initial years of the revolution emphasize the exclusions of liberals and moderates from government institutions, the increasing consolidation of power under the leadership of Fidel Castro, the narrowing of debate throughout the 1960s, and the culmination of this narrowing in the codification of limitations on the freedom of expression in 1976.[4] The date of the final straw is not always the same, but in general these accounts tell the story of how the initial euphoria and burst of unfettered political and creative activities following the ousting of Batista were squelched by an increasing political repression as the 1960s wore on. This repression reached its climax during the Gray Years between 1971 and 1976, when powerful bureaucrats, under the spell of orthodox socialist realism, determined the appropriate content of artistic, literary, and intellectual production, making those who failed to conform suffer personally and professionally. In these accounts, Cubans, and particularly artists, writers, and intellectuals, were forced to choose conformity to an increasingly narrow official ideology, or exile, imprisonment, or obscurity. Free expression was a possibility only because of compromise with state institutions and official ideology, which necessarily harms artistic and intellectual production by politicizing it.[5] Those on the left who participated in the revolution, falsely believing themselves free to act as they wished, did not realize that they, too, would be forced out of the government apparatus, the public sphere, and ultimately the country. The large numbers of artists and intellectuals who had left the island by the end of the 1960s attests to the experience of revolution as increasingly intolerant and repressive.[6] The institutional terrain has been more expansive and forgiving during some periods than others, and this, rather than ideological agreement alone, has influenced the decision of whether an individual sought to negotiate with the system at all.

This picture is too simple. The quantity and sophistication of many discussions throughout the 1960s contradicted the view that "ideology" in Cuba, and socialist ideology specifically, meant only one thing: narrowing and crushing of debate.[7] Political thought is political because it develops in specific contexts, which are never free of constraints. For some who have considered the meaning of socialist ideology, these constraints specific to the revolution have been constitutive of Cuban socialist ideology, and not simply obstacles to thinking about it. Some Cuban intellectuals and artists have thought similarly about their role in the revolution and about the relationships between art, culture, and intellectual production, on the one hand, and radical political change, on the other. Some have seen themselves neither as intellectual functionaries nor as a creative class stifled by the political demands of the state, but rather as active participants in the revolutionary process. The frustrations of these participants, the decision by some to leave (and even to dismiss their earlier activities as naive, shortsighted, or coerced), the failure of their contributions to translate into policy, or their apparent defeat during particularly repressive periods does not negate the contributions they have made to Cuban socialist ideology, nor have the strains of socialist ideology they articulated been permanently suppressed.

In the 1960s, artists and intellectuals attempted to resist a liberal paradigm of intellectual production that suggested that their participation in the revolution necessarily compromised their status as intellectuals. Ironically, it was not only liberals who upheld this paradigm. There were also those within the Cuban leadership and cultural institutions who insisted that intellectual and cultural production was political, while simultaneously arguing against and curbing efforts on the part of intellectuals and artists to participate in revolutionary *politics* as intellectuals and artists. Those who resisted this paradigm argued that while there were distinct spheres of cultural and intellectual production and a distinct official sphere of the political, each with its own sets of techniques and concerns, there was also a zone of participation where cultural and intellectual production overlapped with the official sphere. According to this view, cultural and intellectual production could only be revolutionary if this overlap was permitted. These productions were "within the revolution," because they remained committed to its principles and disagreed with the leadership in the name of those same principles.

The Immediate Postrevolution: New Institutions, New Subjectivities, and New Debates

Upon taking power, the new provisional government, made up largely of members of the 26th of July Movement, began transforming the economic, political, and cultural landscape. In the first nine months, it enacted an estimated 1,500 decrees in response to the increasing demands of a Cuban population frustrated by years of political corruption and ineptitude and eager for socioeconomic change in a country with great disparities in wealth and access to basic services.[8] These decrees appealed to large swaths of the Cuban population, who benefited from wage increases, employment and education opportunities, reduced living expenses, increased access to social services, and other forms of wealth redistribution, and who supported these decrees in the face of bourgeois opposition.[9] In appealing to and satisfying existing demands, the provisional government also created new subjectivities and interests.[10]

The new government began to alter lives and create new constituencies in the area of culture.[11] It often turned to culture as a way to engage with a particular community even as it was formally narrowing that community's political agency. For example, the government's encroachment into the private sphere benefited black and dark-skinned Cubans by redistributing wealth, providing new employment and educational opportunities, and banning racial discrimination and segregation, but these policies can also be understood as paternalistic treatment of black Cubans and an attempt to curb black power and influence. While the state encouraged the celebration of Afro-Cuban culture, and created institutions to support it, it now prohibited black political organizations and limited black political agency.[12]

In a resource-poor environment, culture, like labor power, would be a key resource for revolution.[13] The revolution depended upon mobilizing the Cuban people. Cultural development, and artistic development specifically, would be fundamental to that mobilization.[14] The new government created institutions that would enable it to continue the revolutionary struggle in the cultural realm. These institutions, some more than others, provided spaces from which new debates and positions would emerge. Even before the 26th of July Movement took power, the rebel army, aware of the importance of the "means of mass communication," occupied radio stations and ensured that its message was published in the Cuban press as well as abroad.[15] The revolutionary process, after taking power, was also a "media event," with cameras rolling as the leadership explained new laws and condemned its enemies.[16]

The revolutionary government's first decree concerning cultural affairs was the creation of El Instituto Cubano de Arte e Industria Cinematográficos (ICAIC) in March 1959, after Fidel Castro had taken over as prime minister. It immediately began production of documentaries about the revolutionary struggle. The same month, the National Printing House opened with the "purpose of stimulating literary and scientific production."[17] *Lunes de Revolución*, the literary supplement to the paper of the 26th of July Movement, *Revolución*, also began publication in March 1959. *Hoy*, the paper of the Communist Party, too began publication of a literary supplement. In April, the Cuban Armed Forces began publication of its weekly magazine *Verde Olivo*, which dealt with a wide range of issues related to the changes taking place in Cuba beyond military ones and contained articles, some by Che Guevara, signaling the revolution's Marxist sympathies. Later that same month, Casa de las Américas was created, and it began publication of *Revista Casa de las Américas* in 1960. *Verde Olivo* as well the National Council for Culture (CNC) started in 1960 under the directorship of former Popular

Socialist Party (PSP) member Edith García Buchaca, provided places from which to articulate some of the more orthodox positions on the role of culture in revolution.

By the end of 1959, then, there were several institutional spaces in which to debate the relationship between culture and revolution. The government's use and support of culture did not translate into the imposition of socialist realism or total government control of cultural production, even though some people within these institutions expressed such views. The new cultural institutions created avenues for discourse, at times at odds with that of the leadership or with one another, and allowed many people to discuss what a Cuban socialist culture could be and what it could do. Within the realm of art and literature, there were, at this stage, three main groups participating in the struggle for ideological hegemony—the intellectuals from the prerevolutionary Communist Party; members of ICAIC, many of whom who had in some way been involved in the PSP in the past; and finally, people like Carlos Franqui and Guillermo Cabrera Infante, editors of *Revolución* and its literary supplement *Lunes de Revolución*.[18]

The third group was the most resistant to the direction that Fidel Castro and the leadership began to take the revolution, and specifically to the increasingly strident demands to fall in line with the positions of the Cuban leadership. *Lunes* had no fixed editorial team, and while it came to be seen as a space for intellectuals returning from exile under Batista to publish their views, its first editorial "clearly stated that *Lunes* did not have a previous politico-philosophical position."[19] According to Franqui, it aimed to "break down the barriers that separated elite culture from mass culture."[20]

Neither Franqui nor Cabrera Infante was a member of the old liberal and moderate elite who, though part of the 26th of July Movement, found themselves increasingly excluded from government positions throughout 1959 and 1960.[21] Both men had actively participated in the struggle against Batista and had briefly been members of the prerevolutionary PSP. They would, however, use the pages of *Revolución* and *Lunes* to protect the revolution from creeping Soviet-style Communism in the guise of the "Old Communists" from before the revolution and to push it in a more social democratic and humanist direction.[22] *Revolución*, according to Franqui, was concerned with maintaining autonomy from the government not just for its editorial staff but for those with whom they disagreed as well.[23] He described it as "neither official nor the mouthpiece of any ideology" but rather "the newspaper of the revolution" and one that "posed a challenge."[24]

Thus, while Franqui called for a neutral space for debate and believed that *Revolución* did and should provide that space, he also saw *Revolución* as a champion of an ideological position of anticommunism, political reform, and social justice that went beyond the call for the press to be a site where a variety of views could be expressed. Moreover, he hoped *Revolución* would ideally not just be a participant in a marketplace of ideas, but also the victor in the struggle for ideological hegemony in the cultural sphere. Those involved with *Revolución* wished to participate in the revolution, but as during Batista's reign, they wanted to do so largely as critics.

By their own accounts, a number of events signaled an end to their vision and their participation in the struggle for cultural hegemony. These included the censoring of the 1961 film *P.M.* (Pasado Meridiano), Edith García Buchaca's attack on *Lunes,* and the series of meetings in June 1961, when Prime Minister Fidel Castro as well as President Osvaldo Dorticós, Minister of Education Armando Hart, and other key cultural officials from the government and the CNC met at the National Library to discuss the relationship between culture and revolution, and which culminated in Castro's "Words to the Intellectuals" and the closing of *Lunes*.

P.M. was a short documentary-style account of Havana nightlife, directed by Orlando Jiménez Leal and Sabá Cabrera Infante, Guillermo Infante's brother. According to Ernesto Juan Castellanos, the film was one of the first in the history of Cuban cinema that showed black Cubans enjoying themselves.[25] For the Cuban leadership, however, and harking back to the white paternalism of the 19th-century wars of independence, this enjoyment was not in keeping with what they viewed to be the appropriate image of a heroic and hardworking black population liberated from the vices of the past. Michael Chanan writes that though *P.M.* "presented black people in roles associated with the state of oppression from which they were in process of liberation," its banning was due less to the content of the film than to the fact that it came out right after the Bay of Pigs invasion in April 1961, when Fidel Castro declared the revolution socialist.[26] The film itself is rather innocuous, giving us views of people getting off a ferry in Havana Harbor and then several scenes of a mostly black clientele drinking and dancing to live music. The film appeared on *Lunes en Televisión,* but the Commission for the Study and Classification of Film (CECP) of ICAIC blocked its release on the wide screen in May 1961, arguing that the film offered "a partial picture of Havana nightlife" that did not do justice to the Cuban people's struggles against the counterrevolution instigated by U.S. imperialism.[27] Fidel Castro adopted the position of ICAIC and upheld the ban without having seen the film himself, which gives a sense of the important role ICAIC played as cultural arbitrator.[28]

ICAIC, however, would not always be clearly on the side of censorship. Many of its members eventually challenged calls for censorship, but not on liberal grounds of protecting the independence of the academic and artistic spheres from political control. As Michael Chanan argues, ICAIC resisted efforts to "impose aesthetic formulas like socialist realism on Cuban cultural production"; but it did so, not as liberals, but as leftists, operating "on the principle of Fidel's famous dictum of 1961, 'Within the Revolution, everything; against it [the Revolution], nothing.'"[29] One response to Castro's call to distinguish between friends and enemies of the revolution that is often obscured by a liberal-versus-hardliner lens was to insist that there were a variety of ways in which artists and intellectuals could be friends to the revolution. Exploring these ways was an embrace, rather than a rejection or evasion, of their responsibility as revolutionary intellectuals. According to this view, it was not enough to simply *not* be an enemy, as both liberals and hardliners suggested. Rather, the goal was to be a friend, but *as* an intellectual and artist, even if this meant at times being misrecognized as an enemy.

Politicizing Intellectual Production: Castro's "Word to the Intellectuals"

The oft-cited phrase "within the revolution, everything; against the revolution, nothing" is from Castro's "Words to Intellectuals," which is frequently regarded as evidence of the totalitarian turn of the revolution. However, the speech can be read not just as an expression of an ideology that functioned to discipline or repress Cubans, but also as a framework for later theorizing in Cuba about the relationship between culture and revolution. Those referring to the speech later on would emphasize some of the speech's elements over others, in order to take the repressive logic of the argument further than Fidel Castro himself took it, or to show how one element existed in tension with the another, or in order to explore what it meant to be a Cuban intellectual and a revolutionary.

The now famous phrase is quite ambiguous.[30] Castro drew a clear line between friends of the revolution and enemies who posed an existential threat, but he was less clear about what ideas or behaviors crossed the line.[31] That the friend/enemy distinction lacked content only underlined the extent to which he believed the revolution politicized intellectual production. The statement was not just a warning that certain themes might be off limits but also that those engaged in intellectual production needed to consult regularly with officials to know what these themes were. More broadly, it was a reminder that intellectual production was political. Academic production should both respond to the exigencies of particular historical moments and anticipate the context of its reception. It was as much about the production of a new kind of intellectual—a revolutionary intellectual—as it was about censorship.

In other ways, the speech was quite clear about the new rules. Castro began by privileging the leadership over intellectuals and artists. This privileging was cloaked in humility. Castro explained that the government was not the most qualified to discuss intellectual matters. However, the economic and social revolution of which they were the primary agents led directly to changes in the cultural sphere.[32] Culture "specialists" were only secondary actors. Still, since the revolution had taken place quickly the leadership "did not have all the principal problems solved." It was thus important that all recognize fallibility in their points of view and work together to learn.[33] This participation, rather than one's past revolutionary activities, determined one's revolutionary credentials.

> [I] believe that all of us should have a similar attitude, whatever our deeds have been. No matter how meritorious they may seem, we must begin by placing ourselves in the honest position of not presuming to know more than others do, of not presuming that we have learned everything that can be learned, of not presuming that our points of view are infallible, and not presuming that those who do not think exactly the same way are mistaken.[34]

In what Juan Carlos Quintero Herencia refers to as a deauthorizing move, Castro called upon both the intellectuals ("you") and the leadership ("we") to adopt the appropriate attitude of openness to other points of view.[35] The adoption of this position of openness would lead not to a diversity of opinions, he suggested, but rather to consensus. That consensus would be guaranteed by privileging one criterion: "the revolution itself."[36] According to this logic then, failure to reach consensus indicated both a failure to privilege the revolution and a failure to keep an open mind.

For Castro, there was no contradiction between the call to keep an open mind and the call to maintain the right attitude because the right attitude would create conditions for greater freedom. It made no sense to worry that the revolution would take away freedom of expression, since it was the revolution itself that brought freedom and culture. Only those who were not "certain of [their] revolutionary convictions," he argued, would even concern themselves with the issue of freedom of expression, and while those in such a category were not necessarily counterrevolutionary, they were certainly not revolutionary.[37]

While the government was not going to tell people what to write or paint at every moment, work would be evaluated "through the prism of the revolutionary lens."[38] The revolutionary and nonrevolutionary artists had the same rights, but those rights could not trump the rights of the revolution, he argued, since the revolution took into account the interests of the people, whereas artistic rights were based on merely personal preferences.[39]

However, artists and intellectuals should not fear the hand of the state, for the state too had an interest in culture as a key element in the betterment of all Cubans' lives.

> The revolution cannot attempt to stifle art or culture when one of the goals and one of the basic objectives of the revolution is to develop art and culture, precisely so that art and culture will come to be a genuine patrimony of the people. And just as we have wanted a better life for the people in the material sphere, so do we also want a better life for the people in all spiritual realms and a better life in the cultural realm.[40]

Castro also suggested that the revolutionary state should not be feared since the socialist revolution would eventually do away with it.[41] Faith in the present state authority, including in the cultural sphere, provided the best guarantee against state authority by working for the state's dissolution. Castro also argued that the meetings that had culminated in his speech were evidence that intellectuals and artists had nothing to fear. The government provided "the freedom with which everyone has been able to speak and explain his opinions." There was no reason "for anyone to put its spirit of justice and of fairness in doubt."[42] While his speech left little room for dissent without actually establishing its limits, Castro also provided more concrete examples of what revolutionary artistic freedom might mean, and of the ways in which intellectuals had been exploited prior to the revolution and would benefit from an improvement in material conditions. Before the revolution, the wealthy bought artists' works for a pittance. Without this class of people, the revolution took on the responsibility of ensuring that artists were "guaranteed not only the proper material conditions at present, but also security for the future."[43] He referred to the National Council for Culture provision of guidance and funding to such important institutions as the National Printing House, the Cuban Symphony Orchestra, the Cuban Ballet, the National Library, and ICAIC.[44] The implication of his emphasis on ballet and classical music was that the culture he wished the masses to learn to appreciate was Western European bourgeois culture. When he spoke of culture for the people he meant only the distribution of certain artistic products and tools and of proper training in specific arts. The value of cultural production, in short, was to be judged on the basis of its proximity to Western culture and the extensiveness of its distribution.

Castro's "Words to the Intellectuals," then, involved a constant back and forth, reminding intellectuals and artists of the boundaries the revolution might impose on their production, on the one hand; and appealing to their material interests and their cultural sensibilities, on the other. He called upon intellectuals to join the revolution not only by supporting the government but also by "wag[ing] a war against a lack of culture."

> We are going to fight it, and we are going to test our weapons. Someone does not want to take part? Well, what greater punishment than to deprive oneself of the satisfaction in what others are doing? We were talking about being privileged, because we had learned how to read and to write in a school, and could go to an institute or a university, or at least acquire the sufficient rudiments of education necessary to be able to do something. And can we not call ourselves privileged for being able to live in the midst of a revolution?[45]

Not to participate in this war against the lack of culture was to be left out of history. Respect the fundamental right of the revolution to exist and the revolution would welcome and nurture your artistic and intellectual endeavors in the name of improving the cultural and material lives of all Cubans.

There was, then, some clarity as to what was "within the revolution." Or, to put it another way, his message to the artist and intellectual was the following: You may do your work and you do not have to be a revolutionary, understood either as participating in mass organizations and stating your loyalty or as using your cultural production as a vehicle to exalt the revolution (socialist realism). At the same time, your work should not be counterrevolutionary. One way to know that it is not counterrevolutionary is that it conforms to Western European standards of what counts as valuable cultural production. One's contribution to the revolution was then not directly *through* their art, but rather because of their art. In keeping with a traditional Marxist dialectic, the existence of (Western) culture and its dissemination to the masses was itself a celebration of the revolution and its successes. Bourgeois culture was not negated but socialized. To contribute politically to the revolution as an artist or intellectual was then to keep politics separate from cultural or intellectual production.

There is another way in which the ideology of the speech is less ambiguous than it might first appear. It did frame future discussions, not just in the narrow sense that state institutions, as extensions of the Cuban leadership, would ultimately decide what types of cultural and intellectual production were acceptable (what was within the revolution), but also in the sense that individual intellectuals would use this framework when considering their relationship to the revolution. Using this framework, as we will see, did not necessarily translate into complacency. Instead it served as one source, among others, for some of the principles of Cuban socialism that various groups appealed to in their struggles over cultural hegemony, and specifically their struggles over the definitions and practices of revolutionary intellectualism and artistic production.

Marxism-Leninism and Culture

The first years of the revolution could be characterized not just by the closing and narrowing of debates, but also but the opening of new cultural institutions oriented around the question of what it meant to contribute to the revolution. At the same time that the government was closing *Lunes* and other literary supplements, it created UNEAC (Unión Nacional de Escritores y Artistas Cubanos), which began publication of the journals *Unión* and *La Gaceta de Cuba*. *Cuba Socialista* also began publication in 1961. In the summer of 1961, the government created the Integrated Revolutionary Organizations (ORI) out of the three separate organizations primarily responsible for the overthrow of Batista—the 26th of July Movement, the Directorio Revolucionario (DR), and the PSP—and its members found in *Cuba Socialista* a place to publish their views. In spite of greater institutionalization and the apparently disciplining words of Fidel Castro, debates continued between two of the three groups that were struggling for ideological hegemony at the start of the revolution. Throughout 1963 and 1964, *La Gaceta de Cuba* and *Cuba Socialista* as well as the newspaper *Hoy* served as sites for polemical debates about the class character of culture; the role of the party and government in cultural production; the status of ideological struggle in the revolution; the role of the intellectual in that struggle; and the relationship and responsibility of artists and intellectuals to the Cuban public. On one side of this polemic were people like Edith García Buchaca; Mirta Aguirre (professor in the School of Letters at the University of Havana); the Uruguayan historian and essayist Sergio Benvento (who directed the Department of General History of the School of History at the University of Havana); another Uruguayan professor living in Cuba at the time, Juan J. Flo; and Blas Roca, who, along with Carlos Rafael Rodríguez, was one of the few members of the prerevolutionary Communist Party to occupy any position of power within the postrevolutionary government, albeit in the secretariat, and not in the Politburo or the Central Committee. They generally read Fidel Castro's "Words to the Intellectuals" as a call for artists and intellectuals to rid themselves of prerevolutionary bourgeois ideology in order to better contribute to the fight against imperialism and to the construction of socialism. According to this reading, the Party and government were to take an active role not just in encouraging artistic and intellectual production through the creation of institutions and public funding, but also in guiding and molding the form and content of this production.

On the other side of the polemic were members of ICAIC, most prominently its director, Alfredo Guevara, and the filmmakers Jorge Fraga, Julio García Espinosa, and Tomás Gutiérrez Alea.[46] They took seriously Fidel Castro's call in "Words to Intellectuals" for them to consider their role in the revolution, but they took issue with what they felt to be opportunistic appropriations of Fidel Castro's speeches and vulgar readings of Marxism-Leninism that justified dogmatism and precluded artists and intellectuals from participating in the struggle for socialism *as* artists and intellectuals. In general, members of ICAIC represented themselves as allied against dogmatism and against attempts to disarm the artist and intellectuals by limiting the weapons available to them to fight for and construct socialism in Cuba. Neither side explicitly disavowed socialist realism, but instead contested its meaning. Both sides insisted that they were providing a properly Marxist understanding of cultural production in keeping with Fidel Castro's "Words to the Intellectuals." Each side accused the other of proposing a model of artistic and intellectual production that did nothing to contribute to the construction of socialism in Cuba.

One polemic began in the summer of 1963, after *La Gaceta de Cuba* published a statement signed by several well-known filmmakers at ICAIC including Humberto Solas, Tomás Gutiérrez Alea, Sara Gómez, and Nicolás M. Guillén.[47] Citing Marx and Engels, they argued that culture did not belong to one class, but rather had a universal character.[48] "Attributing a class character to artistic forms," they wrote, "arbitrarily restricts the conditions of struggle and restricts the development of art."[49] Art and culture from before the revolution should not automatically be disqualified on the basis of its origin in bourgeois society.

Alfredo Guevara expressed his general support for the spirit of the filmmakers position in ICAIC's film magazine *Cine Cubano* several months later.⁵⁰ Artistic culture was not just national, but international, and revolutionaries had a duty to engage in global discussions about culture, including engaging with forms from capitalist society. The revolution would not be served by intellectuals sticking their heads in the sand, and, he wrote, the "critical method can't be, nor should be, supplanted by a mechanical copy of critical experience."⁵¹ Discussion "and even polemic" were necessary to the revolutionary struggle. Even prior to the publication of the statement from ICAIC, *La Gaceta de Cuba* had published articles criticizing attempts by some to use the defense of the revolution from external and internal threats as an excuse to define culture in narrow formulaic terms. Juan Blanco wrote that while the revolution had rid Cuba of most enemies of art and culture, including the businessman, the priest, BRAC (Bureau for the Repression of Communist Activities), SIM (the Military Intelligence Service), and imperialism; and while it was not possible to stop the progress of culture in Cuba, there were still some forces to reckon with. Both the "dogmatist of the left" and the "opportunist of the right," argued Blanco, opposed the "ample cultural policy of the revolutionary government and wanted Cuban artists, with their backs turned away from all the achievements of culture, past and present, to adopt only one expressive channel and to cultivate only one form."⁵² In doing so, they failed to see how prerevolutionary forms and culture had advanced before the revolution in spite of conservative attempts to suppress them, and that these could be put to service of the socialist revolution. He wrote: "What we defend, what we want, is the same the revolution defends and wants; the same that our leadership defends: within the revolution fit all artistic tendencies, against the revolution, none of them."⁵³ Julio García Espinosa warned of those who, in the name of ending the chaos of market, tried "to become the owners of man instead of trying to make it so that man becomes owner of himself." Rather than rushing to replace old recipes with new ones, he wrote, it would be better to "learn to live in the rain," to see the "new reality" and to discover the new questions posed by that reality.⁵⁴ While the revolution required new artists, these artists would not emerge by determining the content of their work beforehand. Similarly, revolutionary films that presented an ideal exceptional hero of the revolution did harm to the real heroes who would emerge not by copying ideal types derived from experiences foreign to the Cuban Revolution, but through their participation in the creation of socialism in Cuba. What was needed, he argued in the tradition of José Martí, was not a new model but rather new creators.⁵⁵

The document from ICAIC and ensuing clarifications and defenses of it provoked a variety of critical responses. These critics portrayed the members of ICAIC as naive adventurers who hid their attachment to bourgeois ideology behind the cloak of antidogmatism, and who failed to take a sufficiently critical attitude toward their own ideological baggage and towards prerevolutionary cultural forms. Edith García Buchaca, in her response to ICAIC and to what she called its "Manifesto," insisted that the role of the revolutionary government was not simply to promote art and culture, but also to orient and direct it.[56] The members of ICAIC were right that while each socioeconomic formation produced its own culture, this did not mean that culture from the past was necessarily of no use under socialism.[57] However, she warned against an "eclectic attitude" especially toward cultural forms from abroad. Making use of Cuba's cultural past demanded "a critical attitude" based on the fact that "we are constructing a socialist society and engaging in a relentless fight against an imperialism that does not tolerate ideological concessions, that demands that our people remain constantly alert to the most subtle and apparently inoffensive forces that could undermine the security of Cubans today and that of humanity's future."[58] It meant, argued Mirta Aguirre in a similar vein in *Cuba Socialista*, keeping in mind the dangers of vague discussions about humanity and culture delinked from class.[59] It meant picking those cultural forms from the past that served to illuminate and expose "the most important content of reality," rather than those (like surrealism) that necessarily obscured reality.[60] Whereas art before socialism was used as a fetish to perpetuate myths and falsehoods, argued Aguirre, "in the hands of dialectic materialism" art could and should contribute "to sweeping from the mind of men the dense shadows of ignorance." It should replace "a religious conception of the world with the scientific" and defeat "philosophical idealism."[61] Socialist realism was a "vehicle of truth," "the road to knowledge," and a "weapon for the transformation of the world."[62] Moreover, argued Sergio Benvenuto, the ICAIC signers wrongly presumed that culture was "a no man's land, neutral, like a giant storehouse where Tyrians and Trojans alike supply us with the same products, without us needing to do anything more than extend our arm and remove them from a shelf."[63] The revolutionary task was not to conserve bourgeois culture, but to take the positive elements while destroying the negative ones, and this could only be done if "we are more revolutionary than artist, more Marxist than antidogmatic, more creators than inheritors."[64]

Adopting the proper attitude, then, was fundamental. Indeed, Aguirre argued, while training in materialist philosophy might aid artists in producing socialist realism, it was enough that an artist allied himself "with the proletariat in the class struggle, enough that he refuses abstract metaphysical conceptions of man and society, enough that he possesses creative stature . . . so that the work, inspired by principles of socialist realism, can flow from him naturally, which is the only way, anyway, that it should flow."[65] She criticized artists and intellectuals who, rather than working to rid themselves of "the ideological vestiges of the defeated society within them," were "bent on finding justification for them."[66] Citing "Words to the Intellectuals," she argued that the revolution's only demand was "respect for the revolution" and that threats to the revolution were also threats to the creative spirit.[67] Expressions of concern over attempts to control artistic and intellectual production were evidence of a lack of faith in the revolution and the degree to which many Cuban intellectuals and artists remained attached to bourgeois notions of culture.[68]

The concern of ICAIC members with dogmatism, argued Juan Flo, was simply a foil for ideological confusion.[69] Dogmatism was dangerous, he agreed, but it was more dangerous to challenge dogmatism from the position that the artist "is the custodian of certain eternal values threatened by the uncultured proletariat."[70] Only artists who allied themselves "theoretically and practically" with "the proletariat cause" would be in a position to "combat dogmatism . . . from an authentically Marxist attitude."[71] The statement of the ICAIC members was insufficiently Marxist, argued Sergio Benvenuto, because it treated culture as if it were independent or peripheral to class struggle and its material base, and with its own norms and criteria.[72] The document's diversity of viewpoints and the absence of references to Marxism illustrated its failure to be antidogmatic from a Marxist position. The problem of the dogmatist was not that he subordinated means to ends, but that he did so mechanically.[73] However, the antidogmatic who privileged the end of discussion over the ends about which all discussion had to be directed was worse since this position led to "fantastic confusions of principle." The signers of the ICAIC had mechanistically transferred the "principle" of "within the revolution, everything and against it nothing" onto ideology. While the social process of the revolution might leave space for those who neither actively supported nor opposed it, this did not apply to the ideology of the revolution. According to Benvenuto, a proper understanding of the principle in relation to ideology was the following: "within the ideology of the revolution, everything, and against it, nothing."[74] Just as the social process was not to be confused with the ideology, Marxism could not be confused with eclecticism, antidogmatism with an abandonment of the goals of socialist revolution, and "salon heresies" with the development of revolutionary ideology.[75] "But what systematic heresy can never be," he wrote, "is not even an occasional means in a socialist society based on systematically true and just principles."[76]

The signers of the ICAIC document responded to all these charges and they did so by insisting that it was their critics who had an insufficient understanding of Marxism, and specifically *dialectical* materialism. For instance, to the argument that government should not just promote but also determine the content of art and culture, Jorge Fraga countered that the first implied the second, but that while the general promotion of art and culture would be constant, the exact direction was contingent upon concrete historical conditions, and that García had committed the idealist error of promoting an abstract apolitical and empty culture separate from particular political ends.[77]

> A by-product of this error is the criterion that culture must subjugate itself to the interests of politics. Such a criterion doesn't take into account that the final objective of politics is culture and not the other way around, and [such a criterion] contains, moreover, an abstract vision of culture that forgets the profound identification that exists between politics and culture, because culture is, itself, politics.[78]

This did not mean that idealism should be rejected simply because of its association with bourgeois culture. Intellectuals, far from being unconscious or unreflective pawns of bourgeois ideology, were aware of the importance of Marxism-Leninism to the struggle. This commitment to Marxism-Leninism, however, required a truly dialectical understanding of the relationship between culture and politics, rather than one based on simplistic oppositions.[79] Fraga and others at ICAIC were not disagreeing that culture had a class character, but rather that the class content of culture did not define culture in its entirety.[80] The antithesis between bourgeois culture and proletariat culture was not reducible to the irreconcilable antithesis between bourgeois and proletariat, but instead allowed for the possibility of a higher unity.[81] Thus Fraga agreed that the continuity of culture in the context of revolution and socialism should be selective, but this led him to a different conclusion, that the proletariat could inherit bourgeois culture and that to criticize it wasn't to reject it in its entirety.[82] This was in keeping with Castro's own celebration of Western culture and its importance to the project of elevating the cultural level of the Cuban people. "The task is not to refute idealism," Fraga wrote. "The objective consists in overcoming it, expropriating what it has of value."[83]

Mechanistically juxtaposing idealism to materialism failed to recognize that philosophical idealism and the German philosophical tradition were not simply at the service of exploiters, but also contributed to the development of historical materialism and that at times, idealists such as Hegel were far more important to the development of historical materialism than supposed critics of idealism like Feuerbach.[84] The juxtaposition falsely presumed that all movements based on materialist philosophy were progressive and all those based in idealism were reactionary ones.[85] What determined the truth of an idea, argued Fraga, was not its class origins or function, but rather practice.[86] Through participation one rid oneself of mystification.[87] Even the a priori adoption of Marxism-Leninism served as a point of departure for analysis, rather than a source of all of the answers.[88] Presuming it provided all the answers ahead of time was in fact a negation of it. The study of Marxism had to be accompanied by participation "in the battle of ideas, for the new socialist society."[89] Alienation survived as a result of the survival of classes, private property, and the state, and intellectuals were not the only ones subject to mystification.[90] Excluding intellectuals simply on the basis of their class origins, or what Tomás Gutiérrez Alea referred to as their "original sin," risked excluding important contributions.[91] Because mystification existed everywhere, the ideological struggle was ongoing, and intellectuals had important skills that enabled contributing to that struggle.

If the struggle at the base was clear—the interests of the landowner were irreconcilable with those of the farmer, and force had decided the outcome—this was not so on the "aesthetic terrain," argued García Espinosa, where "the struggle does not develop from positions of force."[92] Exile, law, and politics would deal with those enemies of the revolution who remained. Intellectuals understood the need to participate in the revolution in tangible ways—by working a job and being ready to fight for Cuba—but they also understood the need for the ideological struggle to continue even among supporters of the revolution and socialism. García Espinosa wrote: "To accept the idea that, being politically united, we can express ourselves without any fear [*sobresalto*], and as a consequence of that, to renounce the ideological struggle and the critical attitude is to abandon the [ideological] terrain to mediocrity and conformism."[93] The artist was not "someone who simply adorns and recreates the life of others," but rather was an active participant in the ideological struggle.[94] The critical attitude toward culture that García Espinosa and Aguirre called for would not result automatically from declaring oneself a Marxist or declaring one's allegiance to the proletariat, but rather from being active and critically engaged intellectuals, who saw this as their daily praxis. Cultural policy was "Not to be laid out a priori but rather started from the dialectic relationship with public, artist and party."[95] It was not enough for an artist to have more contact with the people, but also that people understand the problems of the artist. The public was neither an ignorant mass to be ignored, nor like a "newborn" who must have everything already digested. Both views of the public failed to recognize the sophistication of some of the public, but also that the public had "more than one face."[96] However, the public was not the only judge of art. It might need to be taught, suggested García Espinosa, that art should be judged on the basis not just of quantity, but also quality and that there was a "need to experiment, to look for the new."[97]

Artistic Production as "Ideological Mush" or a "Multiplicity of Avenues to Consciousness"

The issue of the relationship between art and the public—and its connection to Marxism-Leninism in general, and to Castro's "Words to Intellectuals"—would become the central focus of another shorter polemic debate, this one about film. It began with the December 12, 1963, publication in *Hoy* of an unsigned article addressing the concerns of a well-known actor that "capitalist cinema" shown to the Cuban public—specifically, Federico Fellini's *La dolce vita*, Pier Paolo Pasolini's *Accattone*, Luis Buñuel's *El ángel exterminador*, and Lautaro Murúa's *Alias gardelito*—depicted the "corruption and immorality of some countries and social classes," but without providing any sort of solution to the problems they presented.[98] The article's author responded that while he had not himself seen the films, comments he had heard from the Cuban public suggested that they should not be shown to the public and to the youth in particular.[99] Film, unlike theater and literature, argued the author, had a particular responsibility to the revolution since its message was much more direct and was received by the masses as a group.[100] It should aid the dissemination and consolidation of ideology by awakening in Cubans "the eagerness to work, lofty ideals, valiant heroism, brotherhood, friendship, [and] selflessness."[101] The author of the article was later revealed to be Blas Roca. Over the next week, there appeared several articles calling for art, and film in particular, to always respond to the immediate demands of the socialist revolution. Intellectuals needed to see their work in direct relation to the satisfaction of the material needs of the Cuban people rather than acting as consumers without concern for the material base that made culture possible.[102] While personal taste played a role in what films people enjoyed, other criteria were needed to assess the value of film, and those criteria privileged the three principal activities of the Cuban Revolution at that historical moment: the defense of the country, the building of the economic base, and consciousness raising. Only those films that provided a clear lesson in these areas were to be shown in Cuba.[103] Art, according to Roca, was to give an account of the lives of the people in their daily struggle to build socialism.[104] Both Roca and the CNC argued that Alfredo Guevara himself had understood this when he decided to censor the film *PM*, even if he now wished to deny responsibility for that decision.[105] Fidel Castro's "Words to the Intellectuals," argued Roca and the CNC, was to guide all decisions related to art. The speech made clear that the objective of the revolutionary artist was "to serve the cause of human redemption, the cause of the redemption of the exploited, the cause of the redemption of the workers, and there will be no conflict in serving that cause with his art, with his creation, with his work."[106]

Responses to such claims from members of ICAIC ensued, all of them arguing that a people who had made revolution would not be easily led astray by films whose revolutionary function might not be simply to provide images of appropriate revolutionary behavior (working and struggling against imperialism, for instance). Quality programming was much more effective in spreading revolutionary ideas than boring programming that treated Cubans as "a stupid child" and thus only alienated them.[107] One of the important contributions of the Cuban Revolution was its "great respect for quality, for art, for culture, for discussion, for imagination."[108] Revolutionary art was not art that trained the spectator, but rather art that "simulated in the consciousness of the spectator the need to give solutions, to change reality, to transform the world."[109] Ten members of ICAIC (including Tomás Gutiérrez Alea) published an article in which they argued that no film alone could incite the Cuban people to oppose the revolution.[110] If that were the case, the Cuban people, long subjected to imperialist popular culture, would never have engaged in revolution in the first place. "Being," they concluded, "determines consciousness and not the other way around."[111]

Alfredo Guevara wrote several individual replies to Roca in *Hoy*. He criticized Roca's superficial treatment of film as a simple medium for directly reflecting the revolutionary process and instead suggested that the task of film was to make the viewer think and to provoke debate.[112] The artist was a "witness" to the revolution, but also a "protagonist and combatant and even a prophet." The artist's task was then not simply to reflect the daily struggles of those building socialism in Cuba, but also to discover "the until now unreachable and insufficiently explored thread of the real world and find a way to express that." While revolutionary art could serve as propaganda, it was not the same, since it meant representing the socialist world in all its complexity, including its suffering.¹¹³ Guevara argued that if socialist realism was about showing the world as it was, a world that was less than ideal, then he did subscribe to socialist realism.¹¹⁴ This understanding of socialist realism showed more respect for the judgment of the masses than Roca's proposal to only show those films with an explicitly revolutionary message.

> If as is expected or recommended, we limited ourselves to exhibiting works either of agitation or reassurance [*tranquilizadores*], then artistic work, and the multiplicity of avenues it can open up for consciousness and perception, would be replaced by propaganda, perhaps sweetened with aesthetic formulas, and the public would be reduced to a mass of "babies" to whom maternal nurses administer "ideological mush," perfectly prepared and sterilized, thereby ensuring its greatest and most complete assimilation.¹¹⁵

How was it that a public who had made a revolution was now not to be trusted to judge films with complex styles and messages? Roca's approach presumed that the Cuban public were children and his approach only contributed to making them dumb. It was not a cultural revolution and not the message of Fidel Castro's "Words to the Intellectuals."¹¹⁶ Castro's "Words," insisted Guevara in another response to Roca, was meant to open up discussion, rather than close it down. Roca's "reactionary and limiting" proposals were "in contradiction to the principles" of the speech, which "far from resolving the complex problems of culture with a series of simplifying formulas, opens to the creator infinite possibilities for tackling reality, and recognizes the public's right to enrich and sharpen its consciousness and sensibility with all the treasures of art from the past, present, and future."¹¹⁷ Those such as Roca who claimed to privilege the proletariat did no such thing since they denied them the means and occasions to critically engage with the world that they were creating.

As we have seen, then, the intellectuals from ICAIC walked a number of fine lines. They refused to denigrate the Cuban public's intelligence and judgment, but they also refused to abandon their role as specialized theoreticians and creators. They recognized their own class backgrounds and skills, but they also considered themselves part of "the public."¹¹⁸ They recognized the class character of culture, but they rejected the ahistorical approach by which the content of socialist culture could be determined independent of material conditions. They recognized that, in keeping with the ideas of Che Guevara, the revolution involved not just a change in leadership or the mode of production, but also a change in consciousness. However, they refused to adopt a facile or mechanistic understanding of that change, as a simple moment of ideological cleansing. "The auto-da-fe," wrote Tomás Gutiérrez Alea, "will have no place inside our revolution."[119] Instead, they understood this transformation as a process, in the same way that the development of Cuban socialist ideology was a process. In this view, the principles of Cuban socialism, far from placing a straitjacket on ideological debate, were what allowed it to flourish. For these intellectuals, their commitment to those principles meant they were unafraid to see the various ways in which the principles would unfold through history.

These debates addressed not just the question of the role of culture, but also how Cubans should understand the relationship between the popular, academic, and official spheres. The debates were not just about the artist's responsibility to the official sphere, but also about the responsibility of intellectuals to the popular sphere. They were also about the question of how much Cubans themselves could be trusted not just to interpret the world around them, but also to understand the relationship between that world, on the one hand, and sophisticated artistic and philosophical forms, on the other.

The members of ICAIC were not the only ones to articulate these kinds of positions. Subsequent debates about intellectual production would have similar contours. They could be seen, for instance, in the polemical debate in 1966 between, on the one hand, Aurelio Alonso, and on the other, Lionel Soto, Félix de la Uz, and Humberto Pérez about the effectiveness of using Soviet manuals to teach Marxism. Here again, one side would argue that Cubans had to be fed Marxism in easily digestible bits, while another would argue that Cubans should be exposed to the original works so as to be better able to use Marxism as a critical tool in the construction of socialism. In February 1967, Alonso's view that Cubans should be given access to original Marxist thought found an institutional home with the creation of the monthly journal *Pensamiento Crítico*. The journal was the result of the founding of the Department of Philosophy at the University of Havana and of the emergence of the journal *Caimán Barbudo*, which began as part of *Juventud Rebelde*.[120] Produced by students and faculty of the University of Havana's philosophy department, *Pensamiento Crítico* published articles representing a wide range of views on the meaning of third-world revolution and Marxism, many of which clashed with the official Soviet positions that became increasingly important politically toward the end of the 1960s. It also published theorists and activists from Western Europe and Latin America. According to Kepa Artaraz, the intellectuals and academics involved in *Pensamiento*

Crítico "embodied many of the characteristics of the new Left," scrutinizing capitalism, imperialism, and "established forms of socialism," and the journals had many parallels to the *New Left Review*.[121] Similar to the New Left, the magazine did not deal much with issues of gender or race, except within the larger context of U.S. resistance movements.[122] The journal, along with the department from which it emerged and the rest of the University of Havana's social science departments with the exception of economics, was shut down by the government in 1971.[123] The closing of *Pensamiento Crítico* signaled increasing intolerance on the part of the Cuban leadership and further alienated European and American leftists who had not already withdrawn their support for Cuba after Fidel's endorsement of the Soviet invasion of Czechoslovakia in 1968.

The Twilight of the Gray Years: Intellectual Naïveté?

By the end of the 1960s, then, it seemed that the kinds of positions articulated by the members of ICAIC, among others, had failed to convince and that the articulators of such positions had been naive to the ways that their own commitment to the revolution left them vulnerable to political and institutional repression. In May 1969, the journal *Casa de las Américas* published the proceedings of a conversation among six intellectuals about the role of the intellectual in the Cuban Revolution.[124] Specifically, the participants discussed what it meant to play the critical function of the intellectual *within* the revolution. What did it mean to be critical, they asked, without being counterrevolutionary?

The participants included Roque Dalton, a Salvadoran poet and revolutionary who had taken refuge in Cuba; René Depestre, a Haitian poet and Communist who helped found Casa de las Americas and had fled to Cuba from the Duvalier dictatorship and who would ultimately break publicly with the revolution in the 1970s; Carlos Maria Gutiérrez, a Uruguayan journalist; and the Cuban writers Roberto Fernández Retamar, Ambrosio Fornet, and Edmundo Desnoes. Desnoes, most famous for his book *Memories of Underdevelopment*—in which a bourgeois intellectual is depicted as being unable either to leave Cuba or to incorporate himself fully into the revolution and which Tomás Gutiérrez Alea made into a film in 1968—would himself leave the country in the 1970s.

In some ways, the points raised in the conversations reflected the narrowing of discussion at the time. In 1965, the government opened up Military Units to Aid Production (UMAP), aimed at rehabilitating nonconformists. While not exclusively targeted for this rehabilitation, homosexuals were disproportionality affected.[125] By the time of the UMAP's closing in 1968, many homosexuals had been purged from the arts, theater, and universities, foreshadowing the institutionalization of homophobia in the 1970s and the increasing intolerance of any opposition, even if not explicit.[126] Throughout 1967 and 1968, *Verde Olivo*, the magazine of the Cuban Armed Forces, had published articles by Fidel Castro and others that criticized intellectuals and, in particular, Herberto Padilla, whose book of poetry won the book award from UNEAC in 1968 in spite of its antigovernment message.[127] Padilla would not be arrested until 1971, but by 1968, the parameters of discussion already appeared to be narrowing and the state seemed to be increasingly intolerant of any dissent. In 1968, the Revolutionary Offensive and Castro's support of the invasion of Czechoslovakia signaled Cuba's closer relations with the Soviet Union and a move away from the freer improvisation of the earlier years.

In light of these criticisms of intellectuals, the discussion of the last ten years can be read as a sort of preemptive and collective self-criticism, in which participants reminded each other of the dangers of intellectual arrogance, the legacy of their own bourgeois backgrounds, and bourgeois categories in general, as well as the ways which they had misunderstood their role in the early 1960s. However, while on the surface, the discussion appeared to be an affirmation of the more strict reading of Castro's "Words to the Intellectuals" and of more recent cultural policy, as a foreshadowing of the Gray Years, the discussion by the six intellectuals, and particularly the views of the Cuban participants, also showed implicitly how Castro's initial formulation of the role of the intellectual, and the interpretation of that formulation by those such as García, Aguirre, Flo, and Roca, had been unsatisfactory.[128] If the participants criticized intellectuals in the first years of the revolution for being insufficiently revolutionary, it appeared that part of the failure to be sufficiently revolutionary came from following Castro's directions too closely. Their harsher view of intellectual responsibility led to a broader understanding of participation than Fidel Castro had proposed, in that they called for both a recognition of the distinct functions of different types of intellectuals, including artists, writers, political leaders, and other Party members, and a recognition of the ways that cultural contributions were also political contributions. In short, and this point was made most clearly by Ambrosio Fornet, the cultural and the political sphere involved distinct functions, but those functions were not distinct because one realm involved purely cultural activities, and the other purely political ones.

Fernández Retamar opened the discussion by recognizing that while the question of the role of the intellectual in revolution had been asked from the beginning, the problem and the answer looked different at each stage and thus required a new approach.[129] Like Fidel's "Words to the Intellectuals," ambiguity, here in the form of a historical materialist understanding of the intellectual, was both constraining and liberating. If the intellectual in the revolutionary context could not defend himself on the basis of an abstract ideal of the intellectual as unrestrained critic, the fact that any definition was historically contingent meant that he could never be permanently contained by one definition. For Fernández Retamar, and others concurred, the revolutionary intellectual had to be evaluated according to what he did, rather according to a timeless and abstract ideal.[130] This, however, placed the intellectual in a precarious position since the criteria by which he was judged were always shifting. These were the stakes of intellectual production in the context of revolution.

Intellectuals during the first years of revolution, however, had acted according to ahistorical ideal definitions of the intellectual, freedom, and culture. According to Edmundo Desnoes, they had created the illusion that there existed complete freedom of expression. They failed to recognize "the demands of a society in revolution" and that the freedom they exercised had been made possible by the revolution itself. This understanding of freedom did not mean an abandonment of critique, and Desnoes ultimately returned to a definition of intellectual as critic. He wrote: "I believe it is a responsibility of the intellectual to maintain a critical attitude, that we must not give this over to the bourgeoisie and give them the right to exercise criticism."[131] To privilege the critical capacities of the intellectual, then, was to protect the revolution by subjecting it to scrutiny by those sympathetic to its ultimate goals. Still, he concluded this criticism had to be "within the revolution." To criticize it, one had to participate in the revolution and *live* the revolution, by participating in education campaigns and agricultural work, for instance. Otherwise to criticize was simply to become an "unconscious enemy of the revolution." According to this formulation, exercising freedom came with a responsibility to the collective, but also ran the risk of overflowing beyond the bounds of the revolution itself. This was a responsibility that Fidel Castro's ambiguous phrase had left the intellectual with.

Ambrosio Fornet also pointed to a certain naïveté on the part of Cuban intellectuals in the early years of the revolution, when they believed their job was to bring culture to the revolution. Though one might argue that bringing culture to the revolution was exactly the task that Fidel Castro had set before Cuban intellectuals, according to Fornet:

We didn't act as revolutionaries, using our own heads to analyze our own problems: we acted on the basis of a sinister conditioned reflex, whose historical motor—whose objective base, to say it that way—we know very well: in the exterior, what we are used to calling the phantasm of Stalin; on the inside, the cordial announcement from the Cultural Council of that time that they defined us suddenly as "transition intellectuals" who very soon would be swept away by the "true" revolutionary intelligentsia.[132]

During this period, he argued, intellectuals were not simply fighting for freedom of creation; they were also struggling for their survival as the same sort of intellectual that existed prior to the revolution, and yet they believed themselves more important than political leaders, economists, technicians, and "pure men of action." Fornet explained: "We were so happy in our little garden, taking care of those splendid flowers, convinced that we would eat alive anyone who dared set foot inside; because there, yes, we were the vanguard."[133] They spoke in the name of the revolution as if they, rather than active members of the 26th of July Movement, had created it. Freedom of expression, argued Fornet, was not an illusion in the first years of the revolution, and it was this freedom to express, create, and publish that enabled intellectuals to believe that they were revolutionaries just for having made the decision to stay.[134] Intellectuals decided, according to Fornet, that the best cultural policy was none at all. "We had acquired a piece of private property—that of high culture—in the middle of a revolution that didn't believe in private property."[135] They had, in other words, believed that they could participate in the revolution even as they believed that the revolution would not and should not affect their identity and activities as intellectuals.

According to Fornet, liberals, in the name of avoiding the mistakes of other socialist countries, came only to concern themselves with defending culture for culture's sake and criticism for criticism's sake, rather than considering the relationship of culture and criticism to revolution and concrete results.[136] They mistakenly believed that this individualized critique meant they were politicized. As a consequence, they became, in the context of revolution, intellectuals in name only ("*intelectuales nominales*"), rather than "functional intellectuals," who understood that while criticism may come from individual intellectuals, "its meaning is always collective."[137] Dogmatics, who insisted that intellectuals abandon their critical function entirely, only served to help them justify their retreat into a purely cultural critical realm, and their retreat, in turn, proved to dogmatics that intellectuals were insufficiently revolutionary.[138] Transforming oneself from a nominal intellectual to a functional intellectual was not about writers becoming politicians or functionaries. All were intellectuals, but with distinct functions that needed to be maintained, respected, and fostered. Neither literature nor politics could be abandoned. Instead, suggested Fornet, intellectuals needed to become more politicized and functionaries needed to become more educated in order to find a common language that was not simply about immediate results.[139] Artists and intellectuals, he argued, needed to be able to represent and defend the revolution *as artists and intellectuals*, not just in the cultural sphere but in more explicitly political realms such as the Committees for the Defense of the Revolution (CDRs) as well.[140] In one sense, Fornet's point began with a critique of Cuban intellectuals reminiscent of Marx's critique of the idealism of the Young Hegelians, yet he concluded that both liberals and dogmatics failed to respect the specific function of the revolutionary intellectual whose cultural contributions were not, but should be, taken into consideration when granting membership in the Party.[141]

It was important, argued Fernández Retamar, not to confuse three separate planes of intellectual activity—the sociological (what is the role of the intellectual and in this society in particular), the ideological (the orientation of the intellectual), and the technical (specific job).[142] Intellectuals, who had not been a strong group prior to the revolution, had been empowered by it, and yet they had acted as if they had always enjoyed the status that the revolution brought to them. The revolution, however, had transformed traditional intellectuals into organic intellectuals, who put their critical skills toward the construction of socialism.[143] Whereas most intellectuals were not Marxist-Leninist ten years prior, they were now.[144] Even so, the revolution asked more of the intellectual than many could give. Still, intellectuals in Cuba had been integrated into society and this meant that they understood the mistakes of the revolution as their mistakes and they took responsibility for them as they took responsibility for the revolution's victories. "The only valid criticism of the revolutionary intellectual, or simply of the revolutionary, is, thus, self-criticism, as has been said here, collective self-criticism."[145] What was essential, concluded Edmundo Desnoes, was that an intellectual avoided complacency and understood that his own identity was related to society and to the larger development of socialism.[146]

Rather than reading this particular moment of collective self-criticism as an example of the triumph of the dogmatists, we might understand it as reaffirmation of the importance of living the principles of Cuban socialism. Far from a sign of having given in to the dogmatists' narrow and sterile understanding of the intellectual, they continued to argue that intellectuals were not immune from the responsibility of actually living the principles that they espoused. Living the principles transformed their identity as intellectuals, but it did not reduce their role to that of simple mouthpieces of the Party. We see that even in their apparent condoning of the suppression of many intellectuals and institutions as antirevolutionary, these thinkers remained committed to an open-ended and shifting definition of revolutionary intellectualism; they continued to operate within the contexts of Marxism-Leninism and Castro's "Words to the Intellectuals," negotiating a stance that remained friendly to the revolution without losing a sense of the difference between cultural and political expression.

Three

What Would Che Say?
Making the Market Socialist

One of the ways that the truth/ideology opposition asserts itself is through the characterization of Cuban economic policy during different periods in postrevolutionary history as either pragmatic yieldings to free-market measures or idealist attempts to move as quickly as possible to communism. Many academic treatments of Cuban economic policy from the 1960s forward rely upon this pragmatism/idealism framework.[1] According to this framework, the 1960s was a period of idealism when economic policy was driven less by a sober evaluation of Cuba's economic, social, and cultural condition than by a revolutionary fervor focused on breaking with Cuba's neocolonial and economically dependent past. Material shortages and inefficiency throughout the 1960s led to waning enthusiasm for the revolution and the government's increasing embrace in the 1970s of various market measures aimed at increasing productivity and maintaining popular support. Such pragmatism can be seen clearly in the adoption of a Soviet-style model of industrialization and planning known as the System of Management and Planning of the Economy (Sistema de Dirección y Planificación de la Economía or SDPE) in 1975. Based on 1965 Soviet reforms, the SDPE aimed to introduce self-financing at the enterprise level and "profitability criterion with its corresponding incentives" and to "promote decentralization, organizational coherence, and efficiency."[2] Although Soviet, the model reflected a greater reliance on market principles, or what was known as economic calculus, than the economic models of the 1960s and specifically the budgetary finance system advocated by Che Guevara.

However, an examination of the discourse, particularly in the press, surrounding the adoption of the SDPE in Cuba complicates this historical narrative and the simple opposition between idealism and pragmatism upon which it is based. The SDPE is a particularly vivid example of the inadequacy of the idealism/pragmatism opposition because it was supposed to be a moment when the (false) ideology of socialism receded in order to make way for market pragmatism. Looking at the discourse in the press surrounding the SDPE, rather than only at the economic policies themselves, shows that during this time of apparent pragmatism, discussions dealt explicitly with the tensions between, on the one hand, material- or market-oriented economic policy focused on increasing productivity (pragmatism) and, on the other hand, a planning system motivated by moral incentives and a desire for equality of distribution (idealism). In general, the press and government officials characterized the SDPE as an attempt to navigate between socialist economic methods such as centralized planning and ideological education, and more market-oriented tools such as material incentives, profit criteria, and enterprise autonomy. The use of these market mechanisms, they insisted, in no way meant a return to capitalism. Technical discussions in the press dealing with accounting, firm autonomy, material incentives, the *libreta* (or ration card), and parallel markets, among other issues, provided explanations of how these methods strengthened, rather than diminished, the project of building socialism. In this sense, the more reliant economic policy was on market mechanisms, the more necessary it was to show how these policies fit within socialist ideology. Idealism did not recede, or remain in a weakened version, but emerged in another form.

The Rectification Campaign of Ideological Errors and Negative Tendencies, first announced by Fidel Castro during the Third Congress of the Cuban Communist Party in 1986, would criticize the SDPE for moving away from socialism because it relied too heavily on economistic solutions and market mechanisms that privileged numerical measures of growth at the expense of real growth based on increased productivity and efficiency for the benefit of society as a whole.[3] At the time of its initiation, however, the SDPE was presented as the best way to consciously control the economy, making the most of the forces of production by using centralized production, and move as rapidly as possible toward socialism and ultimately communism. Articles in *Granma* quoted continuously from the platform of the First Congress of the Communist Party of 1975:

> The SDPE will necessarily be conditioned by and conform to the principles of the socioeconomic regime of socialism, based on social ownership of the means of production, which demands, with the char-

acter of objective law, the planned development of the economy on the basis of a single plan and the appropriate centralized planning through which principal economic decisions are adopted. Likewise the SDPE must be a fundamental instrument for achieving the cardinal objectives of every society that constructs socialism and that has communism as its goal: to satisfy in a rational and growing manner the material and spiritual necessities of human beings through the development of the productive forces and the perfection of relations of production; and to educate men in a new type of human relations and a new attitude toward social duties in conformity with the principles of communist morality.[4]

The period can be understood, then, as a time when principles of Cuban socialism were reshuffled rather than abandoned. The principle of socioeconomic equality continued to anchor these new ideological negotiations, which in some ways had to be more sophisticated than in the 1960s, when theory appeared closer to practice. As in the 1960s, however, these ideological negotiations represented attempts to create a socialist economy while wresting certain goals and principles from their association with liberal ideology. The discourse surrounding the adoption and implementation of the SDPE shows an attempt to resist the necessary juxtaposition of equal opportunity, efficiency, and productivity to socioeconomic justice, and more generally, an attempt to resist the opposition between idealism and pragmatism. It reveals too how the juxtaposition of idealism to pragmatism is both a key element of liberal ideology and also an ideology upon which the leadership has at times relied in order to distance itself from past policies. Even in these instances, however, one might describe this use as principled, as opposed to instrumental, opportunism, since government officials, and the press, with varying degrees of success, attempted to link economic policies to long-standing socialist principles.

The Narrative of Idealism versus Pragmatism in Economic Policy

A straight factual account of some of the key economic policies of the 1960s on up to the period when the SDPE was adopted appears to fit neatly within the idealism/pragmatism framework. According to this narrative of Cuban economic history, the initial years of the revolution represented a period of idealism in the sense that the government's economic decisions were guided by the desire to restructure Cuban society as radically and as quickly as possible, and by a faith that "revolutionary voluntarism, the guerrilla tactic that had been effective in winning the 1956–1959 war against President Fulgencio Batista, could also be applied to governing the country."[5] Part of Cuba's plan for a radical break with the past was the adoption from 1961 to 1963 of intensive industrialization with an emphasis on the production of machines and tools and a move away from monoculture. Industrialization and agricultural diversification was one way to break traditional trade patterns that left Cuba vulnerable to world sugar prices.[6]

Many foreign economic advisors in Cuba during the first years of the revolution complained about the leadership's apparent idealism, expressing dismay and frustration at the leadership's disregard for material and economic considerations.[7] Economist Edward Boorstein, for instance, argued that revolutionary fervor and triumphalism as well as the departure of many professionals frequently meant that those making economic decisions did not understand the limits of revolutionary voluntarism or the limits to the amounts of hard currency in Cuban reserves. They did not want to accept that capitalism would have an influence on the choices among socialist alternatives.[8]

These were not only concerns of foreigner observers. During the "Great Debate" of 1962–65, "the advocates of 'revolutionary ethics' confronted the supporters of economic rationality."[9] The former, represented by Che Guevara, defended the budgetary finance system (also known as the consolidated enterprise system), where all enterprise profits went to the state budget and the state budget covered enterprise losses. Guevara privileged moral incentives over material ones and collective material incentives over individual ones.[10] He argued that creating institutions to foster a socialist consciousness was more important for the long-term success of socialism in Cuba than whatever short-term benefits might accrue from encouraging people to work for individual profit or self-interest.[11] *Estímulo moral* or *conciencia comunista*, as articulated by Guevara, was meant to replace previous modes of economic calculus.[12] Guevara warned against the dangers of the profit motive and individual interest and criticized the tendency toward their use in Eastern European countries experimenting with market socialism.[13] For him, it was an extremely slippery slope between their use and the adoption of capitalism and all its attendant evils.

Supporters of economic rationality, also known as the economic accounting system or self-management system, represented by Carlos Rafael Rodríguez, advocated enterprise self-financing and argued that budgetary financing encouraged enterprises to waste resources by not making them individually accountable.[14] They believed that elements of capitalism such as market signals, profit criteria, and material incentives were necessary, especially in an underdeveloped country, in order to establish a strong material foundation for socialism.

In some ways, the early optimism that Cuba's economy could be radically transformed with hard work and dedication would soon wane. For instance, attempts to move away from sugar monoculture were short lived and in 1964, Cuba accepted that it could not easily overcome its dependence on international trade, and returned to agricultural specialization.[15] However, other events including the apparent triumph of Che Guevara's budgetary finance system in 1966 (Guevara himself was no longer in office), the "Revolutionary Offensive" of 1968, and the 10-million-ton sugar drive of 1970, also appear to support the characterization of Cuban economic policy at this time as idealist.

In 1966, budgetary finance was applied across the board. The government did away with piece payments and bonuses. Individual enterprises were consolidated into larger ones. The Central Planning Board (Junta Central de Planificación or JUCEPLAN), established in 1960, had its powers reduced. Formal one-year planning was replaced by miniplans, which privileged certain sectors by ensuring them sufficient resources (and thus causing bottlenecks in other sectors).[16] The move toward an increasingly centrally planned socialist economy, as advocated by Che, continued with the 1968 "Revolutionary Offensive," when the Cuban state nationalized more than 58,000 small businesses and banned self-employment, significantly increasing the percentage of retail trade and sales controlled by the state.[17] Some owners stayed on, working at their former businesses as employees of the state.

The 10-million-ton sugar drive of 1970 could be seen as Cuba's last attempt at asserting the importance of moral rather than material incentives, since it was hoped that appeals to the good of the country could achieve this high production target. At the same time, it represented an abandonment of previous hopes for greater self-sufficiency, agricultural diversity, and industrialization. Not only did the campaign fail to live up to its goal of 10 million tons of sugar, but it also diverted huge amounts of resources and labor from other areas of the Cuban economy. Frustrated by its failure to move away from the sugar monoculture legacy and by its increasing economic isolation from the rest of Latin America, Cuba adopted an economic strategy of industrialization based on the Soviet model of central planning, which in turn gained Cuba entrance into the Soviet trading bloc, the Council for Mutual Economic Assistance (CMEA), in 1972. Cuba's inclusion in the CMEA, its adoption of the SDPE in 1975, and Castro's support of the August 1968 Soviet invasion of Czechoslovakia often serve as evidence of the Cuban government's increasing pragmatism in the 1970s. All could be said to signal Cuba's increasing alliance with and dependence upon the Soviet Union and its capitulation to the exigencies of the Cold War and the demands of global capitalism.[18]

Upon closer inspection of these policies, however, the idealism/pragmatism distinction is not so neat. For instance, in the case of the Revolutionary Offensive of 1968, over half of the nationalized businesses had opened after 1961.[19] This showed that the revolution was moving not only away from the capitalism of the prerevolutionary period but also from some of the redistributive efforts of the 1960s (set on achieving one type of socioeconomic equality) when those Cubans who remained were either permitted to retain small-scale businesses or given those properties left behind by those fleeing the country. If idealism is understood as moving away from the use of market mechanisms, here was an instance of one form of idealism or one principle (abolishing small-scale capitalist enterprises and businesses and concentrating the means of production in the state) negating a previous instance of idealism or another principle (the redistribution of the means of production to a larger portion of the population previously excluded from such ownership). At the same time, both policies can be seen as pragmatic, with the initial redistribution being an attempt to garner support among the population and the later liquidation of small-scale business an attempt to counteract the power of a new entrepreneurial class in Cuba that was viewed as the source of black market and counterrevolutionary activities.

Similarly, while Guevara's "new man," who worked hard for the sake of his country and whose reward was the virtue of work itself, became the model citizen for all Cubans to follow, this emphasis could be seen as pragmatic in two senses. First, given Cuba's neocolonial status, the absence of an industrial infrastructure and loss of many of its professionals, labor was in fact one of Cuba's greatest resources. It made pragmatic sense to try to exploit this resource as much as possible, even if this exploitation was couched in terms not of increasing capital, but of increasing the country's wealth and confronting imperialism.[20] Second, Guevara saw the limits of his socialist values in the international scene. In a famous televised speech, he held up Cuba's national brand soda, Tropicola, and told the country that their national product was garbage. Such an inferior product could never compete with Coca-Cola. Thus, while he argued that cooperation and brotherhood should replace competition and self-interest at the domestic level, such an ethic at home would not do away with the need for a competitive approach to deal with the realities of the capitalist system. Guevara's emphasis on moral incentives and pride in national brands was an attempt, not simply to create a new socialist society, but to create workers who would produce products that could potentially hold their own in an international world market and reduce Cuban dependence on foreign powers, both capitalist and socialist.

Looking at the discourse surrounding specific policies highlights the problem of distinguishing between pragmatism and idealism, in relation not just to economic policy but to other policies as well. Take, for instance, Castro's public defense of the Soviet invasion of Czechoslovakia, where he struggled with the ideological implications of his support. In his speech, Castro condemned Czech reformers for falling prey to bourgeois definitions of freedom and democracy and for "moving towards a counterrevolutionary situation" that "seriously affected the entire socialist community."[21] At the same time, he gave a nod to the ways that Cuba's support of the Soviet invasion of a smaller independent country might be seen as problematic given Cuba's own experiences with an imperial power to the north.

> Some of the things that we are going to state here will be, in some cases, in contradiction with the emotions of many; in other cases, in contradiction with our own interests; and in others, they will constitute serious risks for our country. However, this is a moment of great importance for the revolutionary movement throughout the world.[22]

Castro referred to the invasion as "traumatic," "bitter," "tragic," and "highly disagreeable." However, he qualified, it could be justified politically as an unfortunate but necessary measure to combat the ideas and influences of Western imperialism. To disassociate the Soviet invasion of Czechoslovakia from possible Soviet or North American incursions into Cuban sovereignty, Castro added that the kind of movement to which the invasion was responding would never take place in Cuba.[23] Castro did remind the Soviet Union that Cuba had the right, according to principle, "to demand that [the Soviet Union] adopt a consistent position with regard to all the other questions that affect the world revolutionary movement."[24] Thus he made the political calculation to condone an act that set a dangerous precedent for Cuba, in order to insist upon greater respect for Cuban input in affairs of the Soviet Union and the socialist world while also reminding the Soviet Union of its responsibility to protect Cuba from North American aggression. This position could be seen throughout the 1970s when, in spite of Cuba's inclusion in CMEA, Cuba would consistently assert its autonomy from the Soviet Union by aligning itself with and actively supporting a number of third-world liberation movements.[25] These sorts of ideological negotiations are not just the privilege of Fidel Castro, but also can be seen in other official expressions of Cuban socialism.

The Cuban Press as Official Ideology

The copious speeches by Fidel Castro have often meant the official point of view is thought to be in the words of one man. This reduction ignores the other arenas, such as the Cuban press, themselves organs of the Cuban Communist Party, in which official ideology and policy are not only publicized and disseminated, but also produced. In many ways, the press is simply a way to bring the ideas of the Cuban government to the general populace. Articles often quote directly from the speeches of party officials or from Communist Party documents. The entire transcript of a speech or large chunks of Party congresses are reproduced with an important section serving as the article's title. Even when Party documents are not directly quoted or cited, it is clear that these are frequently the sources. However, it is also the case that the Cuban press provides instances not simply of ideological regurgitation but also of ideological negotiation.

This should certainly not be confused with ideological diversity. With some exceptions, articles representing hard-hitting investigative reporting on Cuban issues do not really exist.[26] Self-criticism on the part of government officials is the preferred form of criticism. Articles do not call into question the reliability or accuracy of information released by the government unless another government official has pointed to a possible error. No article challenges official reasoning or rationales unless another government official is doing it. There are no legal opposition parties from whom reporters might seek alternative viewpoints, and reporters do not publish the views of Cuba's dissidents and underground parties. The press does not print harsh criticism of government policy coming from the general population or from other independent and illegal organizations. Cuban journalists who operate independently of the state-run media are often censored and can be jailed, while the movement of foreign journalists has been extremely limited and heavily monitored, as is access to certain information inside and outside the country. Groups like the World Press Freedom Committee, Reporters without Borders, and Amnesty International have repeatedly condemned Cuba for jailing independent journalists and for limiting freedom of expression and information. Cuba usually finds itself at the bottom of their rankings based on criteria such as direct violations of press freedom, degree of impunity for those who violate press freedom, state monopoly of the media, access to the Internet, and more.[27] Yet the important point for the purposes of the argument presented here is that even these rankings do not necessarily correlate press quality with ranking. According to Reporters without Borders, for instance, its ranking should not "be viewed as an indication of the quality of the press in the countries concerned," and it "defends press freedom, without taking a position on the quality of the editorial content of the news media." In other words, lack of press freedom does not necessarily tell us about the content or quality of the news produced.

In Cuba, the ideology motivating both the information disseminated and government policy is made explicit. Journalists who work for the official press recognize that their work is ideologically motivated. According to the official web page of the Union of Journalists of Cuba:

> The Cuban press proclaims with pride that it is objective, but not impartial, because one cannot be impartial when given the choice between good and evil, war and peace, justice and injustice, the patriot and the seller of one's country, just as one cannot be impartial about independence and annexation, solidarity and selfishness.[28]

Objectivity, according to the Union, stems from the fact that the Cuban press "does not have to defend the interests of private property, nor those of commercial publicity nor those of a group of politicians." The free press, according to the union's definition, is one that does not defend the interests of capitalism, and which, citing Article 53 of the Cuban constitution, "conforms to the ends of socialist society."[29] This position of the Cuban press makes it particularly useful for understanding official socialist ideology, since its aim is not to limit bias or feign neutrality, but to defend a specific ideology and frame policy within it. This was also the case during the time of the SPDE, when discussions of economic policy in *Granma* and the newsmagazine *Bohemia* took place within certain parameters, which functioned to set the terms of debate, rather than silence it completely.[30] Members of the press in Cuba, more so than government officials, are responsible for reporting the facts of government policy, at the same time as they are expected to defend a particular ideology. That one of the main people covering the SDPE, José Norniella, was a trained economist, shows the degree to which the press was expected not just to repeat the party line, but show how economic policy was consistent with it. It is important to clarify at the outset, though, that the aim of this chapter is not to see the degree to which press coverage accurately reflected how well the SDPE was functioning. Rather, it is to show how official discourse both rejected the idealism/pragmatism framework through its attempts to reconcile the use of tools associated with capitalism with socialist principles and also made use of that same framework for those same ends.

The Principles of the SDPE

The SDPE was approved during the First Congress of the Cuban Communist Party in December 1975. As the passage at the beginning of this chapter illustrates, the language of the platform clearly privileged the goals of socialism and communism. It also emphasized the central role of planning. According to the platform of the Congress, planning was the "principle link that covered all socioeconomic processes and exercise[d] an active influence directed toward the most rational distribution and utilization of material, human, and financial resources." "In order to guarantee the objective of the construction and development of socialist society and the constant elevation in the well-being of the people," emphasized the platform, planning had to be "directed toward scientifically designed short-term, medium-term, and long-term plans" that would be "organically integrated."[31] JUCEPLAN, whose role had been reduced in the late 1960s, would play the primary role in developing and carrying out the plan.[32]

While the SDPE was approved and its main principles outlined during the First Party Congress in December 1975, it would not be fully implemented until 1977.[33] In January 1976, a national commission was created to implement the SDPE.[34] Throughout the following months the press announced that seminars, courses, and meetings were being held to prepare and train those who would be carrying out the SDPE.[35] Articles acknowledged the hitches of implementing the SDPE, pointing out that those responsible for implementing it were still in the process of learning and that there were subjective and objective difficulties with the system.[36] For instance, there needed to be "greater linkage of economic research with the needs of the national economy" and economics professors needed to devote themselves more fully to practical problems of the economy.[37] Some of the core elements of the SDPE were not implemented until 1979 and into 1981. By 1979, articles were already appearing expressing concern over improper use of statistics, financial imbalances, and other shortcomings of the SDPE.[38] Press coverage of the SDPE from the beginning was hardly celebratory and took pains to point out to the myriad challenges of its implementation. According to

Andrew Zimbalist, the SDPE represented "the first systematic attempt to establish in Cuba a system of mature central planning, with stable institutions and defined functions." Such characteristics meant that "when problems appeared, their source was more identifiable and their systematic nature more apparent."[39] This and the primacy the SDPE placed on increasing efficiency by linking salaries to production placed heavy demands on those tasked with showing that the SDPE was consistent with socialist ideology.

Capitalist Means for Socialist Ends

Most of the articles dealing with the SDPE concerned themselves with explaining how the SDPE could make use of tools associated with capitalism for socialist ends. A series of three articles in 1976 dealing with the meaning of accounting under socialism, for instance, recognized that accounting would be seen as associated with financial transactions under capitalism.[40] They pointed out, however, that accounting, understood as the collection of information about firm resources and the calculation of important economic indicators for the national economy, would be all the more important in a centralized economy where decisions were made on the basis of need and availability, rather than on market signals and supply and demand.[41] As a member of the National Commission to Implement the SDPE noted in an interview, Marx and Lenin themselves had placed great emphasis on accounting, which could be adapted to whatever mode of production was in place.[42] Accounting under socialism, explained the commission member, was used by the state to "establish the methods, norms, and procedures so that all the institutions and organizations respond to the fundamental objectives of socialist society."[43] In the "hands of the working class and serving their interests," it could be used to "measure the savings of social work, aid in the results and the efficiency with which organizations of society worked, calculate the expenditures on social services that socialist society offers, and control the planned development of the economy."[44]

As a consequence, the cornerstone or "piedra angular" of the SDPE was to be the new System of National Statistical Information (Sistema de Información Estadístico Nacional or SIEN), which allowed for the collecting and ordering of information such as an inventory of national resources.[45] While firms and farms, which generated earnings, would be responsible for self-financing, other institutions such as schools and hospitals would receive their money straight from the national budget, thereby ensuring that certain services were not subject to the same market disciplining as other sectors. Articles frequently pointed to spheres or areas of the economy that were not subject to market forces as a way of distinguishing Cuba's use of market mechanisms from the full-scale adoption of the capitalist mode of production.

Firm Autonomy in a Centralized Economy

A key element of the SDPE was the granting of greater autonomy to individual firms. This was shown to be a move toward socialism since, as many articles in *Granma* emphasized, individual workers and individual enterprises could be more successful in actually completing the national plan if the role of the state was deemphasized. SDPE's granting of greater autonomy to individual firms and holding them responsible for completing their part of the plan was a way of stimulating workers to be more productive and more efficient.[46] This was not a material incentive, per se, but rather what Zimbalist calls an internal incentive, whereby workers internalized the goals of the firm or the larger economy.[47] Each firm would operate according to "general principles of economic calculus" and would organize production and distribution of material goods and services based on a preestablished sales contract.[48] Firm efficiency, however, was not measured according to "isolated indicators, such as, for example, volume of production, but rather by what was achieved according to a group of interrelated indicators that show efficient functioning in an integrated form."[49] Each firm's responsibilities were as follows:

> A firm is directly responsible for basic resources and their distribution, for the uses to which they are put, for the excessive costs with which it produces, for the low quality of its products, for the failure to complete its production and delivery plans, for high levels of inventory, for exhausting its salary funds without achieving the consequent counterpart of corresponding levels of production and productivity, for not contracting its supplies on time, for the deficient management of its costs and payments, . . . because it is the firm that uses these resources in order to produce in accordance with a plan. . . . Its function within the SDPE is to create methods of control and incentives so that firms complete their plans with efficiency and can develop an economic consciousness among their workers.[50]

Firm autonomy, then, was considered one way to improve worker consciousness and specifically make workers feel individually responsible for the plan, as a larger economic and social goal. It was not presented then as a necessary evil that might compromise workers consciousness in the short run. Firm autonomy did not translate into a type of individualized, private incentive, but was relative. It meant neither that the firms were the private property of anyone nor that the interests of the firm could be separated out from those of the state, the workers, or society as a whole. National norms and procedures were to be respected (base salaries, for instance, could not vary from firm to firm).

> The interests of the workers of each firm are concentrated fundamentally in the activity of the firm, in the achievement of the best results in the firm where they work. Hence, it is necessary to make the interests of the workers coincide with those of the firm and with those of the whole society. This is achieved through the correct application of the principles of economic calculus and state policy, which is fully driven by the absence of antagonistic contradictions between the interests of the workers, of the firm, and of society, thanks to the existence of social ownership of the means of production.[51]

Articles in *Granma* were always careful to explain that enterprise autonomy was meant to encourage greater responsibility on the part of the workers and thus greater productivity and efficiency for the well-being of the country as a whole. This autonomy, however, was always limited by the state and larger economic plans. While planning continued to be an essential element of the SDPE, auto-financing would also play an important role. Enterprises were called upon to generate earnings on top of what they spent, implying a certain level of autonomy. Ultimately, however, the enterprise would be under the control of the Organs of Popular Power (OPP).[52] The OPP were introduced in 1976. They operated at the national level, where they passed annual and five-year plans, approved the national budget and made laws, and at the local level, where they functioned as local government bodies answerable to those who elected them.[53] According to Susan Eckstein, at the municipal level, the bodies did operate democratically, with delegates elected by and responsible to the electorate, but at the time of the SDPE "there was little effective evidence of democratization of governance" at the provincial or national level.[54] In either case, because enterprises were under the OPP, firm autonomy was linked to government decentralization as opposed to government deregulation, thereby distinguishing it from a capitalist enterprise.

Thus the difference between a capitalist enterprise and a socialist enterprise was that the socialist enterprise was not cut off from other enterprises or from the rest of the economic and social entities of the country. The ultimate goal of each individual worker was to fulfill the plan and thus provide for the needs of the national economy. "In socialism, man is interested morally and materially in having the management—the economy of the enterprise—work well, and for that, the first thing is designing a good plan and fulfilling it."[55] It was the responsibility of the firm to "achieve the greatest direct participation of its workers," who would be educated about the plan and given the opportunity to discuss it so that it might be "enriched" by the "suggestions and initiatives of the masses."[56] The 1978 graduation speech from the National School of Economic Planning was titled "The Success of SDPE Will Always Depend on the Conscious and Active Participation of the Workers."[57] Workers were exhorted not just to work harder but also to participate in making realistic plans, which could be completed efficiently. This exhortation, however, was increasingly backed, starting in 1971, with various decrees aimed at making work an obligation, rather than a right. According to Eckstein, survey data suggests that by the mid-1970s, workers viewed unions less as defenders of workers' rights than as educators of workers and geared toward increasing worker productivity.[58] This type of evidence pointed to the myriad ways, anticipated by Che, that the use of economic calculus impacted not just economic outcomes, but worker consciousness.

Economic Calculus at the Service of Human Needs

The issue of economic calculus, as the key to the SDPE, was in particular need of explanation in the press since it appeared to be privileging economic indicators of prosperity over human ones and relinquishing power to the blind laws of capital. Economic calculus within the SDPE was described as "a powerful lever for dynamic and rational efficiency that is based on the utilization of economic laws from the mode of production and on the existence of monetary-mercantile relations and categories (price, cost, profit, etc.) that endure in socialism with a new content."[59] These monetary-mercantile categories and relationships were socialist because they were tools used by the central government to better plan the economy. Hence, they were always subservient, in the final analysis, to the task of providing for the material well-being of the country as a whole. It was the economic planners who were rational, rather than the market.

In the publication of the economics department of the University of Havana, *Economía y Desarrollo*, an article entitled "Theoretical Aspects of the

Economic Planning and Management System" explained that the new system was like a machine, but a machine controlled from inside by the human makers of that machine.

> SDPE is self-governing, directed from within by people, who are the central promoters of all economic relations. Hence, this system of a social character, linked to the diverse actions of men in their economic affairs, is much more complex and has a series of particularities that are different than mechanical systems.[60]

Unlike under capitalism, the objective laws themselves were not rational, which was why harnessing them was necessary, to "rationalize" them. While controlled by the political choices of human beings, the SDPE marked the recognition on the part of economic decision makers that certain objective laws could not be ignored. The solution, therefore, was to understand how these objective economic laws worked so as to better harness and manipulate them to the benefit of society. The act of recognizing these laws linked them to human consciousness just as the workers, in recognizing their structural position within the mode of production, facilitated the destruction of the capitalist system.

> The objective necessity of the economic management system centers around the fact that the socialist economy is based on objective laws that exist independently of our will and consciousness. But economic laws, unlike natural laws (such as the law of gravity, etc.) are mediated by the actions of men. In the interactions of human wills, they continue functioning, imposing tendencies and regularities derived from the fundamentals of the social regime in which they work.[61]

Thus, the law of value, whereby the value of commodities is expressed through fluctuating exchange values (how much of one commodity can be exchanged for another), would be helpful in ensuring that inventories in factories did not sit idle and hold up money that could otherwise be used for other elements of production. As one article explained, "The law of value is precisely one of the mechanisms used by the SDPE to detect these irregularities in the distribution of the means of production."[62]

There was a dialectical relationship between objective economic laws and the economic system in which they functioned. To recognize those objective laws was not to accept them as natural or immutable, nor, however, was it to overturn them overnight or ignore them. Rather, the recognition in and of itself of these objective laws was a prerequisite for the conscious manipulation and ultimate mastery of those objective economic laws to further the goals of the larger society. To further the goals of the larger society, in turn, meant to construct first socialism and then communism, always taking into account the material and historical conditions as well as the level of consciousness of the people.

For this reason, Article 19 under the "political, social and economic principles of the state" of the 1975 Cuban constitution stated that the Republic of Cuba was ruled by "the *socialist principle* of 'from each according to his ability, to each according to his work.'" Many articles published in the late 1970s and early 1980s were devoted to explicating Marx's argument in *The Critique of the Gotha Program* that this principle was necessary during the first phase of the socialist transformation when Communist consciousness had not yet developed sufficiently to enable people to work for the greater good without the motivation of individually assigned material rewards. "Right," argues Marx, "can never be higher than the economic structure of society and the cultural development thereby determined."[63] Unlike the abstract equality of bourgeois political equality, socialist equality is grounded in the historical-material category of labor. When more than labor is taken into account, equality no longer holds. Echoing Marx, some argued that given that mercantile relations still existed within the Cuban economic system, it was impossible to impose the fully developed communist standard of "from each according to his ability, to each according to his need," for such a standard of equality would in practice be imposing inequality in an economic system where people still worked for personal gain. A system where people worked for personal gain meant not just differential salaries, but also markets, known as parallel markets, where those with more money could acquire more and better goods.

Parallel Markets as Material Incentives

The press also relied upon Marx's argument to justify the existence of these parallel markets, and this reliance too refused a dichotomous relationship between pragmatism and idealism. These markets would exist alongside the *libreta* or ration card, which guaranteed everyone a baseline set of goods.[64]

> Distribution according to work is, therefore, the highest achievement of socialism because it signifies true equality of man before the means

of production, since for everyone the principle that work and only work is the source and base of consumption, governs. Socialism cannot give total equality to everyone. It can produce equality, yes, before the means of production, but, for the moment, it cannot produce it before consumption. With relation to consumption, there exist temporary differences [*diferencias temporales*], since he who works more, participates more in consumption.[65]

In spite of differences in consumption, there still existed a "moral, educational element," because workers began to realize that they were working for themselves as a class, as owners of the means of production, and not for an exploiter. Some Cubans still did not realize that socialist property was the property of all, and therefore stole from the factory or did not take proper care of equipment.[66] Moral education was therefore necessary before another standard of equality could be established.

The system was presented as distinct from capitalism because in Cuba, while some received more than others because of the quality and quantity of their work, no one was deprived of her basic necessities because of the quantity or quality of her work. The ration card, guaranteed employment, and the provision of social services meant that no one was left completely at the mercy of the market.

> In socialism, the distribution of consumption and use articles manifests a double character. The fundamental part is distributed according to work, whereas the other part, on account of the social consumption fund, is distributed without taking into account the portion of labor of each member.[67]

Thus, the Cuban who had three children *becados* (enrolled in high school, which in Cuba was a boarding school run by the state) was actually earning more than the 150 pesos a month he received as salary.[68] The parallel market, however, was a material incentive, necessary during a certain phase of development. "He who works more and better has the right to receive more from society" stated another article that year on the parallel markets.[69]

The leadership and the press worked together to ensure that people understood why parallel markets and ration cards existed and how they worked. Discussions of these two key issues appeared not just in *Granma*, but also in the pages of more popular and accessible publications such as the magazine

Bohemia, which published several pieces in 1979 in which the president of JUCEPLAN, Humberto Pérez, discussed various aspects of the SDPE. Pérez was a Party technocrat who did not play a key role in the struggle against Batista.[70] He appeared, then, to personify a departure from the 1960s, and the early 1960s in particular, when posts in the government were handed out on the basis of one's revolutionary, rather than professional, credentials. However, his task of explaining the nuts and bolts of the SPDE did not preclude linking it to a long-term socialist project aimed at a shift not just in the mode of production but in people's consciousness as well. Moreover, Pérez's explanations showed an even greater concern than press accounts in *Granma* with linking policy to socialist *principles*, as found in the works of both Karl Marx and Ernesto "Che" Guevara, and with arguing that what might appear to be an abandonment of principles was actually an instance of their reshuffling.

Ideology of a Bureaucrat: Negotiating Idealism and Pragmatism

In 1979, *Bohemia* published an interview with Pérez by the exiled Chilean journalist Marta Harnecker entitled "Objective Problems of Our Revolution: What the People Should Know."[71] Harnecker's status as a foreign exile might have given her more leeway in the types of questions she asked Pérez, and this might partially account for the greater emphasis he placed on principles.[72] Pérez's answers to questions about the *libreta* and the parallel economy demonstrated a complicated back and forth between idealistic and pragmatic considerations. If he wished to explain key elements of the SDPE, he did so without ever delinking those elements from the larger goal of socialism. In response to the question of whether the *libreta* was a sign of scarcity, Pérez argued that the *libreta* was the best and fairest way to satisfy people's basic needs and while this in some way might detract from economic stimulation, depriving people of basic needs was a tool of capitalism, not socialism. Both the *libreta* and the parallel market, where goods were sold at higher prices, were necessary as "instruments for social justice for certain products and in certain moments, and elements that help to neutralize the effects of inflationary processes caused by monetary surpluses."[73] Furthermore, he argued, satisfying everyone's needs did not mean providing the same products to everyone. People could not simply rely on the *libreta* since what it provided did not take into account people's different preferences. One way around that, argued Pérez, was that people could swap rations depending on what items they valued more (e.g.: coffee for cigarettes). The problem with this, he qualified, was that such swapping opened up a space for intermediaries and the growth of the black market. For this reason, the *libreta* had to be used in concert with the parallel market.

While the *libreta* assumed a certain uniformity of needs and preferences, the parallel market, explained Pérez, allowed for some freedom in terms of selection and quantity and functioned to stimulate an increase in the quality and variety of goods. In that sense, it functioned as a sort of "vanguard" that advanced the production of distinct articles that could later be produced in larger quantities for distribution to the general population. Demand, then, was understood as a need, but also in the more market-oriented sense as a consumer preference. The sale of such products in the parallel market also helped to combat the black market, which operated because of those who, according to Pérez, "by not working, dedicated themselves to waiting in lines or to obtaining certain products that were distributed by the *libreta* but were not used, buying them at one price and reselling them at a higher price."[74] While the prices of the parallel market were "higher than the prices of similar products distributed through rationing . . . these prices [were] frequently lower than the similar products obtained on the black market." According to Pérez, the most important justification of the need for a parallel market where products were sold at higher and different prices was that it was the only way to operate "according to the socialist principle of distribution in accordance with work" since "we all know that the principle to each according to needs belongs to Communism from which we are still separated by a great space."[75] "In socialism," he explained in keeping with a similar emphasis in *Granma*, "the principle is from each according to his ability, to each according to his work."[76]

Pérez told the interviewer that "the goal of the worker is not money but what can be bought with the money," which was why it was important to have higher-priced goods and services that only those who earned more money could buy. This, said Pérez, was

> a necessary motivation for development, increased production and productivity and the elevation of workers' technical abilities, and for all of those reasons, it [was] definitively a necessary motivation for the improvement of society and of workers in general, including those who earn less and do not in all cases have the possibility of acquiring these products at higher prices.[77]

Pérez hastened to add, however, that material incentives did not extend to the most fundamental of human needs. Under socialism, he explained, negative material incentives such as the threat of unemployment, illness, lack of educational opportunities, lack of care during old age, homelessness, and deprivation of basic nutrition were absent. In other words, material incentives took the form of carrots, rather than sticks. Promise of greater material reward, rather than threats of deprivation, were still necessary because the consciousness of Cubans was "still not sufficiently developed" so as to be able to act on the basis of moral incentives alone. It was therefore necessary to have, for instance, a balance between the provision of goods and services that were free or below value and mechanisms that pushed people to work. As a consequence, certain prices were artificially raised, so that salary differentials would be effective incentives.

On the one hand, according to Pérez, the principles of socialism forbade the kind of incentive system established under capitalism, and indeed this incentive system would do nothing to elevate the consciousness of Cubans. On the other hand, these principles could not be taken so far as to ignore the ways in which certain tools of capitalism, such as material incentives, were not only appropriate to a certain stage in the development of socialism, but also less damaging to the socialist project in the long run than pure principle. Although Pérez did not say so, he was suggesting that to be pragmatic was not to abandon principle but to adopt a secondary principle, "to each according to his work," that did greater justice to the larger principle of equal distribution than the larger principle itself could. Pragmatism, then, involved not an abandonment of principles, but their reshuffling. According to Pérez:

> If we let ourselves be carried away by romantic altruism towards which all revolutionaries feel ourselves inclined and if we let ourselves be won over by an egalitarianism that does not correspond to the socialist phase in which we are living, without realizing it, we will be harming, and not benefiting, society and . . . the same workers of lower incomes, although it is true that for the moment they cannot obtain some of the these products and services of the parallel market because they are sold at higher prices. However, the way to improve the quality of the products that are acquired for lower prices, to expand the range of goods offered and to make everyone work more and better, and as a consequence produce goods in greater quantities and of better quality, is by stimulating all to work with greater efficiency and with greater productivity and to improve their technical skills. That is the way to develop ourselves, that is the way that for now, products can exist in sufficient abundance and at lowered prices, because there already exists enough for everyone.[78]

What is striking about Pérez's logic is that it represents a convergence of two ideologies (that of Karl Marx and Adam Smith) as opposed to the abandonment of ideology and the triumph of pragmatism. Pérez is clearly making the Marxist argument, articulated most explicitly in Marx's *The German Ideology*, that abstracting ideals from their historical and concrete conditions is not only naive but harmful to the socialist project since doing so leaves it open to the charge of utopianism.[79] Also Marxist is Pérez's emphasis on the ways in which people acting according to the rules of one system lay the groundwork for the rise of another kind of system whether they are aware of it or not.[80] According to Pérez, it is only by appealing to people's individual self-interest that one will achieve the socialist principle of to each according to his work, but this principle is only necessary in order to move toward the even higher principle of mass material abundance, which in turn is the precondition for distribution regardless of work and according to pure necessity.

The first steps of this logic also share something in common with Smith's political economy. The desired outcome of greater material abundance for all is supposed to be achieved as a result of people's individual self-interest.[81] This appeal to individual self-interest was the concern of those such as Guevara who had worried that these temporary appeals to self-interest would work to the detriment of the longer-term goal of a communist society. Yet Pérez's argument seemed to suggest that it was not the appeal to self-interest itself that was intrinsically nonsocialist, but rather its position among a variety of other socialist principles.

Even Better Than Marx? Enlisting the Ideas of "El Che"

The charge that the SDPE was a move away from Cuba's socialist project was made with sufficient frequency to provoke the publication in *Bohemia*, several months after the publication of his 1979 interview, of a speech given by Pérez at the closing of a congress of the National Association of Cuban Economists. Pérez's speech reflected the leadership's concern with presenting the SDPE, not as a break with the idealism of the sixties, but as a continuation, at least in terms of common goals. Pérez's task involved emphasizing certain ideas and statements of figures such as Che Guevara at the expense of those elements of Guevara's thought that might call the SDPE's dedication to socialism into question. In the speech, Pérez responded to the characterization of SDPE by "some publications in the exterior" as "an abandonment of the ideas of Guevara [and] as a retreat from the struggle for the objectives that he mapped out," arguing that "since the departure of Guevara from our country, the greatest, most systematic, most organized, most intense, most persistent and most integrated effort has been made to carry out the most essential aspects of his economic thought."[82] Pérez referenced Guevara's writings to show that they did not reject material incentives and to argue that the differences between Guevara's budgetary finance system and economic calculus were ones of emphasis rather than principle. Regardless of whether he understood Guevara, Pérez believed that he was being pragmatic, but not simply in the sense of doing what was necessary, but also by creating ideological consistency. Ideological consistency, in other words, was part of what it meant to be pragmatic, and this form of pragmatism was particularly important in Cuba.

At the same time, Pérez's explanation for the failure of the budgetary finance system to take hold belied an underlying unwillingness or failure to recognize the ways in which these minor differences in Guevara's system had principled implications. In the following section of Pérez's speech, Pérez, in justifying the failure of the budgetary finance system to take hold, also suggested, echoing criticisms from the Great Debate, that Guevara's system was not appropriate to the level of development of productive forces that Cuba had in the early sixties.

> Because in that initial period until 1965, convulsions produced by the social transformations of the first years stood in the way, moreover our productive forces were not as developed as they are today; our people, our cadres did not have the experience, the skill and the consciousness that they have today, nor was the internal and external political situation the same and because, moreover, in that period—as Fidel explained in his report to the First Congress of the party—two systems for managing the economy coexisted: that of the budgetary finance system, defended by Guevara, that comprised the greater part of industry; and economic calculus that was applied in a very incipient, partial and limited way to agriculture, external trade and a small part of industry. It is without a doubt that under those conditions, the efforts of Guevara, although backed by his great authority, his great intelligence, tenacity and organizational capacity, would not have been able to have the level of integration and systematization on a national scale that today we are achieving in the process of applying the SDPE, agreed upon in the First Congress of the Party.[83]

In spite of this initial explanation for the failure of Guevara's budgetary finance system, Pérez continued through the speech to argue that the difference between the budgetary finance system and the system of economic calculus, also known as self-management or auto-finance, was simply one of scale. Furthermore, Pérez's speech borrowed heavily from Guevara's 1964 article "On the Budgetary Finance System" in which Guevara explained the difference between his system and economic calculus. At times, Pérez cited Guevara but much of the speech made use of Guevara's ideas even when the ideas weren't attributed to him directly.

Pérez explained that profitability in Guevara's system "did not have to measure itself as a difference between the earnings and the expenses at the level of each individual firm." At the level of the firm, profitability was "measured in relation to the costs in advance of productivity and as a lowering of costs," whereas "relative profitability" or the profitability of each firm in relation to one another was only used as an index since what was of greater concern within Guevara's system was the "profitability of the productive apparatus on the scale of the entire country."[84] The SDPE, he explained, also gave importance to "global profitability of the entire economy but according to each firm within this economy." Earnings and profitability were still important in Guevara's system, argued Pérez, who cited as evidence Guevara's statement that "firm profitability was an essential condition for the development of communism." Another difference, said Pérez, was that the role of the bank was much reduced in Guevara's system, whereas the SDPE relied on the banks and credit to "compel and stimulate firms to save resources and reduce costs" since the use of more resources required the use of loans granted at a higher interest rate.

In the end, argued Pérez, differences in terms of firm organization and the level of autonomy of each firm and the relationship between material and moral incentives were not qualitative differences but only differences of emphasis and then in terms of secondary and quantitative criteria. These were "major differences only in appearance and not in fact" since both systems in the end relied on "economic technical cohesion, a common destination for their production and equally a particular territorial unit."[85]

Pérez concluded the speech by citing instances of Guevara's reliance on material incentives. While Guevara prioritized moral incentives, said Pérez, he never "denied in any moment that it was necessary to eliminate material incentives even when considered a hindrance from the past against which it was necessary to work to create the conditions that would lead to its disappearance in the process of development of a society on its way towards Communism." And, added Pérez, Fidel's comments during the First Party Congress in 1975 had displayed a continuing concern with the role of moral incentives.

Many of the ideas in Pérez's speech could be found in the writings of Guevara himself and in that sense his speech was not a purely selective review of those points of Guevara's work that might sanction the SDPE. Guevara himself argued that the difference between the two systems was one of means, rather than ends. Both economic calculus, to which Guevara was opposed because of what he viewed as too great a reliance on market mechanisms, and the system of budgetary finance, sought a "more efficient way of reaching communism," and in that sense, there was "no discrepancy in principle."[86] According to Guevara, "Economic calculus has proved that it yields practical results, and, based on similar principles, both systems seek the same ends. But we believe that our system's plan of action, if properly developed, can increase the effectiveness of economic management by the socialist State and deepen mass consciousness."[87] In addition, Guevara argued that "under both systems the general State plan is the supreme authority."[88] In support of Pérez's initial explanation for the failure of the budgetary finance system, Guevara had also pointed to the system's "lack of maturity" and the lack of trained cadres to carry it out.[89] Finally, he did argue that communism needed material progress to sustain itself.[90]

That said, there were elements of Guevara's argument and in particular his argument against using material incentives and the law of value that Pérez underplayed. If Guevara saw the need for material incentives at a particular stage of building socialism, he was always sure to qualify exactly what kinds of material incentives those would be as well as the dangers of too heavy a reliance on them. In "On the System of Budgetary Finance," he wrote:

> We must make clear that *we do not deny the objective need for material incentives* [italics in original]. But we are unwilling to use them as the primary instrument of motivation. We believe that, in economics, this kind of device quickly becomes a category per se and then imposes its power over man's relationships. It should be recalled that this category is a product of capitalism and is destined to die under socialism.[91]

The death of this category, he explained, would not be hastened by using it, since "direct material incentives and consciousness are contradictory terms."[92] In direct opposition to Pérez's defense of direct material incentives as a way of increasing the quantity and quality of goods available en masse, he wrote that "the development of consciousness does more for the development of production in a relatively short time than material incentives do." In deciding whether material interest should be appealed to, it was also necessary to answer the question of whether it was "a collective expression of the masses' wants" or "an individual presence, a reflection in the worker's conscience of old society's habits."[93]

That workers who surpassed their quota should be rewarded, acknowledged Guevara, "was a necessary evil during a transitory period." What he was less willing to accept was economic calculus's interpretation of the maxim "from each according to his ability, to each according to his labor" to mean "full payment in extra wages for the amount exceeding a given quota."[94] Here Guevara accused proponents of economic calculus of being guided too much by a principle that was only supposed to be temporary and thereby coming to depend upon and institutionalize it. As proponents of economic calculus argued, knowledge of certain objective economic laws, such as the law of value, meant that they could make conscious use of them, but, he warned, controlling them in order to do away with them was quite different from adopting and perfecting them as useful and permanent tools for planning. This marked a "profound difference" between economic calculus and the budgetary finance system.[95] Recognizing the limitations of a particular historical moment did not mean accepting wholesale all that remained from the society one was trying to overcome.

> The *tendency* should be, in our opinion, to eliminate as fast as possible the old categories, including the market, money, and, therefore, material interest—or, better, to eliminate the conditions for their existence. The contrary would be to assume that the task of building socialism in a backward society is in the nature of a historical accident and that its leaders, in order to excuse the *mistake,* should strive to consolidate all the categories inherent in the intermediate society.[96]

Elsewhere, Guevara posed similar questions about how the rationale of economic calculus reflected on the legitimacy of the Cuban Revolution. In his essay "The Meaning of Socialist Planning" he asked why it was that if the "right" objective conditions for revolution did not exist in Cuba but there was a socialist revolution anyway, economic policy would have to be led by these same objective conditions after the revolution.[97] Being led by them not only ran the risk of entrenching them but was also damaging in the short term. For instance, in Cuba, where dependence on international exchange was great, prices signaled not just domestic demand but external demand as well. Producing more of what was most profitable might mean ignoring that a product might have "strategic value" later on or simply be "of greater benefit to the people."[98]

This, for Guevara, was not simply a problem of emphasis, but a problem of principle since he saw communism as "a goal consciously pursued by man."[99] In the same essay "On the Budgetary Finance System" from which Pérez drew, Guevara pointed to the "humanistic character" of Marx found in his *The Economic and Philosophic Manuscripts of 1844* and wrote: "Man is a conscious actor in history. Without this consciousness, which embraces his awareness as a social being, there can be no communism."[100]

In the case of Pérez's use of Guevara, he emphasized those moments of Guevara's thought that appeared most pragmatic. An examination of Guevara's own discussion of the difference between the budgetary finance system or consolidated enterprise system, usually associated with idealism, and the economic accounting system or economic calculus, usually associated with pragmatism, shows, however, that the simple distinction between idealism and pragmatism was one that did not easily encapsulate either system. Guevara's account of the budgetary finance system and the dangers of using the tools of capitalism focused both on the goal of communism as an ideal and on the most effective way of arriving there. His pragmatism, however, took a different form than that of proponents of economic calculus. Indeed, his arguments suggested that proponents of economic calculus were being led astray by abstract economic principles that could not be separated out so easily from the market in practice. One could not assume that the law of value, for instance, could be harnessed and given an entirely new content under socialism, for its effects could not be easily controlled or isolated.[101]

As Pérez himself argued in relation to the *libreta*, pragmatic and short-term considerations had their limits and one had always be careful of the ways in which these considerations played out in the long run. Articles in *Granma* would continually deal implicitly with the kinds of arguments that had been made by Guevara and attempt to show the moral element of the SDPE, but they would do so without specific mention of Guevara himself. Appealing to the ideas of each posed its own unique challenges. In one way, appealing to el Che, and not only to Marx, was more dangerous since the works of Guevara and the debates in which he participated were directly related to the Cuban reality and also more accessible and familiar to the Cuban public than the works of Marx. On the other hand, disagreeing with Che as one interpreter of Marx was something that had been done publicly in Cuba since 1959, whereas disagreeing with Marx could be seen as a far greater challenge to the entire revolutionary project.

Economic Stimulation Funds

The issue of economic stimulation funds was another aspect of the SPDE that required particular ideological attention, especially in light of Che's warning about the dangers of individual material incentives. Economic stimulation funds were taken either from the net earnings of the individual enterprise if the enterprise was profitable or from subsidies granted by the state if the enterprise was not profitable.[102] These funds were then distributed to either outstanding individual workers within an enterprise or used to build housing and public spaces for cultural and social events.[103] The point was to use economic stimulation to encourage productivity and efficiency while at the same time rewarding collective behavior. Prizes taken from the stimulation funds were not, reminded one article, "a gift but rather stimulation for the collective efforts of a firm, translated into an improvement of determinate indicators that society is interested in improving in order to achieve greater efficiency."[104] While each enterprise decided what to do with these funds, these decisions were bounded by a JUCEPLAN resolution explaining the general purpose of these funds within the SDPE. Funds were to be used to "emphasize the results of socialist emulation and organize places to display the rewards that the enterprise has received or its establishments for the merits of the work achieved by the collective."[105] Earnings of enterprises and individual workers could be used to stimulate greater efficiency and productivity and thus improve the enterprise and society as a whole, but they could never be used against the interests of the people.[106] While there were salary differentials based on the quantity and quality of work, articles also explained that this in no way meant a move toward a capitalist system where the labor force was treated as merchandise since under socialism the means of production were owned by the workers. Those working more hours or more skillfully were simply receiving their share of what they had put in. "In socialist society, the salary is part of the national rent that, expressed in money, corresponds to workers for their personal consumption and its quantity depends on the quantity and quality of the work carried out by each."[107] Wage differentials as well as wage increases were necessary to increase productivity. There was not a one-to-one relationship between the sum of salaries and national rent, however. Productivity always had to rise ahead of the growth of salaries in order to guarantee economic development and ensure that there was enough merchandise so that people could use their salaries to buy what they needed.

Thus, the general challenge for the SDPE was to find just the right relationship between moral and material incentives in order to make the most of the productive forces without chipping away at the collective consciousness. According to an article in *Granma*:

> The SDPE needs to establish an adequate combination of moral and material incentives that stimulate the creation of plans closely directed toward extracting the most from existing productive possibilities, that promote an elevation in economic effectiveness, that invigorate the development of the collective spirit of the workers, and that inspire the struggle for a higher economic consciousness and a greater sense of responsibility for fulfilling social duty.[108]

While the general principle of to each according to his work and the granting of prizes to individual workers seemed to detract from the socialist project, articles were also quick to point out that these workers received these bonuses because their interests were ultimately nonmonetary. After receiving the prize for best worker, one worker was quoted in *Granma*: "For me, the moral aspect of the prize has such a high value that not even all the money in the world could pay for it."[109]

Although the prize bonuses were supposed to be, in the final analysis, moral rather than material incentives, the use of voluntary labor came under sharp criticism within the press, not because it was in some way forced, but because it was harder to calculate into the overall economic plan. Enterprises were failing to report the contributions made by voluntary labor. In doing so, they were attributing greater productivity to greater efficiency with the same quantity of labor rather than to the effort of this voluntary labor. Such omissions meant that enterprises were failing to report all costs and, in essence, robbing both the state and the workers who provided the voluntary labor. This, in turn, was complicating larger countrywide economic calculations, and this, again, was harmful to each individual Cuban.

> When a firm receives voluntary work and does not pay for it, it is appropriating value that does not belong to it insofar as the value is not the result of its economic efforts, but rather of a greater use of the labor force that does not belong to it nor to which it is accountable, and which materializes in the final product of the firm. This is the reason why it is necessary to account for voluntary work and pay for it.[110]

Another article from the same year focused on the achievements at one particular factory, arguing that the SDPE's emphasis on efficiency meant that firms no longer had to rely on voluntary labor to fulfill their quotas.[111] The moral aspect of voluntary labor was undermined by the difficulties it presented for keeping track of economic efficiency and productivity, which were equally important aspects of a socialist society focused on providing people with material needs. Voluntary labor, then, came to be seen as a waste of time.[112] Any positive effects of voluntary labor on individual and collective consciousness were outweighed by the problems it posed for economic calculus.

The Priority of the Plan and the Weaknesses of SDPE

The plan took priority over socialist values of sharing and nonmonetary exchange. Articles in *Granma* throughout 1980 criticized firms for their failure to take economic calculus seriously enough, particularly in relation to firm autonomy and the keeping of proper accounts at the level of each individual firm or group of firms. Articles in *Granma* pointed to an increasingly disharmonious relationship between the various mechanisms of the SDPE, between the firms and the state, including its banks, and to the need to establish a national system of arbitration to act as a neutral judge in disputes and relations between the state organs and the firms.[113] There was also the problem of sloppy bookkeeping on the part of firms. This, strangely, was attributed to lack of firm autonomy, which "conspired" against proper economic management. The problem, however, was that when faced with this "grave financial situation," firms did not demand the autonomy that was "their legitimate right" because they wished to push responsibility onto the larger administrative bodies.[114] Firm autonomy was presented not necessarily as a different sort of incentive structure but rather as a condition imposed upon firms that would force them to be more productive and efficient. According to one article, "Economic calculus obliges managers and workers of firms to plan their work using other conceptions because it is the first time that they are truly managing the resources at their disposal, using them according to economic and rational criteria."[115] Firms were not simply responsible for administering a particular plan but also for managing it economically, for it was only then that they would feel the consequences of their decisions and make economically astute choices.

One mechanism for encouraging greater firm autonomy and responsibility was the Markets for Consumer Goods, where buyers and sellers met to make production and sales contracts. The markets were useful in a variety of ways; they provided a way around the problem of unnecessary inventory and encouraged better use of transport; they encouraged firm autonomy by requiring firms to cover their own expenses; they provided a way for sellers to display their products for the upcoming year and get a sense of how much to produce and whether to produce certain items at all. Finally, the markets were useful for better linking planning, the circulation of goods, and the demands of the population. It was the market's use of "some economic laws of great importance to the SDPE" such as levels of supply and demand and the law of value that made them effective.[116]

If the Markets for Consumer Goods might encourage greater use of the laws of the market, state administrative bodies needed to audit individual firms or groups of firms to make sure that their accounting books corresponded to their actual operations. This was necessary to avoid larger errors in the overall plan.[117] One problem was that firms did not charge for the merchandise they sold. While this would appear to be positive for those firms receiving free goods, it was in fact extremely harmful in that accounting books registered artificial growth in earnings and this in turn led to errors in the National Systems of Costs and Payments. At those firms receiving free goods, economic stimulation funds grew but not because of greater efficiency. Not charging for goods simply hid the true economic state of a firm, thereby making it more difficult to correct mistakes and reducing the incentives that a true growth in earnings would give to workers. The biggest problem was that failure to charge for goods meant that some firms were getting credit for the efforts of others, and this was hardly in keeping with the oft repeated principle of "to each according to his work."[118]

All these problems, however, were not presented in the press as flaws of the overarching SDPE but rather as lack of understanding of the SDPE on the part of managers and workers. Throughout the fall of 1980 and spring of 1981, five years after the SDPE was announced, articles appeared about the importance of educating technicians and those specializing in carrying out the SDPE. For instance, one article announced the adoption of "disciplinary measures against the functionaries of entities that did not conclude economic contracts within the established time period."[119]

By 1981, articles were still talking about the gradual implementation of SDPE,[120] meetings to analyze the successes and failures of the SDPE,[121] the dependence of SDPE's success on workers' understanding of economic calculation,[122] the importance of proper rewards for work done, and the advantages of using price signals.[123] Several articles that spring and summer pointed to the continuing inadequacy of financial management at the level of the firm. One article reported that "the immense majority of firms and budgeted units" did not understand how to "capture primary information" that was necessary for larger statistical analyses and censuses of the national economy.[124] Firms were also failing to report on time their norms of consumption or average consumption for the year.

> Norms of consumption constitute the basis for the calculation of the firm plan. Without them, the plan is something very abstract and very difficult to evaluate. If expenses are not known, how will the level of production of a firm be determined with the exactitude that economic calculus demands[?][125]

Still, emphasis was placed on perfecting SDPE and adjusting solutions to the particular situation of each province rather than on scrapping it entirely. According to one article dealing with deficiencies in one province:

> The majority of difficulties are concentrated in questions of the organization of work and salaries, and questions of banking, the automized system of management, statistics, and planning. Almost all of these can be solved with the application of organizational and managerial solutions, and some of them can be fixed effectively in this province, for they have their origin in technical questions.[126]

The Balance of Statistics on Intersectorial Relations (BRIE), established in April 1981, was credited with improving financial discipline within the firms. BRIE was responsible for collecting statistics on all the economic activities of the country and ordering that information into tables that "express how production is distributed throughout all the branches of the economy and what is consumed in all branches of the economy."[127]

Explanations for the shortcomings of SDPE often focused on individual failings. A 1982 article described the "subjective reasons" for the problems with SDPE as "incomprehension, subvaluation, and a lack of attention to and control of the problems and tasks of the SDPE." Objective factors included "limited material resources" and closely related to the subjective factors, "limited skilled personnel." Again, the problem with the SDPE was not attributed to the general idea of economic calculus but rather to failures on the part of firm accountants and to the underdevelopment of consciousness on the part of the workers. One article entitled "Principal Tasks of the SDPE for the Next Years" cited extensively from Castro's analyses of the SDPE during the Second Party Congress in 1980. According to the article and to

Castro's analyses,[128] the country had done well at introducing and applying economic calculation but neither efficiency nor worker consciousness was yet good enough. In this sense, the argument was a subtle vindication of Che's argument since it seemed to imply that the consciousness of the people had to be sufficiently socialist to even use the methods of capitalism.

In addition, went the argument of the article and Castro's analysis, economic conditions were worse than they were at the time of the Second Party Congress. World sugar prices had dropped dramatically, with a pound of sugar worth 15% of what it was worth at the end of 1980. The U.S. blockade continued to impose problems in terms of access to international credit, while the cost of imports from capitalist countries had risen. These "objective" conditions, however, explained why it was more important than ever to make the SDPE work. Making it work proved difficult, however, and the press became more and more silent about the issues of the SDPE.

The Pragmatism of Rectification

In 1981, five years before the Rectification Campaign of Ideological Errors and Negative Tendencies began, discussions of the SDPE in *Granma* were fewer and farther between and less inclined to speak of its virtues for the overall socialist project.[129] In 1983, there were only thirteen references to the SDPE, and few of these articles focused on balancing material and moral incentives or the virtues of economic calculation. A January article pointing to the failure of agricultural firms both to fulfill their contracts and to demand that the firms with which they did business fulfill theirs, did tell readers that "firms should always take into account that nonfulfillments in agriculture mean that products don't get to the population." "In socialism," continued the article, "this aspect is much more important than monetary compensation between firms."[130] However, the larger point of the article was simply to warn against the rise of *amigoism* whereby firms were not holding each other accountable for fulfilling the plan. The general silence on larger ideological issues was striking given the press's overall defense of particular ideological positions and the intensity with which it had dealt with tensions between the market and socialism and between material and moral incentives in 1980. In 1984, there were only seven references to the SDPE, and while the number rose to fifteen in 1985, the overall decline suggested that pragmatic considerations had become of greater importance than during the discussions of the supposedly pragmatic SDPE. In other words, one might see the increasing silence on the issue of the SDPE as a greater indication of ideological crisis than when the press had been justifying the use of monetary mercantile categories throughout the end of the 1970s and beginning of the 1980s.

The abandonment of the SDPE and the announcement by Fidel Castro in 1986 of the Rectification Campaign of Ideological Errors and Negative Tendencies appears to fit neatly into the pragmatic/idealist mold, since the campaign criticized the institutionalization of the 1970s and 1980s and praised the experimentation of the 1960s. However, the campaign also warned against committing the idealist errors of the past.[131] Moreover, as Susan Eckstein has argued, the campaign was no more ideological than the SDPE and was "rooted in emergent government concerns" that "would have been politically risky to implement if not ideologically justified."[132] As with the SDPE, ideology itself was fundamental to government pragmatism.

Four

Political Unity and Spheres of Difference

Social Scientists and Censorship in the 1990s

Political unity is the principle of Cuban socialism that appears most vulnerable to manipulation by those in power and most likely to overwhelm other principles. What is political unity, after all, but the call from those in power to rally behind the decisions they have already made, regardless of the content of those decisions? Is not the principle of political unity fundamentally totalitarian, antidemocratic, and always swallowing up the other principles of Cuban socialist ideology? Political unity that is in theory at the service of socioeconomic equality can easily become a goal in and of itself, especially when appealed to under conditions of material scarcity and external threats. In Cuba, real threats from the United States, especially in the first years of the revolution, have helped to fuel the tendency, present in any revolutionary movement that has acquired state power (and part of the logic of sovereignty more generally), to prioritize survival, at the expense of specific goals and principles for which it struggled.

As Boaventura de Sousa Santos has pointed out, in Cuba the dual pillars of the revolution, resistance and forging an alternative, have existed in tension with each other, with the former often taking precedence over the latter.[1] At least in the short and medium term, resistance has demanded political unity to a degree that providing an alternative has not. Resistance, easily understood in militaristic terms, involves providing a united front against an enemy, whereas providing an alternative, and especially a socialist one, requires collective efforts, and even the voicing of a wide range of views to better seek out an alternative program. Even so, the meaning of political unity has been contested in Cuba, although in ways that do not represent a direct challenge to state power or a call for an autonomous, private, and apolitical realm of civil society. This call for a different understanding of political unity has often been made, not in the name of expanding civil society in opposition to the state or in the name of freedom of speech as an abstract principle, but rather in the name of defending the academic sphere as a space with its own rules and criteria for participating in the construction and preservation of socialism.

This argument was made in the case of the Centro de Estudios sobre América (Center for the Study of America) or CEA, a research institute in Havana whose members were dispersed in 1996 as part of a more general government campaign to reign in what was viewed as the growth of potentially antagonistic nongovernmental organizations. The members of CEA were not the most outspoken or critical intellectuals at the time or earlier. Others, and particularly visual artists, writers, musicians, and those associated with academic disciplines in the humanities, have always provided the most direct challenges to state power without necessarily allying themselves with official dissident organizations on the island. However, the status of the CEA members as social scientists identified with the Party, as well as the availability of the records of their conversations with the Party leadership, provides the opportunity to see an example of a disagreement that proposed an alternative both to the state monopoly on power and to a liberal understanding of academia that claims neutrality and denies political responsibility. The case of CEA illustrates two different versions of political unity: both the state and CEA academics acknowledged the fundamentally political nature of academic activities, but CEA academics insisted that academic political responsibility was different from that of the state, and that unity was only possible when each could play its role.

Though no one at CEA or any of the other NGOs that were targeted by the government campaign were jailed or banned outright from working in Cuba, the event was an instance of the leadership disciplining academic production and independent political organizations on the island.[2] At first glance, then, the case would appear to be another example of political unity being used by the leadership as a weapon to enforce conformity with the party line and another lesson in the dangers of a one-party state, where the fundamental right to freely express oneself is not guaranteed. Those explanations are part of the story. However, an analysis of the work done by CEA researchers, of discussions that went on between them and party bureaucrats, and of my own conversations with several of the researchers from CEA shows that even those attacked by the leadership drew upon principles of Cuban socialism to defend themselves. When academics from CEA were accused of betraying the revolution and the Party, they agreed with the leadership that their role as academics could not be divorced from political considerations. However, they also insisted that organic intellectuals were not the same as politicians and that in the academic sphere, the criteria for judging academic production were political in a different way. The political consequences of academic production could not be assessed with the same immediacy. Allowing for the distinct *political* role of the organic intellectual helped to protect, rather than weaken, the socialist project. Their defense, then, involved challenging the leadership's narrow understanding of political unity by showing how their definition of political unity was dependent upon other key principles of Cuban socialism—equality (both economic and political) and social justice—and how difference might fortify, rather than weaken, a political unity always justified by its commitment to socioeconomic equality.

Cuban Studies and the Objectivity Problem

During their discussions both the leadership and the CEA academics acknowledged that the events surrounding the Cuban government's actions against Cuban NGOs did not take place in a vacuum and therefore could not be judged as if they had. The academic study of the Cuban political and economic system has not been immune to the ideological war between the United States and Cuba. Some background on the perils of academic production on Cuba and the stakes of academic exchange in the 1990s is therefore in order.

No academics, least of all those engaged in studies of the political and economic systems, can divorce their work entirely from particular ideological agendas and political positions.[3] The situation of academics working on Cuba is particularly tenuous because they are working in what are akin to wartime conditions. The blockade has extended not just to trade but to information as well. The Cuban government is suspicious of academics working on Cuba who are not affiliated with Cuban institutions, while the U.S. government is suspicious of any Cuban academic who *is* affiliated with Cuban academic institutions. Government officials in both countries judge academic work less by its success in illuminating phenomena or its innovative methodology, than by the extent to which it supports or opposes the Cuban revolutionary project.[4] In this sense, the U.S. and Cuban governments are in complete agreement. U.S.-based academics, however, are not, for U.S.-based academics see the governments' politicized criteria as flying in the face of the democratic values the United States claims to espouse. If pure objectivity is impossible, there are ways in which to move closer to it.

Such has been the philosophy of the U.S.-based journal *Cuban Studies*, started in 1970. The birth of the journal represented a shift in Cuban studies away from a broad-brush polemical approach.[5] In keeping with its editorial aim of publishing "scholarly articles which not only represent an ideological balance but also cover a broad range of interests," the journal made efforts especially in the early 1980s to increase the number of Cuban authors published in its pages.[6] The initial exchanges between Cuban and U.S.-based scholars in the pages of *Cuban Studies*, however, revealed the difficulties of removing the study of Cuba from more immediate political conflicts. Cuban scholars writing in the pages of *Cuban Studies* registered their suspicion of liberal pluralism and their distrust of non-Cuba-based scholarly production because of what they perceived to be its ideological bias against the revolution.

An exchange between two Cuban academics in a 1983 issue of *Cuban Studies* illustrates the negotiation of Cuban ideology in the academic sphere. Cuban social scientist and CEA researcher Hernán Yanes wrote a critique of an article by U.S.-based scholar Jorge Domínguez on Cuban foreign policy included in the same issue. Domínguez had argued that Cuban foreign policy in the Caribbean and Central America could be characterized by the two primary goals of ensuring the survival of the revolution and generating economic resources and the three secondary goals of promoting good relations with nonleftist governments, seeking influence within international political movements of the Left, and supporting revolutions.[7] According to Yanes, Domínguez's article wrongly emphasized political opportunism in Cuban foreign policy at the expense of the revolution's principled commitment to socialist internationalism and peaceful coexistence (as opposed to "conciliatory compromise").[8] Yanes saw Domínguez's work as contributing to a larger body of American academic work known in Cuba as "Cubanology," defined by Yanes as the study of the Cuban system from ideological positions or politics opposed to the revolution.[9] Cubanologists in the United States, concluded Yanes, could only "contribute to a better understanding of Cuba" by "reject[ing] anti-Communist Manichaeism with its absurd aberrations" and "dispos[ing] themselves to exercise scientific judgment before political prudence."[10] Yanes thus made the same argument against academics living off the island that the United States made against Cuban academics living on the island: that Cuban academics were simply spouting the party line and unable to produce quality academic work.[11]

Domínguez responded to these charges by turning the tables on Yanes.

His own work was not inherently counterrevolutionary. Rather, Yanes's own prejudices caused him to attribute to Domínguez conclusions that he did not make (that Cubans were responsible for the civil war in El Salvador, for instance) and to fail to see how Domínguez's positions were in agreement with many of Yanes's statement about Cuban foreign policy (Cuba's relative autonomy from the Soviet Union in foreign affairs in Latin American, for instance).[12] Yanes, wrote Domínguez, "appears unwilling and unable to conceive that scholarly works may have some autonomy from partisan political life. Thus he reads my article only at one level: what propaganda purpose does it serve to defame the Cuban Revolution?"[13] Domínguez concluded his defense by suggesting that increased exchange between Cuban scholars and U.S.-based scholars might make "these kinds of misunderstandings . . . less likely."[14] Twelve years later Dominguez restated this position in the pages of *Cuban Studies:* "truth, always elusive, should emerge from the engagement between contrasting ideas."[15]

Those like Yanes did not share this view of truth and instead saw academic production as implicated in politics, whether its practitioners believed it to be or not. His position was presumably the one officially sanctioned in Cuba, and Yanes would later distance himself from it.[16] It was reiterated three years later, in 1986, when *Cuban Studies* published an exchange between José Luis Rodríguez García (an economist and assistant director of the Center for Research on the World Economy in Havana and one of the most vocal Cuban critics of Cuban studies in the United States) and U.S.-based Cuban economist Carmelo Mesa-Lago. The exchange between Rodríguez and Mesa-Lago resembled some of the disagreements between Yanes and Domínguez earlier.[17] Significantly, for Rodríguez, one could not escape the label of Cubanologist (aka soldier in the ideological struggle against the Cuban Revolution), as Domínguez and Mesa-Lago had attempted to do, by showing the ways in which one defended or supported the revolution.

If the editors of *Cuban Studies* invited Cuban academics to publish in the pages of their journal as a way of demonstrating their commitment to freedom of expression and debate and Cuban academics' value for understanding the Cuban reality, those Cubans who published in *Cuban Studies* at this time did so to call these commitments into question and to insist, repeatedly, that academic production was implicated in politics, whether its practitioners believed it to be or not. According to Rodríguez, European and North American scholarship supported "directly or indirectly, consciously or unconsciously, the political struggle of the United States against socialism in Cuba."[18] While the relationship between these academic works and U.S.

policy was "neither linear nor direct," he argued, they helped to create favorable environment for the development of hostile North American policy toward Cuba.[19] The mistrust of academic work on Cuba produced outside the country made academic exchange between the United States and Cuba difficult and set the tone of those exchanges that did occur.

A Shift in the Nature of Academic Exchange

In the late 1980s, a number of institutional and foreign policy changes increased the likelihood of exchange between the United States and Cuba. Cuban and U.S. academics began participating together in more conferences and joint projects.[20] The philosophy surrounding their exchanges also shifted. The members of CEA, of which Yanes was one, responded to the call of U.S. academics for debate and dialogue. These more recent exchanges began with the assumption that ideological bias was inevitable, that scholars' ideological starting points were distinct from the overall quality of their scholarly work, and that in spite of ideological differences, Cuban and U.S.-based academics could cooperate in their search to understand specific phenomena in Cuban history, politics, economics, and society.

For instance, in 1989, CEA member Rafael Hernández coedited a book on U.S./Cuban relations with Jorge Domínguez (of the 1983 *Cuban Studies* debate).[21] The collection represented a joint effort to understand U.S.-Cuban relations following the inauguration of a new U.S. president and in light of what appeared to be increasing cooperation between the two countries in recent years on issues such as migration and South Africa. The carefully crafted introduction by Domínguez and Hernández reflected, sometimes obliquely and sometimes explicitly, the politically charged nature of such an undertaking. The editors spoke of the "importance of understanding the 'lenses' through which we seek individually to make sense of events." They explained that the book included two chapters on each topic—one by a Cuban academic and one by a U.S.-based academic—to illustrate "the utility of being aware of different national, ideological, and analytical lenses" and the importance of recognizing disagreements between scholars from the two countries.[22] "The purpose of scholarship," they wrote, "is to shed light on issues, not to settle disputes that lie properly in the domain of government officials. However, scholars can respond to moments when officials review issues to confirm existing policies or to change them."[23] At the start of the 1990s, then, it appeared that Domínguez's position stated earlier—that the clash of differing views was the best way to weed out ideological bias—had won out and the number of academic and scholarly exchanges between the United States and Cuba (and between Cuba and elsewhere) increased dramatically.

This apparent détente coincided with a shift in the destabilizing tactics of the U.S. government. In 1992, during the height of Cuba's Special Period, and in the wake of transitions in Eastern Europe and Russia driven by civil society, the U.S. Congress passed the Cuban Democracy Act, also known as the Torricelli bill. In addition to the traditional approach of economic sanctions, which had incurred criticism on humanitarian grounds, a second component known as Track II was added. Track II allowed the U.S. government to provide assistance, via NGOs and other external partners, to individuals and organizations working to promote nonviolent change on the island at a time when the Cuban government was struggling to maintain legitimacy in light of severe economic hardship. While wary of Track II, the Cuban government, like the U.S. government, also saw it as a "practical way to gain intelligence."[24] Cuban institutions saw increased exchange as an opportunity to increase much-needed revenue. They also saw it as an opportunity to provide a more positive view of Cuba than the one presented by U.S. academics, and as a consequence, Cuban academics were encouraged to participate in these exchanges.[25] However, they were always to keep in mind the dangerous terrain of academic exchange in light of Track II.

The Academic Production of CEA Researchers

CEA was established by the Central Committee of the Cuban Communist Party (CC of the PCC) in 1977. According to the statutes of CEA, approved by the Central Committee, CEA was to carry out research "of an economic, political and economic character" on Latin America, the Caribbean, the United States, and Canada and on imperialism with a particular emphasis on its U.S. form. While the statutes did not explicitly prohibit working on Cuba, it was clear that the focus was to be on Latin America more generally, and not on the domestic challenges facing Cuba specifically or the ways that the Cuban experience provided the occasion to reconsider Marxism-Leninism and vice versa. The Ministry of Justice granted CEA status as an Asociación Científica Jurídicamente Autónoma y No Gubernamental in 1987 in an effort to attract international funding and to facilitate academic exchanges between CEA and other countries by projecting a more independent image.[26] The change was largely one of image, rather than independence, since CEA remained under the control of the Party, which continued to establish its governing norms and rules and to approve its annual and five-year plans.[27] Its changed status produced the desired effects and CEA's international relations increased throughout the 1978 to 1990 period.

CEA had thirty-nine members, eight of which played a key role in discussions with the central committee.[28] The eight included the sociologists Haroldo Dilla, Luis Suárez, Aurelio Alonso, Rafael Hernández, and Juan Valdés Paz and the economists Pedro Monreal, Luis Gutiérrez, and Julio Carranza Valdés. While all were Communist Party members, all had published articles dealing with the effects of the Special Period and the need to reconceptualize, but not abandon, Cuban socialism in light of these changes. Examples of their work could be found in CEA's journal *Cuadernos de Nuestra América* (hereafter *CNA*), in books published in Cuba, and in journals and edited volumes published outside Cuba.[29] What united the work was a general concern with the direction that Cuba's reforms would take as well as the consequences of those reforms for socialism in Cuba. The work, then, exceeded CEA's original mandate by dealing with Cuba and Cuban socialism.

CNA began publishing such work as early as 1992, but particularly significant was Haroldo Dilla's 1993 article examining Cuba's structural reform process from a critical perspective.[30] In "Cuba, Crisis and Rearticulation of Political Consensus (Notes for a Socialist Debate)," Dilla argued that economic restructuring had to be accompanied by greater political openness if socialism was to be preserved in Cuba. The article traced problems emerging during the Special Period not to U.S. imperialism or global capitalism alone, but also to the persistence of an overly centralized Soviet political model. A shorter English-language version appeared almost a year later in the U.S.-based journal *Latin American Perspectives* and would later be used by the committee investigating CEA as evidence of its members' failure to censor their own criticisms properly when presenting their views to foreign audiences.[31]

While Dilla praised the introduction of democratic institutions (People's Power in the 1970s and direct local elections and indirect elections at the level of parliament and state organs), he also wrote that the changes were "obliterated by the persistence of paternalistic vertical patronage which worked well with the centralized economy."[32] This model would become particularly problematic for socialism and Cuban democracy, he argued, in light of *state-led* economic restructuring that facilitated "worker discipline but not true participation."[33] While Dilla rejected liberal pluralism and the reduction of pluralism to a multiparty system, the article called for a "reconceptualization of the relationship between democracy and governability in a socialist context, where only the expansion of democracy . . . is capable of ensuring the stability and governability of the system."[34] His reconceptualization did not entail an abandonment of Cuba's "political and ideological arsenal," but it did "imply a substantial change in the bipolar relationship between politics and ideology, such that political practice assumes a more determinate role in the production of ideology, and not as was usual with the experiences with true socialism, in which preestablished ideology established sacred political canons."[35]

In his article, Dilla suggested not just that the government needed to take a different path during a particular historical juncture, but also that *what had all along been a weakness of the Cuban system* was now coming to threaten the existence of any sort of socialism in Cuba. The article implied, although did not state explicitly, that it was the Cuban government itself that was threatening the future of socialism in Cuba and not just foreign enemies, antisocial elements, U.S. mercenaries or petty capitalists. The economic crisis brought hardship but also the opportunity to rectify what had long been "missing in Cuban politics: the maturation of a pluralism, understood as the recognition of the diversity and autonomy of the subject participants, and as a consequence of conflict as a moment in the creation of consensus."[36] Political unity, then, could not be achieved by assuming it at the outset. Dilla had also dealt with the issue of popular participation elsewhere, arguing that high participation did not translate into real popular power and suggesting that official claims about the success of its participatory system were subject to empirical verification.[37]

In 1996, Dilla took an even more critical approach to Cuban democracy when he edited a volume of essays entitled *La democracia en Cuba y el diferendo con los Estados Unidos* (*Democracy in Cuba and the Difference with the United States*).[38] The book was the fruit of a workshop held at CEA in 1994 and attended by both Cuban and North American academics. It included articles, like Dilla's articles published in the exterior, pointing to the failure of Cuba's high level of popular mobilization and participation to translate into real political power. What was distinct, however, was that the book was published and released inside Cuba, in Spanish, and included articles by U.S.-based academics critical of Cuba's political system and its claims to its brand of democracy. Jorge Domínguez's contribution, for instance, concluded:

> If Cuba had a political system that was really democratic, there would be free elections, whose results would not be known ahead of time, open to government and opposition parties, in order to thus determine whom the majority supports and where national consensus was in reality situated. Only in this way would national sovereignty be consolidated in the international system that now exists, only in this way

would a democracy "with all" be achieved—not because everyone is in agreement with baseline issues but rather because all would consent to the rules that must govern in a democracy—and only in this way would an approximation of a society *for the good of all* be achieved.[39]

This was no small contribution, not just on the part of Domínguez, but on the part of Dilla as well, since it was Dilla as editor of the book who had decided to include the article. It was hardly common for books published legally in Cuba to include an article by an academic that the government deemed complicit, intentionally or not, in an aggressive propaganda campaign against the Cuban Revolution. In his criticism of the Cuban political system and call for liberal democratic reform, Domínguez appealed to certain principles of Cuban socialism such as unity, national autonomy, and social justice, as evidenced in his strategic use of Martí's phrase "With all, for the good of all."

Dilla's essay in the volume did not share many of Domínguez's conclusions about the superiority of liberal democracy, but it did ask the question, "In what way must Cuba be more democratic?" On the one hand, Dilla argued that liberalism provided "humanity with principles inseparable from the construction of any type of democracy." Dilla advocated political pluralism whereby differing views were not simply tolerated, but could also be registered at the point of decision-making, and whereby minority views were recognized in accordance with established rules of the game.[40] Unfortunately, these values had become trapped in a larger framework whose "cornerstones" were private property and capitalist accumulation.[41] According to Dilla, the privileging and legitimating of private property and capitalist accumulation worked against, rather than with, the individual liberties that were fundamental to the construction of any democracy. Socioeconomic considerations, he insisted, were equally inseparable from the construction of democracy. Free time and education were keys to a citizen's effective participation in political life.[42]

While the latter part of his argument appeared to be a clear endorsement of the Cuban model of democracy, Dilla warned that Cuba had to become more democratic precisely to protect this socioeconomic equality that was increasingly threatened by the possibility that the market (an unavoidable tool) would "become the organizing principle of society and politics."[43] Dilla's contribution, while clearly working well within the bounds of the Marxist tradition, including the Guevarist tradition, was not a wholehearted endorsement of current Cuban policy. The issue that the leadership would ultimately raise, however, was not simply the content of the article but its publication alongside an article by a person who clearly advocated a complete overhaul of the existing political and economic system. It was not considered the time or place to propose alternatives.

CEA's economists, too, published articles in *CNA* and elsewhere pointing to long-standing problems with Cuba's economic and political system. One of the most significant analyses of the Cuban economy came in 1995 when Julio Carranza, Luis Gutiérrez, and Pedro Monreal published *Cuba: La restructuración de la economía: una propuesta para el debate* (*Cuba: The Restructuring of the Economy: A Contribution to the Debate*).[44] In it, the authors argued that the disappearance of the Soviet trading bloc had exposed Cuba to the world market but also made preexisting economic inefficiencies "more apparent and damaging." What was therefore needed, they argued, was a "profound restructuring" of the economy involving a redefinition of the bases of accumulation, reinsertion into the global economy, and reform of the economics system while at the same time maintaining social justice and national independence.[45] They pointed to the importance of strengthening popular participation and the value of "unions and other social organizations so as to defend the interests of workers in the conflicts generated by the new context."[46] London's Institute of Latin American Studies published this book in the exterior in 1996.[47]

The economists' work appeared less threatening than Dilla's, however, for it stayed primarily at the level of the economic and was more in keeping with the official position that the crisis was economic, not political. During a meeting with Dilla in Havana in 1998, Dilla told me that while Cuba lacked a "culture of debate," there were what he called "positions" within academia on the nature of reforms in Cuba. The orthodox or official position, in keeping with the government position, was that changes to the Cuban economy were simply adjustments and that it was possible to maintain a controlled market. CEA members, he said, tended to identify with two other positions. A second position, which Dilla associated with economists Pedro Monreal and Julio Carranza, promoted market socialism and social democracy, but focused on economic reform and saw too much popular participation as an obstacle to economic adjustment. According to Dilla, their analysis "remain[ed] at the level of the economy," and "they did not think of the social effects." The third position, according to Dilla, was the position of those such as Aurelio Alonso and Juan Valdés, who were not economists and who believed that the social effects of economic adjustment could not be treated separately. Their concern, he told me, was not just with governmentality but also with social shifts, democratic politics, firm autonomy, and worker participation. According to Dilla, while all three positions wished to maintain social services, the first two positions differed mostly on technical questions such as the amount of market mechanisms that could be introduced into the economy, what types of property were acceptable, and the extent to which the state was to be involved. For those with an orthodox position, explained Dilla, the state would play an even greater role in the administration of the economy while justifying economic change within the existing ideological framework, while the position occupied by economists proposed decentralized planning and a smaller role for the state.[48]

The belief most of the researchers at CEA shared was that socialism was not going to be reinvented by the leadership alone and that society, under whose heading they placed themselves, would need to play an important part in such an endeavor. They believed too that they had been called upon by the leadership in the early 1990s to play this role. By 1996, however, the Cuban government sent them a very different message.

Raúl's Words to the Intellectuals: Isolating CEA

On March 23, 1996, in a "Report to the Political Bureau on the Political and Social Situation of the Country and the Corresponding Work of the Party," delivered during the Fifth General Meeting of the Cuban Communist Party, Raúl Castro accused Cuban NGOs (naming CEA as one example) of "abandoning classist principles," of being tempted "to travel and edit articles to the liking of those who could finance them," of getting "caught up in the spider's web spun by Cubanologists," and of stating opinions in public that pleased Cuba's enemies.[49] Castro's report to the Political Bureau was read aloud on television the next day and published in *Granma* a week later.

Raúl's speech, like Fidel Castro's 1961 "Words to the Intellectuals," was a warning to intellectuals that the revolution's survival took precedence over all else. In the speech, he dealt with many of the social and ideological repercussions of Cuba's three-year experiment with economic reform, and spoke of the negative consequences of self-employment, tourism, foreign investment, and the intensification of the blockade while emphasizing the "ideological work" (*la labor ideológica*) that would be necessary to combat such consequences.[50] Of particular concern for Raúl Castro were the ways in which the U.S. economic blockade against Cuba (what he referred to as Track I) was increasingly being combined with a second track (Track II) of "internal subversion" intended to slowly "eat away at [Cuba] from within."[51] According to Raúl Castro, the use of the term "civil society" by the U.S. government was little more than "theoretical cover" for the United States to impose its will on Cuba. Unlike in the past, however, when Cuban dissidents were targeted as the primary Trojan horses through which the U.S. exerted its influence, Raúl Castro now focused his attention on the "so-called nongovernmental organizations established in Cuba in recent times."

While he cited the North American solidarity organization Pastors for Peace as evidence that not all NGOs "throughout the world" were "enemies of the people," he did not spare Cuba's own internal NGOs and CEA in particular. While the creation and existence of such NGOs was and continued to be "justified," argued Raúl, the Party had not controlled them enough. According to Raúl:

> Taking one step today and another tomorrow, in which ingenuousness was mixed with pedantry, and combined with an abandonment of classist principles with the temptation to travel and edit articles to the liking of those who could finance them, several comrades got caught up in the spider's web spun by foreign Cubanologists, in truth servants of the United States in its policy of fomenting a fifth column. This is what happened at the Center for the Study of America. Of course, we must distinguish, and we do in said Center [CEA] and everywhere, between the Cuban researcher who may think differently about whatever subject but does so from positions of socialism and within the framework appropriate to it, and that researcher who in fact has become a Cubanologist with Cuban citizenship and even with a Party card, spreading their positions to the satisfaction of our enemies.[52]

Without naming anyone in particular, Raúl argued that research and analysis should be focused on the needs of the country and not determined by the desires of outside funding sources who would exploit Cuba's need for dollars by determining and manipulating academics working at these Cuban NGOs. It was particularly important for Cuban researchers to keep in mind that there were certain contexts in which some research or analyses might not be appropriate for public consumption inside and outside of Cuba. It was the researcher's responsibility to be vigilant about the ways in which enemies of the revolution might use the content of their work, and particularly criticisms of government policies, as ammunition.

Cuban publications were publishing articles that "scarcely differ from those produced by North American academic enemies of the revolution and that use a supposedly revolutionary language that appears destined to serve as a smoke screen for their true intentions."[53] Raúl Castro drew a parallel to the case of *Pensamiento Crítico,* which, according to Raúl Castro, "played a diversionist role in the 1960s" by publishing materials that "corresponded, consciously or not, to those who wished to encourage the emergence of fifth columnists in Cuba."[54]

Raúl felt not just that certain research or analyses were dangerous but that to take the position of academic neutrality was to take the position of the enemy.

> Institutions have to serve the interests of our people, above all, without losing their basic characteristics or language. And their researchers and directors cannot overlook this when it comes to discussing or establishing their positions in workshops, seminars, etc. inside and outside of Cuba. Adopting a neutral or confused position, in order to avoid a confrontation or elude a thorny topic, is a show of unacceptable weakness before one's adversary; it is tantamount to admitting that the adversary's position is the correct one.[55]

Unity among academics of diverse opinions and ideological positions on the basis of academic neutrality was for Raúl a false unity or artificial unanimity that made the country "easy prey to foreign domination."[56] True unity was based on consensus around an agreed upon ideological position arrived at through consultation with the Cuban people and the leadership.

The Party, warned Raúl, had begun and would "continue to take all the necessary measures in the face of present and future situations and challenges on all fronts, particularly on the ideological one." Prior to the Fifth Congress, between June and December 1995, the director of CEA, Luis Suárez, met three times with members of the Political Bureau of the Cuban Communist Party's Central Committee who criticized Suarez's work as a researcher and as director of CEA. In Suárez's last meeting, Political Bureau member José R. Balaguer approved CEA's plan for 1996 to 1998 while at the same time criticizing economists working at the institute. In March 1996, Suárez was removed from his position as director and replaced by Dario Machado, an academic bureaucrat and former head of the Center for Sociopolitical Studies and Public Opinion.[57] While members of CEA were unhappy with the change, the greatest shock would come one week after the Fifth Congress with the March 27 publication of Raúl Castro's speech in *Granma.* In the beginning of April, the Political Bureau of the Central Committee of the Cuban Communist Party established a commission headed by Balaguer to examine the case of CEA. For the next seven months, members of CEA would meet repeatedly with the commission.

First as Tragedy, Then as Farce: Parallels to *Pensamiento Crítico*

The attack on CEA recalled the case of *Pensamiento Crítico* in a variety of ways. Both cases signaled the triumph of dogmatics within the Party and marked the end of what were considered periods of lively and open debate in Cuba. Both CEA and *Pensamiento Crítico* were cases of intellectuals who were members of the Cuban Communist Party working at universities and research institutes affiliated with the state and who saw their intellectual identities and responsibilities in relation to the interests and goals of the Cuban Revolution. They were not dissidents attempting to operate outside the legal system established by the government, nor did they believe that their academic work could or should exist independent of political considerations relevant to the revolution. Rather they saw themselves as organic intellectuals whose scholarly work was intricately connected to the construction of a distinctly Cuban variant of socialism.[58]

There was, however, a key difference between the two cases. While *Pensamiento Crítico* challenged Soviet Marxism at the philosophical level, the work done at CEA and published in its journal, *Cuadernos de Nuestra América*, used Marxism to deal specifically with the challenges facing post-Soviet Cuba, and it did so during a time when the leadership was unsure of itself and wary of making sense of things ideologically and when Track II was firmly in place.

During the meetings following the 1996 publication of criticisms of CEA and other research institutes in Cuba, researchers repeatedly referred both to the 1986 Rectification Campaign of Ideological Errors and Negative Tendencies following the Third Party Congress and to *el llamamiento* ("the call") made prior to the Fourth Party Congress. According to Dilla, it was in the years following the collapse of the Soviet Union that "Cuba experienced the freest and most democratic public debate in its history."[59] Party members, on the eve of the Fourth Congress, scheduled for 1991, saw the need to permit democratic debate as a way of tapping into the minds of the Cuban people. Discussions took place in public spaces throughout the island. The Center for Psychological and Social Research, the Center Félix Varela, and other research institutes as well as various departments at the University of Havana provided settings for debate on the crisis of state socialism. In 1994, an independent women's organization called Magín formed in an attempt to provide a feminist vision alternative to that of the traditionally minded Federation of

Cuban Women (FMC).⁶⁰ The magazine *Temas*, which came under the directorship of Rafael Hernández in 1995, also made contributions to the debate on Cuban socialism. The journal was "dedicated to the theory and analysis of problems of culture, ideology, and contemporary society," and expressed its openness to views of people from Cuba, the Caribbean, Latin America, and other countries. Topics addressed by a wide range of scholars in its issues of 1995 and 1996 included the meaning of Cuban studies, postmodernism, the relationship of postmodernism to Marxism, the role of Marxism in Cuba, civil society and hegemony, Cuban race relations, Cuban daily life, and Cuban popular participation. *Temas*, *CNA*, and the journal *Criterios*, among others, continued publishing in spite of material scarcity.⁶¹

Yet, as two former members of CEA, Alberto F. Álvarez García and Gerardo González Núñez, argued in their 2001 book *¿Intellectuals versus revolution? El caso del Centro de Estudios sobre América, CEA*, it was the government's "need to survive" and its "relative weakness" that forced the state to tolerate debate. It was not, they argued, a decision that the government would have made if leaders had really had the choice.⁶² It reflected a desire to co-opt intellectual dissent during a time of crisis. The Cuban government's role in these discussions, they suggested, was in no way a productive one. It did not so much create the conditions for discussion as refrain from squelching them. The silencing of the intellectuals at CEA was the inevitable outcome of a system in which certain fundamental rights were not guaranteed. According to Álvarez and González, the cases of both *Pensamiento Crítico* and CEA

> demonstrate that attaining the link prescribed by Marxist theory between socialism and democracy must happen inexorably through the construction of a State of Rights and not through the demand for a supposed "opening of spaces of discussion" that the controlling group in power can change according to their whims and to the immediate requirements of the national and international political juncture.⁶³

In general, articles and books off the island dealing with the case of CEA portrayed the researchers as valiant and dedicated reformers who had come up against the limits of the system in which they operated. Italian writer Maurizio Giuliano visited the island, spoke with some members of CEA, and gained access to the documentation of most of the meetings between the members of CEA and the Political Bureau's commission.⁶⁴ In 1998, after considering the possible repercussions of publishing his account for the members of CEA, most of whom had remained in Cuba and were still working as academics, Giuliano published *El caso CEA: Intelectuales e inquisidores en Cuba ¿Perestroika en la isla?* (*The Case of CEA: Intellectuals and Inquisitors in Cuba Perestroika on the Island?*).[65] In the book, Giuliano suggested that there were three types of intellectuals in Cuba—the *oficialistas*, the fearful, and those who "really express their opinions, at the cost of contradicting the official line and of possible sanctions by the apparatus"—and he placed the members of CEA clearly in the third camp.[66] The researchers at CEA, wrote Giuliano, "believe in the ideals of the Cuban Revolution, independence and sovereignty," "the triumph of 1959, agrarian reform and the search for better conditions for the least privileged social sectors."[67] The researchers, whose courage he admired, had made the most of "spaces of tolerance" opened up in the beginning of the 1990s. These spaces, however, were "not conceded consciously and voluntarily by the regime." Rather they emerged as a result of "the confusion that the tremendous ideological and economic crisis caused" when "the leadership had nothing to say." According to Giuliano:

> The government had to let the people speak on whatever topic, within certain limits, because the leadership was interested in "learning" from other sectors, so as to be able to come out of the crisis and survive. The dollarization of the economy, self-employment, constitutional reform, and the reopening of the farmers markets were the result of that process.[68]

CEA was able to survive as long as it did, according to Álvarez and González, because it was protected by liberal bureaucrats, because of its national and international reputation, and because the researchers always defined themselves as organic intellectuals whose "efforts were oriented in the direction of supporting, in the best way possible, the socialist project and its development."[69] Far from believing themselves exempt from Party control, the researchers made clear that they too were required to play by the rules of the game established by the leadership.

> In order to avoid that the contradictions of their work with the party lead to a rupture, CEA knew how to move strategically and tactically with relation to this, negotiating each initiative, postponing those that were not politically advisable, reformulating objectives if it was necessary, classifying expressions and reflections in accordance with the circumstances.[70]

That CEA was accustomed to such maneuvering made the attack on it even more unexpected. According to Álvarez and Gonzalez, the researchers had no intention of coming into conflict with the leadership but rather had been carried away by the period of openness that began in 1990 and forgot that any openness under the current government was inherently unstable.[71]

Insisting on the Inside: CEA's Defense

There is no doubt that Raúl's public attack was a shock for the researchers.[72] They had declared their loyalty to the revolution and they had taken into account the reaction of the Party when disseminating their work. They were also well aware of Track II and the political implications of their academic production. The decision to maneuver within the Party's parameters was a conscious one that involved a willingness to adopt a political understanding of academia. The researchers objected not to the argument that critics of the Cuban Revolution had manipulated their work for political purposes, but rather to the public denunciation by the Party to which they were loyal. In other words, *they objected to the Party's own failure to live up to the principle of unity*. If their experience serves as evidence of the dangers of conditional freedom of expression, their actual defenses and their actions following the event demonstrate that they did not see themselves as innocent victims lulled into a false sense of security. Rather, it is evidence that to some degree they willingly accepted the terms on which academic production operates in Cuba. Insofar as the Party claimed to speak and act in the name of the principles of social justice, unity, and nationalism, these academics allied themselves with the Party and saw their work as motivated and guided by these concerns.

The suggestion that these researchers were not aware of the ways in which their work might be perceived as dangerous by the leadership or that they were carried away in a moment of openness shares striking similarities to the arguments made against CEA by the leadership. As the researchers insisted throughout the meetings following CEA's denunciation, they at no moment were unconscious of the political implications of their work or of their responsibility as organic intellectuals. However, they disagreed that their work's actual content was detrimental to the revolutionary project.

Even prior to the public denunciation of CEA, its researchers had begun meeting to discuss the repercussions of a series of measures taken by the Central Committee, including the replacement of CEA's director Luis Suárez with Dario Machado, for whom the remaining researchers at CEA had little respect and who would participate during the following seven months of meetings as one of CEA's harshest critics. On April 11, following a week of intense discussion among the members of CEA, the group issued a written response to the charges leveled against them by the Party. They characterized the criticisms of CEA as "unfair" and "disproportionate" and disagreed with the Party's public dissemination of the criticisms, while reminding the commission that the work of CEA had received the "systematic support of the Department of International Relations and the Office of Administration and Services of the CC of the PCC."[73] These departments, they pointed out, had not only approved CEA's works but also made use of them. CEA researchers, they added, were incorporated into national commissions to deal with internal and external problems, while the Cuban mass media provided CEA with the means to publicize its results.[74] Citing a 1986 speech by Raúl Castro, they argued that far from breaking with the mandates and desires of the Party, CEA was actually following Raúl's call during the speech to "promote debate" and avoid complacency.[75] They were also heeding "the call" of the Fourth Party Congress to "combat all that has the tendency to tell us only what we want to hear" while recognizing that "dialogue is speaking, listening, and rectifying."[76] CEA's method of defense was thus from the outset to cite the Party itself to demonstrate that CEA's activities represented the utmost loyalty to the revolution and were responsive to the requests of the leadership.

CEA's researchers argued that if CEA had become a world-class research institute, whose scholars traveled and published abroad, this was due to its allegiance to its original 1977 mandates from the PCC to focus on the phenomenon of imperialism in Latin America, rather than to a desire to stray from them. The researchers also made clear that far from believing themselves intellectuals whose research agendas responded to personal interest in terms of fame, money, and privilege, they saw themselves as a part of a collective body of *academic workers* that geared its work toward the creation of Cuban foreign policy in the Americas.

> The mandate received by the highest leadership of the party was absolutely clear: the collective of workers of CEA was called upon to work arduously for the formation of a highly professional academic and scientific institution that, by means of national resources and international collaboration, will gradually be able to carry out theoretical contributions and significant proposals for devising policy toward the hemisphere.[77]

Yet there was one aspect of CEA's research that did reflect a shift from its original mandates, and that was the studies published in *CNA* that focused entirely on Cuba. In their defense, the researchers cited their relatively small number and the fact that Party officials approved and sought out some of the books produced by CEA that focused on Cuba specifically. Another element of their defense, however, did not appeal to original mandates but rather to a broader understanding of the academic responsibilities of revolutionary intellectuals and to the importance of the Cuban Revolution overall. How could they, as intellectuals organic to the revolution, possibly call themselves such while ignoring the very important challenges facing the revolution?

> It is difficult, if not impossible, to prohibit a Cuban researcher who is intellectually and politically committed to the revolutionary reality that surrounds him, from studying those problems of our country that have an organic relation with the research projects that we are developing individually and institutionally [as it is difficult, if not impossible] to try to keep him from putting his knowledge—with modesty and honesty—to the service of transforming our society.[78]

Not talking about Cuba, they argued, would hurt their credibility as organic intellectuals in Cuba and their international academic reputation as Cuban social scientists specializing in studies of the Americas. How, they asked, would it look if such an important research center remained silent and failed to provide "serious reflection on the problems of one of the most important countries on the continent"? This rationale for studying Cuba, they were careful to emphasize, had been initially approved by the Party.[79] So too had been the publication of *CNA* and the consequent decision to free the articles of *CNA* from Party approval. Here, however, the researchers diverged from Party-imposed uniformity by suggesting a model of academic production focusing on the plurality of points of view within CEA and the right of researchers to claim a particular point of view as their own and take responsibility for it. At the same time, they recognized limits to that plurality by explaining that their "collective responsibility" as editors of *CNA* was to "guarantee that the form, content, and political opportunity of what is published in every specific moment is committed to the principles of the revolution and to socialism." Thus the publication of a foreign academic work containing "contentious points of views or points of views adverse to those principles" of the revolution and socialism was accompanied by "a profound critique so that national and foreign readers were in a position to judge the content of the debate and the ideological and political positions of our antagonists."[80] The leadership could interpret this too as heresy, since it implied that the role of *CNA* was not simply to repeat the position of the Party but to provide readers a framework within which to judge the material for themselves.

The researchers at CEA rejected the charge that they had attempted to provide an "alternative" way of thinking about the revolution and socialism, arguing that even if certain work reflected "points of view critical of our reality and particular policies," the overall work of CEA reflected a "commitment to the principles of the revolution." Indeed, the criticisms and suggestions themselves came not from criteria established outside the revolution, but were rather "formulated from the position of defending the principles of the Cuban Revolution."[81] If this commitment to the principles of the revolution was not always crystal clear, argued the researchers, it was because of the nature of academia as a whole.

> We are conscious of our work forming part of the ideological struggle from which the political position, revolutionary principles, and confrontation with the enemy are inseparable. But, in the case of CEA, this struggle transpires in complex scenarios, in which enemies, neutrals, friends, and allies participate at the same time and who are not easily identifiable and in all cases under certain rules specific to the academic world. We consider the primary ideological struggle of CEA to happen through its academic production [*proyección*], through the sustained debate [*la sustentación argumentada*] of its positions, through the verification of data concerning reality, and through rigorous conceptual frameworks.[82]

Academia operated according to a set of rules related to, but also distinct from, politics. Politics defined the principles guiding their scholarly work but did not define their methods or their vocabulary. While the ideological struggle took place in the academic realm, it did so according to an entirely different set of standards, where evidence, logic, and theory played a much larger role. The academic framework also meant that while the researchers were responsible for their political commitments, they were not responsible for the ways in which their work was received and used by colleagues outside Cuba. To impose such a standard, they argued, would have been to disqualify them entirely from the academic realm outside of Cuba while making academic production indistinguishable from political rhetoric. Such a fusion would not benefit the revolution that the political rhetoric championed.

It was on the basis of this division between the academic and political realm that the commission challenged CEA. During the commission's meeting with CEA on April 12, at which time CEA presented its report, commission members appeared to pull back from Raúl Castro's initial attack, saying that at no point were the revolutionary credentials of CEA researchers called into question. What was missing, they argued, was a recognition on the part of CEA researchers of the ways in which CEA's work might have been manipulated or misused by foreigners. To disagree with the Party was one thing, said one commission member, but it was irresponsible of the CEA researchers to not take into account the context in which those criticisms were made. To break with the party line in front of the American press, for instance, was to play into the hands of people who "love[d] to show the discrepancies between what academics say and what officials say." The academics at CEA had no business "questioning harshly things referring to the constitution, to the participation of the people, to political economy, when we leaders have to get up every day, and figure out how to give milk to the children who need it."[83] Academic investigation, implied the official, was a decadent practice in light of more urgent concerns. The researchers at CEA might think themselves revolutionaries, added another member, but one could think oneself a revolutionary without actually being one.[84] Thus the commission disagreed with the researchers' claim that academics could only be responsible for what their work intended and not how it was received and that academics and functionaries played different roles in the ideological struggle. "Independent thought," concluded the commission, "has to have political unity, between academics and politicians, because you are academics but also politicians."[85]

What the commission was ignoring, countered CEA member Julio Carranza, was that academics could not control the ways in which their work was twisted or distorted. What mattered and what was missing from the critique of CEA was the ways in which the group had defended the revolution outside of Cuba. The commission needed, argued Haroldo Dilla, to distinguish between whether CEA had actually presented itself as an alternative to the Party and whether it had the image of an alternative to the revolution. If the center proposed alternatives, they were "alternatives and solutions from the social sciences to specific questions that have to be resolved" and they were alternatives not just in Cuba, but also alternatives to neoliberalism in Latin America and the Caribbean more generally. Furthermore, Dilla argued, the publication of foreign works was not meant to call into question the revolution but rather to show the weakness of those works. In this sense, the publication of different points of view was not about a commitment to pluralism but rather part of an ideological battle that took place in the academic realm as well.[86] If academics were to take part in debates on Cuba that took place outside of the country, added Pedro Monreal, it was inevitable that those wishing to discredit the revolution would manipulate their arguments.[87] Other members of CEA reiterated this point throughout the meeting. They also insisted, as they had in their initial report, that academic production in Cuba had a responsibility to the revolution and that they, as organic intellectuals, embraced that responsibility, but that the terms of that responsibility were dramatically different from those of the political realm. Juan Valdés told the commission:

> [I] feel like the horse saddled up in the revolution from which I have not gotten down nor will I get down, but I believe that the way to confront the differences in academic and intellectual work is through debate at that same level and not with restrictive methods or with a debate of intellectuals who must act like functionaries.[88]

Valdés was not arguing that such academic and intellectual work was apolitical, but rather that the language of functionaries was not always the most useful language for convincing those unfamiliar with the ideology of the revolution. Conceding the academic realm its own methods and language in no way meant granting it neutrality. Indeed, added, Rafael Hernández, the reasons for the CEA researchers' contact with the foreign press was to ensure the information that the press received was correct. As academics, the group was more likely to be trusted by those suspicious of Cuban officials. To recognize this reality, said the CEA researchers, was not to suggest that official language was dogmatic but only that in certain contexts, and in particular the context of the "enemy," the language of academics would be more successful in both conveying information and convincing critics.[89]

Aurelio Alonso added that dogmatism was indeed a problem not just because not all understand the principles of the revolution or trust the language used by officials, but because it was too often used to silence those with whom one did not agree. This dogmatism, he argued, was harmful not just to those individuals silenced by it but also to Marxist and socialist thought in general.

> I don't like to use the term dogmatism simply for those who do not share my opinion, . . . but I want to say that there exists, objectively, dogma and that in the history of socialism it has had a consistent weight and price. The future thought of Marxism and socialism can-

not pass through the logic of dogmatization, and this is a challenge in the ideological struggle, not as imminent as the threat from the United States but yes, consistent and permanent.[90]

Members of the commission, however, would continue to insist in subsequent meetings that CEA researchers were confusing dogmatism with the need for political unity. The fact that the Party had approved work that was deemed damaging to the revolution, argued commission member Balaguer in the second meeting, was irrelevant as was CEA's claim that academic language served as a distinct form of revolutionary discourse. It was the responsibility of the academics to gauge accurately the appropriateness of the settings in which their work was disseminated by paying close attention to official discourse produced at particular historical junctures by Fidel Castro and by those such as Carlos Lage who later reproduced that discourse in relation to particular government policy. That discourse, rather than a more generalized set of revolutionary principles, was to guide CEA's work and it was only within those bounds that opinions could be expressed.

> No academic crime is committed if there is no distance from official language. Official language is the language of Fidel Castro, and to that, add the language of the minister of the economy, of Carlos Lage, etc. That is the official language and when we try to distance ourselves from official language, we have to ask ourselves what image we are looking for in the exterior, because official language is the language of the revolution.[91]

By operating in a language that was not the official language, the academics at CEA, argued members of the commission, had given the impression both inside and outside Cuba that they were providing an alternative to official policy, whether they intended to or not. They had been carried away by the success, money, and foreign travel that their alternative image won them. Their distance from official ideology made their work vulnerable to manipulation.[92]

The commission suggested not just that the researchers should keep to official language but that the idea of meeting with foreigners to defend the revolution implied that the official language itself was somehow wanting and inadequate. While the researchers had resisted making this claim explicitly, there were several ways in which they did implicitly. Most significantly, while the commission members repeatedly referred to the importance of the leadership, they rarely mentioned the term "socialism." The researchers, however, frequently spoke of their commitment to socialism and to the revolution in the same sentence, thereby refusing, even if only rhetorically, to concede that socialism's fate lay only in the hands of the leadership. At the same time, the researchers were careful to emphasize that their understanding of socialism was consistent with fundamental principles of the Cuban Revolution such as self-determination and anti-imperialism. In CEA's third meeting with the commission, the researchers stated:

> We believe that an objective examination of the production of the center will find that it is based on the principles of the revolution, it has been consistent with the policy of our party, its inspiration has been *Martiana* [Martí-an] and Marxist and its project has been invariably anti-imperialist and socialist.[93]

There was, they argued, a common "political commitment to the revolution, its historical leadership and its Party, and to defend our socialism from any attacks of the enemy."[94] For instance, Dilla told the committee during the second meeting: "I am a Marxist and what I say, everybody knows; yes, I believe that Cuba must be more democratic and it must be so through something that we give to ourselves and that nobody can impose upon us."[95] What Dilla was saying was that he had not withheld his true beliefs while in Cuba only to express them abroad in the presence of hostile forces eager to hear criticisms of Cuba's political and economic system, and that in his mind, his beliefs were consistent with his dedication to Marxism. His choice of words was important, for it told the commission that his loyalty was to the Cuban Revolution insofar as it was Marxist and socialist. At the same time, his reference to the importance of Cubans' choosing their own form of democracy served two functions. One was to recognize that his Marxism was a Cuban brand where anti-imperialism and self-determination played key roles. The other, and this one can only infer from Dilla's wording and his larger interest in participatory democracy, was that the principle of self-determination meant that the leadership could not impose a particular form of democracy on Cuba. Instead Cuban society, including Cuban academics, should decide upon it.

Throughout the meetings, CEA academics consistently pointed to the role of the organic intellectual in the revolution and the need for the leadership to allow the ideological struggle to take place not just in other spaces such as schools, conferences, journals, and outside Cuba, but also on other terms and within other frameworks even defined by different theoretical or disciplinary traditions. While they were willing to put academia to the service of socialism, they were unwilling to reduce academia to political discourse. As an example, Dilla argued that citing Marx in an academic work did not make the work good. What mattered, rather, was how Marx was used within that work to help illustrate and guide a theoretical and practical problem.[96]

It was in this way that the researchers believed that they could participate in the ideological war. To participate in this ideological war, it was not sufficient to simply claim one's allegiances to the revolution at the outset. In this sense, they agreed that one could not hide behind good intentions or claim that one's work was revolutionary simply because it was meant to be. "The efficacy of our participation in this struggle," read CEA's April 22 report to the commission, "depends not only on our deep ideological conviction—an essential but not sufficient element—but also on the intelligence, aplomb, and extreme conscientiousness with which we work."[97] Their role as academics did not release them from their responsibility to the revolution, but rather made their political responsibility all the greater, precisely because their work necessarily ran the risk of being used by the enemy to argue that Cuban intellectuals were suggesting a "project that departs from the way of the revolution." It was the responsibility of academics to operate within the academic sphere while being vigilant to this possibility.[98] The researchers argued that they needed to be careful of the ways in which enemies might try to use them to divide the revolution but they could not simply repeat official positions as articulated by the Cuban leadership. Simple repetition was just as vulnerable to manipulation and excluded Cuban intellectuals from participating in the ideological struggle within the intellectual realm outside of Cuba. If the members of CEA had "always understood that their work—both theoretical and practical—forms part of the revolution's ideological struggle," that struggle took place on terms which were not always of the intellectuals' choosing. The academic milieu was complex and imposed its own norms upon the academics. Their work was for an external audience and this meant it needed to demonstrate loyalty to the revolution while being accessible to those unfamiliar with the history of the revolution and its key principles. Their audience included "friends, enemies, neutrals, academics and politicians" all with "different theoretical and political ideological perspectives" with which the researchers at CEA had to engage.

This written self-analysis by CEA did recognize that CEA researchers "should have emphasized the component of ideological struggle of their work," adjusted better to what the party was saying and anticipated the ways in which foreign enemies might have used their studies. They saw these failures, however, as bureaucratic or procedural and not ideological, and again they refused to concede the distinctiveness of academic production in the overall ideological struggle. Recognizing the distinctiveness of academic work did not make it less political, while recognizing the political nature of academic work in no way meant that academic work necessarily had to challenge official discourse.[99] Strangely, their argument appeared to be that while their role as organic intellectuals responding to a particular historical juncture demanded that they address the Cuban reality using the methods of social science, the apparent irrelevance of the social sciences to actual policy rendered it subservient to official language and politics. In other words, the social sciences were political insofar as they responded to political events and looked back upon previous political events to understand and analyze the present, but not political in the sense of influencing or producing actual policy.[100] According to the researchers, to distinguish between politics and social science was to show the utmost respect for official discourse that could "not be substituted" nor emulated. "The message of revolutionary policy," stated CEA's report on its own deficiencies, "is sufficiently explicit, structured, consistent with principle, well-argued and clearly presented such that any attempt to limit oneself to translate or paraphrase it runs the risk of futility or an impoverished schema." While official language contained "obligatory referents" for any analysis of the Cuban Revolution and the Cuban reality, its political and thus strategic nature meant that it was not sufficient for explaining "social, economic, and ideological processes." Scientific or academic language, on the other hand, could take into account information that political discourse, by its very nature, could not.[101]

What troubled the commission, however, was not only that "taking into account the totality of reality and existing contradictions" involved empirical research, analyses, and conclusions that might not coincide with political discourse, but also that the academics had taken the task of recognizing the totality of reality and existing contradictions to the level of academic exchange and had incorporated it into the ideological war with the enemies of the revolution.[102] The researchers at CEA had begun to recognize academic work critical of the revolution, not because they agreed with it, but because they saw engagement with it as serving several functions. One was simply that engagement with it increased the likelihood that the work of Cuban academics would be disseminated outside of Cuba. This was valuable because it might draw audiences who were wary of official language but also open, as scholars, to different points of view. It was also valuable as a way of breaking the dominance in international discussions of Cuban events of work produced outside of Cuba by nonrevolutionary scholars.

It was a testament to the strength of the principles of the Cuban Revolution that they could stand up to debate. Dilla, for instance, defended his inclusion of Domínguez's work, arguing that he had also included works critical of Domínguez, but also that the inclusion illustrated his "trust in the intelligence of the Cuban people and their political capacity to discern what the revolution ha[d] taught them."[103] He defended pluralism, but on the basis of a deep respect for a political language and culture that had sufficiently prepared the Cuban public to read articles such as Domínguez's critically and incorporate his criticisms into an even stronger defense of the revolution.[104]

During the third meeting, CEA read its assessment of its own deficiencies but its account did not satisfy the commission.[105] The CEA researchers continued to express a willingness to examine any deficiencies of CEA, while attributing those deficiencies to a lack of guidelines for dealing with issues such as funds from abroad rather than to any lack of revolutionary commitment. They insisted that their presence at the meetings represented their commitment to the revolution. That same commitment to the revolution also meant, however, that they would never agree with all of the conclusions of the commission. To admit errors simply to please the commission would be a far greater betrayal of the revolution. Julio Carranza:

> There are considerations that out of respect for myself I cannot accept, because errors aside, there are matters that we can't accept as revolutionaries. It would be easier for us to produce a report that didn't irritate anyone but that would be opportunistic. I insist that we did this with honesty.[106]

Political opportunism, then, was not only a danger on the outside, but within the Party as well. True commitment to the principles of the revolution meant not just defending them from outside attacks but also staying true to the work inspired by those principles even when the leadership itself took issue with the work. What Carranza and other researchers did, although not explicitly, was to redefine the meaning of political unity. Political unity did not entail repeating official language regardless of time and place, disengaging from the international academic community, abandoning the academic plane entirely or withdrawing from any sort of conflict or debate either with friends or enemies of the revolution. Political unity, instead, involved maintaining a loyalty to principles of the revolution in spite of the circumstances in which one found oneself. Political unity involved debate and discussion in order to strengthen the revolution.

What dismayed the researchers at CEA so much was that they were being criticized for answering a call which the leadership itself had made. Julio Carranza pointed to the fact that he had recently presented material to no criticism at a conference at which members of the commission were present, and that officials high up in the Party including Fidel Castro himself had requested copies of one of his books.[107] Pedro Monreal told the commission that CEA members had taken seriously the concerns of the commission, and thus demonstrated their commitment to political unity, but that recognition of those concerns had to be accompanied by a defense of a space in which to establish just what were the criteria for political unity. In other words, political unity had little substantive meaning if the leadership appealed to it when requesting CEA scholars' input but also when suggesting that their input was counterrevolutionary. To accept that their work was counterrevolutionary, albeit unintentionally, was to reject the very political unity upon which their participation in the revolution was based.

> We recognize that we have brought political problems [*inconvenientes políticos*] but also we have to defend a space for discussion. . . . That space has to exist. . . . My duty as a scientist and a revolutionary is to give opinions in the space that they give me. I believe it is unacceptable that you ask us for suggestions and then later say that what CEA proposed was counterrevolutionary. That has to be clear because down deep, I believe that it [the claim made against CEA] cannot be demonstrated. We recognize [some] things here, but there are others that we are not going to accept.[108]

Refusal to accept the conclusions of the commission was, for the commission, evidence of a lack of political unity on the part of the members of CEA. The members of CEA, however, continued to insist upon their own understanding of political unity. They did this by using the commission's accusation that they were presenting an alternative to the leadership as an illustration of political unity. Given the diversity of opinions within CEA, they repeatedly told the commission that the charge that they were proposing one single alternative to the leadership made little sense. At the same time, they argued that CEA's general commitment to searching for alternatives was perfectly commensurate with the goals of the leadership. In other words, it was precisely the search for political and economic alternatives to the dominant arrangements in the world that allied CEA with the revolution. To quote Aurelio Alonso:

> I don't believe that the center has an alternative project, because among ourselves, there is quite a lot of debate. For us the only alternative . . . is the Cuban alternative project of socialism and I think that that project that is built day by day is an alternative to the supposed capitalist solutions and also is an alternative to a failed socialism; and it is toward that alternative project of Cuban socialism that the *Direccion de la Revolución* is constructing every day, that I have worked and will continue to work.[109]

The researchers' appeals to their revolutionary credentials would have little effect on the opinions of the members of the commission, who continued to emphasize that even honest and dedicated revolutionaries could be wrong.[110] For the researchers at CEA, however, it was the commission, rather than CEA, that was dividing the revolution from within. In CEA's final report on the proceedings, they objected neither to the commission's emphasis on external threats nor to the possibility that some of their work might have been better left unpublicized but rather to the method in which CEA was investigated.[111] While they argued that they had approached the meetings with a willingness to recognize errors and weaknesses at CEA, they had hoped that the calls for political unity issued from the commission would have been reciprocated rather than having to endure a prolonged process that damaged not just the image of the individual researchers but of CEA itself.[112] To remedy this damage, the researchers requested a retraction of the charges against CEA in Cuba's mass media. The deficiencies of CEA, which both the members of CEA and the commission had agreed upon, did not match the initial criticisms made of CEA. The commission again appealed to political unity when it rejected these requests on the grounds that even the Left might use the retraction to further divide the revolution. The members of CEA, of course, argued the opposite. A public rectification of the initial charges was an important element in maintaining political unity. In a letter sent directly to Fidel and Raúl Castro in August, the members repeated their requests that the commission publicly retract its harshest criticisms of the researchers at CEA and expressed concern that the "political and moral disqualifications of the collective of CEA could be affecting the image of the revolution, internally and externally, disorient objectives of the ideological struggle, be useful to enemies and confuse friends."[113]

Distinguishing between Friends and Enemies

If political unity was to mean more than a simple call to be silent and the closing of an increasingly small number of ranks, the members of CEA were right. The attack on CEA and particularly its public form provoked dismay on the part of Cuban intellectuals and their colleagues abroad. The union of writers and artists (UNEAC) sent a letter to Fidel Castro expressing concern over a possible repeat of the kind of repression that took place in Cuba in the 1970s and also organized a meeting at UNEAC to discuss the meaning of Raúl's remarks. Alfredo Guevara and Culture Minister Armando Hart made indirect references to the importance of creativity and openness to the revolution.[114] The American political scientist Carollee Bengelsdorf drew a parallel to the shutting down of *Pensamiento Crítico*, arguing that in both cases the revolution only hurt itself, first by silencing some of its best social scientists, and second by hurting its reputation abroad.[115]

> Remarkably, despite the obstacles they face, the young Cuban intellectuals at CEA—who were born or came of age with the revolution itself—still believe in the project about which they write. They experienced the recent government action as a stunning blow. After Raúl's speech, there were no parties in Cuba. The only celebration was held in the offices of Radio Martí in Miami.[116]

The commissioners made increasingly clear throughout their discussions with CEA that their concerns were not with the particular content of the studies at CEA but rather with its failure to coincide exactly with the official discourse produced during a particular historical moment. CEA members had wrongly believed, argued the commission, that they could produce studies using criteria, even socialist criteria, that were distinct from those of the leadership. "Discrepant criteria," argued the commission, "are criteria that are alternative to the party, even if within socialism."[117] CEA was prohibited from continuing its work on Cuba specifically since the institute itself was not equipped to monitor the political impact of those studies. In this way, academic work was not simply political in the sense that research projects were motivated by a desire to improve Cuban socialism, defend it from against attacks from abroad, and understand better its internal dynamics. Rather, it was political, according to the standards of the commission, in the sense that every step of the academic process, from the topics chosen, the questions posed, the data collected, the method of investigation, all the way to the conclusions drawn and the forum and time of their dissemination, was to be measured against the criteria of the party.

Such stringent criteria effectively erased all distinction between academia and politics. The researchers relied upon this distinction not simply to defend a space in which to discuss but also to defend the revolution. To reduce political unity to a phrase invoked to censure threatened to turn one principle of Cuban socialism—political unity—into its be-all and end-all. Socialism itself could be sacrificed in its name. Paradoxically, the failure to distinguish between politics and academia produced precisely the opposite of its intended effect. If academics measure their work according to the criteria of the Party at every step of the way, they themselves can shrug off responsibility for understanding the relationship between the various levels of their work. As the researchers themselves pointed out, the Party approved their work, yet the researchers were still willing to take responsibility for the unintended consequences of their work. This responsibility, they believed, strengthened their work intellectually and politically.

When the members of CEA found themselves under attack by the leadership, they did not defend themselves or their academic ground on the basis of an appeal to the liberal principles of unfettered freedom of expression and thought. To do so would have been to place key principles of the Cuban Revolution in a secondary position. Rather, they had to show how they themselves were "within the revolution." This did not involve a renunciation of those elements of their research and the proposals arising from it that ran counter to official policy positions. Instead, they attempted to draw a distinction between the academic and political realm that did not deny the role and responsibility of the organic intellectual in maintaining and defending the principles of Cuban socialism as a political, economic, and social project. In short, these intellectuals accepted to a large extent not only the maxim laid down by Fidel Castro in 1961 that some intellectual production fell outside the realm of the revolution but also his call for them to take part in the revolution. They agreed that what counted as acceptable academic production was dependent upon the time and place of its dissemination and that their role as academics could not be divorced from political considerations. They themselves had suffered the consequences of the thin distinction between political and scholarly responsibility and between the silencing of clear enemies of the revolution and all those who are unwilling to provide unconditional and uncritical support of the revolution at all times. However, their concern was not with presenting themselves as victims, but rather with demonstrating that too fine a line between the academic and political realm threatened to empty the revolution of all its content and reduce, rather than encourage, political unity based on a socialist alternative.

The Dispersal of CEA's Members and Their Afterthoughts

Members of CEA disagreed about just how far political unity should be taken. Each dealt differently with the aftermath of the meetings. Dilla would continue to emphasize the need to decentralize political power particularly in light of the increasing role of capital in the Cuban economy. Valdés, Alonso, and Hernández would argue that there were parts of the revolution that depended on the state for their survival, but that greater openness was also needed to ensure that the principles of the revolution would not be lost. To quote Valdés, "The absence of democracy means that there is not a voice to say that the king has no clothes."[118]

The letter that CEA's members wrote to Fidel Castro went unanswered. No public retraction of the way CEA's work had been characterized was ever issued. Their requests to be able to continue working on Cuba at CEA and their rejection of Party functionary and middling academic Dario Machado as the new director of CEA also went unheeded. The sociologists, for the most part, were transferred to institutes that had little to do with their interests and specialties.[119] The economists, perhaps because their work's focus on the economic level was less threatening, were also sent to respected academic institutes where they could continue their work.[120]

Even the sociologists who found themselves at research institutes where their expertise was not used to its fullest continued to work on Cuba. Rafael Hernández, in particular, who had been sent to the Center for Research and Development of Cuban Culture "Juan Marinello," would continue on as editor of *Temas*, in whose pages many of his former CEA colleagues would continue to publish along with other Cuba scholars from throughout the world. In 1999 Hernández published books dealing with Cuban foreign policy following the Cold War and on Cuban culture and civil society.[121] In 2001, he would coedit a book with Harvard's John H. Coatsworth, on cultural exchange between the United States and Cuba. The two would work together again to publish the 2004 edited volume on the Cuban economy in the 21st century.

If Hernández and Alonso inserted themselves back into Cuban academia, Dilla would have more difficulties navigating the academic terrain without irritating the authorities. After his expulsion from the Party in 2001, he moved to the Dominican Republic, from where he would register more explicitly his opposition to the lack of civil liberties in Cuba. Following the 2002 crackdown on dissidents, when seventy-five were arrested, he signed the "Statement Protesting Repression in Cuba" put out by the Campaign for Peace and Democracy and signed by prominent leftists.[122] That same year, he published in the Dominican Republic "Cuban Social Sciences: Between Knowledge and Power," in which he discussed what he called "the inhibitory relationship between Cuban academics and political power." The closer a discipline came to politics in Cuba, he argued, the lower its quality. As a consequence, sociology had suffered greatly.[123] Dilla warned of the fine line between "silent complicity" and "political loyalty." Mistaking the former for the latter threatened to undermine the revolution itself, for it allowed the censure of precisely those parts of Cuban society that the revolution had empowered and upon which its survival was ultimately based.

> A society that eliminates its own critical thought only wins momentary peace at the high price of mortgaging its future. And since the Cuban academic world is in the last instance a result of revolutionary work, for that reason its repression paradoxically implies that that revolution begins to take away from its own achievements.[124]

In a sense, Dilla's words harked back to Fidel Castro's "Words to the Intellectuals." It was this promise to facilitate and encourage intellectual production and include it in the construction of the revolution that was one of the more appealing elements of his speech. Yet this call had always been tempered by Castro's insistence upon an unconditional loyalty.

The terms "silent complicity" and "political loyalty," explained Dilla, came respectively from Cuban writer Jesús Díaz and from Dilla's former CEA colleague Aurelio Alonso. Both Díaz and Alonso had been affiliated with *Pensamiento Crítico* but had since taken very different positions on the extent to which the principles of Cuban socialism could be compromised in the name of political unity. Their differences were made public during a panel on the role of the intellectual in the Cuban Revolution at the 2000 Latin American Studies Association Congress in Miami, later reproduced in *Encuentro de la Cultura Cubana*, the magazine Díaz founded in 1996 following his exile to Spain in 1991. Díaz and others in exile and on the island had started the magazine in the hopes of encouraging Cuba's discovery of "the roads of democracy and consensus" and the development of "historical memory and the capacity for critical analysis as foundations for a peaceful future."[125] For Díaz, such a project was impossible in Cuba proper, where, along with all other similar projects, it was doomed to failure. Díaz explained his mind-set after arriving to Spain from Cuba in 1991:

> By then, I had already accumulated more than sufficient frustrations to recognize that all attempts to modify Castroite totalitarianism from within were condemned by definition to the most absolute failure, and I began to gather the courage to critically analyze both the Cuban Revolution and my own past, without ceasing for those reasons to be a man of the Left. My friends and colleagues from *Pensamiento Crítico* and *Caimán Barbudo*, more stubborn and obstinate than I, drew other conclusions. But they never became enemies, nor denounced each other, nor obtained special privileges from the regime.[126]

Díaz displayed here and elsewhere in the essay his clear loyalty to and respect for the integrity and character of those who continued to try to change the revolution from within. But this was inevitably tempered by his belief that they were participating in a project whose failure the existing Cuban system guaranteed.

Strangely, Aurelio Alonso's response to Díaz, a man calling for greater political openness and an end to Castro's rule, was the same as Alonso's response to the commission investigating CEA. His role in *Pensamiento Crítico* and in CEA, argued Alonso, did not disqualify his status as a "militant revolutionary." These two events, he argued, could be used to show the hopelessness of the revolutionary process or to illustrate the strength of his commitment to the revolution. "That unhappiness can be part, however, of another happiness, I believe, because it increases the merit of the intellectual committed to maintain his commitment when he feels that his commitment is rejected."[127] Alonso did not deny that there were many "miseries" in Cuban revolutionary history. Concentration camps (UMAPs) for antisocial elements and the Padilla Affair of the 1970s were only a few. Yet he asked whether one should resign oneself to the miseries rather than continue to fight for what good the revolution had done. "Do we remain loyal to the vocation of saving the great things or do we quit, crushed by the miserable things?" asked Alonso.[128]

Thus, this harsh definition of political responsibility can serve as an incentive for Cuban academics to stay. According to another member of CEA, "One's self-image becomes linked to the country, and this can take you good places or bad places."[129] He used the metaphor of a boat to explain his commitment to the revolution.[130] One had an ethical commitment to the collective in Cuba and one could not request to get off before the boat sank. One could not say that one likes free education and health care but does not like politics. While this did not mean that people could not criticize or want something different, it was necessary to resolve those desires within the revolution. Rejecting politics, the CEA member argued, was in reality to express the desire for another politics. He disagreed with those who believed that the "system is so determined by historic power that it's impossible to introduce reforms." Such a view took one far too close to being a counterrevolutionary. Instead, he insisted that it was necessary to make one's revolution within the country and the existing state structures. This endeavor did not entail absolute silence, however. He believed it was important that official discourse provide a balance between triumphalism even in the worst of times and a concern with explaining to people the difficulties of their everyday lives. "If there is no bread," explained Valdés, "a speech does not resolve the problem."[131]

In many ways, CEA had responded to the frustration of Cuban people with the failure of the leadership to make sense of the economic crisis of the early 1990s. CEA's work was respected. The researchers have attempted to continue this project. In 2003, Rafael Hernández told me that the articles in the magazine *Temas* were directed to all Cubans, and not simply academics, and that articles addressed issues that all are concerned or worried about, such as drugs, marginalization, and prostitution. These issues, he added, are not often addressed on the news or on television. While the articles in *Temas* did not necessarily provide solutions, they provided "a systematization of problems so that people could think them through."

Thus when Valdés and Alonso speak of loyalty, they speak of loyalty to those in Cuba who are unwilling to remove themselves from the system yet also unwilling to reduce their loyalty to the revolution to complacency or uncritical thought. For many this loyalty necessarily means compromising critical thought, while for others, this same loyalty demands critical thought. What is important, and also significant for academics outside Cuba, is that this calculation—does political loyalty, or political unity, compromise or actually *require* critical thought?—is a political calculation. The recognition that that judgment is a political one has inspired debate as well as silenced it. The arguments that first incited CEA's interesting work, and then suppressed it, demonstrate that critical contestation is claimed by some as a central feature of Cuban socialism, rather than a threat to it.

Five

"Sales + Economy + Efficiency = Revolution"?

In 2000, in the entranceway of the shopping complex Plaza Carlos III in Central Havana, a sign announced, "En el nuevo milenio, venta + economía + eficiencia = revolución" ("In the New Millennium, Sales + Economy + Efficiency = Revolution") (see figure 5). Another sign inside read "Juntos para defender lo nuestro" ("Together to defend what is ours") and was credited to Cuba's largest trading company and the firm that runs the shopping complex.[1] These signs, in a place that seemed only to represent the inequality brought about by the legalization of the dollar in 1993 and to exhort long-demonized mercantilism and consumerism, appeared as poignant examples of how desperately those managing the Cuban economy and its propaganda machine wished to hold onto the rhetoric of the Cuban Revolution in spite of the increasing marketization of the economy and growing social and economic inequality. Well-known revolutionary slogans such as "Patria o Muerte!" (Fatherland or Death!), "Hazlo por Cuba!" (Do it for Cuba!), and "Creemos en el socialismo" ("We believe in socialism") still remained on the walls in the streets of Havana and throughout the island, but new slogans had to be invented to try to link current developments to the revolutionary tradition (see figure 6).

While the signs at Plaza Carlos III and other shopping complexes could simply be dismissed as bad advertising in a country that spent thirty years trying to rid itself of capitalist elements—and did so fairly successfully—few dispute that post-Soviet Cuba, or "Special Period" Cuba was a place of contradictions that the leadership had a hard time smoothing over. What is disputable, however, is how new and particular to Cuba these contradictions were, how they functioned, and to what end. Taking these contradictions at face value or trying to reconcile them too quickly, as many outside observ-

Fig. 5. "En el nuevo milenio! Venta + Economía+ Eficiencia = Revolución" (In the new millennium! Sales + economy + efficiency = revolution). Sign at the entrance of Plaza Carlos III, Havana, 2000.

Fig. 6. "Creemos en el Socialismo" (We believe in socialism). Slogan painted on the wall of the corner of Prado and the Malecón, Havana, ca. 1998.

ers did, failed to grasp how Cuban socialist ideology continued to be transformed even during this moment of crisis. Seeing such transformation, however, meant looking outside the state to those spheres most often associated with opposition to it, and presumably with opposition to socialism as well.

Cuban popular reactions to the economic policies implemented in Cuba in the 1990s—particularly those represented through popular music—suggest that although the economy was de facto in crisis, this did not immediately translate into the death of the ideology with which it was associated, but rather into its renegotiation and reevaluation. Popular expressions of discontent incorporated such implicit principles of Cuban socialism as unity, equality, and nationalism to complain about its shortcomings—both the living conditions it provided and the policies the state promoted—at a particular historical juncture. Frustration with the failure of socialist principles to manifest themselves in daily life did not necessarily indicate a lack of faith in the principles of socialist ideology or lead to the conclusion that it could only survive as dogma imposed by the leadership.

While the Cuban government clung to the logic of revolutionary progress, of history as progress, to smooth over contradictions produced by its selective use of market reforms, various popular expressions of Cuban socialism, particularly in the arts, challenged the state to remain true to its socialist principles in practice. Popular expressions of discontent dealt frankly with the myriad ways in which socialist principles were compromised by market measures and logics that were increasingly part of the fabric of Cuban daily life. They challenged, for instance, the increasingly consumer-oriented activities of the Cuban public sphere and the state's increasingly narrow definition of Cuban socialism. These challenges to consumerism were not always uncomplicated or purely ideological articulations. For instance, as Esther Whitfield notes, much of the Cuban literature during the Special Period, with its critiques of consumerism and accounts of the seedy side of life during those years, responded to foreign demand and foreign markets.[2] Exploring consumerism in art and literature appealed to the global marketplace, to the benefit of not just individual writers and artists whose work sold outside of Cuba, but to the state, which had schooled them in the socialist labor ethic and now taxed their incomes as a source of hard currency.[3] However, in highlighting contradictions and tensions, these expressions of discontent maintained Cuban socialism as a living ideology. The expressions represented not just challenges to the state's monopoly on socialist ideology, but also represented a different and more robust understanding of ideology than that of the state. While the state tended to fetishize ideology, locating its power within the ideology itself so as to make the truth tolerable, popular articulations used ideology to call their reality into question and call for change. In other words, while the leadership treated ideology as distinct from practice, to be preserved and protected, popular articulations treated ideology as contingent and contradictory, as something lived and living.

Capturing the Contradictions in Images and the Danger of Juxtaposition

During the Special Period, official socialist rhetoric in Cuba often appeared to be mocked by daily life. Street hustlers wore T-shirts condemning the blockade or urging the return of Elian while they worked in the illegal economy and hoped to meet a foreigner who would take them out of the country. Crumbling buildings in the old section of Havana sat alongside new hotels, beyond whose lobbies Cubans were not allowed to enter. T-shirts displaying the face of Che hung in dollar stores, whose goods were out of reach for most Cubans (see figure 7). A billboard with peeling paint reading "Tenemos y tendremos socialismo" (We have and we will have socialism) appeared next to a neon sign for Havanatur, a state-run tourist agency that caters to foreigners with hard currency. It was not difficult to find images that displayed the contradictions and tensions between official rhetoric and daily life in Cuba and between principles and practice.

All economic systems have justifying ideologies that do not match exactly with practice. Capitalism, too, has failed to come through on its promises, yet capitalist ideology, as Marx pointed out, presents the particular interests of capital in the form of the universal good and natural laws. Capitalist ideology holds that the market takes on a life of its own independent of political agendas and yet, ultimately, it benefits all (as illustrated by Smith's invisible hand). Capitalism thus escapes the kind of scrutiny given to socialist economies, which make clear the subservience of purely market-driven considerations to social welfare goals, at least at the level of political rhetoric and ideology. The Cuban government's practice of making clear its ideological commitments makes it particularly vulnerable to the use of images, juxtaposing revolutionary slogans to the Cuban reality. While these images capture certain difficult realities of the Cuban situation that demand attention, they are often taken as proof of what was already assumed about the possibilities of socialism and alternative projects in general, rather than as a point of departure for further examination of the issues the images raise.

"Sales + Economy + Efficiency = Revolution"? • 161

Fig. 7. T-shirts with the image of Che in the window of a storefront in Manzana de Gómez, the first shopping mall in Havana, Old Havana, ca. 2000.

Anthropologist Paul Ryer has pointed to the dangers of these kinds of images of Cuba. He used two images as examples. One was a photo of a decrepit wall on which the slogan "Socialism or Death" appeared in faded paint. Another was a picture on the book jacket of a North American journalist's account of Special Period Cuba.[4] This picture featured a woman in high heels and a spandex suit with the design of the American flag on it.[5] In reference to these types of images, Ryer wrote:

> Both [the] commercial North American representation of a Cuban appropriation of a U.S. symbol and [the] image of a decaying revolutionary slogan too easily map onto Western complacencies regarding the inevitability of capitalism and the futility of alternative ideologies or resistant practices. Image consumption of this sort not only naturalizes a not–New World Order, it also implicates the consumer: the star-spangled woman pictured is not actually waiting for Fidel, but for a dollar rich foreign client—one of the very persons mostly likely to find a comfortable irony, eroticism, or pathos in such photographs.[6]

As Ryer points out, such a complacent reading of the images means that history and politics drop out entirely. The images are used to illustrate a position already preserved. Images juxtaposing revolutionary slogans to Cuban daily life and practice preserve the position, assumed at the outset, that Cuban socialist ideology can only exist as dogma imposed by the leadership and that most Cubans reject that ideology.

Reading Dialectical Images

For German social theorist Walter Benjamin, images had valuable critical and revolutionary potential, as a challenge to the myth of progress, which political ideologies on both the right and left used to justify programs regardless of the effects on those groups the programs claimed to be benefiting. Benjamin's points of reference were Stalinism and the ideologies opposing it, but this myth operates today. International lending institutions insist that economic development be defined in terms of a macroeconomic growth, but such growth often comes at the greatest cost to poorest populations of these countries. The myth operates in Cuba, where the government insists that labor unions and other independent organizations representing the interests of workers, darker-skinned Cubans, women, and farmers, to name a few, are superfluous to the socialist revolution made in their name. In both cases, one measure of progress occludes another measure of equal importance and the voices of those actually affected by these policies drop out. Apparently opposing ideologies produce similar results.

Benjamin criticized the notion of history as progress because he believed it served as a code word for the continuation of existing power relations despite technological change. Precisely because "things 'just keep on going,'" progress is in reality catastrophe.[7] The chain of events known as history is, in fact, one enormous catastrophe, which appears as wreckage piling higher and higher into the sky as time moves forward. Benjamin's angel of history sees the wreckage and "would like to stay, awaken the dead and make whole what has been smashed," yet the strong wind of progress pushes him forward into a "future towards which his back is turned."[8] The wind is difficult to resist, for it tells us that what we have was the only possible outcome. It denies that things could have been otherwise and that what we have does not have to be. It paralyzes political agency by making all change seem futile in the face of history's incontrovertible movement. Benjamin's angel of history is useful for discussions of post-Soviet Cuba because his framework provides a way of navigating between the acceptance of the cheap shots that Ryer critiques and blind apology for all that the Cuban government does.

In the place of universal history, Benjamin places a brand of historical materialism that sees the present in transition and not as some final culmination of the past. The historical materialist, Benjamin's angel of history, is one who acknowledges history's possibilities and who "blast[s] open the continuum of history."[9] Before one can even construct an alternative to the status quo, one must arrest the flow of events, showing the world through dialectical images that juxtapose what progress claims to provide and what it in reality produces.

According to Benjamin, a useful dialectical image is one that "puts the trash to use" by bringing into the present that which has been discarded and ignored.[10] This involves, not a change in criteria and object of inquiry, but rather "a shift in point of view."[11] It means looking at the ways in which "things" that have lost their use value and become alienated from themselves take on different meanings through time. The task of the dialectical materialist is to "catch dialectics at a standstill," at this point of undifferentiation, in an image that makes the past clear and knowable.[12] "Thinking," argues Benjamin, "involves not only the flow of thoughts, but their arrest as well."[13] Dialectical images should cause the viewer to pause and rethink rather than to affirm what one already believed. During these pauses, one can reexamine not just the present but also the past and what could have been.

Considering Dialectical Images in Cuba

Consider, for instance, two signs that I saw during a visit to the eastern city of Holguin in 2000. Neither sign was as new as it might have appeared to the casual observer, and each contained a story that complicated both the official narrative of revolution and socialism in Cuba and that of the opposition.

On the front of the bus station there was a picture of Cuban revolutionary hero and martyr Abel Santamaría accompanied by the words "Morir por la patria es vivir" (To die for the fatherland is to live) (see figure 8). The slogan, often cited as an example of Cuban Communist fanaticism, is in fact a line from the Cuban national anthem written in 1868 by Pedro Figueredo, a follower of Carlos Manuel de Céspedes, whose *Grito de Yara* sparked Cuba's first war for independence that same year.[14]

As we saw in chapter 1, both supporters and opponents of the Cuban Revolution appeal to Cuba's wars of independence from Spain. Cuban official history marks the 1959 revolution as the continuation of the struggle to rid Cuba not just of Spanish domination but of U.S. domination as well. This history points to U.S. attempts to annex Cuba and otherwise thwart Cuban independence throughout the nineteenth century, to Cuba's repeated occupa-

Fig. 8. "Morir por la Patria es vivir" (To die for the homeland is to live). Slogan with image of Abel Santamaría on the front of the bus station in Holguín, Holguín Province, ca. 2000.

tion by U.S. troops following the end of the Spanish-American War, and to the passage of the 1901 Platt Amendment giving the United States the right to intervene for "the maintenance of a government adequate for the protection of life, property, and individual liberties." Socialism, according to this account, was the logical outcome of a radical nationalism that had been brewing since the late nineteenth century, and it was socialism that enabled Cuba to achieve the true independence that the United States snatched away.[15]

Others, however, argue that Castro did violence to the Cuban nation, the prize of independence, by allying it with another foreign power, the Soviet Union, and by forcing the country to divide itself between supporters of the revolution and enemies, between those on the island and those in exile.[16] Because the platform of the 26th of July Movement that ousted then dictator Fulgencio Batista and brought Fidel Castro to power in 1959 was based on reforms to the existing system rather than its complete overthrow, they argue that Castro's 1961 declaration of the socialist nature of the revolution represented a betrayal of what was initially a popular, broad-based movement.[17]

Abel Santamaría, an Ortodoxo activist and follower of Fidel Castro, was tortured and killed following the failed attack on the Moncada Barracks in 1953. He did, indeed, die for the fatherland and he came to be an important symbol of the sacrifices made by the Cuban revolutionary youth in their fight against Batista. Santamaría's sister reported that he was an avid reader of Lenin and other Russian revolutionaries. However, his ideology, like that of many of the members of the revolutionary movement that Fidel Castro organized, was not explicitly socialist, nor was he allied with the PCC. His image, then, points to the contested and complicated history of the Cuban Revolution before 1959.[18]

The other sign in Holguin, which reads "Lo Más Importante es Seguir Buscando Eficiencia" (What is most important is to continue searching for efficiency), points not to the choice between reform and revolution, but to the options within the socialist paradigm itself. This slogan, which would seem to represent Cuba's concern with economic viability in the 1990s, actually harks back to the second half of the 1970s, when Cuba adopted the System of Management and Planning of the Economy (SDPE). While this particular slogan focused on the importance of economic efficiency, chapter 3 illustrates how much of the press coverage of the issue at the time dealt explicitly with the tension between material- or market-oriented economic policy, on the one hand, and a planning system motivated by moral incentives and a desire for equality of distribution, on the other. The press and Party officials frequently cited Che Guevara and Karl Marx to explain and justify Cuba's increased use of market mechanisms such as pricing, supply and demand, and the profit motive, and to show that their use represented not an abandonment of the socialist project, but rather attempts to do greater justice to it in the long term. Guevara would probably not have supported either the SDPE or the ideological and political justifications for it. Nor do Guevara's own writings support the claim made in 1979 by Humberto Pérez, the man in charge of economic planning at the time, that the differences between the economic calculus used by the Soviet model and Guevara's more centralized budgetary finance system were ones of emphasis rather than principle. However, the use of Guevara's work by the Cuban leadership and press to justify economic policy makes it difficult to characterize periods of Cuban economic policy as either wholly pragmatic or wholly idealistic.

Thus the two signs in Holguin point to a past where principle and practice were never separated and where decisions were made and options discarded. The two signs also represent two elements of Cuban socialism that have at times conflicted, but at others have supported one another. Both signs exhort sacrifice in the name of the country—to defend it militarily or to build it up economically. From the moment that Cuba declared itself a socialist republic, Cuba has struggled with the issue of just what the right balance of moral and material incentives should be. This issue, broached first during the Great Debate of 1962–65, would emerge again and again, in the late 1960s with the Revolutionary Offensive; in the early 1970s with the failure of the 10-million-ton sugar drive and Cuba's subsequent inclusion in the Soviet trading bloc; in the late 1970s when SDPE was being implemented; and again in the late 1980s with the Rectification Campaign of Ideological Errors and Negative Tendencies, when the leadership felt that small-scale capitalism threatened Cuba's egalitarian ethos and urged a return to the ideas of el Che (even though his ideas had been used to justify precisely those policies the Rectification Campaign was now rejecting).

The signs and histories these debates recall illustrate that many of the tensions brought about by the collapse of the Soviet trading bloc had long existed. It was not the first time Cuba had grappled with the relationship between national liberation and the need for economic links to foreign powers, or the relationship between economic growth and redistribution. Market mechanisms, including private property, material incentives, and pricing signals, were not new to Cuban economic policy in the 1990s, nor were the ideological questions that arose from their use. Indeed, Cuban socialist ideology had gone through many permutations before the 1990s even as basic principles of socioeconomic equality, inclusive nationalism, and unified leadership remained key. It was not as if there existed a clear and unchanging definition of Cuban socialist ideology that was forced for the first time to adjust to historical conditions.

The severity of the economic free-fall in the 1990s did, however, bring these long-standing tensions into high relief. At the same time, the straight empirical narrative of this free fall threatened not just to erase Cuban history before 1991 but also to obscure the fact that while the crisis may have limited Cuba's choices, it did not do away with them completely, particularly at the level of ideology.

The Empirical Narrative of the Economic Crisis

Cuba was extremely dependent upon the Soviet trading bloc, known as the Council for Mutual Economic Assistance (CMEA), which it joined in 1972, and from whose subsidized prices and generous terms of trade it benefited greatly. Before CMEA's termination, Cuba conducted 85% of its total (import-export) trade with CMEA countries (70% of that with the USSR), and realized 95% of its foreign exchange operations with socialist countries.[19] By 1989, the Soviets provided all the wheat with which Cuban bread was made, 65% of the powdered milk, 50% of fertilizers, and 40% of its rice.[20]

While there is hardly consensus as to what the fundamental flaws of the Cuban economy are and when they began to manifest themselves,[21] there are few who do not identify the disappearance of the Soviet bloc as the most immediate source of Cuba's economic crisis.[22] The statistics documenting the effects of the decline and ultimate disappearance of CMEA are dramatic.

Between 1989 and 1993, Cuba's import bill decreased by 70%, the Soviet Union decided to stop automatically covering Cuba's trade deficits, and Cuban national output fell by more than 50%.[23] During the same period, the GDP fell by 35%,[24] private consumption dropped by 30%, and gross investment decreased by 80%. By the end of 1993, the fiscal deficit was almost a third of GDP.[25] Between 1989 and 1992, total trade with the member countries of CMEA fell 93%.[26] Between 1984 and 1989, sugar accounted for nearly 77% of Cuba's exports.[27] In 1994, Cuba paid for 2.5 million tons of petroleum with 1 million tons of sugar, a third of what it used to sell for.[28]

In 1990, Cuba was threatened with the prospect of "option zero," which called for zero use of energy, electricity, and transportation.[29] While option zero was never put into practice, fuel deliveries to state and private sectors were reduced by 80%. Bicycles and ox-drawn carts replaced fuel-consuming cars and tractors. The nickel-processing plant and oil refinery were both shut down to save energy. Food and clothing rationing was reinstated.[30]

Daily living conditions of Cubans during this period present the crisis more vividly. Schools and factories shut down. Electricity was scarce and blackouts a daily occurrence. Hospitals operated under wartime conditions. While laid-off workers continued to receive 60% of their salaries, the money in their pockets was of little use as there was nothing to buy with it. Soap was a rare commodity and people turned to making their own. Weekly cooking shows explored various recipes whose primary ingredient was banana peels. Used coffee grinds were set out in the sun to dry so that they could be used for a second, third, or fourth time. People were left temporarily blind from vitamin deficiencies.[31] The government newspaper *Granma* became a weekly publication rather than a daily in order to save paper. Newspapers, Bibles, and other thin-papered books became high-ticket items as replacement for toilet paper. While the government attempted to move people to the countryside to support the drive for food self-sufficiency, those in the countryside flocked to Havana in the hopes of acquiring hard currency and scarce goods.

The situation reached a head in the summer of 1994. In July, there were a number of boat and ferry hijackings including one that left forty-one dead after Cuban authorities tried to intercept the ferry. In August, in what is known as the *Maleconazo*, several hundred mostly young men took the streets of central Havana in a rare *public* display of dissatisfaction with conditions in the country. Though the spontaneous protest was brief, it precipitated the *balsero* crisis, when tens of thousands of Cubans left the country in boats and makeshift rafts (*balsas*) after the Cuban government announced, as it had in 1980, that it would not stop them. The exact number of Cubans who died at sea is unknown.[32]

The Significance of Crisis versus Shock

In the early 1990s, lurid tales of hardship could be heard across the island, and they abounded in accounts of Cuba that juxtaposed images of poverty to the revolution's promises of material progress.[33] If material shortages were not new to Cuba, Cubans in postrevolutionary Cuba had only come close to such extreme deprivation in the late 1960s. By the 1980s, their expectations for a comfortable standard of living were high. Cuba and Colombia were the only two economies in Latin America whose per capita incomes were higher at the end of the 1980s than at the beginning.[34] Thus, the economic free-fall of the 1990s was a shock. However, the term "shock," understood as Benjamin understood it, and missing from most accounts of the Special Period, suggests a dramatically different interpretation of events since it does not lend itself so easily to the language of history as progress—whether it be the narrative of socialism's inevitable decline worldwide, or that of the Cuban leadership who suggested that the period represented a temporary derailment from an otherwise healthy and uncontested path of socialist construction, as evidenced in the leadership's use of the phrase "Special Period in Times of Peace."

For many inside Cuba, this shock functioned as a dialectical image, calling everything into question and unmooring commonly held assumptions. While the shock called for change, it did so within a tradition inside Cuba that saw creative innovation as a key element of Cuban socialism. It pointed to the need to seriously examine not just the current juncture but also longstanding deficiencies of the Cuban system, and yet many found the impetus for this project in the same tradition that was now open to interrogation. To quote Cuban literary and art critic Desiderio Navarro:

> In their respective moments of participation in the public sphere, a majority of Cuban critical intellectuals have believed, more so than

many of the politicians, in socialism's capacity to bear open criticism. They have believed that criticism, far from being a threat to socialism, is its "oxygen," its "motor": a necessity for the survival and well-being of the revolutionary process. The critical intellectuals believe that social criticism can constitute a threat only when it is silenced or even met with reprisals, when it is confined to a close guild or institutional enclave, when it is placed in a communication vacuum under a bell jar, or—and this above all else—when it goes unanswered or when, recognized as correct, it is not taken into account in political practice.[35]

The Cuban leadership in the first half of the 1990s appeared to hold a similar belief. In March 1990, on the eve of the Fourth Congress of the Communist Party scheduled for 1991, Raúl Castro, second secretary of the Central Committee of the Cuban Communist Party and head of the Cuban armed forces, issued what was known as *el llamamiento* or "the call." Citing "the creative tradition of Cuban revolutionary thought," Raúl Castro emphasized the need to "continue to foster a climate of openness that reflects the richness of social thought and encourages the knowledge and participation of the people on all fronts of the revolution."[36]

According to Cuban sociologist Haroldo Dilla:

Millions of people in thousands of settings (schools, labour halls, community centres) exercised their right to criticize, to propose solutions or simply to offer opinions on questions ranging from daily life to public policy. The results of these debates were never published, but from various reports and comments they reflected a demand for profound renewal of the system within the framework of an enduring commitment to social objectives and national independence. The Cuban political class had access to more than enough information to judge the state of mind, aspirations and opinions of the majority of the Cuban people.[37]

Many of the complaints were about the inefficiencies of the Cuban economy and bureaucracy and about the inability of ordinary Cubans to participate more actively in the institutions where decisions affecting their lives were made.[38] According to Rafael Hernández, some of the issues that emerged included decentralization, the possibility of nonstate forms of property, the need for more avenues for public participation (as opposed to mobilization), the need for more room for NGOs, and a rejection of bureaucratic thinking in exchange for more "cultural expression, social thought and ideological debate."[39] It is difficult to tell how much of this information was heeded by the Cuban government because little of the public discussion could be found in print. What remains from the period between 1991 and 1995 is a large body of academic work produced at research institutes in Havana and published in Cuba and internationally, much of it united by a belief that economic restructuring in Cuba had to be accompanied by greater political openness if socialism was to be preserved. While these academics did not call for multiparty elections, they expressed concern that ordinary Cubans would be left powerless to defend their interests as producers and consumers in the conflicts emerging in an increasingly decentralized economy run by technocratic and bureaucratic elites.

Once the leadership began to settle on specific economic policy, it grew less tolerant of those suggesting that it might be done another way or that the leadership could not make changes in the economic sphere while resisting change in its political and social program. By 1996, as we saw in chapter 4, some of the academics that the government had consulted in the first part of the decade, including Haroldo Dilla, were now being accused of and reprimanded for a variety of sins, including straying from the official path. What was threatening to the leadership about much of this academic work was its argument that many of the economic and political problems of the 1990s were not caused, but only intensified, by the collapse of the Soviet Union and that Cuban socialism could not be salvaged simply by narrowing its definition to a few key "achievements" of the revolution and then holding that definition above scrutiny. While 1996 marked the end of greater openness in Cuba, it did not mark the end of discussion, particularly in the cultural sphere.

It is not surprising that these discussions within the socialist paradigm were lost to accounts treating the shock simply as evidence of the ideology's global demise and juxtaposing the consequences of that shock to socialist slogans. What is worthy of note is that the Cuban government itself was complicit in perpetuating this framework. The following account of some of the most significant economic policies adopted by the Cuban government to respond to the shock illustrates the difficulty of the leadership's rhetorical attempts to distinguish between, on the one hand, a pure yet narrowly defined socialist ideology to serve as the revolution's guiding light in an exceptional moment, and, on the other, a series of economic measures that they argued were not ideal but unavoidable.

Economic Policy and Narrowing Options Rhetorically

Cuba's overall economic strategy in response to this macroeconomic crisis was characterized by economic opening in order to attract foreign investment and encourage long-term growth, promotion of export industries including biotechnology and electronics, attempts to limit imports by moving toward greater agricultural self-sufficiency, and development of foreign tourism as a way of earning foreign exchange.[40] This sectoral approach was designed to keep market mechanisms from contaminating the rest of the social and economic fabric.

These strategies, however, had many shortcomings. Income on biotechnology exports would be slow in coming and might never provide Cuba with the currency it needed to lift itself out of the crisis. Food self-sufficiency was unrealistic. While tourism grew, it required importing many goods not available in Cuba and aggravated political tensions and contradictions. Most of the foreign investment activity at that time took place in the tourist industry, which fostered short-term investment with high rates of return but very little stability.[41]

In 1993, the Cuban government began introducing and, in some cases, reintroducing market mechanisms into the internal logic of the economy and creating and strengthening institutions resembling private property. One of the first measures taken was to legalize the possession of U.S. dollars (Law-Decree 140) and set up dollar stores[42] where Cubans with access to dollars, mostly those with family in the United States, would be able to buy imported goods.[43] This policy provided another door for the entrance of hard currency into the country and into the hands of the government and alleviated some of the pressures arising from shortages of basic goods. The text of the law stated bluntly that legalizing the possession of dollars would reduce the number of acts deemed punishable by the law and thus alleviate the workload of the police and courts. The increased police workload was, of course, the consequence of a shortage of goods and people's consequent attempts to acquire them illegally. In general, the tone of the law's text was pragmatic. It stated that "the conditions of the Special Period" and the economic difficulties of the country "made it necessary to introduce new regulations and methods in relation to the possession of convertible currency [U.S. dollars]."[44] Similarly, the text of the 1993 self-employment law (Law-Decree 141), which legalized self-employment in 117 occupations,[45] argued that the necessities of the moment justified legalizing self-employment but that it should be heavily monitored by the state in order to avoid the values of entrepreneurship from contaminating those values and practices fostered by socialism.[46]

Also that year, the government transformed most state farms into worker-run cooperatives called Unidades Basicas de Producción Cooperativas (UBPC or Basic Units of Cooperative Production) where the land was still technically owned by the state but workers had use rights permanently deeded to them.[47] Law-Decree No. 142 stipulated that the cooperative owned what it produced, would have managerial autonomy, including its own bank account, and could collectively elect representatives who would report to members on a periodic basis. Salaries were to be directly related to productivity.[48]

In addition, the government reopened free agricultural markets. It had shut down the markets eight years earlier during the Rectification Campaign when Castro criticized them for promoting profiteering and thus threatening Cuba's social equality.[49] The reopened farmers markets allowed individual farmers to sell their surplus above the state quota at unregulated prices and introduced a wealthier social group into Cuba's egalitarian society. By 1994, most Cubans had high levels of savings because of a lack of consumer goods, and the markets alleviated this monetary overhang by soaking up excess currency. The markets also facilitated an appreciation of the Cuban peso from 120 pesos to the dollar in 1994 to between 20 and 22 pesos to the dollar by 1995.[50] The government reduced its deficit by implementing new taxes, reducing subsidies to state firms that lost money, and increasing certain state prices.[51] This move from soft budget constraints to hard budget constraints helped to improve efficiency within the surviving state enterprises.

In 1995, the government replaced the 1982 foreign investment law (Law-Decree 50), which had closed most sectors of the Cuban economy off to foreign investment, with a new law (Law-Decree 77) permitting foreign investment in almost all sectors of the Cuban economy except education, health, and the armed forces. The text of the new foreign investment law, like the texts of the laws legalizing dollars and self-employment, argued that foreign investment was the only way that Cuba could maintain its revolutionary achievements in light of current changes to the global economy, since a redistributive economy must also be a growing economy.

> In today's world, without the existence of the socialist camp, with a globalizing world economy and strong hegemonic tendencies in the economic, political, and military camps, Cuba, in order to preserve its achievements and, moreover, subject to a fierce blockade, lacking capital and certain technologies—often market technologies—and need-

ing to restructure its industry, can obtain through foreign investment, only on the basis of the strictest respect for national sovereignty and independence, benefits: by introducing new and advanced technologies, modernizing its industries, greater productive efficiency, creating new jobs, improving the quality of products and services offered, reducing costs, improving competitiveness in foreign markets, and accessing certain markets, which together would support the efforts that the country needs to make in order to develop economically and socially.[52]

The law emphasized the need to always take national sovereignty into account when dealing with foreign investors.[53] The Cuban government plays a large role in monitoring foreign investment and contracting. Cuban labor is provided to foreign firms by a Cuban agency that sets wages and work conditions and, by converting dollar salaries paid to the agency into pesos, siphons off a large percentage of the salary.[54] In general, foreign investment was approached with caution and skepticism even when there was recognition that there was no other choice in the matter.

Also legalized in 1995 were private restaurants. During the following two years, the government implemented a procedure to collect income taxes and private taxi services were legalized. In 1997, the government passed Law-Decree 171 regulating the private bed and breakfasts that had been legalized in 1993. The law is similar to that which legalized self-employment and, according to Ted Henken in his study of Cuban bed and breakfasts, is best understood not as a decision made unilaterally by the government, but rather as "an administrative response to a multitude of (mostly illegal) homegrown economic survival strategies developed by the Cuban people."[55]

However, the texts of these laws emphasized that they were not decisions reflecting shifts in the ideology of the Cuban people or in the nature of the system as a whole, but policy responses to changes in the global economy and, to a lesser extent, people's behavior. Such a distinction, however, was harder to maintain when dealing with the consequences of these economic measures and particularly the legalization of the dollar.

The Repercussions of Dollarization: What Cubans Do and What Cubans Say

Critics pointed to the consequences of dollarization as evidence that any attempts to salvage socialism in Cuba only undermined it in other ways and, thus, that Cuban economic policy was only a series of stopgap measures to forestall the inevitable collapse of the system. As with the situation in the country immediately following the collapse of the Soviet Union, conditions of material scarcity, social and economic inequality, and participation in illegal activities in Cuba provided abundant material with which to argue that ideology in Cuba was exhausted or that, while the 1990s provided exciting material with which intellectuals could theorize about socialism, most Cubans had little interest in and time for such activities.[56] A straight empirical account of 1990s Cuba that locates ideology in the Cuban government and experience in the Cuban people appears to support these conclusions. But if one shifts one's point of view, as Benjamin suggests, to look not just at how Cubans were behaving in the 1990s but also at how they themselves made sense of these social shifts, the argument that ideology is dead in Cuba or that theoretical discussions take place only in the academic realm is far less compelling.

No one denies that the legalization of the dollar created severe divisions in a society that was previously highly egalitarian.[57] Those with family abroad who can send remittances and those with links to tourism and the dollars that tourists bring have had much higher incomes than those living on state salaries.

Since the Special Period, very few people in Cuba actually have lived on a state salary. If they work a government job, they supplement their income in a variety of ways. A university secretary may do manicures out of her house. The elderly supplement their social security by selling cigarettes from their ration cards or buying up newspapers in the morning to sell at a slightly higher price on the streets.[58] One member of a family may work for the state either because she likes her job or certain material perks from it (free lunch, transportation, access to computers, email, and internet), while another member of the family might work in the illicit economy as a way of acquiring dollars. Even state jobs sometimes give people access to dollars either because part of the salary is in dollars or because workers can steal from the state and resell the goods. Workers at cigar factories, for instance, may siphon off some of the goods to sell to tourists on the street at a lower price.

A lot of people don't even bother with their government job. A doctor may have abandoned practice all together to devote himself full time to shuttling people around in a bici-taxi. Then there are the full time *jineteros* (which literally means jockeys, because they ride on the backs of tourists), who are guides, middlemen, or prostitutes. The story of the doctor or engineer turned cab driver or prostitute is now familiar. Few can say that they do not participate in illegal activities, or at least benefit from participation, and yet there is a great deal of finger pointing, especially at those who have fewer outside resources.

The finger pointing implicated racial and gendered stereotypes whose resurgence the conditions of the Special Period facilitated. While the revolution never eradicated racism or sexism, particularly at the level of everyday practice, it did reduce their institutionalized forms and alleviate racial and gender inequality by bringing up the standard of living of many black and darker-skinned Cubans and of women and offering them jobs and educational opportunities that had previously been closed off.[59] With the increased reliance on dollars in the 1990s, black and darker-skinned Cubans found themselves at a disadvantage economically.[60] The earlier education benefits were no longer helpful because there was no longer a clear link between education and income.[61] Work in the tourist industry was frequently off-limits.[62] Black Cubans were less likely to be legally self-employed. They also had fewer relatives abroad from whom they could receive much-needed dollars. These conditions meant that black Cubans were at a disadvantage relative to white Cubans.[63] White Cubans too engaged in *jinterismo*, yet these activities were not marked as deviant in the same way as they were when nonwhite Cubans engaged in them.[64] Thus the Special Period led to the resurgence of stereotypes of black criminality.

Women bore the brunt of the crisis in a variety of ways. One of the achievements of the revolution had been its incorporation of large numbers of women into the workforce, which freed them from economic dependence on men.[65] During the initial cutbacks of the early 1990s, however, women were fired first from state jobs and their work opportunities curtailed.[66] This decision was not made on the basis of gender-neutral criteria, but rather under the assumption that women would find other work more easily in the nonstate sector and that women staying at home was more acceptable than men staying at home. At the same time, women, many of whom lived in multigenerational nonnuclear families, continued to bear primary responsibility for the household and family in spite of the passage of the Family Code in 1975.[67] By 1994, most *cuenta-propistas* were men, and the traditional sexual division of labor was being reproduced within the informal sector, with many women taking jobs that they filled before the revolution or in much smaller numbers since 1959.[68] One of those jobs was *jinetera*.

As with *jinterismo* more generally, the label of *jinetera* was often applied selectively depending on who was engaging in particular activities. The leadership reserved its sharpest criticisms for women engaging in *jineterismo*. Fidel Castro and Vilma Espín of the Federation of Cuban Women argued that prostitution was not the result of necessity, but the path chosen by women who liked sex or were looking for easy money and a luxurious lifestyle rather than taking advantage of the educational and work opportunities offered to them by the revolution. Male *jineteros* were not subject to the same disdain. Black and darker-skinned and poorer Cuban women involved with foreign men were more frequently subject to the label *jinetera* than white and middle- to upper-class Cuban women whose relationships would be likely to be seen as motivated by more than sex and economic need.[69] According to Coco Fusco, wealthier and mostly white women, unaccustomed to competition from black and darker-skinned Cuban women marrying Europeans at higher rates, "often resort[ed] to moralizing rhetoric as a mask for their resentment."[70]

For Fusco, however, *jineteras* are neither antisocial pleasure seekers (the official Cuban government position) nor passive victims of a totalitarian state (the position of critics). The rise of *jineterismo*, she argues, is due not just to economic necessity. In addition, it reflects both a more casual attitude toward sex since the revolution, and also a "desire among the populace for the non-productive leisure and pleasurable consumerism that the revolutionary government had once linked with capitalist corruption."[71] Yet this desire is a challenge not just to "Communist bureaucrats" but also to "prudish liberals" and "fanatic Catholics."[72] In other words, *jineteras* too refused the easy categories of liberal versus communist.

The language surrounding all the activities of *jineterismo* also suggests that certain behaviors and ways of talking about Cuban daily life cannot immediately be understood as proof of opposition to socialism. The use of the term *jinetera*, rather than prostitute, implies a job that fits with a particular time period in Cuban history and can be more easily combined with classic revolutionary terms that have been reinvented to fit present circumstances. It is easier to say that a *jinetera* is *luchando* (struggling to make do), just as it is far easier, and more palatable, to say that working for dollars or finding needed goods on the black market is *inventando* (inventing) or *resolviendo* (resolving). Such terms seem far more heroic and dignified. They also challenge the idea of passive third-world subjects who either are taken advantage of by foreigners or have abandoned all their pride and principles to scrape by in difficult circumstances.

What the use of these terms indicates, therefore, is not the failure of socialist rhetoric in Cuba but rather its continued use, not as static slogans, but as a language that continues to appeal to people's sensibilities and helps make sense of their lived conditions. Saying someone is inventing rather than stealing, or struggling rather than prostituting themselves, may appear only to be an extreme rationalization. Calling prostitution or stealing by another name does not change the bitter reality of these activities, but it is in the bending of these terms that they survive as more than slogans and instead as issues to be interrogated.

Anthropologist Alexei Yurchak argues that it was the Soviet people's continued allegiance and reformulation of Communist ideology that "made its 'collapse' appear completely unimaginable and surprisingly fast" both to most foreign observers and to the Soviet people.[73] People engaged in the reproduction of ideological forms, attending meetings and mass rallies, for instance, but they did not assign the same meaning to those activities as the Party did. This was not an instance of what is often referred to in Cuba as double morality, where one does one thing and says another, but instead an instance of people reassigning meaning to certain activities so that they could continue to participate in Soviet society according to what they saw to be important Communist values.

> Contrary to the Party claims, many Soviet people, especially the younger generations, creatively reinterpreted the meanings of the ideological symbols, deideologizing static dogmas and rendering communist values meaningful on their own terms. The act of the reproduction of form with the reinterpretation of meaning, which this paper theorizes as a *heteronymous shift*, cannot be reduced to resistance, opportunism, or dissimulation; indeed, it allowed many Soviet people to continue adhering to Communist ideals and to see themselves as good Soviet citizens.[74]

Yurchak suggests, then, that because practices running counter to socialism were couched in socialist terms, the actual collapse of the system was unanticipated. In Special Period Cuba, however, there was a much clearer recognition of the gap between ideals and daily life. This recognition was expressed in the form of *cuentos* or ironic jokes, which, as anthropologist Sachuko Tanumo argues, should not be understood as a cynical rejection of any utopian political projects or agreement with dissidents, but instead as an "ironic affection towards revolutionary ideals."[75] Irony, she argues, was a "means of escaping the pro-socialism versus anti-socialism binary" understood as either naive support for a flawed socialist system as articulated by the Cuban leadership or outright rejection of it, and instead provided a means to register complaints without allying oneself with those opposed to the revolution.[76]

The Leadership's Rationalizations

The leadership during the Special Period generally argued that, in spite of these social shifts, the crisis was economic and that measures to tackle the crisis were unavoidable. In a 1993 interview, then secretary of the Cuban Council of Ministers Carlos Lage Dávila was asked whether the economic problem was worse than the political. He answered that Cuba's problems were "economic, not political" and that only those who were not familiar with Cuban "reality" would ask Cuba to make political changes. Applying political solutions to economic problems was, argued Lage, "like treating a stomach ache with aspirin, with the danger moreover of producing gastritis and aggravating the problems."[77]

Lage, a pediatrician by training, was one of the main architects of economic reform in Cuba, and during the 1990s he increasingly took over the task of articulating and justifying the dramatic changes that took place in the Cuban economy after 1991. While Fidel Castro remained the main ideological and political force of the country in the 1990s, he tended to focus on economic questions not particular to Cuba such as globalization, neoliberalism, and third-world debt[78] and domestic issues such as the negative effects of the U.S. blockade and the importance of culture and ideas for the revolution.[79] According to one Cuban academic, Castro had not used the term "Cuban economy" itself since 1996 because it was not "an agreeable theme." He left the stickier issue of Cuba's domestic economy and macro-data to Lage.

In a 1994 piece entitled *Las estrategias ante la situación económica actual* (*Strategies to Confront the Present Economic Situation*), Lage argued that Cuba had two choices given the new situation in which it found itself after the collapse of CMEA. The first option was to impose a program of structural adjustment by raising prices, closing factories, cutting social-welfare programs, and decreasing social security, thus imposing great hardship on the Cuban people. The second option was to "apply a policy that corresponded with the ideology, the ideas, the aspirations and the objectives of the revolution: to share among everyone the weight of [the] grave economic consequences" of Cuba's economic isolation.[80] While far superior to the first option, argued Lage, the second option had negative consequences, which were well known before they manifested themselves. Nevertheless, the second option was seen as the solution most consistent with Cuban socialism since it focused on preserving achievements of the revolution such as health care, education, and social security and on distributing the burden of the crisis evenly throughout Cuban society. According to Lage:

> To choose this second way meant that, with time—and the time depended on the capacity of the country to face its problems and recover—the population would acquire more money, which [without legal ways in which to spend it] would inconveniently accumulate in excess, thereby leading to the expansion of the black market. At the same time, there would be an increase in the contradictions between, on the one hand, the circumstances in which the population lived and, on the other, the need to stimulate and encourage a market and an activity like tourism, which demanded the guarantee of certain resources and free-market conditions for their development. These hitches, which thrived given the circumstances of the country, had been seen in advance. Notwithstanding, this road was much more humane and bearable for the population than applying adjustment methods in such abrupt and deep crisis conditions.[81]

By characterizing the economic measures in the mid-1990s as the lesser of two evils and isolating the crisis in the economic realm, officials hoped to link the longer-term survival of the Cuban Revolution to the maintenance of basic social services—such as health care, education, housing, regulated prices, and low inflation—and Communist Party control.[82]

Banking on Social Services

The government managed to weather the 1990s with the majority of the "revolution's achievements" intact. According to the World Bank's 2001 edition of World Development Indicators (WDI), Cuba not only maintained the revolution's achievements in low infant mortality rates, primary education, and health care, but improved them despite the presence of the U.S. trade embargo and the collapse of the Soviet trading bloc.[83] Many of these impressive statistics could be attributed to high public spending in these areas. In 2001, for instance, spending on education amounted to 6.7% of the gross national income.

In spite of critics' contention that these kinds of services were not sustainable,[84] statistics like these were the government's constant defense in light of increasing economic and social inequality,[85] material scarcity, overt and subtle discrimination against Cubans in their own country, often harsh crackdowns on those trying to make their way in Cuba's illicit economy or seeking political change in Cuba, and continuing attempts by Cubans to leave their country.

There is support among the Cuban population for maintaining these social services. A 1995 poll showed that 75% wished to keep education free and 77.9% wished to keep public health care free; 22.1 % wished to keep education partially free and 19.6% wished to keep health care partially free. The remaining percentages either opposed free or partially free education and health care or were not sure.[86] Those who have done research in Cuba and spoken with Cuban people generally recognize that in spite of the Cuban people's dissatisfaction with such things as state salaries upon which they cannot subsist, the poor purchasing power of the Cuban peso, and a new class system based on access to dollars, the majority of Cubans continue to value and depend upon the Cuban social welfare state and do not wish to see it disappear under the weight of a hyperindividualistic consumer society.[87] My own conversations with people in Cuba support these general conclusions.

While one may be suspicious of an opinion poll carried out by the government of a one-party system or question the objectivity of the type of foreign researcher who would even be given permission to enter Cuba, a complete dismissal of this data would fail to take into account several important considerations. The fact that not all Cubans supported absolutely free education and health care demonstrates that people were sufficiently honest to express at least a mild opposition. It is significant that many of the dissident organizations on and off the island also support some sort of welfare state.[88]

By the Special Period, the government's ideology had achieved hegemony. According to anthropologist Mona Rosenthal: "the hegemonic political ideology, the centralist planned structure and the planned economy pervade everyday life" and "no one in Cuba can avoid being affected by socialist ideology in one way or another, whether one accepts its premises or not."[89] To use Gramscian terms, as Rosenthal does, the state does not rule from above by imposing certain rules and norms on preconstituted subjects. Rather, it sets the standards of appropriate behavior and provides the structures through which individuals interpret their situations, thereby producing and maintaining subjects who come to view law and other forms of coercion, not as something externally imposed, but as freedom, since they have been taught to believe that these laws contain moral or social value.[90] Thus, for instance, a man I knew in Holguín who described himself as an *opositor* complained that the bakery's provision of *pan doble* after a day without bread was not truly the double provision of bread but simply the provision of what he was owed to him according to the ration card. The problem, even for this *opositor*, was not that the state monopolized bread production, but that it failed to provide what it had promised. Martin Holbraad argues that the revolution, by constantly demanding self-sacrifice from the Cuban people and defining itself as an all-encompassing "political universe" with "no outside" creates an "ontological firewall," such that the revolution, embodied in the Cuban state, never becomes the object of discontent even as people consistently complain about daily living conditions. For this reason, he argues, the liberal framework in which individuals choose or reject ideologies fails to grasp the way in which the revolution has entirely redefined what subjectivity means.[91]

There is no doubt that the discursive framework in Cuba is limited by these considerations, and one should not underestimate the various forms of direct oppression that the state uses.[92] However, these conditions can too easily be used to ignore any popular expressions of support for socialism as necessarily coerced or unreflective. Recognizing the ways in which subjectivity itself has been redefined in Cuba may unintentionally reaffirm liberalism's pretenses to monopolize individual agency. In Cuba one can find anarchists, Jehovah's Witnesses, Quakers, and followers of a whole range of ideologies that do not match either Cuban socialism in a broad sense or official definitions of it, and it cannot be assumed that only these views are truly expressed or acquired consciously. One must also ask if belittling Cuban popular opinion does not make one complicit in the same logic used by the Cuban government to dismiss displays and expressions of dissatisfaction with daily living conditions as the work of antisocial elements or mercenaries of the U.S. government.[93]

The complexity and variety of the responses of Cubans themselves to Cuba's situation call into question the simplistic categories of criminal antirevolutionary elements, active and thinking opponents to the system, fearful citizens of a totalitarian state, or fanatical hard-line Communists and party elites. The fact that Cuban responses are rarely knee-jerk repetitions of party slogans poses a problem for those wishing to dismiss Cuban public opinion as the product of either Communist indoctrination or foreign influence. It makes it harder to sustain the image of the Cuban government as the protector of a pure or dogmatic socialism and the Cuban population as the source of a reality that calls that socialism into question.

For instance, a friend of mine, who studied sociology at the University of Havana, was a member of the Union of Communist Youth (Unión de la Juventud Communista) and regularly did voluntary labor (a thing associated with either the idealism or tyranny of the 1960s). At the same time, she refused to sign a national referendum in support of the Cuban constitution and against the Varela Project,[94] even when the local representative from the neighborhood CDR (Committee for the Defense of the Revolution) came to her door and made her write a letter explaining why, and even though her refusal might have made future advancement difficult. For her, supporting the revolution, as she does, was not compatible with signing a document that argues that the constitution is "untouchable." For her, giving such power to the constitution was antirevolutionary. At the same time, she helped with neighborhood voluntary programs and worked for a government office in Havana. She is equally critical of the Cuban press, however, and finds the Cuban cultural-studies magazine *Temas*, which publishes a variety of academic article by both Cuban and foreigner authors, too compromised.

Another friend who is a thirty-two-year-old independent artist emphasized the necessity of an economic base for socialism and the tendency of the people to rationalize the situation in Cuba by referring to the provision of social services. At the same time, she saw socialism as providing good things. "Cuban socialism for me is a set of ideas favorable to man, but in reality these ideas would be more viable if there was a more solid economic base. Sometimes socialism loses its meaning in reality because it does not have structural support. . . . Yes, there are benefits to socialism, but they are precarious, because they want everybody to have them without having an economic base." Thus she pointed to what she saw as a trade-off between social welfare and individual wealth accumulation. When I asked her whether she would sacrifice free health care for a higher salary, she told me she would not. At the same time, she was critical of the ways in which the provision of social services in Cuba served to justify severe inadequacies to the system. When I asked if socialism for her amounted only to free education and medicine, she told me, "That is the banner that people raise here. People protect themselves with this." But again, she did not see these rationalizations of the government's failure in Cuba as a sign that socialism, in the sense of decommodification, did not have its virtues. Thus, when I asked if she would want to leave Cuba, she told me she wouldn't because "money corrupts" and causes problems.

I reference these responses not because they represent the views of all Cubans, but because the arguments illustrate active engaged negotiations of Cuban socialist ideology and raise difficult questions both for the leadership and for those suggesting that socialist ideology in Cuba no longer has any meaning for most Cubans. The government's calculation that its continued legitimacy rests on its ability to provide Cubans with health care, education, and subsidized prices is one that it can feel relatively secure about, given that the provision of these services continues to be important to most, although certainly not all, Cubans. However, as the above anecdotes suggest, not all Cubans are willing to accept the state's narrow definition of social services. Nor are Cubans willing to allow the Cuban state to fetishize these achievements by delinking them from all the Cuban individuals whose daily work is to provide these same services. In other words, it is not simply a question of not wanting savage capitalism, and therefore supporting some sort of welfare state. Rather, popular reactions to government economic policy reflect a concern that attempts to salvage a narrow definition of socialism may well work to undermine the possibility of a true political consensus around the state's governing ideology. To quote Haroldo Dilla again:

> The slow commercial colonization of socialized areas of the economy has posed challenges at many levels to the most central of all political questions—the distribution of power. If we take as axiomatic the fact that a combination of militant anti-imperialism and the provision of free social services does not amount to socialism, we are left with the question as to the real depth of these systemic changes: first, at the social (and more specifically the class) level and second, at the level of the rearticulation of the whole of political life.[95]

If Cuba is heading toward marketization, with the state increasingly allying its interests with capital, it becomes increasingly important for discussions of Cuban socialism to center on the elements of Cuban socialism most important for its long-term survival—not simply as dogma imposed from above, but as a continual project in which the entire nation is involved. Marketization may help to maintain the social-welfare state, but what happens when the state comes not just to identify with capital but to define Cuban socialism? What happens when the government would rather reconcile socialist ideology with the market than share the project of defining socialism with the populace? The point now becomes not that the Cuban government is facilitating market contamination or that it attempts to bring the rhetoric of revolution to bear on present circumstances but rather that a government monopoly on socialist ideology implies that there is only one way to renegotiate it. This monopoly contributes to stagnation by obstructing an understanding of ideology as a set of principles that are constantly being negotiated and assembled in a variety of ways. Survival may entail a particular combination of these principles, with some emphasized at the expense of others, but the insistence that this is the only possible combination ultimately reduces the number of options available to the government as well.

Returning to Carlos III and Dialectical Images

The shopping mall mentioned at the beginning of this chapter is a useful dialectical image that illustrates the problem the government faces. Plaza Carlos III and other shopping complexes like it in Havana testify to the expanding role that consumption plays in public life in Cuba even as the number of people who can consume diminishes. The stores and prices demonstrate the vast differences between the peso and dollar economy. The identity of its shoppers represents class shifts and a new system of remuneration. One must possess dollars (now convertible pesos) to buy anything at Carlos III.[96]

Opened in October 1998, Plaza Carlos III is a self-contained mall (see figure 9). It is a space full of the new with few reminders of the scarcity and dilapidation of Havana outside. The mall offers everything: home appliances, cosmetics and perfume, clothing, pet supplies, shoes, and a food court. In 2000, when the sign reading "Sales + Economy + Efficiency = Revolution" greeted its customers, there was a Benetton store where T-shirts for children cost $25. The grocery store sold sugar cereals, peanut butter, imported apples that cost up to a dollar each, olive oil, and other tinned products that most Cubans could never afford. There was even an "everything for a dollar" store in the tradition of the United States where one could buy plastic toys and flowers, buckets, and pencils, much of it made in China. There were often long lines outside these stores (see figure 10). Everything was "only a dollar" even when a dollar could buy you 60 bus rides (120 if you rode the infamous *camello* instituted during the Special Period, and now discontinued), ten cinema tickets, ten pounds of oranges, or five packs of unfiltered cigarettes. However, a dollar in the world of dollars in Cuba got you very little. In the grocery store like the one in Carlos III, a can of *Tropicola*, the Cuban cola, cost 45 cents and a beer cost 60 cents. A stick of butter could cost up to a dollar, more than what it cost in the United States. Toilet paper cost $1.40 for four rolls. Eggs cost from 10 to 15 cents each.[97] When the highest salary in Cuba at that time was 40 dollars a month, these prices were very high indeed.[98]

Carlos III provides Cubans with a window onto the goods they may not have access to in the peso economy. It is not simply a store; it is a shopping experience. Just like the malls in the United States, it's a place where people congregate by virtue of their commonality as consumers. Just as in the United

Fig. 9. Plaza Carlos III, 2001.

Fig. 10. "Todo x $1.00." Waiting in line to enter the "everything for a dollar" store, Plaza Carlos III, Havana, 2000.

States, it is a place where one has agency as a buyer and where one can take control of one's life by adding new objects to it. And, just as in the United States, this agency as a buyer does not translate into political power. Unlike the United States, however, this realm of consumer culture falls directly under the purview of the state.

Thus those who go shopping at Carlos III are "defend[ing] what is [theirs]" by helping to keep the economy functioning.[99] Sales plus economy plus efficiency does equal revolution if the revolution has come to mean nothing but the influx of hard currency to keep the economy going, the government afloat, and basic social services intact. Other activities—such as domestic production, popular political and direct participation, and the search for Cuban-sourced solutions—are absent from this equation. If "sales + economy + efficiency = revolution," then revolution in Cuba is reduced to economic calculation and conspicuous consumption, which are not only activities that few Cuban can actually participate in, but are also principles fundamentally at odds with such important principles of Cuban socialism as unity, equality, and nationalism.

It is tempting to conclude from this that Cuban socialist ideology is doomed to lose all meaning under the weight of a capitalist logic increasingly insinuating itself, with the help of the Cuban government's economic policies, into daily life. It is also tempting to conclude that there is no place for pragmatism within socialism—that the use of the market necessarily implies a move away from socialism. These are the kind of critiques that the government has set itself up for by insisting upon being the primary, and at times sole, articulator and protector of an extremely narrowly defined socialist ideology.

But while the welfare state is not the same as socialism, it is a very important element and one that the Cuban government has done a fairly good job of maintaining. The calculation that "sales + economic + efficiency = revolution" is pragmatic but also focused on maintaining services that are either lacking or under attack in much of the world. To insist upon their importance is to hold crucial ground. But such insistence is different from insisting on converting them into the only achievements of the revolution and the only ones worth salvaging. Social services are not the only surviving legacies of the revolution. And nationalism takes the form not only of anti-imperialism but also of pride in the historical significance of the Cuban Revolution or simply pride in things Cuban. Cubans may express annoyance at constantly being told by the government to sacrifice and share, but such values have seeped into everyday life. Government responses to the demands of global capitalism may have changed social relations, but existing social relations, themselves partially a product of the Cuban government's provision of services such as free education, have also molded the way that the market is received and used.

Precisely because of the socialist Cuban revolution, consumer culture is not the same as popular culture. Yet because of the changes to Cuban economic policy, popular culture is increasingly beyond the control of the state even as the state attempts to mediate between Cuban cultural production, on the one hand, and the world market, on the other. The revolution itself has produced a set of principles and traditions with which to make sense of daily life, and yet the conclusions drawn extend beyond the ideological confines set by the state. Even when the forms that popular culture take represent foreign and commercial influences, those forms are often converted into vehicles for exploring the contradictions of Cuban socialism, rather than adopted uncritically to be used as further empirical evidence by both critics and the Cuban government that Cubans themselves are vulnerable to the forces and whims of the global market.

The realm of popular culture has not bound itself, as the state has, to representing a pure socialist ideology that can then be juxtaposed to particular policies or material conditions. Popular culture has not necessarily dedicated itself to facile juxtapositions either.[100] Instead, it has provided a space in which to examine the relationship between the various principles of Cuban socialism and even to maintain, rather than suppress, what may be irreconcilable but productive tensions. One such realm is that of music, where lyrics provide examples of popular responses that criticize state censorship, material shortages, and racism, to name a few a issues, while at the same time drawing attention to the ways in which capitalism creates new forms of domination and material scarcity. Critical engagement could be found in Cuban films, art, and literature in the 1990s as well.[101] I focus here on music because of its closeness to the popular sphere more generally and to the revolutionary tradition.

Cuban Popular Culture: Critiquing Consumerism and Expanding the Bounds of Socialism

Since the 1960s, the Cuban musical form *nueva trova* has served as a vehicle for social commentary, and the 1990s provided much material for it, although critiques now focused inward, rather than outward. The songs of Cuban *trovador* Carlos Varela dealt with Cubans' self-censorship and fear ("Like Fish" [Como los peces], "Walls and Doors" [Muros y puertas]), the irony of a system that says that all is for you but forbids you to change it ("Like They Did to Me" [Como me hicieron a mí]), and the failure of the Cuban news media to report on the ugly realities of Cuban life ("Politics Doesn't Fit in the Sugar Bowl" [La política no cabe en la azucarera]).[102] Yet Varela's concern with greater freedom of expression in Cuba and his criticisms are not unproblematic embraces of consumer society. His 1989 song "Tropicollage" (a play on "tropical collage") addresses both the ways in which Cuba's desire for dollars damaged Cubans' respect for one another and the ways in which Cuba was commodified by its reliance on the tourist industry. "I know that the dollar makes the economy like flour makes bread," sings Varela, "but what I don't understand is why money confuses people so much that if you go to a hotel they treat you badly because you are not a foreigner."[103] In the same song, Varela reminds the typical tourist who never goes to the places where Cubans actually live and work that Cuba can neither be bought nor be captured in a photograph.

Frank Delgado's 1995 song "Trovatur" is about Cuban musicians who pander to tourists' romantic vision of Cuban revolutionaries. "I was a tropical virus, Communist Latin lover, trafficking in the revolution and its points of views." In "Johnny, the Babaloa," Delgado sings of Afro-Cuban religious figures whose spiritual concerns have been clouded by their entrepreneurial aspirations and who accept only dollars and name brand rum.[104]

Cuban hip-hop, itself an import from the United States but also a hybrid form drawing from the Caribbean, functions as an important vehicle for critiquing state power and ideology and forging alternative black identities.[105] Yet Cuban hip-hip often cites the country's long revolutionary tradition ("Roof of rebelliousness, essence of my country," sings the group Anónimo Consejo) and is skeptical of certain political and cultural products from abroad. Thus the rap group EPG&B tell its listeners in one song not to be a "Miki" ("Mickey Mouse"), which means to be a copycat and a blind consumer of American culture, but rather to be *Carabalí*, in reference to Cuba's African cultural origins and influences.[106] The point is that rap loses its critical and revolutionary potential if Cuban rappers simply imitate the lyrics and styles of their American counterparts. Cuban youth may "consume" rap but they also transform it, calling upon principles of the revolution to criticize and celebrate daily life.[107] Such lines are not a clear condemnation of the market but rather a warning about its reception. Even *jineterismo* reflects a concern with maintaining an active role in the transformations taking place in Cuba.

The rock group Buena Fe's song "Psychology of Today" (Psicología al día)[108] portrays capitalism as something that "grab[s] you by the neck" and demands that you resign yourself to it.

Te atraparé por el cuello	I will grab you by the neck
y te lo voy a apretar,	and squeeze it
mas te exijo firmemente	but demand firmly
no te puedes quejar.	you cannot complain
Porque me da jaquecas,	Because it annoys me
me pone mal humorado	it puts me in a bad mood
si a fin de cuentas	if at the end of the story
estar ahorcado no es tan mal	being hanged isn't so bad
Mirémoslo así	Look at it this way
Seamos positivistas,	Be positive
desde el punto de vista: Humanista	From a humanist point of view

The song's verses go on to describe the ways in which capitalism appears to provide freedom but in fact creates forms of obligation for which capital does not compensate in the end. Thus one stanza of the song refers to the situation of the underdeveloped country that must squander its natural resources and its environment in order to acquire loans which it will be paying off indefinitely. Each chorus ends with a different "point of view" whether it be ecological or humanist, and the chorus itself shows the extent to which that particular view has been perverted by capitalism. Humanism, for instance, is about resignation to the inequality of a world where people exist to enjoy their own individual lives. If one looks on the bright side, goes the song, at least poverty and suffering can be profitable.

The final verse deals with wealthy countries that argue that they need more money in order to be able to share it with the world and forget that this condition for accumulation means that the world remains profoundly unequal. "How am I going to donate?" asks the song, if to do this, "I first must educate my will and have more than enough money."

The final chorus tells the listener that the desired result of this ideological and economic onslaught is that people themselves ask to be grabbed by the neck and promise that they won't complain since "at the end of the story, being hanged isn't so bad." The final lines conclude that "you will see it in this way, in a conformist way, from the slavish point of view."

No vamos a parar	We are not going to stop
hasta oírte decir	until we hear you say,
lo que otros por ahí	what others over there,
repiten sin cesar.	endlessly repeat.
Atrápame por el cuello	Grab me by the neck
y me lo puedes apretar,	and you can squeeze it
te prometo firmemente	I firmly promise you that
no me voy a quejar,	I won't complain,
no te daré jaquecas,	nor annoy you,
ni te pondré enfadado	nor make you angry
si a fin de cuentas	if at the end of the story
estar ahorcados no es tan malo . . .	being hanged isn't so bad.
Yo lo verás así,	You will see it this way,
de modo conformista	in a conformist way
desde el punto de vista: esclavista	from the slavish point of view

The song represents precisely the kind of Gramscian dynamic that Rosenthal uses to describe Cuba. What begins as coercion ends in consent. Yet, in this case, it is explicitly a critique of neoliberalism and its attempt not simply to impose a certain world order, but to make it appear as if this is what people really wish.[109] Given the limitations on freedom of expression in Cuba and the use of codes and double meanings in Cuban cultural production, many would suggest that the explicit message of Buena Fe's song is simply a cover for criticizing people's cooperation with the government's "repressive machinery." However, such a conclusion falls too easily into the kinds of strict dichotomies (ideology versus reality, theory versus practice, pragmatism versus idealism) that dominate discussions of Special Period Cuba and indeed much social science. The song's ambiguity is a reflection not only of political censorship but also of the dilemmas facing the country at a particular historical juncture.

Criticisms of the Cuban government and of daily living conditions can be found not just among the dissident community but also in the streets and in popular culture. However, expressions of dissatisfaction with the status quo do not represent a straightforward embrace of the free market. Nor, however, do these expressions represent claims to revolutionary ideological purity. Rather, they treat Cuban socialist ideology as a set of ever-evolving principles whose relationship to one another is just as important as each one taken independently. This is something that neither the Cuban state, which believes itself to be the primary protector of Cuban socialism, nor the critics of socialist projects, who appear often to share the same belief, wishes to recognize. Recalling Benjamin's critique of history as progress, accounts of Special Period Cuba from apparently opposing ideological standpoints actually work together to make it seem as if the choices in Cuba are much more limited than might in fact be the case.

Conclusion

Another View of Ideology

Cuba and Beyond

Nadie sabe qué cosa es el comunismo
y eso puede ser pasto de la censura
Nadie sabe que cosa es el comunismo
y eso puede ser pasto de la ventura

[No one knows what communism is
And that can be fodder for censorship
No one knows what communism is
And that can be fodder for fortune]

Silvio Rodríguez, *Reino de todavía*
(Kingdom Yet to Come), 1996

A common question people ask about Cuba is what the future holds and whether change is on the horizon. Speculating on the subject, however, is rarely an innocent exercise, and it relies upon assumptions that this book has questioned throughout. One of those assumptions is that Cuba is always in transition, in crisis, and on the verge of radical change with its future linked to the health and well-being of the Castro brothers, who are the glue that keeps the system together.[1] In this scenario, Cuban socialist ideology is static, fixed, ahistorical or, conversely, always fully subject to the whims of the Cuban leadership and the pressures of realpolitik. Thus the question of what the future holds for Cuba is not simply a request for more information. It reflects an ideological position, whereby only certain events, actions, and decisions constitute real change and the past is seen as always the same.

Instead of speculating on Cuba's future, then, this book ends by asking how the preceding chapters help to reframe Cuba's past and present, to rethink Cuban socialist ideology, but also ideology elsewhere and in general. It explores these questions by returning to a specific place, Plaza Carlos III, the mall from the previous chapter, and to three specific later moments, 2007, 2011, and 2013. These moments appear to trace socialism's decline in Cuba, yet, if examined through the framework offered by this book, tell a *different* story of loss, but also of socialist continuity and transformation.

Returning to Plaza Carlos III

By January 2007, the U.S. dollar was no longer in circulation and the slogan at Carlos III, "Sales + Economy + Efficiency = Revolution," had been replaced with a much lengthier and moralizing description of revolution, taken from the beginning of a May 1, 2000, speech of Fidel Castro.[2] It read:

> Revolution is an awareness of historic moments
> It is changing everything that must be changed
> It is full equality and liberty; it is to be treated
> And to treat everyone as a human being
> It is emancipating ourselves by ourselves and with
> our own efforts; it is to challenge powerful dominant forces inside
> and outside of the national and social sphere
> It is defending values in which one believes
> at the price of whatever sacrifice; it is modesty, disinterest,
> altruism, solidarity and heroism; it is to struggle
> with audacity, intelligence, and realism; it is never lying
> nor violating ethical principles; it is a deep conviction
> that there does not exist a force in this world powerful enough to
>   crush
> the power/force/strength [*fuerza*] of truth and ideas. Revolution is
>   unity,
> independence, it's fighting [*luchando*] for our dreams
> of justice for Cuba and for the world, which is the foundation
> of our patriotism, our socialism and our
> internationalism.

Near this lengthy passage in the entranceway sat a bust of Jose Martí accompanied by a sign with three of his quotations from various sources. They read: "These times now are ones of honor. There is an eagerness to be useful, and sacrifice becomes fashionable again"; "For me, all just and generous men have been born in Cuba"; and "There is no impossible task, only incapable men."³ All of these quotations in some way emphasize the voluntarist and individualist elements of Cuban socialism. Latin American Marxism in general has found in voluntarism and nationalism a way to forge a specifically Latin American path to socialism independent of the directives of the Soviet Comintern.⁴ Che linked voluntarism and *Cubania* to a form of individualism, where one distinguished oneself by thinking beyond one's immediate self-interest and by modeling selfless behavior presumably latent in all Cubans.⁵ Linking Cuban nationalism to voluntarism functioned quite successfully during the first years of revolution to mobilize Cubans to work for the construction of socialism, at a time when material incentives were scarce and revolutionary fervor was high. This voluntarist element became harder to maintain as the years wore on, as chapters 3 and 5 illustrated.

While the first two phrases of Martí are less well known, the last quotation emphasizing the primacy of individual initiative and fortitude in taking on difficult tasks, often appears on the walls of state-run firms, large and small (see figure 11). So too does the lengthy passage from Fidel quoted above, which also would serve to introduce the guidelines of the Sixth Party Congress in 2011 (see figure 12). State-run firms, which are oriented toward production, national industry, and the satisfaction of basic needs (bakeries often display Fidel's definition of revolution), do not pose the same challenges to Cuban socialism as a place like Carlos III, geared to consumption and with items for sale that are often not of national origin. It is hard to see the immediate connection between buying goods produced abroad and the spirit of messages like the ones above and others from Fidel Castro at Carlos III in 2007 like "We can construct the most just society in the world" and "Revolution is unity, independence, and fighting for our dreams of justice for Cuba and for the world."⁶

By 2007, then, snappy slogans reducing revolution to a mathematical equation had been replaced by a labored and detailed description of all the moral virtues of revolution. Unlike "sales + economy + efficiency = revolution," fabricated by bureaucrats working for CIMEX in an attempt to reconcile mall culture with revolution, now the slogans on the signs drew from purer sources in an effort to remind shoppers of that other, original revolution, of Martí and Fidel, which demanded individual and collective struggle, discipline, sacrifice, and strength. One could shop at a place like Carlos III, but thinking always of one's revolutionary principles, which did not include consumption, sales, economy, and efficiency even as means to the end of so-

Conclusion · 195

Fig. 11. "No Hay Tareas Imposibles sino Hombres Incapaces. Revolución es convicción profunda de que no existe fuerza en el mundo capaz de aplastar la fuerza de la verdad y las ideas" (There are not impossible tasks, just incapable men. Revolution is the profound conviction that there exists no force strong enough to crush the force of the truth and of ideas). "Base Receptora Suchel Cetro, Firmes y Anclados con la Revolución" (Suchel Cetro Receiving Station, firmly anchored to the revolution). Sign outside Cuban state soap company, Regla, Havana province, 2011.

cialism. If earlier signs linking revolution to purely market-oriented activities showed the corrupting possibilities of attempting to synchronize ideology with practice, the 2007 sign reciting traditional revolutionary rhetoric in a place of buying and selling showed how a concern with purity could make ideology appear as a historical relic and irrelevant to the present.

These are the high stakes of ideological negotiation that this book has explored. It has examined instances of ideological discussion and contestation over the meaning and relationship of socialist principles within and between different spheres. Far from providing an exhaustive account of all ideological debate in Cuba, however, the book's framework of spheres opens up the possibility for further research in Cuba, by focusing on other spheres—such as the sphere of work or education—that did not receive focused attention

Fig. 12. "Revolución es unidad, . . ." (Revolution is unity . . .). Sign on factory wall, Havana, 2013.

here. Seen as different modes of ideological negotiation, Cuban socialist ideology no longer appears monolithic, as either genuine because it is entirely consistent with practice, or entirely false because it clashes with it. Instead one sees it as made up of different principles or strands that can be combined in different ways or emphasized more at particular historical junctures. The issue is one of emphasis, rather than complete abandonment or complete faith. Viewing it this way allows us to see the dangers, the risks, and the costs of these ideological negotiations, which are unavoidable, but which make political actors no less accountable for the ways they choose to navigate a particular ideology. Once it becomes a question of ideological negotiation, rather than whether or not ideology exists, we can see the politics in Cuba that are hidden by a framework that juxtaposes reality to ideology, idealism to pragmatism, principled to opportunistic, or theory to experience. We can see the politics of the state and its institutions (including the press), but also the politics that escapes the state's control and that is occluded by an account that sees the state as the owner of ideology and the people as either passive recipients or liberal opponents.

As I have shown throughout the book, ideology does not silence political activity, but rather enables it. The Cuban state's adherence to and preoccupation with ideology makes critique possible. Even at its most repressive, the Cuban state has historically justified repression ideologically, and this justification has opened up avenues for contestation, in spite of the Cuban state's prohibition of most organized opposition. The inevitable contradictions of political ideologies are preferable to ideological silence (which should be distinguished from its impossible absence).

In this light, the relatively few attempts by May 2011 to link the word "revolution" to the shopping experience at Carlos III can be seen as yet another ideological strategy, with its own sets of costs and consequences. In 2011, the entranceway had no more signs about the meaning of revolution or busts of Martí. In the entrance was a giant photo of the Cuban national baseball team and then, a little further in, a large yellow sign for Western Union, to whose offices the remittances from the United States had increased after Obama's election. Money received was money to be spent. Hanging banners celebrated Mother's Day. A large electronic sign at one end of the mall flashed images of Visa and Mastercard and then "GIRON: 50 years of Victory" followed by a invitation to visit the stores of Carlos III and information about what items were available for sale (spices, condiments, parts and accessories for cars).

By this time, the stores of the mall at Carlos III had also changed. While in 2007 the number of "everything for a dollar" stores had increased, in spite of the fact that the U.S. dollar had been taken out of circulation in 2004, by 2011 there were no longer any "everything for a dollar" stores at all. The dual-currency system remained, with the peso-convertible serving as the currency of exchange inside Carlos III, and the Cuban peso outside on the streets. Prices at Carlos III were still prohibitive for anyone without access to foreign currency, although the amount of remittances flowing into the country had grown dramatically.[7] The contrast between the merchandise available at Carlos III and outside was less stark than in 2000, when items on the street were largely limited to homemade food and coffee. The streets of Cuba looked more like other Latin American countries. Part of the new economic plan launched by the Sixth Party Congress in April 2011 included the authorization of more self-employment, while state employees deemed redundant were laid off.[8] Residential entrances now housed *cuentapropistas* selling a wide range of items including CDs, plumbing parts, shoes, and clothing (see figures 13, 14, and 15).

Back inside Carlos III, one explicitly political sign hung above the food court and exhorted people: "TO WORK HARD" (A TRABAJAR DURO) (see figure 16). These were the words with which Raúl Castro had ended his address

Fig. 13. *Cuentrapropista* storefronts on Carlos III Avenue, Havana, 2013.

Fig. 14. *Cuentrapropista* selling clothing and sneakers on stoops outside private homes on Carlos III Avenue, Havana, 2013.

Fig. 15. *Cuentrapropista* selling clothing, Carlos III Avenue, Havana, 2013.

Fig. 16. "A Trabajar Duro" (To work, hard). Sign at the entrance to Plaza Carlos III, Havana, 2011.

to the Sixth Party Congress in which the leadership had outlined its new economic plan to give the market an greater role in what was previously the domain of the state. By this time, Fidel Castro had passed power to Raúl, who was elected president in early 2008. Carlos Lage, credited with reforms of the 1990s that rescued Cuba from the worst of the Special Period, had been passed over for a leadership position and was also no longer part of the government, having renounced his Party and state positions in March 2009, following Fidel Castro's public criticism of unnamed Cuban officials.[9] The challenges of balancing growth with equity that Lage faced in the 1990s, however, persisted.

Among the *lineamientos* of the Sixth Party Congress, efficiency played an important role, but so did work itself. There were no references to Che, but the message resonated with his insistence that Cubans must work hard not just for the immediate satisfaction of material needs, but for the nation's wealth and international reputation.[10] Indeed, Raúl ended the Fourth Congress of the Union of Communist Youth in April 2010 insisting that "the economic battle today constitutes, more than ever, the principle task and the focus of the ideological work of the cadres, because on the economy depends the sustainability and preservation of our social system."[11] The future of socialism in this case rested not on sales, economy, and efficiency, but on hard work, which was valued not because it enabled people to buy things, but because it contributed to the nation's wealth.

Thus, while socialist ideology within the mall was more silent than ever before, even here, there was an echo back to previous debates within socialist ideology, particularly from the 1970s and 1980s, about the importance of work within a socialist society, and specifically in a country like Cuba, where labor was a particularly valuable commodity. This was no less true in the 21st century, when economists emphasized the importance of Cuba's educated and skilled labor force to the future of the Cuban economy, and when many of Cuba's professionals were emigrating out of frustration with low salaries in Cuba and with the fact that increasingly education had little bearing on wealth. *Cuentapropistas* and farmers had significantly more earning power and wealth than professionals. This had consequences for racial inequality as well.[12] On the one hand, this was something relatively new. There was now much more dramatic wealth inequality that in some ways broke down according to traditional class and racial hierarchies due to the importance of remittances. This inequality also challenged the professional hierarchy that partly but not completely challenged prerevolutionary class structures, because professionals were no longer at the higher end of the earnings scale. On the other hand, these changes were by this time familiar enough to Cuban history that the ideological arsenal already contained certain ways of grappling with the questions these new problems posed. Specifically, as we saw chapter 3, Cuban socialist ideology had already had to consider the question of how to get people to work for something other than material gain, but also how to use material incentives to foster greater moral consciousness, rather than less.

One of the aims of this book has been to show that many of the problems and dilemmas facing Cuba at particular historical junctures have histories to them. These, as noted in chapter 1, go back to the 19th century, even if 19th-century Cuban nationalist and proto-nationalist political thought does not lend itself clearly to either supporters or critics of the Cuban Revolution. The history of Cuban socialist ideology is not just a history of grand patriotic slogans splashed across billboards in an effort to distract Cubans from their everyday woes, but one of attempting to articulate, actualize, legitimate, and understand an alternative socioeconomic system. The Cuban state has always faced the challenge of how to create new socialist subjectivities. Importantly, Cubans themselves, as individuals and collectives—whether they be the socialist workers discussed in chapter 3, the socialist intellectuals of chapters 2 and 4, or the revolutionary artists of chapter 5—too have engaged with this question of socialist subjectivity, sometimes or in part as a response to state coercion, but also out of commitment to the revolution, which those outside the Cuban leadership have also viewed as their own. Cuba's apparent abandonment of those egalitarian elements of its system is a story of loss, not just for the Cuban leadership or for Cuban elites, but for these others as well. The leadership's appeals to ideology during times of economic liberalization and restructuring run the risk of making socialist ideology appear at best stale and outdated, and at worse a cover for authoritarian neoliberalism. However, ideological silence signals neither the absence of power and a weakening of the state, nor the abandonment of socialist ideology on the part of those in other spheres of Cuban society.

By January 2013, there were even fewer political references within the walls of Carlos III. The flashing electronic sign announcing all of the store's offerings occasionally flashed a reminder of Cuba's "Five Heroes" sentenced for espionage and doing time in the United States and the most recent cause around which the Cuban state called upon the Cuban people to rally, via slogans on billboards and posters in state institutions (see figure 17). The "Five Heroes" replaced the earlier campaign around the return of Elian and complemented the ever-present project of pointing to the injustice of the U.S. blockade. Frequently it is argued that this reliance on foreign threats to unify the Cuban people is evidence of the flimsiness of Cuban socialist ideology. Given the arguments of this book, however, one might see it instead as an example of a weaker version of Cuban socialism, based on a negative definition of the principle of unity and buttressed by the existence of threats to Cuban sovereignty.

The entranceway of Carlos III now reminded shoppers of the upcoming holiday. There were even more *cuentapropistas*, not just outside of Carlos III but throughout Havana, where entranceway after entranceway of buildings on busy thoroughfares was occupied by Cubans selling their wares. As one Havana resident and friend put it, parts of Havana looked like any other capitalist country. Havana's streets had an even higher volume of American cars, which, due to the loosening of restrictions on selling certain goods across provincial lines, were being brought to Havana from other provinces to serve as taxis as part of the burgeoning zone of self-employment. Cuba was never an entirely socialist country, but rather, as one Cuban friend put it, "a country with certain socialist characteristics," yet there is little question that a variety of important changes over the past ten years mean those characteristics are fewer and fewer.

Fig. 17. "Será hoy, será mañana, volveran! Libertad para los cinco héroes: Antonio, Fernando, Gerardo, Ramón, René (Whether it's today or tomorrow, they will return! Liberty for the five heroes). Slogan on a wall calling for the release of the Cuban Five, Regla, Havana Province, 2013.

Evidence of this decline include talk of getting rid of the *libreta* or providing it on an as-needed basis; massive layoffs of state employees that began after the Sixth Party Congress and affected large numbers of workers who were considered redundant and were left without any means of support to replace their lost salaries; the closing of the Escuelas del Campo long charged with instilling the socialist and *Martiano* work ethic in younger generations; greater economic, social, racial, and gender inequality; compromised public services even in the area of health, which has long been the pride and joy of the Cuban socialist project; increased self-employment; and the expansion of the sphere of buying and selling, including what is permissible to buy and sell (e.g., private homes).[13]

The official understanding of these changes seems to have shifted. The leaders in the 1990s presented Cuba's situation as one of crisis and their policies as ones of stabilization. Now they present changes taking place in Cuba in the last ten years not just as reactions to external shocks during special times, but also as more permanent adjustments. The leadership no longer presents market liberalization as a temporary measure, and as of the Sixth Party Congress in 2011 set about to address the inefficiencies of economic centralization and bureaucratization. Economic practices previously deemed unacceptable under socialism, or tolerable only as temporary measures, now seem to be permanent parts of the Cuban landscape. Even here, however, rather than a complete abandonment of socialist principles, there is a return to an emphasis on the socialist principle of "from each according to his ability, to each according to his work," as opposed to "from each according to his ability, to each according to his need."[14]

Dilemmas made most apparent in the 1990s also remained in 2013. Recent market liberalization, as in the 1990s, has not been accompanied by political opening for the most part. Freedom of information, assembly, and movement is still restricted. There have been some significant policy shifts. In 2008, Cubans were permitted to own cell phones and stay in hotels. In 2010, the government released the dissidents that still remained in jail from the 2003 "crackdown," when the Cuban government jailed, tried, and convicted seventy-five dissidents for violating rarely used laws related to Cuban national sovereignty.[15] Most recently, the hated exit visa was abolished. Yet on the whole the same problem of economic liberalization without political pluralization raised in chapter 5 remained, but in even more dramatic form. In the name of preserving socialism, by the end of the first decade of the 21st century, the Cuban leadership was indirectly encouraging a neoliberal definition of civil society as the realm of economic activities rather than political participation. The transformation of the public realm into one of buying and selling, and the closing of state enterprises ostensibly focused on production, suggests a future of mercantile capitalism that can hardly be a long-term solution to Cuba's economic woes or provide the conditions for a robust and engaged debate about the meaning of Cuban socialism in the 21st century. Even the government's most recent turn against market activities does not represent a clear embrace of an inclusive socialist project. This criticism, however, does not simply point to the tension between theory and practice, or between ideology and reality. It is not that the Cuban state fails to respect the autonomy of civil society, but rather that it fails to distinguish between civil society and political society. This type of criticism becomes available when we understand socialist ideology in Cuba as constituted by principles that are negotiated within different spheres of a society.

When it comes to the Cuban state in particular, there often appear to be two choices, especially for those on the left (whether Cuban revolutionaries or fellow travelers from elsewhere): They can either offer naive, unquestioning, and/or hypocritical support of policies they would likely criticize and refuse to tolerate in other countries; or they can admit that liberalism is the only system that provides an avenue for freely engaged and meaningful political activity. Throughout this book, we have seen the different ways that Cubans invested in the revolution and Cuban socialism have challenged particular state policies or the state's understanding of Cuban socialist ideology, but in ways that escape the opposition between a liberal understanding of politics and an authoritarian one, between opportunism and naive idealism. Chapter 4, for instance, showed how Cuban intellectuals provided several examples of this: they argued that diversity rooted in the principles of Cuban socialism was more conducive to the preservation of socioeconomic equality than a political unity based on blind conformity with the words of the leadership; that the autonomy of the academic sphere did not imply an apolitical or purely theoretical academic sphere; that difference might be used to fight inequality rather than perpetuate it.

The framework proposed by this book suggests an alternative way to criticize the Cuban state, but it also enables us to see socialist ideology elsewhere in Cuba. It allows us to see that Cuba's public spaces are far more than spaces of burgeoning mercantile capitalism. For instance, a mile from Carlos III toward Old Havana one arrives at the Parque de la Fraternidad, where a variety of sexual and political currents converge—prostitutes charging in Cuban pesos, *jineteras*, police, and taxi drivers. Nearby, at the Parque Central, one can find a wide range of discussions taking place that are either directly or indirectly political. Anthropologist Benjamin Eastman has documented, for instance, the ways that baseball, and specifically player defections, becomes an occasion to discuss other issues related to "the deprivations and distortions of an economy and cultural order in crisis."[16]

In addition to these types of informal spaces for political discussion, are more formal ones, with only some or no affiliation with the Cuban state. For instance, Desiderio Navarro's Centro Teórico-Cultural Criterios, which he founded in 2003 in Havana, hosts a variety of events related to the cultural and political sphere in Cuba.[17] The center is also home to Navarro's journal and editorial collective *Criterios*, founded in 1972, which translates and publishes theoretical work on literature, art, culture, and society. Additionally, in 2002, the offices of the magazine *Temas*, whose offices are across the street from those of *Criterios*, began holding "Last Thursday" (Último Jueves), a monthly panel on a selected cultural, political, or social issue.[18] These spaces can be contentious in ways that highlight how difficult ideological work takes place in spaces not entirely monopolized by the Cuban state, neither fully supporting nor attacking party lines, but contesting the meaning of lived Cuban socialism.

By way of examples, we might consider some of the diversity of political positions that events in these spaces have generated. Panelists of *Temas*'s "Last Thursday" event have included former CEA members Rafael Hernández and Aurelio Alonso, as well as other academics and intellectuals. While the panelists might express views in disagreement with the state, the event is not without its exclusions, especially of those affiliated with illegal organizations on the island. In 2009, for instance, members of Arco Democrático Progresista, a coalition of social democratic opposition parties many of whose members are black, were refused entrance to an event dealing with racism on the island. The same year, Yoani Sanchez, who is undoubtedly the most well-known opposition Cuban blogger, was refused entrance to the meeting and was expelled after it was discovered that she had entered in disguise. According to one participant, not all those who disagreed with her views were pleased with her expulsion, having been deprived of the opportunity to debate her. For him and others, the greatest threat to socialism is not dissidence, but the absence of discussion, to which they attribute socialism's decline in the former Soviet Union.[19]

These contentious events, and reactions to them, illustrate how lively political contestation within Cuba can be flattened when it is put into the context of Cuban-U.S. state relations, whether that is done by the Cuban state or those opposing it internationally. When the Cuban state prohibits opposition groups and dismisses them as mercenaries of the U.S. government, it casts them as being opposed to all the principles of Cuban socialism, though many of them are not. The U.S. defense of these opposition groups often does little to challenge this. Thus international responses to certain Cuban government actions, such as the near universal condemnation of the 2003 crackdown on Cuban dissidents, tend to assert the primacy of individual rights, but in doing so, they allow the Cuban state to lay claim to principles of Cuban *socialism* that it does not in fact have exclusive ownership over.[20] Another consequence of this emphasis on individual rights is that only those dissidents who actively espouse this ideology are given international recognition. Their voices come to be the true voices of Cuba, when in fact spaces of debate (the blogosphere is one example) are occupied by a diversity of voices from within Cuba.[21]

Paradoxically though, even some of the activities of opposition groups aimed at bringing liberal democracy and free-market capitalism to Cuba in fact promote through their practices an understanding of the public sphere as a place of debate and political participation, rather than mere buying and selling. Antonio G. Rodiles's organization, Estado de SATS, aims to create "a space where different visions, from art, thought and social activism, come together and affect the sketch of a diverse and plural Cuba."[22] In addition, the legacy of socialism in Cuba and the ways in which public spaces were reconfigured and expanded led to an understanding of the public that has served to defy both liberal understandings of the political and the narrowly defined institutional venues of the Cuban government.[23] One particularly illustrative example of an attempt not simply to encourage debate, but also to occupy and create "public spaces," is the multidisciplinary Cuban arts collective known as Omni Zona Franca.[24] Another example is that of the urban gardens that have sprung up since the Special Period. The group Red Observatorio Crítico makes up part of what political scientist Samuel Farber has referred to as the "new critical left."[25] They have called for a delinking of socialism from the state and Party leadership, instead calling for worker self-management and cooperatives.[26] In all these cases, despite the forces working against a robust practice and understanding of the public sphere in Cuba—forces that at times include the Cuban state and its enemies as strange bedfellows—we see that Cubans within and without the state engage in the work of ideology by debating the meaning of Cuban socialism and claiming its legacy.

Ideology in Cuba and Beyond

Cuban socialist ideology was not simply the creation of Fidel Castro or an ideology invented to legitimate authoritarian rule. The various articulations of Cuban socialist ideology have drawn on a variety of strands of political thought, both indigenous and foreign. But Cuban politics is no more or less driven by ideology than is politics anywhere else. What is distinct about Cuba, however, is the degree to which the government explicitly *deploys* socialist ideology in its management of Cuban society. While it is tempting to interpret the government's use of ideology solely as a means of political repression, this interpretation ignores several important aspects of Cuban politics. One is the degree to which activity in other spheres of society has contributed to the development of Cuban socialism. Actors in these spheres have articulated Cuban socialist ideology in order to make demands upon the Cuban state, to respond to calls to consider the meaning of Cuban socialism, or to challenge the state's understanding of it. While the leadership imposes decisions from the top down, it has also, in many cases, made decisions on the basis of such demands. Thus, while the political structure has always been more or less vertical with an emphasis on mobilization rather than participation, focusing on these formal structures means failing to see the political activities and ideological contributions of other spheres of Cuban society that have not been so easily disciplined or contained. This is no less true today than it was in the 1960s.

This brings us to a second aspect of Cuban society the significance of which is occluded by the equation of ideology with repression: While the state's emphasis on ideology disqualifies certain participants from the outset, it has also facilitated ideological discussion and debate that is not simply a reflection or repetition of the party line. Moreover, the state's insistence upon explicitly linking its policies to ideology has made it accountable in a way that a tacit reliance on ideology would not have. When viewed this way, the tacit ideological dynamics of liberalism and liberalization may not necessarily be any less politically troubling than political repression that is ideologically justified. Both impede accountability through silence about their ideological foundations.

The Cuban state's emphasis on ideology also has international implications. It is not just the content of Cuban socialist ideology that is threatening to the United States and other liberal democracies. These states are also threatened by the Cuban government's insistence upon highlighting the ideological nature of *all* political discourse. This insistence forces liberals, who often hide behind a veil of universalism, to concede the ideological character of liberalism, and with it the particular interests and agendas it represents.[27]

The Cuban state and other spheres of Cuban society highlight the working of ideology in distinct, and at times dramatic, ways. My account of Cuban socialism is useful for understanding ideology in other socialist and non-liberal-democratic countries where ideology is presumed to be state-imposed and subject to the state's whims; but also and perhaps more surprisingly in liberal democracies where ideology is either naturalized or used as an epithet. In the United States, liberalism is so naturalized that we don't recognize it as such. North American students intuitively understand the arguments of John Locke because they already think this way. To teach his work as an ideology, and so to expose the hegemonic pretensions of liberalism, does little to deter its adherents from believing that they have freely chosen it from the marketplace of ideas and that other actors have as well.

At the same time, in the United States there is a general distrust of ideology as such. Politicians frequently criticize each other for allowing their ideology to get in the way of serving the best interests of their constituents. For instance, in 1998, then New York state representative Charles Schumer criticized his Republican opponent and incumbent senator, Alfonse M. D'Amato, for supporting cuts in federal spending on education (part of Newt Gingrich's "Contract with America"). According to Schumer, D'Amato had "let [New York's] children down" and was "putting ideology ahead of people."[28] In 2007, in response to mounting foreclosures, Schumer criticized President Bush's refusal to "adjust his radical ideology" and approve legislation allowing a temporary lifting of portfolio caps on the biggest mortgage associations.[29] President Obama, who has presented himself as a representative of a postpolitical, postracial, and postideological politics, also shares this view of ideology as harmful and corrupting to the political process. Thus, in his 2009 President's Message on the budget he declared: "We need to put tired ideologies aside, and ask not whether our government is too big or too small, or whether it is the problem or the solution, but whether it is working for the American people."[30]

As this study of Cuba has shown, however, it is ideology that enables us to make political (and pragmatic) judgments at all. Moreover, it facilitates not just judgment but action. Maligning ideology as a source of political corruption and intransigence has gone hand in hand with the increasingly rightward creep of U.S. political discourse and policy and has allowed a particular ideology to function all the more undetected. The source of this disdain for ideology, however, was not U.S. conservatism but, rather the belief of liberals that the welfare state and the incorporation of the working class and unions into an industrialized society geared toward consumerism made ideologies of the Left and Right irrelevant to U.S. politics.[31]

Against postpolitical conceptions of politics according to which ideology is supposed to be transcended, this study has suggested that ideology is the *language* of politics and to do away with ideology is to do away with politics. Thus, the question in Cuba and elsewhere is not whether a particular policy or political project is ideological or not; but rather, whether the ideology being used to explain and justify it is compelling or not. How well does the ideology make sense of that project's history, its current goals. and what it aims for in the future? How well does it reflect upon itself? A strong version of ideology is still subject to criticism, but it is the strength of the ideology, rather than its weakness, or worse, its supposed absence, which provides the foundation for political contestation and negotiation.

Slavoj Žižek points to the irony that contemporary defenders of capitalism, faced with mounting evidence of its failures, resort to the same defenses for which they criticized socialist ideologues in Eastern Europe and the Soviet Union, whereby all failures of the system reflected failures in practice, rather than ideology.[32] Ideology, then, operates in "fetishistic mode" to make the truth tolerable.[33] It rationalizes, contains, and thus depoliticizes politics. As we saw in Cuba, however, exposing a particular ideology as hegemonic can produce other results. Exposing the pervasiveness of an ideology can open it up to examination and rearticulation. If Althusser is right that there is nothing outside of ideology, this study suggests that much can be done within it. When examined as relations of principles the variability, and also the limits, of a particular ideology can be seen. Similarly, when its operation and negotiation is examined within specific sites, one can see how ideologies are informed by related sets of norms and considerations.

Applying this framework to the United States would highlight the ways that ideology functions not just as a legacy of the Founding Fathers or a reflection of the Constitution, but as a set of principles that frame, without determining, political debates and their outcomes. In doing so, my framework puts responsibility for politics back in the hands of all North Americans by showing its actors how they participate in ideological reproduction, as both its products and its agents. It allows us to see ideology outside the platforms of the two main parties or in the words and decisions of the U.S. president, and to see how ostensibly oppositional movements on both the right and the left are operating within this same ideology. Just as in Cuba, seeing the operation of shared principles need not lead to facile conclusions about the futility of political action and radical change. Instead, it might force greater accountability and political responsibility upon political actors as agents of an ideology that, just as in Cuba, is neither blindly followed nor freely chosen.

Just as the framework of spheres opens up new avenues for studies in Cuba, so too might it be a fruitful way to study how ideology works outside the government in the United States and elsewhere. When we consider ideology the domain of the state or nation, civil society becomes a depoliticized remnant. Unlike a focus on civil society, which presumes a space in which predetermined identities defend their interests, the framework of spheres recognizes the ways in which subjectivities emerge out of participation in specific activities associated with different spheres. Unlike the term "civil society," the term "spheres" does not presume opposition or conformity at the outset, nor does it privilege the private as the realm of freedom. Unlike the concept of the "public sphere" or its cousin, the "counterpublic," the concept of spheres also does not privilege the public as the site of politics nor presume that inclusion is the ultimate goal of participation within these spheres.[34]

This book's approach to examining political dynamics and forms of political thinking specific to Cuba also makes Cuba seem less exceptional. It opens up new ways of seeing how ideology, understood as a set of principles and practices, functions elsewhere. Moreover, a focus on spheres allows us to consider the distinct norms and constraints governing specific spheres, and thus the different modes of political participation.

Taken together, the insights in this book contribute to a view of ideology as a lived practice that organizes and gives life to politics. In doing so, it opens up, rather than forecloses, possibilities for the future. This opening is particularly important to consider in a place like Cuba, where ideology can resist neoliberal and state ideologies, masked as pragmatism.

Postscript

As this book goes to press, speculation about dramatic change in Cuba seems more warranted than ever. In mid-December 2014, following over a year of secret talks between the two countries, President Obama announced the restoration of diplomatic relations with Cuba. While the embargo still remains, and would have to be lifted by Congress, immediate changes included easing restrictions on travel, remittances, and trade with Cuba and the return of three imprisoned Cuban spies. Cuba, in turn, promised to allow greater Internet access, released 53 jailed dissidents and, on humanitarian grounds, returned Alan Gross, the jailed USAID contractor. The traditional Republican supporters of the previous policy of embargo, isolation, and destabilization rushed to condemn the decision as a naïve faith that economic opening would translate into political opening in Cuba. Obama, however, received praise from large swaths of the political establishment for his willingness to break with a tired policy that had long failed to produce the results it promised. In general, however, both praise and criticism operated within the same overall ideological framework wherein freedom and change is equated with the introduction of free market capitalism and liberal democracy. Evidence thus far suggests, however, that while most Cubans welcome these recent diplomatic changes, there is no direct link between economic liberalization and a thriving political sphere. The stifling of political protest can coincide with the arrival of Netflix, which announced operations in Cuba at the beginning of February 2015. It is my hope though that this book will encourage Cuba watchers to see socialist ideology outside the state, to look for politics in unexpected places, and to understand Cuban society as diverse and multifaceted, both in spite of, and because of, its socialist legacy.

Notes

Introduction

1. Ethnographic evidence includes material gathered from interviews and informal conversations. Between 1996 and 2014, I visited the island fifteen times, often for two months at a time. Between 2000 and 2002, I was there for a period of seven consecutive months with a student visa, and another period of six consecutive months. I spent the most time in Havana, and mostly in the neighborhoods of Habana Vieja, Centro Habana, and El Vedado, with some extended stays in the town of Velasco in Holguín Province. The book, as a consequence, focuses on events and people in Havana.

2. Michael Freeden, *Ideologies and Political Theory: A Conceptual Approach* (Oxford: Clarendon Press, 1996), 4.

3. Ibid., 1.

4. The phrase has been used to describe the particularly difficult years between 1990 and 1996, but the question of when and if this "Special Period" ended is the subject of much discussion.

5. The term "functionary" refers to those who are official representatives of the Cuban government and who spoke largely on behalf of it. Some functionaries are also academics. My observations are based primarily on conversations with the following people: a Cuban diplomat in Havana, an academic at the Escuela Superior del PCC, "Nico López," who was working on a doctoral thesis entitled "The Ideology of the Revolution in Cubanology: Reflections from Cuba," and a student liaison at the University of Havana who was assigned to me as part of my independent study at the University of Havana's Department of Philosophy and History. I do not include all Cuban academics within the category of functionary, in spite of the tendency to presume that their status as employees of organs of the Communist Party makes them so.

6. For a textual version of this position, see, for instance, Darío L. Machado Rodríguez, *Cuba: Ideología revolucionaria* (Havana: Editora Política, 2000).

7. Most of the academics with whom I have met were at one time or another associated with the Center for the Study of America. Some, such as Haroldo Dilla, have since left Cuba.

8. See Stuart Hall's discussion of the meaningfulness of bourgeois political economy and the ways that it accounts for real concrete practices under the capitalist mode of production. Stuart Hall, "The Problem of Ideology: Marxism without Guarantees," in *Critical Dialogues in Cultural Studies*, ed. David Morley and Kuan-Hsing Chen (New York: Routledge, 1996), 25–46.

9. Antoni Kapcia, *Cuba: Island of Dreams* (New York: Berg, 2000), 15.

10. Mona Rosenthal, *Inside the Revolution: Everyday Life in Socialist Cuba*, ed. Roger Sanjek (Ithaca: Cornell University Press, 1997), 156.

11. Michel Foucault, "Truth and Power," in *Power/Knowledge: Selected Interviews and Other Writings, 1972–1977*, ed. Colin Gordon (New York: Vintage, 1980), 119.

12. Michel Foucault, *Discipline and Punish: The Birth of the Prison*, trans. Alan Sheridan (New York: Vintage Books, 1995).

13. Louis Althusser, "Ideology and the State," in *Lenin and Philosophy and Other Essays*, trans. Ben Brewster (New York: Monthly Review Press, 1971), 171.

14. Terry Eagleton, *Ideology: An Introduction* (London: Verso, 1991), 8.

15. E.g., Banu Bargu, *Starve and Immolate: The Politics of Human Weapons* (New York: Columbia University Press, 2014); George Ciccariello-Maher, *We Created Chávez: A People's History of the Venezuelan Revolution* (Durham: Duke University Press, 2013); Juliet Hooker, *Race and the Politics of Solidarity* (Oxford: Oxford University Press, 2009); Megan Thomas, *Orientalists, Propagandists, and Illustrados: Filipino Scholarship and the End of Spanish Colonialism* (Minneapolis: University of Minnesota Press, 2012).

16. E.g., Leigh Jenco, "'What Does Heaven Ever Say?' A Methods Centered Approach to Cross-Cultural Engagement," *American Political Science Review* 101 (2007): 741–55; Farah Godrej, "Towards a Cosmopolitan Political Thought: The Hermeneutics of Interpreting the Other," *Polity* 41 (2009): 135–65.

17. Freeden, *Ideologies and Political Theory*, 26.

18. These organizations included the Committees for the Defense of the Revolution (CDRs), Central Organization of Cuban Trade Unions (CTC), National Association of Small Farmers (ANAP), Union of Communist Youth (UJC), Federation of Mid-Level Students (FEEM), Federation of Cuban Women (FMC), and the Federation of University Students (FEU).

19. Julia E. Sweig, *Cuba: What Everyone Needs to Know* (Oxford: Oxford University Press, 2009), 46.

20. Carollee Bengelsdorf, *The Problem of Democracy in Cuba: Between Vision and Reality* (New York: Oxford University Press, 1994), 85.

21. Marx characterized civil society as a sphere of concrete inequality that allowed the state to claim to represent the universal interest. Equal citizenship was based on an abstract equality that only existed because all real distinctions based on wealth, rank, class, etc. had been displaced onto the realm of civil society. Karl Marx, "On the Jewish Question," in *The Marx-Engels Reader,* edited by Robert C. Tucker (New York: W.W. Norton, 1972), 26–52.

22. E.g., Juan Carlo Espinosa, "Civil Society in Cuba: The Logic of Emer-

gence in Comparative Perspective," *Cuba in Transition*, vol. 9 (Washington, DC: Association for the Study of the Cuban Economy, 1999), 346–67; Juan J. López, *Democracy Delayed: The Case of Castro's Cuba* (Baltimore: John Hopkins University Press, 2002); Gerardo Otero and Janice O'Bryan, "Cuba in Transition? The Civil Sphere's Challenge to the Castro Regime," *Latin American Politics and Society* 44, no. 4 (Winter 2002): 29–57.

23. Bert Hoffman, "Cuba: Civil Society within Socialism—and Its Limits," in *Modern Political Culture in the Caribbean*, ed. Holger Henke and Fred Reno (St. Augustine, Trinidad and Tobago: University of the West Indies Press, 2003), 311.

24. See, for instance, Amelia Rosenberg Weinreb's discussion of "unsatisfied citizen consumers" in *Cuba in the Shadow of Change: Daily Life in the Twilight of the Revolution* (Gainesville: University Press of Florida, 2009) and Ted Henken, "Condemned to Informality: Cuba's Experiments with Self-Employment during the Special Period (the Case of the Bed and Breakfasts)," *Cuban Studies* 33 (2002): 1–29.

25. Irving Louis Horowitz, "Epilogue," in *Cuban Communism, 1959–1995*, ed. Irving Louis Horowitz (New Brunswick, NJ: Transaction, 1995), 862–64. Julie Marie Bunck takes a similar position in *Fidel Castro and the Quest for a Revolutionary Culture in Cuba* (University Park: Pennsylvania State University Press, 1994).

26. Wayne S. Smith, "Castro: To Fall or Not to Fall," in Horowitz, *Cuban Communism*, 699.

27. Jorge I. Domínguez, "Why the Cuban Regime Has Not Fallen," in Horowitz, *Cuban Communism*, 698; Marifeli Pérez-Stable, "The Invisible Crisis: The Exhaustion of Politics in 1990s Cuba," in *Toward a New Cuba: Legacies of a Revolution*, ed. Miguel Angel Centeno and Mauricio Font (Boulder: Lynne Rienner, 1997), 25; Damián J. Fernández, *Cuba and the Politics of Passion* (Austin: University of Texas Press, 2000).

28. As with the rest of Latin America under neoliberalism, an increase in the number of NGOs could be understood not necessarily as a flowering of democratic participation, but instead as a product of a weakened state eager to pass on or share its former responsibilities to the public with nonstate organizations. George Yúdice, *The Expediency of Culture: Uses of Culture in the Global Era* (Durham: Duke University Press, 2003), 107; David Harvey, *A Brief History of Neoliberalism* (Oxford: Oxford University Press, 2005), 78.

29. The category is called Asociación Científica Jurídacamente Autonoma y no Gubernamental (Juridically Autonomous and Nongovernmental Scientific Association).

30. Alexander I. Gray and Antoni Kapcia, "Setting the Stage for a Discussion of Cuban Civil Society: The Nature of Cuban 'Communism' and the Revolution's Political Culture," in *The Changing Dynamic of Cuban Civil Society*, ed. Alexander I. Gray and Antoni Kapcia (Gainesville: University Press of Florida, 2008), 11.

31. Some of these NGOs have been relabeled "neogovernmental organizations," "national NGOs," or "controlled government organizations" because they were previously state institutions or made up of bureaucrats and others who previ-

ously worked for the state. Hoffman, "Cuba: Civil Society within Socialism," 307; Fernández, *Politics of Passion*, 133.

32. Many of these dissident groups prefer not to use the term "NGO," because such a label would appear to legitimate the Cuban government, although some did unsuccessfully seek legal recognition in the 1990s. Hoffman, "Cuba: Civil Society within Socialism," 308.

33. See, for instance, Fernández, *Politics of Passion*; and Gillian Gunn, "Cuba's NGO's: Government Puppets or Seeds of Civil Society?" Cuba Briefing Paper 7, Washington, DC: Center for Latin American Studies, Georgetown University, 1995.

34. For a discussion of the ways in which the ideological content of dissident organizations is obscured by the war of words, see chapter 3: "Sharing Principles of Unity, Nationalism, and Social Welfare: Diversity Among Dissidents," in Katherine Gordy, "The Theory and Practice of Ideology: Navigating the Principles of Cuban Socialism," PhD diss., Cornell University, 2005.

35. Michelle Marín-Dogan, "Civil Society: The Cuban Debate," in Gray and Kapcia, *Changing Dynamic*, 40–64.

36. Hoffman, "Cuba: Civil Society within Socialism," 311.

37. Jorge Acanda, "Sociedad civil y hegemonía," *Temas* 6 (1996): 87–93; Rafael Hernández, *Mirar a Cuba: Ensayos sobre cultura y sociedad civil* (Havana: Editorial Letras Cubanas, 1999).

38. Haroldo Dilla Alfonso, "Comrades and Investors: The Uncertain Transition in Cuba," in *Global Capitalism versus Democracy: Socialist Register 1999*, ed. Leo Panitch and Colin Leys (New York: Monthly Review Press, 1999); Haroldo Dilla and Philip Oxhorn, "The Virtues and Misfortunes of Civil Society in Cuba," *Latin American Perspectives* 29, no. 4 (2002): 11–30.

39. Sujatha Fernandes, *Cuba Represent! Cuban Arts, State Power and the Making of New Revolutionary Cultures* (Durham: Duke University Press, 2006).

40. Robin D. Moore, *Music and Revolution: Cultural Change in Socialist Cuba* (Berkeley: University of California Press, 2006), 7–9.

41. Ariana Hernández-Reguant, "Copyrighting Che: Art and Authorship under Cuban Late Socialism," *Public Culture* 16, no. 1 (2004): 24.

42. Adrian H. Hearn, *Cuba: Religion, Social Capital and Development* (Durham: Duke University Press, 2008).

43. P. Sean Brotherton, *Revolutionary Medicine: Health and the Body in Post-Soviet Cuba* (Durham: Duke University Press, 2012).

44. Katherine Gordy, "Beside the State: Anarchist Strains in Cuban Revolutionary Thought," in *How Not to Be Governed: Readings and Interpretations from a Critical Anarchist Left*, ed. Jimmy Casas Klausen and James Martel (New York: Lexington Press, 2011), 47–64.

45. People's different ways of talking about socialism do not map easily onto public acceptance of domination and private questioning and thus I do not rely upon James C. Scott's distinction between public and hidden transcripts in this study. James C. Scott, *Domination and the Arts of Resistance: Hidden Transcripts* (New Haven: Yale University Press, 2009).

Chapter 1

1. Antoni Kapcia points to this surprising absence in *Cuba: Island of Dreams*, 15.
2. See, for instance, Václav Havel, *Living in Truth* (Boston: Faber and Faber, 1990).
3. See, for instance, Theodore Draper, *Castro's Revolution: Myths and Realities* (New York: Frederick A. Praeger, 1962); Irving Louis Horowitz, "Epilogue," in *Cuban Communism*; but also more sensationalist works like Georgie Anne Geyer's *Guerrilla Prince: The Untold Story of Fidel Castro* (Boston: Little, Brown, 1991).
4. Richard Boucher of the U.S. State Department, for instance, justified the denial of visas to sixty-seven Cuban academics hoping to attend the Latin American Studies Association 2004 Congress, arguing that these academics were employees of the Cuban government and should not be permitted to come to the United States "to spout the party line" and "enjoy the free and open discussion" the country allowed. Boucher, "Cuba: Denial of Visas to Group of Cuban Academics/Basis for Decision," Washington, DC: U.S. Department of State, 2004.
5. See, for instance, José Luis Rodríguez García, *Crítica a nuestros críticos* (Havana: Editorial de Ciencias Sociales, 1988); and Hernán Yanes Quintero, "Comment," *Cuban Studies* 13, no. 2 (1983): 112–17.
6. See Carmelo Mesa-Lago, "On the Objectives and Objectivity of Cubanology: A Response to a Critic from Cuba," *Cuban Studies* 16, no. 1 (1986): 225–33. Mesa-Lago complains that those on the left criticize him for not recognizing the achievements of the revolution while those on the right criticize him for recognizing them too much and omitting the costs at which these achievements came.
7. See, for instance, Jorge I. Domínguez, "Twenty-Five Years of *Cuban Studies*," *Cuban Studies* 25 (1995): 7–22.
8. Carmelo Mesa-Lago, "Three Decades of Studies on the Cuban Revolution: Progress, Problems, and the Future," in *Cuban Studies since the Revolution*, ed. Damián J. Fernández (Gainesville: University Press Florida, 1992), 25.
9. Three groups in Cuba were key players in the struggle against Batista: The 26th of July Movement, headed by Fidel Castro, and based in both the Sierra and the cities; the Revolutionary Directorate (DR), based primarily in the cities; and the Popular Socialist Party (PSP), which gave its support late in the struggle. The first two groups did not openly espouse socialism.
10. Fidel Castro, "I Shall Be a Marxist-Leninist to the End of My Life," in *Selected Speeches of Fidel Castro*, 11–40 (New York: Pathfinder Press, 1979).
11. Daniel James, *Cuba: The First Soviet Satellite in the Americas* (New York: Avon, 1961), 84.
12. See, for instance, James, *Cuba: First Soviet Satellite*; Nathaniel Weyl, *Red Star over Cuba: The Russian Assault on the Western Hemisphere* (New York: Devin-Adair, 1960); Fulgencio Batista, *Cuba Betrayed* (New York: Vantage Press, 1962).
13. Draper, *Castro's Revolution*, 34–42; Hugh Thomas, *Cuba; or The Pursuit of Freedom*, updated ed. (New York: Da Capo Press, 1998), 814; Kapcia, *Cuba: Island of Dreams*; Carlos Franqui, *Family Portrait with Fidel*, trans. Alfred MacAdam (New York: Random House, 1981), 152–53.

14. Draper, *Castro's Revolution*; Theodore Draper, *Castroism: Theory and Practice* (New York: Frederick A. Praeger, 1965); Andrés Suárez, *Cuba: Castroism and Communism, 1959–1966*, trans. Joel Carmichael and Ernst Halperin (Cambridge: MIT Press, 1967); Edward González, *Cuba under Castro: The Limits of Charisma* (Boston: Houghton Mifflin, 1974).

15. Draper, *Castroism*, 49. Draper continues to be cited for his "revolution betrayed" thesis. See, for instance, Marifeli Pérez-Stable, *The Cuban Revolution: Origins, Course, and Legacy* (New York: Oxford University Press, 1993).

16. Gonzalez, *Cuba under Castro*, 41.

17. Draper, *Castro's Revolution*, 75.

18. Draper, *Castroism*, 50.

19. E.g., Suárez, *Cuba: Castroism and Communism*.

20. Ibid., 238.

21. According to Carlos Franqui, "The Soviet Union was very interested in what it called 'the heroic island,' a revolutionary people, fighting against imperialism, only ninety miles away from the United States." Franqui, *Family Portrait with Fidel*, 184. According to Cuban sociologist Aurelio Alonso, it is not until 1972 that the Soviet Union referred to Cuba as a socialist country. Prior to that it was described as, for instance, "a progressive country" or "a revolutionary country," but not a socialist country. Aurelio Alonso, interview with author, Havana, Cuba, February 15, 2002.

22. Kapcia, *Cuba: Island of Dreams*, 132.

23. Nelson P. Valdés, "Ideological Roots of the Cuban Revolutionary Movement," Occasional Paper No. 15, Glasgow: Institute of Latin American Studies, University of Glasgow, 1975, 5.

24. Kapcia, *Cuba: Island of Dreams*, 132.

25. Susan Eva Eckstein, *Back from the Future: Cuba under Castro* (Princeton: Princeton University Press, 1994).

26. Ernesto "Che" Guevara, "A New Culture of Work," in *Che Guevara Reader: Writings on Politics and Revolution*, ed. David Deutschmann (New York: Ocean Press, 2003), 142.

27. Cited in ibid., 6.

28. Lee Lockwood, *Castro's Cuba, Cuba's Fidel* (Boulder: Westview Press, 1990), 154.

29. Ibid., 155.

30. In his 1961 speech "I Shall Be a Marxist-Leninist to the End of My Life," Castro also attributes certain prejudices against Communism to his education, but also argues that they were not able to entirely "instill the counter-revolutionary spirit" in him. Fidel Castro, "I Shall Be a Marxist-Leninist," 38.

31. Lockwood, *Castro's Cuba, Cuba's Fidel*, 156.

32. Ibid., 162.

33. Fidel Castro Ruz, *La historia me absolverá: Discurso ante la sala primera de urgencia de la audiencia de Santiago de Cuba, 16 de octubre de 1953* (Havana: Editora Política, 1994), 31–32.

34. Lockwood, *Castro's Cuba, Cuba's Fidel*, 164.
35. Ibid., 159.
36. Franqui, *Family Portrait with Fidel*, 152. Draper also expressed concern with approaches that relied upon most recent events to make sense of the entire revolutionary process. "Each stage has told us more and more, but no stage has told us so much about the whole process as the latest one." *Castro's Revolution*, 115.
37. Ibid., 161.
38. Examples include C. Wright Mills, *Listen Yankee: The Revolution in Cuba* (New York: McGraw-Hill, 1960); Jean-Paul Sartre, *Sartre on Cuba* (New York: Ballantine Books, 1961); Richard Fagen, *The Transformation of Political Culture in Cuba* (Stanford: Stanford University Press, 1969); Leo Huberman and Paul Sweezy, *Cuba: Anatomy of a Revolution* (New York: Monthly Review Press, 1961).
39. Sartre, *Sartre on Cuba*, 153.
40. Fagen, *Transformation of Political Culture*, 163.
41. Ibid., 56.
42. Ibid., 35.
43. Ibid., 57. Other more contemporary examples might also apply. For instance, the campaign to return Elián González to Cuba appealed not to explicitly socialist values, but rather to the importance of family.
44. During my time in Cuba, I often heard older people speak proudly of their participation in the Literacy Campaign. The documentary *Maestra*, directed by Catherine Murphy, shows the ways that the campaign transformed women participants, in particular, many of whom reported that the experience gave them a sense of freedom and escape from conventional gender norms.
45. Louis Pérez Jr., review of *The Limits of Charisma: Cuba under Castro*, by Edward Gonzalez, in *The Americas* 3, no. 3 (January 1976): 489.
46. See, for instance, Huber Matos, *Cómo llegó la noche* (Barcelona: TusQuets, 2004); Franqui, *Family Portrait with Fidel*; Guillermo Cabrera Infante, *Mea Cuba* (New York: Farrar, Straus and Giroux, 1994).
47. Frank Fernandez, *Cuban Anarchism: A History of a Movement*, trans. Charles Bufe (Tuscon: See Sharp Press, 2001); Franqui, *Family Portrait with Fidel*.
48. María del Pilar Díaz Castañón, *Ideología y revolución: Cuba, 1959–1962* (Havana: Editorial de Ciencias Sociales, 2001), 16; Jorge Ibarra, *Cuba: 1989–1958, Estructura y procesos sociales* (Havana: Editorial de Ciencias Sociales, 1995), 236; Jorge Ibarra, *Prologue to Revolution: Cuba, 1898–1958* (Boulder: Lynne Rienner, 1998), 181.
49. Díaz Castañón, *Ideología y revolución*, 29. All translations not otherwise attributed are the author's. Díaz Castañón's call to look to the work of Gramsci reflected a more general interest in his work on the part of Cuban intellectuals at that time.
50. Antonio Gramsci, "State and Civil Society," in *Selections from the Prison Notebooks*, ed. and trans. Quintin Hoare and Geoffrey Nowell Smith (New York: International, 1971), 247.
51. As Michael Freeden points out in *Ideologies and Political Theory*, the "ideological baggage" of classical liberalism is often present in the work of political philosophy.

52. Antonio Gramsci, "The Study of Philosophy," in *Prison Notebooks*, 324, 232.

53. Draper's argument also survived the 1960s in other forms, particular in popular arguments that attribute the revolution's survival to Fidel Castro's ability to focus attention on U.S. hostility during those times when socialism and the government are in crisis. Draper is cited, at times with an insufficient understanding of his argument, to emphasize Fidel Castro's opportunism. Georgie Anne Geyer, for instance, refers to Draper to argue that ideology for Fidel Castro was simply a suit that he put on to hide what were at base "sheer Machiavellian power tactics." *Guerrilla Prince*, 52.

54. Kapcia also notes the parallel between these earlier works and Medin in *Cuba: Island of Dreams*, 6.

55. Tzvi Medin, *Cuba: The Shaping of Revolutionary Consciousness*, trans. Martha Grenzback (Boulder: Lynne Rienner, 1990), 167.

56. Louis A. Pérez Jr. also suggests that the United States "served as both a standard and a source of modernity and offered an alternative framework within which to envision the dismantling of colonial structures." *On Becoming Cuban: Identity, Nationality, and Culture* (Durham: University of North Carolina Press, 1999), 62.

57. Medin, *Cuba: Shaping of Revolutionary Consciousness*, 53.

58. Ibid., 14.

59. Michel-Rolph Trouillot, *Silencing the Past: Power and the Production of History* (Boston: Beacon Press, 1995), 50.

60. According to a list put out by the Commission of Human Rights of the Christian Democratic Party of Cuba, there are nine organizations in Martí's name, four in Varela's name, three in Máximo Gómez's name, two in Antonio Maceo's name, and three in Ignacio Agramonte's name.

61. John M. Kirk, *José Martí: Mentor of the Cuban Nation* (Tampa: University Presses of Florida, 1983), 3.

62. Louis A. Pérez, "History, Historiography, and Cuban Studies: Thirty Years Later," in Fernández, *Cuban Studies since the Revolution*, 63.

63. Fidel Castro Ruz, *José Martí: El autor intelectual* (Havana: Editora Política, 1983), 235.

64. Kirk, *José Martí*, 12.

65. Castro, "I Shall Be a Marxist-Leninist," 33; Donald E. Rice, *The Rhetorical Uses of the Authorizing Figure: Fidel Castro and José Martí* (New York: Praeger, 1992), 82.

66. Roberto Fernandez Retamar, "Martí en su (tercer) mundo," in *Ensayo de Otro Mundo* (Santiago de Chile: Editorial Universitaria S.A., 1969), 36–37.

67. Ibid., 50.

68. Ibid., 50–51.

69. Carlos Rafael Rodríguez, "José Martí," in *Letra Con Filo*, vol. 3 (Havana: Ediciones Union, 1987), 215.

70. Ibid., 216–19.

71. Ibid., 219.

72. Kirk, *José Martí*, 14, 16.

73. Cited in ibid., 16.
74. Carlos Rafael Rodríguez, "Nuestro Tiempo," in *Letra Con Filo*, 555.
75. See, for instance, their characterizations in Eduardo Torres-Cuevas and Oscar Loyola Vega, eds., *Historia de Cuba 1492–1898: Formación y liberación de la nación* (Havana: Editorial Pueblo y Educación, 2001), 136, 47; and Isabel Monal and Olivia Miranda Francisco, eds., *Pensamiento cubano: Siglo XIX*, vol. 1 (Havana: Editorial de ciencias sociales, 2002), 186, 392.
76. Louis A. Pérez, "Introduction," in *Slaves, Sugar, and Colonial Society: Travel Accounts of Cuba, 1801–1899*, ed. Louis Pérez (Wilmington, DE: Scholarly Resources, 1992), xxi.
77. Between 1764 and 1868, 752,000 slaves were introduced into Cuba. Levi Marrero, *Cuba, economía y sociedad: azucar, ilustración y conciencia (1762–1868)*, 15 vols., vol. 1 (Madrid: Editorial Playor, 1983), 2.
78. Marrero, *Cuba, economía y sociedad*, 34. For a detailed account of Aponte's endeavors, see José Luciano Franco, *La conspiración de Aponte* (Havana: Consejo Nacional de Cultura, 1963) and Matt D. Childs, *The 1812 Aponte Rebellion in Cuba and the Struggle against Atlantic Slavery* (Chapel Hill: University of North Carolina Press, 2006).
79. Marrero, *Cuba, economía y sociedad*, 34; Pérez, "Introduction," in *Slaves, Sugar*, xv.
80. Pezuela worked to actualize the decree throughout 1854, while adding others promising to free all slaves for whom the planters did not have a title. Given that titles only began to be used in 1820, the decree automatically called for the liberation of all slaves brought in prior to that date. Hugh Thomas, *The Cuban Revolution*, 2nd ed. (New York: Harper and Row, 1971), 221. *Emancipados* were Africans who had been freed from captured slave ships but kept "under direct control of the government, treated almost exactly like slaves, and employed in a limited number of enterprises." Rebecca Scott, *Slave Emancipation in Cuba: The Transition to Free Labor, 1860–1899* (Princeton: Princeton University Press, 1985), 223.
81. Félix Varela, "Consideraciones sobre el estado actual de la isla de Cuba (1824)," in Monal and Miranda Francisco, *Pensamiento cubano, Siglo XIX*, 282.
82. José M. Hernández, "¿Fue Varela el primer revolucionario de Cuba?" *Cuban Studies* 28 (1998): 78.
83. José Antonio Saco, "Ideas sobre la incorporación (1848)," in *Contra la anexión: Recopilación de sus papeles, con prólogo y ultílogo de Fernando Ortíz*, ed. Fernando Ortíz (Havana: Instituto Cubano del Libro, Editorial de Ciencias Sociales, 1974), 100.
84. José Antonio Saco, "Origen del movimiento anexionista en Cuba," in Ortíz, *Contra la anexión*, 87.
85. José Antonio Saco, "Párrafos de la 'Réplica a V. Vásquez Queipo en la polémica con J. A. Saco sobre el incremento de la población blanca en Cuba' (1847)," in Ortíz, *Contra la anexión*, 85.
86. José Antonio Saco, "Párrafos del 'Paralelo entre la Isla de Cuba y algunas colonías inglesas' (1837)," in Ortíz, *Contra la anexión*, 79.

87. Saco, "Ideas sobre la incorporación de Cuba en los Estados Unidos (1848)," in Ortíz, *Contra la anexión*, 96.
88. Ibid.
89. Ibid., 97.
90. Ibid.
91. Thomas, *The Cuban Revolution*, 226.
92. Contracts were made with Gallegos, Canary Islanders, Irishmen, and Indians from the Yucatán, but the Chinese were the most coveted source of labor, with 130,000 introduced between 1853 and 1872. Thomas, "Cuba, c. 1750–c. 1860," in *Cuba: A Short History*, ed. Leslie Bethell (New York: Cambridge University Press, 1993), 18. In 1862, Chinese slaves made up 10% of all slaves. In 1877, they made up 17.5%. Juan Pérez de la Riva, *Demografía de los culíes chinos: 1853–1874* (Havana: Pablo de la Torriente Editorial, 1996), 43.
93. Philip S. Foner, *Antonio Maceo: The "Bronze Titan" of Cuba's Struggle for Independence* (New York: Monthly Review Press, 1977), 15.
94. Carlos Manuel de Céspedes, "Declaración de independencia (1868)," in Monal and Miranda Francisco, *Pensamiento cubano, Siglo XIX*, 4.
95. Ibid., 5. "We have unanimously agreed to name a single leader who will direct operations using his full capacities, and is authorized especially to name a second and other subordinates that he needs in all the areas of administration for as long as the war lasts."
96. Carlos Manuel de Céspedes, "Decreto de 27 de diciembre de 1868: Carlos Manuel de Céspedes, Capitán General del Ejército Libertador de Cuba y encargado de su gobierno provisional (1868)," in Monal and Miranda Francisco, *Pensamiento cubano, Siglo XIX*, 6.
97. Ibid.
98. Matt D. Childs notes that while the Cuban black intellectual Walterio Carbonell and others traced Cuban national identity back to figures like Aponte, the mostly white leadership of the Cuban revolution has not. However, on occasion, notes Childs, Aponte has received greater recognition, such as in a 1962 issue of *Bohemia*, which portrayed him as a precursor to the 1959 revolution. Childs, *The 1812 Aponte Rebellion*, 11–12. See also Walterio Carbonell, *Cómo surgió la cultura nacional* (Havana: Ediciones Bachiller, Biblioteca Nacional José Martí, 2005).
99. See Ignacio Agramonte y Loynaz, "Decreto de Extinción de la Esclavitud (1869)," in Monal and Miranda Francisco, *Pensamiento cubano, Siglo XIX*.
100. Ignacio Agramonte y Loynaz, *Patria y mujer* (Havana: Publicaciones del Ministerio de Educación, 1942), 33.
101. Ibid., 36.
102. Ibid., 38–40.
103. Ibid., 47.
104. These texts include the following: "Comunicación del Comité Revolucionario del Camagüey a la Junta Revolucionaria de la Habana (1869)"; "Decreto de extinción de la esclavitud"; "A representantes de la Cámara del Camagüey"; "Carta a José Manuel Mestre," in Monal and Miranda Francisco, *Pensamiento cubano, Siglo XIX*.

105. Agramonte, "Comunicación del Comité Revolucionario," 15.
106. Luis E. Aguilar, "Cuba, c. 1860–c. 1930," in Bethell, *Cuba: A Short History*, 25.
107. Foner, *Antonio Maceo*, 20.
108. Ibid., 7, 17.
109. Thomas, *The Cuban Revolution*, 255.
110. Aguilar, "Cuba, c. 1860–c. 1930," 26.
111. Foner, *Antonio Maceo*, 74.
112. Ibid., 75.
113. Thomas, *The Cuban Revolution*, 266.
114. Aguilar, "Cuba, c. 1860–c. 1930," 26–27.
115. At that time, Puerto Rico was losing many of the 1868 concessions. Foner, *Antonio Maceo*, 92.
116. Ibid., 93.
117. Ibid., 94.
118. Antonio Maceo, "Proclama ¡Viva Cuba Independiente! (1879)," in *Ideología política: Cartas y otros documentos* (Havana: Editorial de Ciencias Sociales, 1998), 46.
119. See, for instance, Antonio Maceo, "A los cubanos de color," in *Ideología política*, 112.
120. Maceo, "Al General José Lamothe," in *Ideología política*, 108.
121. Aguilar, "Cuba, c. 1860–c. 1930," 27.
122. Kirk, *José Martí*, 77.
123. José Martí, "Bases del Partido Revolucionario Cubano (1892)," in Monal and Miranda Francisco, *Pensamiento cubano, Siglo XIX*, 299.
124. See, for instance, José Martí, "Lectura en la reunión de emigrados cubanos (1880)," in Monal and Miranda Francisco, *Pensamiento cubano, Siglo XIX*.
125. Gerald E. Poyo, *"With All, and for the Good of All": The Emergence of Popular Nationalism in the Cuban Communities of the United States, 1848–1898* (Durham: Duke University Press, 1989), 52.
126. C. Neale Ronning, *José Martí and the Émigré Colony in Key West: Leadership and State Formation* (New York: Praeger, 1990), 4.
127. Poyo, *With All*, 70.
128. Ibid., 71. Labor issues were even more important in the newer Florida émigré colony of Ybor City. Ibid., 81.
129. Ibid., 82.
130. Rice, *Rhetorical Uses*, 25.
131. José Martí, "Our America," "My Race," and "The Montecristi Manifesto," in *Selected Writings*, ed. and trans. Esther Allen (New York: Penguin, 2002), 288–95, 318–20, 337–45.
132. José Martí, "Tributes to Karl Marx, Who Has Died" in *Selected Writings*, 130–39.
133. Martí, "Our America," 291.
134. Jeffrey Belnap, "Headbands, Hemp Sandals, and Headdresses: The Dialectics of Dress and Self Conception in Martí's 'Our America,'" in *José Martí's "Our America": From National to Hemispheric Cultural Studies*, ed. Jeffrey Belnap and Raúl Fernández (Durham: Duke University Press, 1998), 191–209.

135. Martí, "Our America," 290.
136. Enrico Mario Santí, "'Our America,' the Gilded Age, and the Crisis of Latinamericanism," in Belnap and Fernández, *José Martí's "Our America,"* 179–90.
137. Martí, "Our America," 296; "My Race," 318–20.
138. Alejandro de la Fuente, *A Nation for All: Race, Inequality, and Politics in Twentieth Century Cuba* (Chapel Hill: University of North Carolina Press, 2001), 29–30.
139. Kapcia, *Cuba: Island of Dreams*, 6, 22.
140. Ibid., 6.
141. Ibid., 15.
142. Ibid., 14.
143. Ibid., 17.
144. Ibid., 137.
145. Karl Mannheim, *Ideology and Utopia: An Introduction to the Sociology of Knowledge* (New York: Harcourt, 1936), 151.

Chapter 2

1. Che Guevara, "Algo nuevo en América: A la sesión de apertura del Primer Congreso Latinamericano de Juventudes, 28 de julio de 1960," in *Che Guevara habla a la juventud* (Havana: Casa Editora Abril, 2001), 29.
2. Che also hinted at the Marxist nature of the revolution in the pages of the newly created magazine of the Cuban armed forces, *Verde Olivo*, where he contributed a column under the pseudonym *Francotirador*.
3. Guevara, "Algo nuevo en América," 30.
4. Examples of firsthand accounts, although not necessarily written at the time of the events, include Franqui, *Family Portrait with Fidel*; Cabrera Infante, *Mea Cuba*; Reinaldo Arenas, *Before Night Falls* (New York: Viking, 1993). Examples of secondary accounts include Bunck, *Castro and the Quest*; Medin, *Cuba: Shaping of Revolutionary Consciousness*; Linda S. Howe, *Transgression and Conformity: Cuban Writers after the Revolution (*Madison: University of Wisconsin Press, 2004).
5. Howe, *Transgression and Conformity*.
6. Moore, *Music and Revolution*, 68.
7. Néstor Kohan, "*Pensamiento Crítico* y el debate por las ciencias sociales en el seno de la Revolución Cubana," in *Crítica y teoría en el pensamiento social latinoamericano*, ed. Fernanda Beigel (Buenos Aires: CLACSO, 2006), 389–437.
8. Louis A. Pérez, *Cuba: Between Reform and Revolution* (New York: Oxford University Press, 1988), 319. As advocates of the "revolution betrayed" argument liked to point out, 1950s Cuba ranked high in terms of several standard-of-living indexes. However, there were also high levels of unemployment and dramatic socioeconomic disparities between rural and urban Cuba, between black and white Cubans, and between workers and the middle and upper classes. For a discussion and evidence of the rural/urban inequalities in 1950s Cuba, see Samuel Farber, *The Origins of the Cuban Revolution Reconsidered* (Chapel Hill: University of North

Carolina Press, 2006), 9–21; Pérez-Stable, *The Cuban Revolution*, 27–31; and Richard Fagan, *The Transformation of Political Culture in Cuba* (Stanford: Stanford University Press, 1969), 22–23.

9. Michael Chanan, *Cuban Cinema* (Minneapolis: University of Minnesota Press, 2004), 118.

10. Díaz Castañón, *Ideología y revolución*, 16.

11. Moore, *Music and Revolution*.

12. Fuente, *A Nation for All*, 273, 28; Mark Q. Sawyer, *Racial Politics in Postrevolutionary Cuba* (Cambridge: Cambridge University Press, 2006), 53–55. The narrowing of private spaces was less complicated and its negative effects more pronounced when it came to Cuba's gay population, who, with the reduction of the private spaces into which they had previously been pushed, found themselves increasingly in a public realm that was hostile and unwelcoming both in terms of rhetoric and policy. Ian Lumsden, *Machos, Maricones, and Gays: Cuba and Homosexuality* (Philadelphia: Temple University Press, 1996), 62. Yet, even in this case, the story is complicated by the ways that the universal provision of certain services might have buffered gay Cubans from private forms of discrimination.

13. Culture, then, was not commodified, but rather called upon to do work usually left to politics and economics. I use George Yúdice's understanding of culture as a resource here, although Yúdice discussed culture as a resource in the context of neoliberalism. Yúdice, *The Expediency of Culture*, 2.

14. Doreen Weppler-Grogan, "Cultural Policy, the Visual Arts, and the Advance of the Cuban Revolution in the Aftermath of the Gray Years," *Cuban Studies* 41 (2010): 144.

15. Chanan, *Cuban Cinema*, 119. See, also, Herbert L. Matthews, *The Cuban Story* (New York: George Brazillier, 1961) for an account of his role as a *New York Times* reporter in publicizing the Cuban Revolution.

16. Sandra del Valle, "Cine y Revolución: La política cultural del ICAIC en los sesenta," *Perfiles de la cultura Cubana*, January–February 2008, 1.

17. Pamela Maria Smorkaloff, *Readers and Writers in Cuba: A Social History of Print Culture* (New York: Garland, 1997), 83.

18. Ambrosio Fornet, "La lucha por la hegemonía," intervention from the presentation of the book *Quinquenio Gris*. Document received from personal communication with Desiderio Navarro, June 2011.

19. Kepa Artaraz, *Cuba and Western Intellectuals since 1959* (New York: Palgrave Macmillan, 2009), 34.

20. Franqui, *Family Portrait with Fidel*, 129.

21. By the end of 1959, few of the members of the first provisional government cabinet, which "assembled the best of liberal Cuba," remained. Pérez-Stable, *The Cuban Revolution*, 62. Within months of taking power, the prime minister, José Miró Cardona, a lawyer and professor at the University of Havana, resigned and was replaced by Fidel Castro. In mid-July, the first provisional president, Judge Manuel Urrutia Lleó, resigned and was replaced Osvaldo Dorticós Torrado, who would remain as president until 1976. British historian Hugh Thomas describes the

period between 1959 and 1961 as "The Eclipse of the Liberals." *Cuba; or The Pursuit of Freedom*, 1065–66.

22. Franqui, *Family Portrait with Fidel*, 80. They criticized the old Communists for being too dependent on Moscow and for being guilty of collaborating with Batista.

23. Ibid. Throughout 1959 and 1960, *Diario de la Marina*, *Prensa Libre*, and *Avance* and other papers criticized the revolution or provided space in their pages for others to do so. In December 26, 1959, the Union of Newspaper Printers required newspapers to include footnotes, called *coletillas*, criticizing those articles or editorials that were not in agreement with the government. The newspapers *Avance* and *El País* were shut down in January and February 1960 for failing to comply with this new regulation. In May 1960, the last large-scale national opposition papers, *Diario de la Marina* and *Prensa Libre*, were shut down. Thomas, *Cuba; or the Pursuit of Freedom*, 1261, 1268, 1281.

24. Franqui, *Family Portrait with Fidel*, 17.

25. Ernesto Juan Castellanos, "El diversionismo ideológico del rock, la moda y los enfermitos," conference paper presented at Centro Teórico-Cultural, Havana, on October 31, 2008. Available at http://www.criterios.es/pdf/9castellanosdiversionismo.pdf.

26. Chanan, *Cuban Cinema*, 133.

27. Cited in Castellanos, "El diversionismo ideológico," n. 2.

28. Chanan, *Cuban Cinema*, 138.

29. Ibid., 15.

30. José Quiroja, *Cuban Palimpsests* (Minneapolis: University of Minnesota Press, 2005), 116; Juan Carlos Quintero Herencia, *Fulguración del espacio: Letras e imaginario institucional de la Revolución Cubana (1960–1971)* (Rosario: Beatriz Viterbo, 2002).

31. This understanding of the political—as irreducible to the ideological, the economic or the moral, etc.—is one various political theorists have articulated. See Carl Schmitt, *The Concept of the Political* (Chicago: The University of Chicago Press, 1996).

32. Castro Ruz, *Palabras a los intelectuales* (Havana: Departmento de ediciones de la Biblioteca Nacional "José Martí," 1991), 5.

33. Ibid

34. Ibid., 6.

35. Quintero Herencia, *Fulguración del espacio,* 351.

36. Castro, *Palabras a los intelectuales*, 8.

37. Ibid., 9.

38. Ibid., 21.

39. Ibid., 13.

40. Ibid., 13–14.

41. Ibid., 16.

42. Ibid., 18.

43. Ibid., 23.

44. Ibid.

45. Ibid., 29.

46. Alfredo Guevara had been an activist in the urban underground and a member of the Communist Youth League in the 1950s before joining the 26th of July Movement. He had also been part of the journal *Nuestro Tiempo*, started in 1954, which published emerging Latin American writers and was guided by the principle of bringing the people to art.

47. "Conclusiones de un debate entre cineastas cubanos," in *Polémicas culturales de los 60*, ed. Graziella Pogolotti (Havana: Editorial Letras Cubanas, 2006), 17–22. Originally published in *La Gaceta de Cuba* 2, no. 23, August 3, 1963.

48. Ibid., 18–19.

49. Ibid., 21–22.

50. Alfredo Guevara, "Sobre un debate entre cineastas cubanos," in Pogolotti, *Polémicas culturales,* 23–25. Originally published in *Cine Cubano* 14–15, October–November 1963.

51. Ibid., 24.

52. Juan Blanco, "Los herederos del oscurantismo," in Pogolotti, *Polémicas culturales*, 7. Originally published in *La Gaceta de Cuba* 2, no. 15, April 1, 1963.

53. Ibid., 8.

54. Julio García Espinosa, "Vivir bajo la lluvia," in Pogolotti, *Polémicas culturales,* 10. Originally published in *La Gaceta de Cuba* 2, no. 15, April 1, 1963.

55. Ibid., 11–12.

56. Edith García Buchaca, "Consideraciones sobre un manifiesto," in Pogolotti, *Polémicas culturales,* 26–27. Originally published in *La Gaceta de Cuba* 2, no. 28, October 18, 1963.

57. Ibid., 29.

58. Ibid., 34.

59. Mirta Aguirre, "Apuntes sobre la literatura y el arte," in Pogolotti, *Polémicas culturales*, 62, 70. Originally published in *Cuba Socialista* 3, no. 26, October 1963.

60. Ibid., 45, 65.

61. Ibid., 43.

62. Ibid., 53, 59.

63. Sergio Benvenuto, "¿Cultura pequeñoburguesa hay una sola?" in Pogolotti, *Polémicas culturales*, 129–30. Originally published in *La Gaceta de Cuba* 3, no. 33, March 20, 1964.

64. Ibid., 133.

65. Aguirre, "Apuntes sobre la literatura," 53–54.

66. Ibid., 70.

67. Ibid., 62, 71.

68. Ibid., 71. García Buchaca also made this point. "Consideraciones sobre un manifiesto," 33.

69. Juan J. Flo, "¿Estética antidogmática o estética no Marxista?" in Pogolotti, *Polémicas culturales*. Originally published in *La Gaceta de Cuba* 3, no. 31, January 10, 1964.

70. Ibid., 108.
71. Ibid., 110.
72. Benvenuto, "¿Cultura pequeñoburguesa hay una sola?" 128, 130.
73. Ibid., 135.
74. Ibid., 138.
75. Ibid., 139.
76. Ibid., 140.
77. Jorge Fraga, "Ambigüedad de la crítica y crítica de la ambigüedad," in Pogolotti, *Polémicas culturales*, 39. Originally published in *La Gaceta de Cuba* 3, no. 31, January 10, 1964.
78. Ibid., 40.
79. Jorge Fraga, "¿Cuántas culturas?" in Pogolotti, *Polémicas culturales*, 73, 81. Originally published in *La Gaceta de Cuba* 2, no. 28, October 18, 1963.
80. Ibid., 73.
81. Ibid., 74.
82. Ibid., 75.
83. Ibid., 81.
84. Ibid., 79–82.
85. This latter point would have obvious appeal to those who drew inspiration not just from the works of Marx and Lenin, but from Latin American Marxists like José Carlos Mariátegui and Che Guevara, who emphasized the importance of myth, spirit, and will.
86. Fraga, "¿Cuántas culturas?" 80.
87. Ibid., 84.
88. Fraga, "Ambigüedad de la crítica," 36.
89. Fraga, "¿Cuántas Culturas?" 84.
90. Ibid.
91. Tomás Gutiérrez Alea, "Notas sobre una discusión de un documento sobre una discusión (de otros documentos)," in Pogolotti, *Polémicas culturales*, 99. Originally published in *La Gaceta de Cuba* 2, no. 29, November 5, 1963.
92. Julio García Espinosa, "Galgos y podencos," in Pogolotti, *Polémicas culturales*, 86. Originally published in *La Gaceta de Cuba* 2, no. 29, November 5, 1963.
93. Ibid., 87.
94. Ibid., 88.
95. Ibid., 91.
96. Ibid., 92.
97. Ibid.
98. "Preguntas sobre películas," in Pogolotti, *Polémicas culturales*, 145–48. Originally published in *Hoy*, December 12, 1963.
99. Ibid., 145.
100. Ibid., 147.
101. Ibid., 147–48.
102. "El camino trazado por nuestra revolución," in Pogolotti, *Polémicas culturales*, 159. Originally published in *La Tarde*, December 17, 1963.

103. "¿Cuáles son las mejores películas?" in Pogolotti, *Polémicas culturales*, 166. Originally published in *Hoy*, December 18, 1963.

104. "Respuesta a Alfredo Guevara (I)," in Pogolotti, *Polémicas culturales*, 181. Originally published in *Hoy*, December 19, 1963.

105. "Respuesta a Alfredo Guevara (II)," in Pogolotti, *Polémicas culturales*, 185. Originally published in *Hoy*, December 20, 1963; Consejo Nacional de Cultura, "El Consejo Nacional de Cultura contesta a Alfredo Guevara," in Pogolotti, *Polémicas culturales*, 189. Originally published in *Hoy*, December 20, 1963.

106. "Respuesta a Alfredo Guevara (III)," in Pogolotti, *Polémicas culturales*, 197–98. Originally published in *Hoy*, December 21, 1963.

107. "¿Qué películas debemos ver? Las mejores," in Pogolotti, *Polémicas culturales*, 150. Originally published in *Revolución*, December 14, 1963.

108. Ibid., 151.

109. "Eligen críticos *El ángel exterminador* y *Viridiana*," in Pogolotti, *Polémicas culturales*, 160. Originally published in *Revolución*, December 17, 1963.

110. "Carta de Severino Puente y de directores del ICAIC," in Pogolotti, *Polémicas culturales*, 152–57.

111. Ibid., 156.

112. "Alfredo Guevara responde a las 'aclaraciones,'" in Pogolotti, *Polémicas culturales*, 169. Originally published in *Hoy*, December 18, 1963.

113. Ibid., 170–71.

114. Ibid., 171.

115. Ibid., 172–73.

116. Ibid., 174.

117. Alfredo Guevara, "Declaraciones de Alfredo Guevara," in Pogolotti, *Polémicas culturales*, 200. Originally published in *Hoy*, December 21, 1963.

118. Tomás Gutiérrez Alea, "Donde menos se piensa salta el cazador . . . de brujas," in Pogolotti, *Polémicas culturales*, 112–13. Originally published in *La Gaceta de Cuba* 3, no. 33, March 20, 1964.

119. Ibid., 112.

120. Kohan, "*Pensamiento Crítico*," 17.

121. Artaraz, *Cuba and Western Intellectuals*, 48.

122. Ibid., 80.

123. Néstor Kohan attributes its closing to both external and internal causes. The Department of Economics remained on the grounds that it was a hard science.

124. Roque Dalton, René Depestre, Edmundo Desnoes, et al., "Diez años de la Revolución: El intellectual y la sociedad," *Casa de las Américas* 56 (September–October 1969): 6–48.

125. Lumsden, *Machos, Maricones and Gays*, 67.

126. Ibid., 72–73.

127. Chanan, *Cuban Cinema*, 312.

128. The non-Cuban participants in particular, perhaps because they had been engaged in revolutionary struggles for political power in their own home countries, articulated more traditional Marxist-Leninist views about the role of the intellec-

tual and his relationship to the masses. Roque Dalton, in particular, in spite of being a poet, seemed to have the least imaginative and most dogmatic contributions to the discussion.

129. Dalton et al., "Diez años de la Revolución," 7.
130. Ibid., 40.
131. Ibid., 12.
132. Ibid., 17.
133. Ibid.
134. Ibid., 18.
135. Ibid.
136. Ibid., 19.
137. Ibid., 21.
138. Ibid., 20.
139. Ibid., 22.
140. Ibid., 24.
141. Ibid., 22–23.
142. Ibid., 27.
143. Ibid., 29.
144. Ibid., 40.
145. Ibid., 31.
146. Ibid., 47.

Chapter 3

1. See, for instance, Carmelo Mesa-Lago, *Cuba in the 1970s: Pragmatism and Institutionalization* (Albuquerque: University of New Mexico Press, 1974); Mesa-Lago, "The Cuban Economy: Patterns of Continuity and Change," paper presented at the Latin American Studies Association Annual Meeting, Miami, 2000; Mesa-Lago, *Dialéctica de la Revolución Cubana: Del idealismo carismático al pragmatismo institucional*, Biblioteca cubana contemporánea (Madrid: Playor, 1979); Medin, *Cuba: Shaping of Revolutionary Consciousness*; Pérez-Stable, *The Cuban Revolution*.

2. Andrew Zimbalist, "Incentives and Planning in Cuba," *Latin American Research Review* 24, no. 1 (1989): 72.

3. For discussions of the Rectification Campaign, see Max Azicri, "The Cuban Rectification: Safeguarding the Revolution While Building the Future," in *Transformation and Struggle: Cuba Faces the 1990s*, ed. Sandor Halebsky and John M. Kirk (New York: Praeger, 1990); and Eckstein, *Back from the Future*.

4. *Tesis y resoluciones: Primer congreso del Partido Comunista de Cuba* (Havana: Editoral de ciencias sociales, 1978), 189.

5. Max Azicri, *Cuba Today and Tomorrow: Reinventing Socialism*, ed. John M. Kirk (Gainesville: University Press of Florida, 2000), 49.

6. Pérez-Stable, *The Cuban Revolution*, 85–86.

7. Edward Boorstein, *The Economic Transformation of Cuba* (New York: Modern Reader Paperbacks, 1968); and René Dumont, *Cuba: Socialism and Development*, trans. Helen R. Lane (New York: Grove Press, 1970).

8. Boorstein, *Economic Transformation of Cuba*.

9. Bertram Silverman, ed., *Man and Socialism in Cuba: The Great Debate* (New York: Atheneum, 1971), 3.

10. Zimbalist, "Incentives and Planning in Cuba," 68.

11. Guevara, "On the Budgetary Finance System," in Silverman, *Man and Socialism*, 134.

12. Robert M. Bernardo, *The Theory of Moral Incentives in Cuba* (University: University of Alabama Press, 1971), 27.

13. "The new generation [in Yugoslavia]—its mentality and attitudes have been and are being shaped by an economic system in which the goals and initiative of the individual are indistinguishable from those of capitalism. The types produced by such an environment range from the philistine through the unprincipled opportunist to the greedy corruptionist." Guevara quoted in ibid., 9.

14. Zimbalist, "Incentives and Planning in Cuba," 68.

15. Pérez-Stable, *The Cuban Revolution*, 86.

16. Zimbalist, "Incentives and Planning in Cuba," 68–69.

17. Pérez-Stable, *The Cuban Revolution*, 117–18.

18. CMEA was established in 1949 to facilitate political and economic relations between the socialist countries. Trade among the CMEA countries was conducted on a barter basis using a transferable ruble. No other country's currency was transferable. Ronald H. Linden, "Analogies and the Loss of Community: Cuba and East Europe in the 1990s," in *Cuba after the Cold War*, ed. Carmelo Mesa-Lago (Pittsburgh: University of Pittsburgh Press, 1993), 20.

19. Pérez-Stable, *The Cuban Revolution*, 118.

20. Guevara, "A New Culture of Work," 142–45.

21. Fidel Castro, "On the Events in Czechoslovakia," in *Selected Speeches*, 112.

22. Ibid., 110.

23. Ibid., 112.

24. Ibid., 123.

25. See Jorgé I. Domínguez, *To Make a World Safe for Revolution: Cuba's Foreign Policy* (Cambridge: Harvard University Press, 1989); and Piero Gleijeses, *Conflicting Missions: Havana, Washington, and Africa, 1959–1976* (Chapel Hill: University of North Carolina Press, 2002).

26. This may be less true today than it was between 1976 and 1986.

27. In 2013, Cuba ranked 171 out of 179 countries surveyed in the World Press Freedom Index. http://en.rsf.org/press-freedom-index-2013,1054.html. In 2004, it ranked 65 out of 166 countries surveyed. World Press Freedom Committee, Resolution on Cuba: Jailed Journalists in Cuba, May 3 2004, cited June 16, 2004; available from www.wpfc.org/index.jsp?page=Resolution%20-%20Cuba.

28. Unión de Periodistas de Cuba, "Dos fuerzas negativas: El bloqueo y los llamados independientes," web page, 2004, cited August 13, 2004; available from www.cubaperiodistas.cu/libertaddeprensa/principio3.htm.

29. Ibid.

30. How the Cuban readership responded to this press coverage is beyond the scope of this chapter.

31. *Tesis y resoluciones*, 192.

32. Ibid., 193.

33. In September 1976, *Granma* announced that the minimum conditions were being created to fully implement the program in January 1977. "Comenzó reunión operativa sobre cumplimiento de algunas tareas de cronograma," *Granma,* September 3, 1976.

34. "Creada la Comisión Nacional de Implantación del Sistema de Dirección y Planificación de la Economía," *Granma,* January 23, 1976.

35. "Inauguró Raúl tres cursos de la Escuela Nacional de Dirección de la Economía," *Granma,* March 4, 1976; Leon Choy and Alex Shelton, "Extenderán el pago por rendimiento a 230 mil trabajadores este año," *Granma,* April 2, 1976; and Alex Shelton, "Preparase Cuba para adoptar formas superiores de organización del trabajo," *Granma,* March 17, 1976.

36. "Efectuase en Santa Clara, Plenaria Provincial sobre la eficiencia económica ya la implantación del SDPE," *Granma*, September 1, 1977. This would be an enduring theme. In January 1979, for instance, *Granma* published the entire section of the First Congress dealing with the SDPE and reminded readers again that things would not go smoothly right away, just as they had reminded readers two years before.

37. Álvarez Quiñones, "Proponen mayor vinculación de investigaciones económicas con necesidades de la economía nacional," *Granma,* December 5, 1977.

38. "La indisciplina estadística atenta directamente contra la normal coordinación que debe existir entre todos los subsistemas que conforman el SDPE," *Granma*, December 20, 1979; José Norniella, "Por cada modelo del SIED utilizado para enviar información estadística, las empresas emiten 1,5 modelos no aprobados: Esta violación de la disciplina estadística se conoció por las auditores realizadas por el CEE en 403 empresas y unidades presupuestas acerca de la emisión de modelos no aprobados," *Granma,* December 18, 1979; and "Señalan incumplimientos y deficiencias en la aplicación del SDPE en la provincia Santiago de Cuba," *Granma,* December 25, 1979.

39. Zimbalist, "Incentives and Planning in Cuba," 72.

40. José Norniella, "La contabilidad en el socialismo (I): Su relación con la formación económico-social," *Granma,* August 4, 1976; José Norniella, "La contabilidad en el socialismo (II): La Contabilidad y el Sistema de Dirección y Planificación de la Economía," *Granma,* August 5, 1976; José Norniella, "La contabilidad en el socialismo (final): El contador y la implantación del Sistema de Dirección y Planificación de la Economía," *Granma,* August 6, 1976.

41. Norniella, "La contabilidad en el socialism (II)."

42. Norniella, "La contabilidad en el socialismo (I)."

43. Ibid.

44. Ibid.

45. Fernando Dávalos, "Entrará en vigor en enero del año próximo el nuevo Sistema de Información Estadística Nacional (SIEN)," *Granma,* September 4, 1976.

46. "Características de las empresas socialistas en Cuba (I)," *Granma,* January 12, 1977. "The material responsibility of firms in the utilization of available resources

and the completion of all its obligations constitute a powerful incentive for the collective of each firm to be vitally interested in the development of the firm's activities and in the greatest efficiency of its management."

47. Zimbalist, "Incentives and Planning in Cuba," 66.

48. Ibid.

49. "Características de las empresas socialistas en Cuba (II)," *Granma*, January 13, 1977. "La eficiencia de la gestión de la empresa no se mide por el cumplimiento de un índice aislado, como, por ejemplo, el volumen de producción, sino por lo alcanzado según un conjunto interrelacionado de indicadores que muestran un funcionamiento eficiente en forma integral."

50. José M. Norniella, "¿Cuántas empresas conocen las consecuencias que entraña el principio de la responsabilidad material por el incumplimiento de los planes?" *Granma*, October 14, 1978.

51. "Características de las empresas socialistas en Cuba (I)."

52. Fernando Dávalos, "Cuatro principios de la gestión empresarial," *Granma*, January 5, 1980.

53. Eckstein, *Back from the Future*, 27.

54. Ibid. This would change to some degree in 1992.

55. Fernando Dávalos, "El artículo 3 del Reglamento General de la empresa estatal: Cálculo económico en Cuba," *Granma*, February 13, 1980.

56. "Características de las empresas socialistas en Cuba (I)."

57. José Norniella, "El éxito del SDPE dependerá siempre de la participación consciente y activa de los trabajadores," *Granma*, July 10, 1978.

58. Eckstein, *Back from the Future*, 44.

59. "El artículo 3 del Reglamento General de la empresa estatal."

60. Hector Ayala Castro and Frank Hidalgo-Gato, "Aspectos teóricos del sistema de dirección y planificación de la economía," *Economía y Desarrollo* 57 (1980).

61. Ibid.

62. José Norniella, "El control de los inventarios en la construcción es un ejemplo positivo que todos debemos imitar," *Granma*, January 7, 1980.

63. Karl Marx, *Critique of the Gotha Program* (New York: International Publishers, 1966), 10.

64. The ration card provides every Cuban resident with certain food staples at subsidized prices. The food items have varied depending on availability and time period, but staples such as rice, beans, eggs, coffee, toothpaste, soap, and cigarettes were long the most common. As of 2012, the number of goods available on the ration card had been severely reduced.

65. José Norniella, "El mercado paralelo: El trabajo y sólo el trabajo es la fuente y la base del consumo," *Granma*, February 2, 1980.

66. Roberto Álvarez Quiñones, "Propiedad social, eficiencia económica y ahorro," *Granma*, February 4, 1980.

67. Roberto Álvarez Quiñones, "La ley económica de distribución según el trabajo," *Granma*, February 2, 1980.

68. Ibid.

69. José Norniella, "A propósito del mercado paralelo (III): Quien trabaje más y mejor tiene derecho a recibir más de la sociedad," *Granma*, October 16, 1980.

70. Pérez-Stable, *The Cuban Revolution*, 132.

71. Marta Harnecker, "Problemas objetivos de nuestra revolución: Lo que el pueblo debe saber," *Bohemia*, February 16, 1979.

72. Harnecker is the author of *Cuba: Dictatorship or Democracy?* (Westport, CT: Lawrence Hill, 1980).

73. Harnecker, "Problemas objetivos de nuestra revolución."

74. Ibid.

75. Ibid.

76. Ibid.

77. Ibid., 77.

78. Ibid., 78.

79. Marx was highly critical of those such as utopian socialists and the Young Hegelians who believed they could operate only at the level of theory and moral imperatives, while ignoring the degree to which the ideas they believed to be radical were in fact products of the very conditions they wished to overthrow. Karl Marx, *The German Ideology* (New York: International Publishers, 1947).

80. The bourgeoisie are a revolutionary class because they usher in the capitalist mode of production, but in doing so, they also lay the foundations of socialism by developing the productive forces, socializing production, and bringing into being the proletariat. Karl Marx and Friedrich Engels, "Manifesto of the Communist Party," in *The Marx-Engels Reader*, ed. Robert C. Tucker (New York: W.W. Norton, 1967).

81. This is Smith's invisible hand. Adam Smith, *An Inquiry into the Nature and Causes of the Wealth of Nations* (Chicago: University of Chicago Press, 1976).

82. Humberto Pérez, "Humberto Pérez en el Congreso de la ANEC. Che El más destacado economista de nuestro país después del triunfo de la revolución," *Bohemia*, June 22, 1979, 52–53.

83. Ibid., 53.

84. Ibid.

85. Ibid., 55.

86. Guevara, "On the Budgetary Finance System," 131.

87. Ibid., 131–32.

88. Ibid., 133.

89. Ibid., 151.

90. Ibid., 130.

91. Ibid., 134.

92. Ibid.

93. Ibid., 135.

94. Ibid., 138.

95. Ibid., 140.

96. Ibid., 142.

97. Che Guevara, "The Meaning of Socialist Planning (1964)," in Silverman, *Man and Socialism*, 102.

98. Che Guevara, "On Production Costs and the Budgetary System (1963)," in Silverman, *Man and Socialism*, 117.

99. Guevara, "On the Budgetary Finance System," 130.

100. Ibid., 123–24.

101. Che Guevara, "Man and Socialism in Cuba (1965)," in Silverman, *Man and Socialism*, 340. "Under capitalism, man is guided by a cold ordinance that is usually beyond his comprehension. The alienated human individual is bound to society as a whole by an invisible umbilical cord: the law of value. It acts upon all facets of his life, shaping his road and his destiny."

102. In other words, if a firm was able to fill planning targets using less money than what was allotted to it by the state and thus diminish its subsidies, it was able to keep the money saved to use for economic stimulation funds.

103. José Norniella, "El premio," *Granma*, May 24, 1980.

104. José Norniella, "Aprobado el reglamento general para la utilización del fondo para medidas socioculturales y construcción de viviendas," *Granma*, January 30, 1980. "No estaría de más recordar que el premio no es una obligación de la sociedad sino el salario. El premio no es un obsequio sino la estimulación por el esfuerzo colectivo de la impresa, traducido en una mejoría de determinado indicadores que a la sociedad le interesa mejorar en aras de una mayor eficiencia."

105. José M. Norniella, "Emite JUCEPLAN la Resolución 576 que establece el reglamento general para la utilización del Fondo de Medidas Socioculturales y Construcción de Viviendas," *Granma*, January 31, 1980. "Destacar los resultados de la emulación socialista y organizar lugares donde se expongan las condecoraciones que haya recibido la empresa o sus establecimientos por los meritos laborales alcanzados por el colectivo."

106. José Norniella, "La implementación del SDPE nos obligó a pensar a como la hacíamos antes, a organizarnos de otra manera, a trabajar pensando en el costo," *Granma*, February 23, 1980.

107. Roberto Álvarez Quiñones, "El salario por rendimiento o destajo, las primas y las normas," *Granma*, February 27, 1980.

108. José Norniella, "Los estímulos económicos en el socialismo," *Granma*, March 12, 1980.

109. José Norniella, "El aspecto moral del premio tiene para mi un valor tan alto que no se puede pagar ni con todo el dinero del mundo," *Granma*, April 2, 1980. Whether the worker meant what he said or simply thought this is what he should say, is another question.

110. José Norniella, "Dejaron de aportar las empresas más de 48 millones de pesos al presupuesto estatal por concepto de trabajo voluntario," *Granma*, February 19, 1980.

111. "Buscando eficiencia los criterios económicos de la empresa evolucionan hasta llegar al campo terminado," *Granma*, June 11, 1980.

112. Carlos Tablada argues that Che Guevara would have been troubled by the SDPE in general, and this in particular. *Economics and Politics in the Transition to Socialism* (New York: Pathfinder, 1989), 41–42.

113. José Gabriel Guma, "Actuarán con independencia e imparcialidad los árbi-

tros estatales que integraran el sistema de arbitraje nacional," *Granma*, January 22, 1980.

114. José Norniella, "Pasó ayer el banco a créditos vencidos los saldos de los sobregiros en las cuentas de operaciones de las empresas," *Granma*, April 2, 1980.

115. José Norniella, "El cálculo económico obliga a dirigentes y obreros de las empresas a proyectarse con nuevas concepciones en el trabajo," *Granma*, August 23, 1980.

116. José Norniella, "¿Qué nos enseñan las ferias de Bienes de Consumo?" *Granma*, August 27, 1981.

117. José Norniella, "La auditoría es una función administrativa del Estado para prevenir a tiempo los errores e indisciplinas," *Granma*, April 3, 1980. See also "Analizan deficiencias y avances presentados por el SDPE en la Provincia en Camagüey," *Granma*, May 9, 1980, which pointed to problems of violations of financial discipline and bad use of bank credits.

118. "Crean empresa para prestar servicios de contabilidad y auditoria a empresas y unidades presupuestadas con el objetivo de facilitar la implantación del Sistema de Dirección y Planificación de la Economía," *Granma*, January 2, 1980.

119. José Gabriel Guma, "Adoptarán medidas disciplinarias contra los funcionarios de entidades que no conciertan los contratos económicos en los plazos establecidos," *Granma*, November 27, 1980.

120. José Norniella, "Se desarrolla y perfecciona la organización masiva de la enseñanza y entrenamiento de cuadros de dirección económica," *Granma*, June 4, 1981.

121. Jesús Mena, "Garantizarán la implantación y perfeccionamiento del SDPE en el MINCOM," *Granma*, June 4, 1981.

122. "Debatir cada uno de los indicadores del plan con los trabajadores y escuchar sus opiniones," *Granma*, April 7, 1981.

123. José Norniella, "Cumplidas importantes tareas en materia de precios que han ido permitiendo al SDPE crear las bases para el establecimiento de un sistema de precios económicamente fundamentados," *Granma*, June 18, 1982.

124. "Muy atrasadas algunas tareas iniciales del balance de relaciones intersectoriales," *Granma*, April 6, 1981.

125. José Norniella, "Atrasadas la mitad de las empresas del país en la entrega de sus normas de consumo," *Granma*, June 4, 1980.

126. José Norniella, "Discuten en Sancti Spiritus los principales problemas que afectan el proceso de implantación," *Granma*, April 1, 1982.

127. José Norniella, "El rescate de la disciplina estadística es el primer gran resultado inmediato logrado por el balance de relaciones intersectoriales estadístico (BRIE)," *Granma*, March 10, 1982.

128. See Fidel Castro Ruz, "El Sistema de Dirección y Planificación de la Economía," in *II Congreso del Partido Comunista de Cuba: Informe Central* (Havana: Editora Política, 1980).

129. The absolute number of articles referring to the SDPE at all had dropped from 117 in 1980 to 48 in 1981 and to 40 in 1982. These statistics come from using the

Latin American Network Information Center's *Granma* archives at http://lanic.utexas.edu/la/cb/cuba/granma/ to do a search on the SDPE for those years.

130. José Norniella, "Inercia y pasividad en materia arbitral son las características dominantes en las empresas agropecuarias," *Granma*, January 15, 1983.

131. Pérez-Stable, *The Cuban Revolution*, 157–58.

132. Eckstein, *Back from the Future*, 60–61.

Chapter 4

1. Boaventura de Sousa Santos, "Why Has Cuba Become a Difficult Problem for the Left?" *Latin American Perspectives* 36, no. 3 (2009): 43–53.

2. This does not mean that some were not subtly encouraged to leave or disillusioned by the experience. Haroldo Dilla, for instance, did leave Cuba after he was placed in the Instituto de Filosofía, known for its dogmatism, rigid readings of Marxism and Marxism-Leninism, and strict adherence to the party line.

3. The question of whether and how it is possible to carry out objective studies occupies most of the philosophy-of-science literature. See, for instance, Pierre Bourdieu, *Outline of a Theory of Practice*, trans. Richard Nice (Cambridge: Cambridge University Press, 1977); Thomas S. Kuhn, *The Structure of Scientific Revolutions* (Chicago: University of Chicago Press, 1964); and Karl Mannheim, *Ideology and Utopia: An Introduction to the Sociology of Knowledge* (New York: Harcourt, 1936).

4. Even those defending Cuban academics against the charge of being mouthpieces of the Cuban state may end up falling back upon such criteria to defend these same academics against criticisms from the U.S. government. In short, evidence of the quality of their academic production is easily elided with evidence that their work is critical.

5. Kapcia, *Cuba: Island of Dreams*, 4.

6. "Editorial Note," *Cuban Studies* 13, no. 1 (1983).

7. Jorge I. Domínguez, "Cuba's Relations with Caribbean and Central American Countries," *Cuban Studies* 13, no. 2 (1983): 80.

8. Quintero, "Comment," *Cuban Studies* 13, no. 2 (1983): 113–15.

9. This is not the only definition of Cubanology. For a discussion of the various meanings of the term, see Nelson P. Valdés, "Estudios cubanos en los Estados Unidos," *Temas* 2 (1995): 5–10.

10. Yanes, "Comment," 117.

11. See Richard Boucher, "Cuba: Denial of Visas to Group of Cuban Academics/Basis for Decision," Washington, DC: U.S. Department of State, 2004.

12. Jorge I. Domínguez, "Response," *Cuban Studies* 13, no. 2 (1983): 119.

13. Ibid., 118.

14. Ibid., 119.

15. Domínguez, "Twenty-Five Years," 20.

16. Yanes emigrated to the United States in 2003 and criticized the Cuban government in the pages of *El Nuevo Herald*. He also expressed concern that the

Cuban military would impose a Chinese- or Vietnamese-style economic system on the island. See Pablo Alfonso, "Muy importantes los militares para el poscastrismo," *El Nuevo Herald*, November 7, 2003.

17. José Luis Rodríguez García, "The So-Called Cubanology and Cuban Economic Development," *Cuban Studies* 16, no. 1 (1986): 211; Mesa-Lago, "On the Objectives," 232.

18. Rodríguez García, *Crítica a nuestros críticos*, 8.

19. Ibid., 8.

20. For a detailed account of the history of educational exchange between Cuba and the United States, see Sheryl L. Lutgens, "National Security the State, and the Politics of U.S.-Cuba Educational Exchange," *Latin American Perspectives* 33, no. 5 (2006): 58–80.

21. Jorge I. Domínguez and Rafael Hernández, eds., *U.S.-Cuban Relations in the 1990s* (Boulder: Westview Press, 1989).

22. Ibid., 3.

23. Ibid., 1.

24. Sweig, *Cuba: What Everyone Needs to Know*, 169.

25. Carlos Alzugaray, "Academic Exchanges and Transnational Relations: Cuba and the United States," *Latin American Perspectives* 33, no. 5 (2006): 52.

26. Centro de Estudios Sobre América, "Balance Político de las Tareas Cumplidas en el Quinquenio 1991–1995 (April 12, 1996)," in *El caso CEA: Intelectuales e inquisidores en Cuba ¿Perestroika en la isla?* ed. Maurizio Giuliano (Miami: Ediciones Universal, 1998), 163.

27. Ibid., 166.

28. Directors: Oscar Pino-Santos, Santiago Díaz Paz, Luis Suárez Salazar. Subdirectors: Julio Carranza Valdés, Camilo Domenech, Aurelio Alonso. Department Head: Rafael Hernández, Juan Valdés Paz, Ilya Villar, Haroldo Dilla Alberto F. Álvarez. Other members: Jorge Hernández, Luis René Fernández, Redi Gomis, Isabel Jaramillo, Alfredo Prieto, Ana Teresa Vincentelli, Jesús Hernández, Fernando Heredia, Ferardo González Núñez, Fausto Sing Yu, Armando Fernández Soriano, Mayra Góngora, Santiago Pérez Benitez, Verónica Loynaz, Ernesto Rodríguez, Ana Julia Faya, Gerardo Timossi, Tomas A. Vasconi, Inés Reca, Alfredo González Pedraza, Jorge Benítez, Pedro Monreal, Hernán Yanes Quintero, Tania García Lorenzo, Lourdes María Regueiro, Luis Gutiérrez, Mercedes Gallardo, Hugo Azcuy. Alberto F. Álvarez Garcia, and Gerardo González Núñez, *Intelectuales vs. Revolución? El caso del Centro de Estudios sobre América, CEA* (Montreal: Ediciones Arte D.T., 2001), 167–68.

29. See, for instance, Centro de Estudios sobre América, ed., *The Cuban Revolution into the 1990s* (Boulder: Westview Press, 1992).

30. Haroldo Dilla, "Cuba: La crisis y la rearticulación del consenso político (notas para un debate socialista)," *Cuadernos de Nuestra América* 10, no. 20 (1993): 20–45. Earlier articles included economist Julio Carranza Valdés's "Cuba: Los retos de la economía" and Aurelio Alonso's "La economía cubana: Los desafíos de un ajuste sin desocialización," in *Cuadernos de Nuestra America* 9, no. 19 (1993).

31. Haroldo Dilla, "Cuba between Utopia and the World Market," *Latin American Perspectives* 21, no. 83 (1994): 46–59.
32. Dilla, "Cuba: La crisis y la rearticulación," 30.
33. Ibid., 34.
34. Ibid., 41.
35. Ibid., 40.
36. Ibid., 44.
37. For a discussion of the relationship between participation and actual power, see, for instance, Rafael Hernández and Haroldo Dilla, "Political Culture and Popular Participation," in Centro de Estudios sobre América, *Cuban Revolution into the 1990s*, 31. See also a study Dilla carried out with other former CEA members: Haroldo Dilla Alfonso, Gerardo González Núñez, and Ana Teresa Vicentelli, *Participación popular y desarrollo en los municipios Cubanos* (Caracas: Fondo Editorial Tropykos, 1994). González Nuñez would go on to cowrite the book *Intelectuales vs. Revolución?* cited at the beginning of this chapter.
38. Haroldo Dilla, ed., *La Democracia en Cuba y el diferendo con los Estados Unidos* (Havana: Editorial de Ciencias Sociales, 1996).
39. Jorge I. Domínguez, "La democracia en Cuba: ¿Cuál es el modelo deseable?" in Dilla, *La democracia en Cuba*, 129.
40. Haroldo Dilla, "Cuba: Cuál es la democracia deseable?" in Dilla, *La democracia en Cuba*, 186.
41. Ibid., 184.
42. Ibid., 171.
43. Ibid., 185.
44. Julio Carranza Valdés, Luis Gutiérrez Urdaneta, and Pedro Monreal González, *Cuba: La restructuración de la economía: una propuesta para el debate* (Havana: Editorial de Ciencias Sociales, 1995). I bought the paperback book in a Havana bookstore during a trip in 1997. The bookstore was near the University and sold books in dollars.
45. Ibid., 3.
46. Ibid., 65.
47. Julio Carranza Valdés, Luis Gutiérrez Urdaneta, and Pedro Monreal González, *Cuba: Restructuring the Economy—a Contribution to the Debate*, trans. Ruth Pearson (London: Institute of Latin American Studies, 1996).
48. Haroldo Dilla Alfonso, interview with the author, Havana, December 1998.
49. Raúl Castro, "Informe del Buró Político," *Granma*, March 27, 1996, 5.
50. Ibid., 2.
51. Ibid., 5.
52. Ibid.
53. Ibid., 6.
54. Ibid. See Machado Rodríguez, *Cuba: Ideología revolucionaria* for his understanding of the role of the intellectual.
55. Raúl Castro, "Informe del Buró Político," 6.

56. Ibid. He cited the Soviet Union's glasnost as an example of this type of disunity that ended up destroying the revolution from within.

57. Giuliano, *El caso CEA*, 151. The center is notorious for its role in reproducing Party dogma and for discouraging its researchers from doing their job too well.

58. Several of the researchers at CEA had participated in *Pensamiento Crítico*. Ibid., 49. Fernando Martínez, Aurelio Alonso, Rafael Hernández, Juan Valdés Paz, Ana Julia Faya, and Hugo Azcuy were members of both collectives. Those CEA researchers who had not participated in *Pensamiento Crítico* were marked by it indirectly, having studied at the University of the Havana in the 1970s when the social sciences had been purged and literature seemed the closest replacement. Carollee Bengelsdorf, "Intellectuals under Fire," *In These Times*, September 16–29, 1996.

59. Dilla, "Comrades and Investors," 232.

60. Magín, which asked for, but did not receive NGO status from the Cuban government, also came under attack in 1996 for threatening Cuban unity. For a discussion of Magín's differences with the FMC and the reasons for its closing in 1996, see Sujatha Fernandes, "Transnationalism and Feminist Activism in Cuba: The Case of Magín," in *Politics and Gender* 1, no. 3 (September 2005): 431–52.

61. Álvarez García and González Núñez, *Intelectuales vs. Revolución?* 65. Álvarez and González had emigrated during academic exchanges prior to the 1996 confrontation with the Party, and were referred to during the meetings as "deserters."

62. Ibid., 54.

63. Ibid., 122–23.

64. Several members of CEA told me they were unclear as to how Giuliano acquired the records.

65. Giuliano, *El caso CEA*. While I have used the case of CEA to make a different argument than the one made by Giuliano, I am indebted to the book for factual information and for its appendices of the main discussions between CEA and the commission.

66. Ibid., 19.

67. Ibid., 148.

68. Ibid., 144.

69. Álvarez Garcia and González Núñez, *Intelectuales vs. Revolución?* 160.

70. Ibid., 161.

71. Ibid.

72. Hugo Azcuy, CEA researcher and former contributor to *Pensamiento Crítico*, died of a heart attack one day after the publication in *Granma* of Raúl Castro's speech attacking CEA.

73. Centro de Estudios sobre América, "Balance político de las tareas cumplidas en el Quinquenio 1991–1995 (April 12, 1996)," in Giuliano, *El caso CEA*, 155.

74. Ibid., 167–68.

75. Ibid., 155.

76. Ibid., 177.

77. Ibid., 157.

78. Ibid., 159–60. Giuliano also found this passage particularly noteworthy and cited the last two sentences in his own discussion of the case, *El caso CEA*, 60.

79. Centro de Estudios sobre América, "Balance político," 160.
80. Ibid., 162.
81. Ibid., 171.
82. Ibid., 176.
83. Centro de Estudios sobre América, "Primera reunión de la Comisión del CC del PCC con el Consejo de Dirección del CEA, April 12, 1996," in Giuliano, *El caso CEA*, 180.
84. Ibid., 183.
85. Ibid., 197.
86. Ibid., 184.
87. Ibid., 186.
88. Ibid., 188–89.
89. Ibid., 189.
90. Ibid., 191–92.
91. Centro de Estudios sobre América, "Segunda reunión de la Comisión del CC del PCC con el Consejo de Dirección del CEA (April 15, 1996)," in Giuliano, *El caso CEA*, 203.
92. Ibid., 210.
93. Centro de Estudios sobre América, "Balance crítico de las deficiencias del Centro de Estudios sobre América en el periodo 1991–1995 (April 22, 1996)," in Giuliano, *El caso CEA*, 219.
94. Ibid., 227.
95. Centro de Estudios sobre América, "Segunda reunión," 209.
96. Ibid.
97. Centro de Estudios sobre América, "Balance crítico," 216.
98. Ibid., 217.
99. Ibid., 223–24.
100. During a conversation with a former CEA member during one of my first visits to Cuba, I asked him why he was an academic if academics had little influence on actual policy. His answer was similar to one that I would have given. Getting paid to read books and write was better than selling pizza.
101. Ibid., 225.
102. Centro de Estudios sobre América, "Balance crítico," 225.
103. Centro de Estudios sobre América, "Tercera reunión de la Comisión del Buró Político con el Consejo de Dirección del CEA (April 26, 1996)," in Giuliano, *El caso CEA*, 241.
104. Ibid.
105. Ibid., 234–37.
106. Ibid., 240.
107. Ibid., 246–47.
108. Ibid., 243.
109. Ibid., 244. While the original Spanish is "dentro de nosotros mismos" and refers to debate within each individual, I have chosen to translate it as "among ourselves," in reference to debate within the center. The ambiguity of the phrasing, however, is worth noting.

110. See, for instance, ibid., 247.

111. Centro de Estudios sobre América, "Consideraciones preliminares de la Dirección del Núcleo del Partido del CEA acerca del proceso de análisis efectuado en el Centro por la Comisión designada por el Buró Político a raíz de los señalamientos del V Pleno del CC del PCC (May 23, 1997)," in Giuliano, *El caso CEA,* 257.

112. Ibid., 264.

113. Centro de Estudios sobre América, "Carta enviada por el Núcleo del PCC del CEA a Fidel y Raúl Castro (August 27, 1996)," in Giuliano, *El caso CEA*, 275.

114. Mimi Whitefield and Juan O. Tomayo, "Raúl Castro's Attack on Intellectuals Stirs Backlash," (Knight_Ridder News Service, 1996, cited September 10, 2004, available from www.hartford-hwp.com/archives/43b/197.html.

115. Bengelsdorf, "Intellectuals under Fire," 27.

116. Ibid.

117. Centro de Estudios sobre América, "Intervención de José Ramon Balaguer en la Reunión de la Comisión del Buró Político con el Núcleo del PCC del CEA (August 14, 1996)," in Giuliano, *El caso CEA*, 267–68.

118. Juan Valdés Paz, interview with the author, Havana, January 23, 2003.

119. Haroldo Dilla, Rafael Hernández, and Juan Valdés were all transferred to research institutions where it was almost impossible for them to do the work in sociology that they had done at CEA. Only Aurelio Alonso was sent to an institute where he could continue his work as a sociologist. At the Center for Psychological and Social Research, he found himself among other researchers, such as Mayra Espina, doing work on the social effects of Cuba's transition in the 1990s. Giuliano, *El Caso CEA*, 130–31.

120. Julio Carranza went to the Center for Studies of the Cuban Economy and Pedro Monreal went to the Center for Studies of the International Economy. Ibid.

121. Hernández, *Mirar a Cuba*; Rafael Hernández, *Otra guerra* (Havana: Editorial de ciencias sociales, 1999).

122. Campaign for Peace and Democracy, "Statement Protesting Repression in Cuba," 2003, cited October 15, 2003, available from http://home.igc.org/~jlandy/cpd/anti-war/cuba-stmt.html.

123. It must be noted that this argument is not one that can only be made outside of Cuba. Valdés Paz also takes this position, arguing that while there is much creativity in the arts, there is much reticence in the social sciences. Juan Valdés Paz, interview with the author, Havana, January 23, 2003.

124. Haroldo Dilla Alfonso, "Las ciencias sociales cubanas: Entre el saber y el poder," *Vértice* 7 (2002): 4–5.

125. Jesus Díaz, "El fin de otra ilusión: A propósito de la quiebra de *El Caimán Barbudo* y la clausura de *Pensamiento Crítico*," *Encuentro de la Cultura Cubana*, Spring–Summer 2000, 119.

126. Ibid., 118.

127. Aurelio Alonso, "Réplica," *Encuentro de la Cultura Cubana*, Spring–Summer 2000, 120.

128. Ibid., 120–21.

129. Juan Valdés Paz, interview with author, Havana, January 23, 2003.

130. The metaphor of the boat is similar to the metaphor of the horse that Valdés used during CEA's meeting with the commission.

131. Interview with author.

Chapter 5

1. This corporation is CIMEX (Corporación Importadora y Exportadora, S.A.). By the end of 2001, it had sold products totaling over $950 million. "CIMEX: Over $950 million USD Revenue in 2001," web page, Digital Granma International, 2001, cited January 21, 2004, available from http://www.granma.cu/ingles/actualidad-i.html. According to CIMEX's own literature, it is a "juridically private firm of Cuban capital" "established in the Republic of Panama according to the existing laws of that country." The firm is made up of seventy-three subsidiaries and twenty-one companies that participate as associations. The nucleus of CIMEX was started in June 1978 and dealt primarily with the tourist industry. The consortium grew rapidly in the 1990s with the legalization of the dollar and the growth of tourism on the island, and the majority of its entities are focused in commercial activities (32%) and tourism (23%). Between 1996 and 2000, CIMEX reinvested no less than $60 million annually into its operations with an average annual earnings growth rate of 8.2% and average annual profit growth rate of 10.1%. The firm employs roughly 21,700 Cuban laborers. Apart from national investment, the firm also counts on the participation of foreign capital in nine mixed ventures; 51% of their products and services come from Cuban national production.

2. Esther Whitfield, *Cuban Currency: The Dollar and "Special Period" Fiction* (Minneapolis: University of Minnesota Press, 2008).

3. Hernández-Reguant, "Copyrighting Che."

4. The blurb on the book jacket of the book *Waiting for Fidel* captures the tone of the book. "This time he sets his sights on Cuba, where crumbling but elegant facades overlook shady street activities, where vintage Ford Fairlanes rumble past Soviet Ladas in the fast lanes of eerily deserted boulevards, and where an aging Fidel Castro is struggling to maintain his grip on a population yearning for *aire libre*, or at least Air Jordans." Christopher Hunt, *Waiting for Fidel* (Boston: Houghton Mifflin, 1998).

5. Images of Cuban women's bodies, and the existence of sex work, were often used in the mainstream media outside of Cuba to portray the economic crisis and point to the failure of socialism. Amalia Lucía Cabezas, "Discourses of Prostitution: The Case of Cuba," in *Global Sex Workers: Rights, Resistance, and Redefinition*, ed. Kamal Kempadoo and Jo Doezema (New York: Routledge, 1998), 79. In spite of the tremendous advances made by Cuban women by world standards, the *jinetera* came to be the representation of Cuban woman in the 1990s. Isabel Holgado Fernández, *¡No es fácil!: Mujeres cubanas y la crisis revolucionaria* (Barcelona: Icaria Editorial, 2000).

6. Paul Ryer, "Millennium's Past Cuba's Future?" *Public Culture* 12, no. 2 (2000): 499.

7. Walter Benjamin, "N [Re the Theory of Knowledge, Theory of Progress]," in *Benjamin: Philosophy, Aesthetics, History*, ed. Gary Smith (Chicago: University of Chicago Press, 1989), 64.

8. Walter Benjamin, "Theses on the Philosophy of History," in *Illuminations*, ed. Hannah Arendt, trans. Harry Zohn (New York: Schocken Books, 1968), 257–58.

9. Ibid., 262.

10. Benjamin, "N [Re the Theory of Knowledge, Theory of Progress]," 47.

11. Ibid., 46.

12. Ibid., 49.

13. Benjamin, "Theses on the Philosophy of History," 262.

14. "To the Battle, Bayameses! / Let the Fatherland proudly observe you! / Do not fear a glorious death, / To die for the fatherland is to live!"

15. Sociologist Marifeli Pérez-Stable has argued that while radical nationalist interpretations of Cuban history are thus far the most convincing and coherent, their analyses are weakened by a teleology that "portrays the Cuban Revolution as the inevitable conclusion of a hallowed destiny." The very fact that the revolution happened means that "the past acquires the logic of radical nationalism and, consequently, contingencies are eliminated." Pérez-Stable, *The Cuban Revolution*, 4.

16. The Cuban American National Foundation, for example, holds this position. CANF (Cuban American National Foundation), n.d. "About CANF," www.canf.org/2005/principal-ingles.htm, cited September 2, 2005.

17. See discussion in chapter 1.

18. In an earlier version of this piece published in *Public Culture*, I misidentified the figure on the bus station billboard as Frank País, who also points to the revolution's contested origins. País was the head of the revolutionary 26th of July Movement's operations in Santiago, Cuba's second largest city, where he was assassinated by police in July 1957. He had long been part of the anti-Batista movement, first as head of the Acción Nacional Revolucionaria in the early 1950s, and then as a leader of the 26th of July Movement's urban faction after much of the opposition had been consolidated under its umbrella. He was a practicing Baptist and an advocate of liberal, rather than socialist, reforms in Cuba. He saw the general strike, rather than guerilla warfare, as the primary "catalyst for nationalist insurrection" (Pérez-Stable, *The Cuban Revolution*, 58). His assassination in 1957 by Batista's police, prior to the triumph and radicalization of the revolution, made it possible for him to remain a popular figure in official Cuban revolutionary history. However, his differences with the ideology that Castro adopted after the revolution's triumph also allow him to be admired by those wishing the revolution had taken a more reformist course. Pérez-Stable argues that had he not been killed, the "urban July 26th Movement might have exercised greater direction of the struggle than the Sierra Maestra guerrillas."

19. Miguel García Reyes and María Guadalupe Lopez de Llergo y Cornejo, *Cuba después de la era soviética* (Mexico City: El Colegio de México, 1997), 25.

20. Ana Julia Jatar-Hausman, *The Cuban Way: Capitalism, Communism and Confrontation* (West Hartford, CT: Kumarian Press, 1999), 39.

21. Between 1972 and 1985, the Cuban economy experienced "a sustained and robust rate of growth" of around 6% per year. Problems began appearing in the second half of the 1980s. Claes Brundenius, "Whither the Cuban Economy after Recovery? The Reform Process, Upgrading Strategies and the Question of Transition," *Journal of Latin American Studies* 34, no. 2 (2002): 366.

22. In the late 80s, Eastern European countries expressed their desire to reform CMEA so as to facilitate trade with the capitalist world and reduce Soviet domination. Talk of reform soon turned to talk of abolition and in June 1991, CMEA was terminated. Linden, "Analogies," 39–40.

23. Manuel Pastor Jr. and Andrew Zimbalist, "Cuba's Economic Conundrum," *NACLA Report on the Americas*, September–October 1995, 8.

24. The official figure is 35%, but unofficial sources have suggested figures as high as 50%. William M. Leogrande and Julie M. Thomas, "Cuba's Quest for Economic Independence," *Journal of Latin American Studies* 34, no. 2 (2002): 343.

25. Brundenius, "Whither the Cuban Economy?" 366.

26. Frank T. Fitzgerald, *The Cuban Revolution in Crisis: From Managing Socialism to Managing Survival* (New York: Monthly Review Press, 1994), 2.

27. Pastor and Zimbalist, "Cuba's Economic Conundrum," 8.

28. García Reyes and Lopez de Llergo y Cornejo, *Cuba después de la era soviética*, 15.

29. Ibid., 27.

30. Jatar-Hausmann, *The Cuban Way*, 49.

31. Sean Brotherton, *Revolutionary Medicine*, 18.

32. Sweig, *Cuba: What Everyone Needs to Know*, 142–43. See also, the documentary *Balseros* (dir. Carlos Bosch and Josep Maria Doménech, 2002).

33. For instance, a 2001 *New York Times* article editorialized: "Though billboards proclaim 'Victorious in the New Millennium' and Fidel Castro still clings to the revolutionary ideals of an earlier generation, the unending scramble to make ends meet and the voices in the streets tell another story." David Gonzalez, "In Cuba, Clashing Voices over Ideals and Reality," *New York Times*, May 30, 2001.

34. John H. Coatsworth, "Preface," in *The Cuban Economy at the Start of the Twenty-First Century*, ed. Jorge Domínguez, Omar Everleny Pérez, and Lorena Barberia (Cambridge: David Rockefeller Center for Latin American Studies, Harvard University, 2004), xvii.

35. Desiderio Navarro, "In medias res Republicas: On Intellectuals and Social Criticism in the Cuban Public Sphere," *Nepantla: Views from South* 2 (2001): 368–69.

36. Raúl Castro, *El futuro de nuestra patria será un eterno Baragua: Llamamiento al IV Congreso del PCC* (Havana: Editora Política, 1990), 13, 15.

37. Dilla, "Comrades and Investors," 232.

38. Bengelsdorf, *Problem of Democracy*, 169.

39. Rafael Hernández, *Looking at Cuba*, trans. Dick Cluster (Gainesville: University Press of Florida, 2003), 99.

40. García Reyes and Lopez de Llergo y Cornejo, *Cuba después de la era soviética*, 15.

41. Pastor and Zimbalist, "Cuba's Economic Conundrum," 9.

42. The stores were aptly named Tiendas Para la Recuperación de Divisas (TRDs) or Stores for the Recuperation of Hard Currency (*divisas*).

43. Cuba is not entirely alone either in its decision to partially dollarize (Ecuador and El Salvador also fully dollarized their economies) or in its aggressive search for remittances (which characterizes the situation of many countries in the Caribbean).

44. CEPAL, *La economía cubana: Reformas estructurales y desempeño en los noventa* (Mexico City: Fondo de cultura económica/CEPAL, 1997), 520.

45. For a list of those activities that qualified under the self-employment law, see ibid., 505–9. The number of permitted activities increased to 157 by 1997. Henken, "Condemned to Informality," 4.

46. CEPAL, *La economía cubana*, 501.

47. Carmen Diana Deere, "The New Agrarian Reforms," *NACLA Report on the Americas* 29, no. 2 (1995): 13.

48. Jatar-Hausman, *The Cuban Way*, 72.

49. Deere, "The New Agrarian Reforms," 13.

50. The rate has continued to stay between twenty and twenty-eight pesos to the dollar.

51. Pastor and Zimbalist, "Cuba's Economic Conundrum," 11.

52. CEPAL, *La economía cubana*, 417.

53. See Raúl Valdés Vivó, "Why Cuba Says No to Privatization," *Workers World*, January 15, 1998, for an official Cuban response to the accusation that Cuba is hypocritical for allowing large-scale foreign investment while continuing to forbid Cuban citizens from investing in small and medium-sized enterprises. The author argued that allowing small-scale domestic enterprise would create a new capitalist class that would "conspire against socialism." According to the official point of view, "In order to be profitable, small and medium-sized private enterprises would have to be based on the super-exploitation of the work force."

54. Mario Sznajder and Luis Roniger, *Politics, Social Ethos and Identity in Contemporary Cuba* (Jerusalem: Harry S. Truman Research Institute for the Advancement of Peace, Hebrew University of Jerusalem, 2001), 6.

55. Henken, "Condemned to Informality," 4.

56. See for instance, Horowitz, "Castro and the End of Ideology," in *Cuban Communism, 1959–1995*, 861–64. and Deirdre McFayden, "The Social Repercussions of the Crisis," *NACLA Report on the Americas* 29, no. 2 (1995).

57. While wage differentials in Cuba have always existed as a way of stimulating productivity, what changed was that pay was based on one's involvement in the dollar economy.

58. Newspapers cost 20 centavos at the newsstands, but they are almost always all gone before noon because the elderly have bought them up to resell at an 80-centavo profit (100 centavos = 1 peso ≈ 5 cents).

59. Alejandro de la Fuente, "The Resurgence of Racism in Cuba," *NACLA Report on the Americas*, 2001, 30; Ilja Luciak, *Gender and Democracy in Cuba* (Gaines-

ville: University Press of Florida, 2007), xvii–xx. Luciak argues that there has been much less progress in transforming substantive gender equality (societal norms and power relation), than formal equality (legal norms).

60. Sarah A. Blue, "The Erosion of Racial Equality in the Context of Cuba's Dual Economy," *Latin American Politics and Society* 49, no. 3 (Fall 2007): 36.

61. Ibid., 54.

62. While black and darker-skinned Cubans have a harder time getting jobs in the tourist industry, which is vulnerable to racist assumptions about what constitutes a "pleasant aspect" (*buena presencia*), "blackness is used in the [tourist] sector's advertising campaigns as an icon of sensuality, music and fun." De la Fuente, "Resurgence of Racism," 32–33.

63. De la Fuente, "Resurgence of Racism," 32–33; Blue, "Erosion of Racial Equality," 35–36.

64. According to Sarah Blue, *jiniterismo* is the only area where blacks and mulattos earn as much as whites and they are only slightly more likely to engage in "riskier informal activities." "Erosion of Racial Equality," 51.

65. Citing Lourdes Casal's work on the subject, Carollee Bengelsdorf notes that the number of women in the workforce increased in spite of the reduction in the number of domestic servants and prostitutes, the increased educational opportunities offered to women, and the disincentive to work offered by the welfare state. Bengelsdorf, "(Re)Considering Cuban Women in a Time of Troubles," in *Daughters of Caliban: Caribbean Women in the Twentieth Century*, ed. Consuelo López Springfield (Bloomington: Indiana University Press, 1997), 236.

66. Ibid., 237.

67. Ibid., 231; Cabezas, "Discourses of Prostitution," 84. The Family Code attempted to distribute household responsibilities equally between male and female partners.

68. Bengelsdorf, "(Re)Considering Cuban Women," 238–40. While the number of prostitutes increased in the 1990s, as Coco Fusco notes, *jineteras* existed in revolutionary Cuba prior to the Special Period, and often worked as spies with the approval of the Ministry of Interior. Fusco, "Hustling for Dollars: Jineterismo in Cuba," in Kempadoo and Doezema. *Global Sex Workers*, 151.

69. Nadine Fernandez, "Back to the Future? Women, Race, and Tourism in Cuba," in *Sun, Sex, and Gold: Tourism and Sex Work in the Caribbean*, ed. Kamala Kempadoo (New York: Rowman & Littlefield, 1999), 87–88.

70. Fusco, "Hustling for Dollars," 160.

71. Ibid., 163.

72. Ibid., 166.

73. Alexei Yurchak, "Soviet Hegemony of Form: Everything Was Forever, until It Was No More," *Comparative Studies in Society and History* 45, no. 3 (2003): 504.

74. Ibid.

75. Sachiko Tanuma, "Post-utopian Irony: Cuban Narratives during the 'Special Period' Decade," *PoLAR: Political and Legal Anthropology Review* 30, no. 1 (May 2007): 57.

76. Ibid., 53.

77. Carlos Lage Dávila, *Enfrentamos el desafío: Entrevista concedida por el Secretario del Consejo de Ministros a Mario Vázquez Raña* (Havana: Editora Política, 1993), 18.

78. See Fidel Castro Ruz, *The Current World Order Is Unsustainable* (Havana: Editora Política, 1999) and Fidel Castro Ruz, *Globalización neoliberal y crisis económica global: discursos y declaraciones, mayo de 1998–enero de 1999* (Havana: Oficina de Publicaciones del Consejo de Estado, 1999).

79. See Fidel Castro Ruz, *A Revolution Can Only Be Born from Culture and Ideas* (Havana: Editora Política, 1999).

80. Carlos Lage Dávila, *Las estrategias ante la situación económica actual* (Havana: Editora Política, 1994).

81. Ibid.

82. Albeit with some important changes to the Cuban constitution in 1992, when the Cuban National Assembly approved various constitutional reforms including direct elections for deputies of the National Assembly and for delegates of the provincial assemblies known as the Organs of Popular Power. Also of significance was the omission of the Soviet Union from the charter's preamble, the elevation of José Martí to father of the nation, the ban on religious discrimination, and finally the decision to call the Cuban Communist Party the party of the Cuban people (*el pueblo cubano*) rather than the party of the Cuban workers. Azicri, *Cuba Today and Tomorrow*, 112–20.

83. Cuba ranked with the Western industrialized nations in many of these indicators. The infant mortality rate was reduced from eleven in one thousand births in 1990 to seven in 1999, which would place it sixth among the Western industrialized nations. The mortality rate for children under five fell from thirteen per thousand to eight per thousand between 1990 and 2001. This is a considerable achievement in a region where the average was thirty-eight per thousand in 1999. Jim Lobe, "Learn from Cuba, Says World Bank," Inter Press New Service Agency, April 30, 2001.

84. See Mauricio Solaún, "On Political Change in Cuba: A Comparative Introduction," in *Cuba in Transition*, vol. 9, 173–77 (Washington, DC: Association for the Study of the Cuban Economy, 1999).

85. The Gini coefficient increased from .22 in 1986 to .41 in 1999. Whereas the upper fifth of the population received 33.8% of the income in 1986, it received 58.1% in 1999. The bottom fifth of the population received 11.3% in 1986 and received 4% in 1999. According to Claes Brundenius, "If this trend continues, income distribution in Cuba will increasingly resemble that of the rest of Latin America." Brundenius, "Whither the Cuban Economy?" 378.

86. Azicri, *Cuba Today and Tomorrow*, 120.

87. See, for instance, Azicri, *Cuba Today and Tomorrow*; Rosenthal, *Inside the Revolution*; Sznajder and Roniger, "Politics, Social Ethos and Identity"; and Miguel Vasquez, "Cultural Integrity in Non-traditional Societies: Cuba Encounters the Global Market System," *Cultural Dynamics* 14 (July 2002) 185–204; Brotherton, *Revolutionary Medicine*.

88. The Miami-based *Cuban Change*, for instance, supports a social-democrat platform.

89. Rosenthal, *Inside the Revolution*, 156.

90. Gramsci, "On Education" and "State and Civil Society," in *Selections from the Prison Notebooks*, 34, 258.

91. Martin Holbraad, "Revolución o Muerte: Self-Sacrifice and the Ontology of the Cuban Revolution," *Ethnos: Journal of Anthropology* 79, no. 3 (2014): 370.

92. Whether the government in Cuba actually knows all does not matter, for it has succeeded in making most Cuban citizens believe that it does. Foreigners wishing to see the best of Cuba often have a difficult time understanding this fear by virtue of their limited time in Cuba, the special treatment they receive, and their ability to leave.

93. For instance, the description in the Museum of the Revolution in Havana of photos of the *Maleconazo*: "Groups of antisocial elements and tramps performed counter-revolutionary riots in two neighborhoods Old Havana and Central Havana." In spite of the fact that many of the participants were working class and black, the description continues: "The workers responded immediately and, without weapons, put an end to the revolts, supported by the presence of Fidel, who had rushed to join the revolutionary people. Huge popular demonstrations followed, frustrating all attempts to create instability."

94. The referendum was called in response to the Varela Project, a petition with roughly 11,000 signatures requesting "a referendum to guarantee Cuban civil liberties: freedom of expression and association, the right to own a private business (foreigners can own businesses in Cuba but nationals cannot), the release of nonviolent political prisoners and the right to directly elect representatives in multi-party elections." Osvaldo Payá, "Cloud of Terror Hangs over Cubans Seeking Rights," *Los Angeles Times*, July 14, 2003.

95. Dilla, "Comrades and Investors," 229.

96. In November 2004, the Cuban government removed the U.S. dollar from circulation and replaced it with what is called the convertible peso. Those with dollars in Cuba are charged a 10% commission for exchanging them into convertible pesos. This policy, however, does not change the general dynamic whereby those with access to hard currency from abroad have access to far more goods.

97. Prices are from the year 2000.

98. They are high even when we take into account the following factors; most people are owners of their housing or do not pay rent; health care and education are free; public transportation is affordable if unreliable; while one cannot survive on the rations provided at minimal cost by the state, they do make up a proportion of people's diet, providing staples such as rice, sugar, beans, powdered milk, lard, salt, potatoes, and bread; the state markets provide low-cost items.

99. As P. Sean Brotherton notes, the launching of Cuba's health tourism industry, Turismo y Salud, S.A., in the mid-1990s *did* help keep socialism alive by providing hard currency to the state, but the private informal health sector was also dependent upon that same state. P. Sean Brotherton, *Revolutionary Medicine*, 148, 163.

100. Linda Howe in *Transgression and Conformity* writes that intellectuals during the Special Period explored "the chasm between seedy reality" and "the ideal socialist island depicted in government propaganda" (4). This was one approach, but certainly not the only one and as James Buckwalter-Arias notes was also partly a response to global market demand.

101. For treatments of Special Period literature, see James Buckwalter-Arias, *Cuba and the New Origenismo* (Rochester, NY: Tamesis Books, 2010); and Whitfield, *Cuban Currency*. For discussions of film and art during the Special Period, see Chanan, *Cuban Cinema*; Fernandes, *Cuba Represent!*; and Holly Block, ed., *Art Cuba: The New Generation* (New York: Harry N. Abrams, 2001).

102. All songs are from Varela's albums *Como los peces* (TRAK, 1995), Nubes (PM Records, 2000), *Monedas al aire* (Anides-Sonido, 1992), and *Jalisco Park* (EGREM, 1989). All translations of lyrics and song titles from Spanish to English in this chapter are by the author. For Carlos Varela's songs, the original Spanish lyrics were taken from www.carlosvarela.com/lirica.asp.

103. The original lyrics are "Yo sé que la divisa hace la economía como hace al pan el trigo. Pero lo que no entiendo es que por el dinero confundan a la gente si vas a los hoteles por no ser extranjero te tratan diferente."

104. Both songs from the album *Trova-Tur* (Mutis, 1995). Spanish lyrics for Delgado's songs were taken from www.trovadores.net.

105. Fernandes, *Cuba Represent*.

106. These lyrics are from the song "Rap con churre" ("Rap with Grunge"), from the album *Con los puños arriba: Compilación de hip hop cubano* (EGREM, 2002). The term *Carabalí* is used in Cuba to refer to descendants of slaves who came from the Calabar region of West Africa (what is now southeastern Nigeria and the western part of Cameroon). The Cubans transposed the consonants, so that *Calabar* became *Carabalí*. Thanks to Lisa Maya Knauer for this point.

107. Certainly not all Cuban rap falls neatly into this category. The terms "commercial" and "underground" have been used in Cuba, as in the United States, to distinguish between rap whose style and lyrics are produced for wide commercial appeal and consumption and rap that is focused on social and political messages. For more in-depth discussions of these distinctions as well as treatments of the history and development of the Cuban hip-hop movement, its transnational links, and its political and social role in post-Soviet Cuba, see Sujatha Fernándes, "Island Paradise, Revolutionary Utopia or Hustler's Haven: Consumerism and Socialism in Contemporary Cuban Rap," *Journal of Latin American Cultural Studies* 12 (2003) 359–75; Ariel Fernández, "¿Poesía urbana? O la nueva trova de los noventa," in *El Caimán Barbudo* 296: 2000, 4–14; Ariel Fernández, "¿SBS Timba con rap? El hip hop de la polémica," in *Revista Salsa Cubana* 17 (2002): 43–35; Roberto Zurbano, "El Rap Cubano: Can't Stop, Won't Stop the Movement!" in *Cuba in the Special Period: Culture and Ideology in the 1990s*, ed. Ariana Hernández-Reguant (New York: Palgrave Macmillan, 2009).

108. From the album *Dejáme entrar* (EGREM, 2001); Spanish lyrics from album liner notes.

109. Among Sujatha Fernandes's examples of "underground rap" in her article on Cuban hip-hop is the song "Contamination and Globalization," by the group Hermanos a la Causa, which contains the lines "Technology controlling your tastes in your mind, you are a slave to the product like many people." Fernandes, "Island Paradise," 365.

Conclusion

1. See, for instance, the cover of the November 2012 issue of *National Geographic* with the feature article "Cuba on the Edge of Change." This sensationalism is not limited to popular journalism. Conferences on Cuba in the United States are frequently structured around the question of Cuba's "transition" away from the existing system toward some form of liberal democracy.

2. "Discurso Pronunciado por el presidente con consejo de Estado de la República de Cuba, Fidel Castro Ruz, en la Tribuna Abierta de la Juventud, los estudiantes, y los trabajadores por el día internacional de los trabajadores, en la plaza de la Revolución, El primero de Mayo del 2000," available at http://www.cuba.cu/gobierno/discursos/2000/esp/f010500e.html.

3. The original Spanish is "Estos tiempos de ahora, son honor. Hay afán de ser útil y el sacrificio vuelve a ser moda"; "Para mi todo hombre justo y generoso ha nacido en Cuba." "No hay obra imposible sino hombres incapaces."

4. See, for instance, José Carlos Mariétegui, *Seven Interpretive Essays on Peruvian Reality* (Austin: University of Texas Press, 1988) and *The Heroic and Creative Meaning of Socialism* (Atlantic Highlands, NJ: Humanities Press, 1996).

5. Ernesto Che Guevara, "Socialism and Man in Cuba," in *Che Guevara Reader*, 212–28.

6. The Spanish versions are "Podemos construir la sociedad más justa del mundo"; "Revolución es unidad, es independencia, es luchar por nuestro sueños de justicia para Cuba, y para el mundo." Both passages come from a 2005 speech of Fidel Castro.

7. For specific data, see Emilio Morales and Joseph L. Scarpaci, "Opening Up on Both Shorelines Helps Increase Remittances Sent to Cuba in 2011 by about 20%," Havana Consulting Group, March 2012. Available at: http://www.thehavanaconsultinggroup.com/.

8. VI Congreso del Partido Comunista de Cuba, *Lineamientos de la política económica y social del Partido y la Revolución*, (Havana: s.n., 2011). Available at http://www.granma.cubaweb.cu/secciones/6to-congreso-pcc/Folleto%20Lineamientos%20VI%20Cong.pdf.

9. Felipe Pérez Roque, who had been the minister of foreign affairs, also resigned from his Party and state positions.

10. Guevara, "A New Culture of Work."

11. "La batalla económica constituye hoy, más que nunca, la tarea principal y el centro del trabajo ideológico de los cuadros, porque de ella depende la sostenibilidad y preservación de nuestro sistema social—General de Ejercito Raúl Castro

Ruz, Clausura del IX Congreso de la Unión de Jovenes Comunistas, 4 de Abril de 2010."

12. Sarah A. Blue, "The Erosion of Racial Equality in the Context of Cuba's Dual Economy," *Latin American Politics and Society* 49, no. 3 (Fall 2007): 35–68.

13. Previously, private housing could only be exchanged.

14. *Información sobre el resultado del Debate de los Lineamientos de la Política Económica y Social del Partido y la Revolución, aprobado el 18 de abril de 2011 "Año 53 de la Revolución,"* 5.

15. For details of the case, see Amnesty International, "Cuba 'Essential Measures'? Human Rights Crackdown in the Name of Security," June 3, 2003, cited 2013, available at http://www.amnesty.org/en/library/info/AMR25/017/2003. For the official Cuban defense of its actions, see Felipe Pérez Roque, "Conferencia de prensa ofrecida por el canciller Felipe Pérez Roque con relación a los mercenarios al servicio del imperio que fueron juzgados los días 3,4,5 y 7 de abril," Havana: Versiones Taquigráficas, Consejo de Estado, 2003.

16. Benjamin Eastman, "Baseball in the Breach: Notes on Defection, Disaffection and Transition in Contemporary Cuba," *International Journal of the History of Sport* 24, no. 2 (2007): 264–95.

17. In February 2012, in celebration of the fortieth anniversary of *Criterios* and its latest edition, which had been blocked at the airport from leaving the country, the center hosted an event entitled "The Meaning of the Public Sphere in Cuba." Participants included, among others, University of Havana philosophy professor Jorge Luis Acanda, filmmaker Arturo Arango, anthropologist Mario Castillo, Rafael Hernández, the author Leonardo Padura, and the blogger Yasmín Portales. The center also published an edited volume of essays dealing with the Gray Years entitled *La política cultural del período revolucionario: memoria y reflexión* (Havana: Centro Teórico-Cultural Criterios, 2007).

18. The content of many of these discussions is available in a four-volume set. Vivian Lechuga, Denia García Ronda, and Rafael Hernández Rodríguez, *Último jueves: Los debates de Temas* (Havana: Ediciones ICAIC, 2004–10).

19. Navarro, "In Medias Res Republicas," 368–69.

20. Following the conviction of the Cuban dissidents, not just the U.S. government but also the European Union and North American and Latin American leftists condemned the jailing, summary trials, and executions. Well-known intellectuals such as Noam Chomsky, Howard Zinn, Edward Said, Cornel West, and Barbara Ehrenreich signed a statement recognizing that the United States was "hardly in a position to preach democracy and human rights," but that "the imprisonment of people for attempting to exercise their rights of free expression [was] outrageous and unacceptable" and called upon Castro to "release all political prisoners and let the Cuban people speak, write and organize freely." Campaign for Peace and Democracy, "Statement Protesting Repression in Cuba," 2003, cited October 15, 2003, available from http://home.igc.org/~jlandy/cpd/anti-war/cuba-stmt.html.

21. For a discussion of the Cuban blogosphere, see Ted Henken, "A Blogger's

Polemic: Debating Independent Cuban Blogger Projects in a Polarized Political Context," in *Cuba in Transition*, vol. 11, 171–85 (Washington, DC: Association for the Study of the Cuban Economy, 2011).

22. State of SATS, http://www.estadodesats.com/aboutstate-of-sats.

23. Gordy, "Beside the State"; Marina Gold, "Urban Gardens: Private Property or the Ultimate Socialist Experience?" in *Cuban Intersections of Literary and Urban Spaces*, ed. Carlos Riobó (New York: State University of New York Press, 2011), 25–48.

24. Marie Laure Geoffray, "Cuba, de la subversion des normes révolutionnaires à la (re) création d'un espace public," *Actes du Second Congrès international pluridisciplinaire du GIS Réseau Amérique Latine: Territoires et Sociétés dans les Amériques, 15–17 novembre 2007, Rennes* (2007).

25. Samuel Farber, "The Future of the Cuban Revolution," in *Jacobin*. Available at https://www.jacobinmag.com/2014/01/the-cuban-revolution/.

26. Pedro Campos, "La revolución socialista no es el gobierno, ni el estado, ni el partido ni los dirigentes." Available at http://observatoriocriticodesdecuba.wordpress.com/.

27. Katherine Gordy and Jee Sun E. Lee, "Rogue Specters: Cuba and North Korea at the Limits of US Hegemony," *Alternatives: Global, Local, Political* 34, no. 3 (2009): 229–48.

28. James Dao, "Schumer Says D'Amato Puts 'Ideology Ahead of People," *New York Times*, October 15, 1998.

29. Jessica Holzer, "Schumer Retools Bill to Lift Caps on GSE's." Posted October 11, 2007. Available at http://thehill.com. In fairness to Schumer, he also argued for the use of ideology as one of the criteria in the judicial selection process. See Charles Schumer. "Judging by Ideology," *New York Times*, June 26, 2001. Available at https://www.senate.gov/~schumer/SchumerWebsite/pressroom/press releases/PR00612.html.

30. Thanks to Peter Breiner for this specific example.

31. I am grateful to Peter Breiner for clarifying this issue for me.

32. Slavoj Žižek, *First as Tragedy, Then as Farce* (New York: Verso, 2009), 19.

33. Ibid., 65.

34. Michael Warner makes similar critiques of the literature on counterpublics, while retaining the term itself. See Warner, *Publics and Counterpublics* (New York: Zone Books, 2002).

Bibliography

VI Congreso del Partido Comunista de Cuba, *Lineamientos de la política económica y social del Partido y la Revolución*. Havana: s.n., 2011. Available at http://www.granma.cubaweb.cu/secciones/6to-congreso-pcc/Folleto%20Lineamientos%20VI%20Cong.pdf.

Acanda, Jorge. "Sociedad civil y hegemonía." *Temas* 6 (1996): 87–93.

Agramonte y Loynaz, Ignacio. "Comunicación del Comité Revolucionario del Camagüey a la Junta Revolucionaria de la Habana (1869)." In *Pensamiento cubano, Siglo XIX*, edited by Isabel Monal and Olivia Miranda Francisco, 15–16. Havana: Editorial de Ciencias Sociales, 2002.

Agramonte y Loynaz, Ignacio. "Decreto de extinción de la esclavitud (1869)." In *Pensamiento Cubano, Siglo XIX*, edited by Isabel Monal and Olivia Miranda Francisco, 17. Havana: Editorial de Ciencias Sociales, 2002.

Agramonte y Loynaz, Ignacio. *Patria y mujer*. Havana: Publicaciones del Ministerio de Educación, 1942.

Aguilar, Luis E. "Cuba, c. 1860–c. 1930." In *Cuba: A Short History*, edited by Leslie Bethell, 21–55. New York: Cambridge University Press, 1993.

Aguirre, Mirta. "Apuntes sobre la literatura y el arte." In *Polémicas culturales de los 60*, edited by Graziella Pogolotti, 43–71. Havana: Editorial Letras Cubanas, 2006.

Alfonso, Pablo. "Muy importantes los militares para el poscastrismo." *El Nuevo Herald*, November 7, 2003.

Alonso, Aurelio. "La economía cubana: Los desafíos de un ajuste sin desocialización." *Cuadernos de Nuestra América* 9, no. 19 (1992): 159–74.

Alonso, Aurelio. "Réplica." *Encuentro de la Cultura Cubana*, Spring–Summer 2000, 120–21.

Althusser, Louis. *Lenin and Philosophy and Other Essays*. Translated by Ben Brewster. New York: Monthly Review Press, 1971.

Álvarez García, Alberto F., and Gerardo González Núñez. *Intelectuales vs. Revolución? El caso del Centro de Estudios sobre América, CEA*. Montreal: Ediciones Arte D.T., 2001.

Álvarez Quiñones, Roberto. "El salario por rendimiento o destajo, las primas y las normas." *Granma*, February 27, 1980.

Álvarez Quiñones, Roberto. "La ley económica de distribución según el trabajo." *Granma*, February 2, 1980.
Álvarez Quiñones, Roberto. "Propiedad social, eficiencia económica y ahorro." *Granma*, February 4, 1980.
Álvarez Quiñones, Roberto. "Proponen mayor vinculación de investigaciones económicas con necesidades de la economía nacional." *Granma*, December 5, 1977.
Alzugaray, Carlos. "Academic Exchanges and Transnational Relations: Cuba and the United States." *Latin American Perspectives* 33, no. 5 (2006): 43–57.
Amnesty International. "Cuba 'Essential Measures'? Human Rights Crackdown in the Name of Security." June 3, 2003. Cited 2013. Available at http://www.amnesty.org/en/library/info/AMR25/017/20032003.
"Analizan deficiencias y avances presentados por el SDPE en la Provincia en Camagüey." *Granma*, May 9, 1980.
Arenas, Reinaldo. *Before Night Falls*. New York: Viking, 1993.
Artaraz, Kepa. *Cuba and Western Intellectuals since 1959*. New York: Palgrave Macmillan, 2009.
Ayala Castro, Hector, and Frank Hidalgo-Gato. "Aspectos teóricos del Sistema de Dirección y Planificación de la Economía." *Economía y Desarrollo* 57 (1980): 37–73.
Azicri, Max. *Cuba Today and Tomorrow: Reinventing Socialism*. Edited by John M. Kirk. Gainesville: University Press of Florida, 2000.
Azicri, Max. "The Cuban Rectification: Safeguarding the Revolution While Building the Future." In *Transformation and Struggle: Cuba Faces the 1990s*, edited by Sandor Halebsky and John M. Kirk, 3–20. New York: Praeger, 1990.
Bargu, Banu. *Starve and Immolate: The Politics of Human Weapons*. New York: Columbia University Press, 2014.
Batista y Zaldívar, Fulgencio. *Cuba Betrayed*. New York: Vantage Press, 1962.
Belnap, Jeffrey, and Raúl Fernández, eds. *José Martí's "Our America": From National to Hemispheric Cultural Studies*. Durham: Duke University Press, 1998.
Bengelsdorf, Carollee. "Intellectuals under Fire." *In These Times*, September 16–29, 1996, 27.
Bengelsdorf, Carollee. *The Problem of Democracy in Cuba: Between Vision and Reality*. New York: Oxford University Press, 1994.
Bengelsdorf, Carollee. "(Re)Considering Cuban Women in a Time of Troubles." In *Daughters of Caliban: Caribbean Women in the Twentieth Century*, edited by Consuelo López Springfield, 229–55. Bloomington: Indiana University Press, 1997.
Benjamin, Walter. "N [Re the Theory of Knowledge, Theory of Progress]." In *Benjamin: Philosophy, Aesthetics, History*, edited by Gary Smith, 43–83. Chicago: University of Chicago Press, 1989.
Benjamin, Walter. "Theses on the Philosophy of History." In *Illuminations*, edited by Hannah Arendt, translated by Harry Zohn, 253–64. New York: Schocken Books, 1968.
Benvenuto, Sergio. "¿Cultura pequeñoburguesa hay una sola?" In *Polémicas cultura-*

les de los 60, edited by Graziella Pogolotti, 126–41. Havana: Editorial Letras Cubanas, 2006.

Bernardo, Robert M. *The Theory of Moral Incentives in Cuba*. University: University of Alabama Press, 1971.

Blanco, Juan. "Los herederos del oscurantismo." In *Polémicas culturales de los 60*, edited by Graziella Pogolotti, 3–8. Havana: Editorial Letras Cubanas, 2006.

Block, Holly, ed. *Art Cuba: The New Generation*. New York: Harry N. Abrams, 2001.

Blue, Sarah A. "The Erosion of Racial Equality in the Context of Cuba's Dual Economy." *Latin American Politics and Society* 49, no. 3 (Fall 2007): 35–68.

Boorstein, Edward. *The Economic Transformation of Cuba*. New York: Modern Reader Paperbacks, 1968.

Boucher, Richard. "Cuba: Denial of Visas to Group of Cuban Academics/Basis for decision." Washington, DC: U.S. Department of State, 2004.

Bourdieu, Pierre. *Outline of a Theory of Practice*. Translated by Richard Nice. Cambridge: Cambridge University Press, 1977.

Brotherton, P. Sean. *Revolutionary Medicine: Health and the Body in Post-Soviet Cuba*. Durham: Duke University Press, 2012.

Brundenius, Claes. "Whither the Cuban Economy after Recovery? The Reform Process, Upgrading Strategies and the Question of Transition." *Journal of Latin American Studies* 34, no. 2 (2002): 365–95.

Buckwalter-Arias, James. *Cuba and the New Origenismo*. Rochester, NY: Tamesis Books, 2010.

Bunck, Julie Marie. *Fidel Castro and the Quest for a Revolutionary Culture in Cuba*. University Park: Pennsylvania State University Press, 1994.

"Buscando eficiencia los criterios económicos de la empresa evolucionan hasta llegar al campo terminado." *Granma*, June 11, 1980.

Cabezas, Amalia Lucía. "Discourses of Prostitution: The Case of Cuba." In *Global Sex Workers: Rights, Resistance, and Redefinition*, edited by Kamal Kempadoo and Jo Doezema, 79–86. New York: Routledge, 1998.

Cabrera Infante, Guillermo. *Mea Cuba*. Madrid: Grupo Santillana de Ediciones, 1999.

Campaign for Peace and Democracy. 2003. "Statement Protesting Repression in Cuba." http://home.igc.org/~jlandy/cpd/anti-war/cuba-stmt.html. Accessed October 15, 2003.

"Características de las empresas socialistas en Cuba (I)." *Granma*, January 12, 1977.

"Características de las empresas socialistas en Cuba (II)." *Granma*, January 13, 1977.

Carbonell, Walterio. *Cómo surgió la cultura nacional*. Havana: Ediciones Bachiller, Biblioteca Nacional José Martí, 2005.

Carranza Valdés, Julio. "Cuba: Los retos de la economía." *Cuadernos de Nuestra América* 9, no. 19 (1992): 131–58.

Carranza Valdés, Julio, Luis Gutiérrez Urdaneta, and Pedro Monreal González. *Cuba: La restructuración de la economía: Una propuesta para el debate*. Havana: Editorial de Ciencias Sociales, 1995.

Carranza Valdés, Julio, Luis Gutiérrez Urdaneta, and Pedro Monreal González.

Cuba: Restructuring the Economy—a Contribution to the Debate. Translated by Ruth Pearson. London: Institute of Latin American Studies, 1996.

"Carta de Severino Puente y de directores del ICAIC." In *Polémicas culturales de los 60*, edited by Graziella Pogolotti, 152–57. Havana: Editorial Letras Cubanas, 2006.

Castellanos, Ernesto Juan. "El diversionismo ideológico del rock, la moda y los enfermitos." Conference paper presented at Centro Teórico Cultural Criterios, Havana, October 31, 2008. Available at http://www.criterios.es/pdf/9castellanosdiversionismo.pdf.

Castro Ruz, Fidel. *The Current World Order Is Unsustainable*. Havana: Editora Política, 1999.

Castro Ruz, Fidel. "El Sistema de Dirección y Planificación de la Economía." In *II Congreso del Partido Comunista de Cuba: Informe Central*, 33–37. Havana: Editora Política, 1980.

Castro Ruz, Fidel. *Globalización neoliberal y crisis económica global: Discursos y declaraciones, mayo de 1998–enero de 1999*. Havana: Oficina de Publicaciones del Consejo de Estado, 1999.

Castro Ruz, Fidel. *La historia me absolverá: Discurso ante la sala primera de urgencia de la audencia de Santiago de Cuba, 16 de octubre de 1953*. Havana: Editora Política, 1994.

Castro Ruz, Fidel. "On the Events in Czechoslovakia." In *Selected Speeches of Fidel Castro*, 110–25. New York: Pathfinder, 1979.

Castro Ruz, Fidel. *Palabras a Los Intelectuales*. Havana: Departamento de ediciones de la Biblioteca Nacional "José Martí," 1991.

Castro Ruz, Fidel. *A Revolution Can Only Be Born from Culture and Ideas*. Havana: Editora Política, 1999.

Castro Ruz, Fidel. "I Will Be a Marxist-Leninist to the End of My Life." In *Selected Speeches of Fidel* Castro, 11–40. New York: Pathfinder Press, 1979: 11–40.

Castro Ruz, Fidel, ed. *José Martí: El autor intelectual*. Havana: Editora Política, 1983.

Castro Ruz, Fidel. "Discurso Pronunciado por el presidente con consejo de Estado de la República de Cuba, Fidel Castro Ruz, en la Tribuna Abierta de la Juventud, los estudiantes, y los trabajadores por el día internacional de los trabajadores, en la plaza de la Revolución, El primero de Mayo del 2000." Available at http://www.cuba.cu/gobierno/discursos/2000/esp/f010500e.html.

Castro, Raúl. "Informe del Buró Político." *Granma*, March 27, 1996, 2–6.

Centro de Estudios sobre América. "Balance crítico de las deficiencias del Centro de Estudios sobre América en el periodo 1991–1995 (April 22, 1996)." In *El caso CEA: Intelectuales e inquisidores en Cuba ¿Perestroika en la isla?*, edited by Maurizio Giuliano, 215–33. Miami: Ediciones Universal, 1998.

Centro de Estudios sobre América. "Balance político de las tareas cumplidas en el Quinquenio 1991–1995 (April 11, 1996)." In *El caso CEA: Intelectuales e inquisidores en Cuba ¿Perestroika en la isla?*, edited by Maurizio Giuliano, 154–77. Miami: Ediciones Universal, 1998.

Centro de Estudios sobre América. "Carta enviada por el Núcleo del PCC del CEA a Fidel y Raúl Castro (August 27, 1996)." In *El caso CEA: Intelectuales e inquisidores en Cuba ¿Perestroika en la isla?*, edited by Maurizio Giuliano, 272–76. Miami: Ediciones Universal, 1998.

Centro de Estudios sobre América. "Consideraciones preliminares de la Dirección del Núcleo del Partido del CEA acerca del proceso de análisis efectuado en el Centro por la Comisión designada por el Buró Político a raíz de los señalamientos del V Pleno del CC del PCC (May 23, 1997)." In *El caso CEA: Intelectuales e inquisidores en Cuba ¿Perestroika en la isla?*, edited by Maurizio Giuliano, 256–60. Miami: Ediciones Universal, 1998.

Centro de Estudios sobre América. "Intervención de José Ramón Balaguer en la Reunión de la Comisión del Buró Político con el Núcleo del PCC del CEA (August 14, 1996)." In *El caso CEA: Intelectuales e inquisidores en Cuba ¿Perestroika en la isla?*, edited by Maurizio Giuliano, 265–71. Miami: Ediciones Universal, 1998.

Centro de Estudios sobre América. "Primera Reunión de la Comisión del CC del PCC con el Consejo de Dirección del CEA (April 12, 1996)." In *El caso CEA: Intelectuales e inquisidores en Cuba ¿Perestroika en la isla?*, edited by Maurizio Giuliano, 178–97. Miami: Ediciones Universal, 1998.

Centro de Estudios sobre América. "Segunda Reunión de la Comisión del CC del PCC con el Consejo de Dirección del CEA (April 15, 1996)." In *El caso CEA: Intelectuales e inquisidores en Cuba ¿Perestroika en la isla?*, edited by Maurizio Giuliano, 198–214. Miami: Ediciones Universal, 1998.

Centro de Estudios sobre América. "Tercera Reunión de la Comisión del Buró Político con el Consejo de Dirección del CEA (April 26, 1996)." In *El caso CEA: Intelectuales e inquisidores en Cuba ¿Perestroika en la isla?*, edited by Maurizio Giuliano, 234–55. Miami: Ediciones Universal, 1998.

Centro de Estudios sobre América, ed. *The Cuban Revolution into the 1990s*. Boulder: Westview Press, 1992.

Centro Teórico-Cultural Criterios, ed. *La política cultural del período revolucionario: Memoria y reflexión*. Havana: Centro Teórico-Cultural Criterios, 2007.

CEPAL (Comisión Económica para América Latina y el Caribe). *La economía cubana: Reformas estructurales y desempeño en los noventa*. Mexico City: Fondo de cultura económica, 1997.

Céspedes, Carlos Manuel de. "Declaración de Independencia: (1868)." In *Pensamiento cubano: Siglo XIX*, edited by Isabel Monal and Olivia Miranda, 3–5. Havana: Editorial de Ciencias Sociales, 2002.

Céspedes, Carlos Manuel de. "Decreto de 27 de diciembre de 1868: Carlos Manuel de Céspedes, Capitán General del Ejército Libertador de Cuba y encargado de su gobierno provisional (1868)." In *Pensamiento cubano: Siglo XIX*, edited by Isabel Monal and Olivia Miranda, 6–7. Havana: Editorial de Ciencias Sociales, 2002.

Chanan, Michael. *Cuban Cinema*. Minneapolis: University of Minnesota Press, 2004.

Childs, Matt D. *The 1812 Aponte Rebellion in Cuba and the Struggle against Atlantic Slavery*. Chapel Hill: University of North Carolina Press, 2006.

Ciccariello-Maher, George. *We Created Chávez: A People's History of the Venezuelan Revolution*. Durham: Duke University Press, 2013.

Choy, Leon, and Alex Shelton. "Extenderán el pago por rendimiento a 230 mil trabajadores este año." *Granma*, April 2, 1976, 1.

"CIMEX: Over $950 Million USD Revenue in 2001." Digital Granma International. http://www.granma.cu/ingles/actualidad-i.html. Accessed January 21, 2004.

Coatsworth, John. "Preface." In *The Cuban Economy at the Start of the Twenty-First Century*, edited by Jorge Domínguez, Omar Everleny Pérez, and Lorena Barberia. Cambridge: David Rockefeller Center for Latin American Studies, Harvard University, 2004.

"Comenzó reunión operativa sobre cumplimiento de algunas tareas de cronograma." *Granma*, September 3, 1976, 4.

"Conclusiones de un debate entre cineastas cubanos." In *Polémicas culturales de los 60*, edited by Graziella Pogolotti, 17–22. Havana: Editorial Letras Cubanas, 2006.

"Constituyen en Guantánamo la comisión provincial del SDPE." *Granma*, June 16, 1977.

"Creada la Comisión Nacional de Implantación del Sistema de Dirección y Planificación de la Economía." *Granma*, January 23, 1976, 1.

"Crean empresa para prestar servicios de contabilidad y auditoría a empresas y unidades presupuestadas con el objetivo de facilitar la implantación del Sistema de Dirección y Planificación de la Economía." *Granma*, January 2, 1980.

Cuban American National Foundation. "About the Cuban American National Foundation." http://www.canf.org/About/aboutmain.htm.

Cuban Committee for Democracy. 2004. "Cuban Committee for Democracy Mission Statement." http://www.us.net/cuban/mission/html.

Dao, James. "Schumer Says D'Amato Puts 'Ideology Ahead of People'." *New York Times*, October 15, 1998.

Dávalos, Fernando. "Cuatro principios de la gestión empresarial." *Granma*, January 5, 1980.

Dávalos, Fernando. "El artículo 3 del Reglamento General de la empresa estatal: Cálculo económico." *Granma,* February 13, 1980.

Dávalos, Fernando. "Entrará en vigor en enero del año próximo el nuevo Sistema de Información Estadística Nacional (SIEN)." *Granma*, September 4, 1976, 1.

"Debatir cada uno de los indicadores del plan con los trabajadores y escuchar sus opiniones." *Granma*, April 7, 1981.

Deere, Carmen Diana. "The New Agrarian Reforms." *NACLA Report on the Americas* 29, no. 2 (1995): 13–17.

Díaz Castañón, María del Pilar. *Ideología y revolución: Cuba, 1959–1962*. Havana: Editorial de Ciencias Sociales, 2001.

Díaz, Jesús. "El fin de otra ilusión: A propósito de la quiebra de *El Caimán Barbudo* y la clausura de *Pensamiento Crítico*." *Encuentro de la Cultura Cubana*, Spring–Summer 2000, 106–19.

Dilla, Haroldo. "Las ciencias sociales cubanas: entre el saber y el poder." *Vértice* 7 (2002): 4–5.

Dilla, Haroldo. "Comrades and Investors: The Uncertain Transition in Cuba." In

Global Capitalism versus Democracy: Socialist Register 1999, edited by Leo Panitch and Colin Leys, 227–47. New York: Monthly Review Press, 1999.

Dilla, Haroldo. "Cuba between Utopia and the World Market." *Latin American Perspectives* 21, no. 83 (1994): 46–59.

Dilla, Haroldo. "Cuba: La crisis y la rearticulación del consenso político (notas para un debate socialista)." *Cuadernos de Nuestra América* 10, no. 20 (1993): 20–45.

Dilla, Haroldo. "Cuba: ¿Cuál es la democracia deseable?" In *La democracia en Cuba y el diferendo con los Estados Unidos*, edited by Haroldo Dilla, 169–89. Havana: Editorial de Ciencias Sociales, 1996.

Dilla, Haroldo, ed. *La democracia en Cuba y el diferendo con los Estados Unidos*. Havana: Editorial de Ciencias Sociales, 1996.

Dilla, Haroldo, and Philip Oxhorn. "The Virtues and Misfortunes of Civil Society in Cuba." *Latin American Perspectives* 29, no. 4 (2002): 11–30.

Dilla Alfonso, Haroldo, Gerardo González Núñez, and Ana Teresa Vicentelli. *Participación popular y desarrollo en los municipios cubanos*. Caracas: Fondo Editorial Tropykos, 1994.

Domínguez, Jorge I. "Cuba's Relations with Caribbean and Central American Countries." *Cuban Studies* 13, no. 2 (1983): 79–110.

Domínguez, Jorge I. "La democracia en Cuba: ¿Cuál es el modelo deseable?" In *La democracia en Cuba y el diferendo con los Estados Unidos*, edited by Haroldo Dilla Alfonso, 117–29. Havana: Editorial de Ciencias Sociales, 1996.

Domínguez, Jorge I. "Response." *Cuban Studies* 13, no 2 (1983): 119.

Domínguez, Jorge I. *To Make a World Safe for Revolution: Cuba's Foreign Policy*. Cambridge: Harvard University Press, 1989.

Domínguez, Jorge I. "Twenty-Five Years of Cuban Studies." *Cuban Studies* 25 (1995): 7–22.

Domínguez, Jorge I. "Why the Cuban Regime Has Not Fallen." In *Cuban Communism*, edited by Irving Louis Horowitz, 691–98. New Brunswick, NJ: Transaction Publishers, 1995.

Domínguez, Jorge I., and Rafael Hernández, eds. *U.S.-Cuban Relations in the 1990s*. Boulder: Westview Press, 1989.

Domínguez, Jorge I., Omar Everleny Pérez Villanueva, and Lorena Barberia, eds. *The Cuban Economy at the Start of the Twenty-First Century*. Cambridge: Harvard University, David Rockefeller Center for Latin American Studies, 2004.

Draper, Theodore. *Castro's Revolution: Myths and Realities*. New York: Frederick A. Praeger, 1962.

Draper, Theodore. *Castroism: Theory and Practice*. New York: Frederick A. Praeger, 1965.

Dumont, Rene. *Cuba: Socialism and Development*. Translated by Helen R. Lane. New York: Grove Press, 1970.

Eagleton, Terry. *Ideology: An Introduction*. London: Verso, 1991.

Eastman, Benjamin. "Baseball in the Breach: Notes on Defection, Disaffection and Transition in Contemporary Cuba." *International Journal of the History of Sport* 24, no. 2: 264–95.

Eckstein, Susan Eva. *Back from the Future: Cuba under Castro*. Princeton: Princeton University Press, 1994.

"Editorial Note." *Cuban Studies* 13, no. 1 (1983).
"Efectúase en Santa Clara, Plenaria Provincial sobre la eficiencia económica ya la implantación del SDPE." *Granma*, September 1, 1977.
"El camino trazado por nuestra revolución." In *Polémicas culturales de los 60*, edited by Graziella Pogolotti, 158–59. Havana: Editorial Letras Cubanas, 2006.
Espinosa, Juan Carlos. "Civil Society in Cuba: The Logic of Emergence in Comparative Perspective." In *Cuba in Transition*, vol. 9, 346–67. Washington, DC: Association for the Study of the Cuban Economy, 1999.
Fagen, Richard R. *The Transformation of Political Culture in Cuba*. Stanford: Stanford University Press, 1969.
Farber, Samuel. *The Origins of the Cuban Revolution Reconsidered*. Chapel Hill: University of North Carolina Press, 2006.
Fernandes, Sujatha. "Island Paradise, Revolutionary Utopia or Hustler's Haven? Consumerism and Socialism in Contemporary Cuban Rap." *Journal of Latin American Cultural Studies* 12, no. 3 (2003): 359–75.
Fernandes, Sujatha. *Cuba Represent: Cuban Arts, State Power and the Making of New Revolutionary Cultures*. Durham: Duke University Press, 2006.
Fernandes, Sujatha. "Transnationalism and Feminist Activism in Cuba: The Case of Magín." *Politics & Gender* 1, no. 3 (September 2005): 431–52.
Fernández, Ariel. "¿Poesía urbana? O la nueva trova de los noventa." *El Caimán Barbudo* 296 (2000): 4–14.
Fernández, Ariel. "¿Timba con rap? El hip hop de la polémica." *Revista Salsa Cubana* 17 (2002): 43–35.
Fernández, Damián J. *Cuba and the Politics of Passion*. Austin: University of Texas Press, 2000.
Fernández, Frank. *Cuban Anarchism: A History of a Movement*. Translated by Charles Bufe. Tuscon: See Sharp Press, 2001.
Fernandez, Nadine. "Back to the Future? Women, Race, and Tourism in Cuba." In *Sun, Sex, and Gold: Tourism and Sex Work in the Caribbean*, edited by Kamala Kempadoo, 81–89. New York: Rowman & Littlefield, 1999.
Fernández Retamar, Roberto. "Martí en su (tercer) mundo." In *Ensayo de Otro Mundo*, 19–51. Santiago de Chile: Editorial Universitaria S.A., 1969.
Fitzgerald, Frank T. *The Cuban Revolution in Crisis: From Managing Socialism to Managing Survival*. New York: Monthly Review Press, 1994.
Foner, Philip S. *Antonio Maceo: The "Bronze Titan" of Cuba's Struggle for Independence*. New York: Monthly Review Press, 1977.
Flo, Juan. J. "¿Estética antidogmática o estética no marxista?" In *Polémicas culturales de los 60*, edited by Graziella Pogolotti, 102–10. Havana: Editorial Letras Cubanas, 2006.
Foucault, Michel. "Truth and Power." In *Power/Knowledge: Selected Interviews and Other Writings, 1972–1977*, edited by Colin Gordon. New York: Vintage Book, 1980.
Foucault, Michel. *Discipline and Punish: The Birth of the Prison*. Translated by Alan Sheridan. New York: Vintage Books, 1995.
Fraga, Jorge. "Ambigüedad de la crítica y crítica de ambigüedad." In *Polémicas cul-

turales de los 60, edited by Graziella Pogolotti, 35–42. Havana: Editorial Letras Cubanas, 2006.

Fraga, Jorge. ¿Cuántas culturas? In *Polémicas culturales de los 60*, edited by Graziella Pogolotti, 72–85. Havana: Editorial Letras Cubanas, 2006.

Franco, José Luciano. *La conspiración de Aponte*. Havana: Consejo Nacional de Cultura, 1963.

Franqui, Carlos. *Family Portrait with Fidel*. Translated by Alfred MacAdam. New York: Random House, 1981.

Freeden, Michael. *Ideologies and Political Theory: A Conceptual Approach*. Oxford: Clarendon Press, 1996.

Fuente, Alejandro de la. *A Nation for All: Race, Inequality, and Politics in Twentieth Century Cuba*. Chapel Hill: University of North Carolina Press, 2001.

Fuente, Alejandro de la. "The Resurgence of Racism in Cuba." *NACLA Report on the Americas* 2001, 29–34.

Fusco, Coco. "Hustling for Dollars: Jineterismo in Cuba." In *Global Sex Workers: Rights, Resistance, and Redefinition*, edited by Kamal Kempadoo and Jo Doezema, 151–60. New York: Routledge, 1998.

García Buchaca, Edith. "Consideraciones sobre un manifiesto." In *Polémicas culturales de los 60*, edited by Graziella Pogolotti, 26–34. Havana: Editorial Letras Cubanas, 2006.

García Espinosa, Julio. "Vivir bajo la lluvia." In *Polémicas culturales de los 60*, edited by Graziella Pogolotti, 9–13. Havana: Editorial Letras Cubanas, 2006.

García Espinosa, Julio. "Galgos y podencos." In *Polémicas culturales de los 60*, edited by Graziella Pogolotti, 86–94. Havana: Editorial Letras Cubanas, 2006.

García, María Cristina. *Havana USA: Cuban Exiles and Cuban Americans in South Florida, 1959–1994*. Berkeley: University of California Press, 1996.

García Reyes, Miguel, and María Guadalupe López de Llergo y Cornejo. *Cuba después de la era soviética*. Mexico City: El Colegio de México, 1997.

Geoffray, Marie Laure. "Cuba, de la subversion des normes révolutionnaires à la (re) création d'un espace public." *Actes du Second Congrès international pluridisciplinaire du GIS Réseau Amérique Latine: Territoires et Sociétés dans les Amériques, 15–17 novembre 2007, Rennes*. 2007.

Geyer, Georgie Anne. *Guerrilla Prince: The Untold Story of Fidel Castro*. Boston: Little, Brown, 1991.

Giuliano, Maurizio. *El caso CEA: Intelectuales e inquisidores en Cuba ¿Perestroika en la isla?* Miami: Ediciones Universal, 1998.

Gleijeses, Piero. *Conflicting Missions: Havana, Washington and Africa, 1959–1976*. Chapel Hill: University of North Carolina Press, 2002.

Godrej, Farah. "Toward a Cosmopolitan Political Thought: The Hermeneutics of Interpreting the Other." *Polity* 41 (2009): 135–65.

Gold, Marina. "Urban Gardens: Private Property or the Ultimate Socialist Experience?" In *Cuban Intersections of Literary and Urban Spaces*, edited by Carlos Riobó, 25–48. New York: State University of New York Press, 2007.

Gonzalez, David. "In Cuba, Clashing Voices over Ideals and Reality." *New York Times*, May 30, 2001.

González, Edward. *Cuba under Castro: The Limits of Charisma*. Boston: Houghton Mifflin, 1974.

Gordy, Katherine. "Beside the State: Anarchist Strains in Cuban Revolutionary Thought." In *How Not to Be Governed: Readings and Interpretations from a Critical Anarchist Left*. Edited by Jimmy Casas Klausen and James Martel, 47–64. New York: Lexington Press, 2011.

Gordy, Katherine. "The Theory and Practice of Ideology: Navigating the Principles of Cuban Socialism." PhD diss., Cornell University, 2005.

Gordy, Katherine, and Jee Sun E. Lee. "Rogue Specters: Cuba and North Korea at the Limits of US Hegemony." *Alternatives: Global, Local, Political* 34, no. 3 (2009): 229–48.

Gramsci, Antonio. "On Education." In *Selections from the Prison Notebooks*, edited by Quintin Hoare and Geoffrey Nowell Smith, 24–43. New York: International Publishers, 1971.

Gramsci, Antonio. "State and Civil Society." In *Selections from the Prison Notebooks*, edited by Quintin Hoare and Geoffrey Nowell Smith, 206–76. New York: International Publishers, 1971.

Gramsci, Antonio. "The Study of Philosophy." In *Selections from the Prison Notebooks*, edited by Quintin Hoare and Geoffrey Nowell Smith, 321–77. New York: International Publishers, 1971.

Gray, Alexander I., and Antoni Kapcia. "Setting the Stage for a Discussion of Cuban Civil Society: The Nature of Cuban 'Communism' and the Revolution's Political Culture." In *The Changing Dynamic of Cuban Civil Society*, edited by Alexander I. Gray and Antoni Kapcia, 20–39. Gainesville: University Press of Florida, 2008.

Guevara, Alfredo. "Sobre un debate entre cineastas cubanos." In *Polémicas culturales de los 60*, edited by Graziella Pogolotti, 23–25. Havana: Editorial Letras Cubanas, 2006.

Guevara, Ernesto "Che." "Man and Socialism in Cuba (1965)." In *Man and Socialism in Cuba: The Great Debate*, edited by Bertram Silverman, 337–82. New York: Atheneum, 1971.

Guevara, Ernesto "Che." "The Meaning of Socialist Planning (1964)." In *Man and Socialism in Cuba: The Great Debate*, edited by Bertram Silverman, 98–110. New York: Atheneum, 1971.

Guevara, Ernesto "Che." "On Production Costs and the Budgetary System (1963)." In *Man and Socialism in Cuba: The Great Debate*, edited by Bertram Silverman, 113–21. New York: Atheneum, 1971.

Guevara, Ernesto "Che." "On the Budgetary Finance System (1964)." In *Man and Socialism in Cuba: The Great Debate*, edited by Bertram Silverman, 122–56. New York: Atheneum, 1971.

Guevara, Ernesto "Che." "A New Culture of Work." In *Che Guevara Reader: Writings on Politics and Revolution*, 143–52. New York: Ocean Press, 2003.

Guevara, Ernesto "Che." "Algo nuevo en América: A la sesión de apertura del Primer Congreso Latinamericano de Juventudes, 28 de julio de 1960." In *Che Guevara habla a la juventud*, 25–42. Havana: Casa Editora Abril, 2001.

Guma, José Gabriel. "Actuarán con independencia e imparcialidad los árbitros estatales que integraran el Sistema de Arbitraje Nacional." *Granma*, January 22, 1980.

Guma, José Gabriel. "Adoptarán medidas disciplinarias contra los funcionarios de entidades que no conciertan los contratos económicos en los plazos establecidos." *Granma*, November 27, 1980.

Gunn, Gillian. "Cuba's NGO's: Government Puppets or Seeds of Civil Society?" Cuba Briefing Paper 7. Washington, DC: Center for Latin American Studies, Georgetown University, 1995.

Gutiérrez Alea, Tomás. "Notas sobre una discusión de un documento sobre una discussion (de otros documentos)." In *Polémicas culturales de los 60*, edited by Graziella Pogolotti, 95–101. Havana: Editorial Letras Cubanas, 2006.

Gutiérrez Alea, Tomás. "Donde menos se piensa salta el cazador . . . de brujas." In *Polémicas culturales de los 60*, edited by Graziella Pogolotti, 111–25. Havana: Editorial Letras Cubanas, 2006.

Hall, Stuart. "The Problem of Ideology: Marxism without Guarantees." In *Critical Dialogues in Cultural Studies*, edited by David Morly and Kuan-Hsing Chen, 25–46. New York: Routledge, 1996.

Harnecker, Marta. *Cuba: Dictatorship or Democracy?* Westport, CT: Lawrence Hill and Company, 1980.

Harnecker, Marta. "Problemas objetivos de nuestra revolución: Lo que el pueblo debe saber." *Bohemia*, February 16, 1979, 60–81.

Hearn, Adrian H. *Cuba: Religion, Social Capital and Development*. Durham: Duke University Press, 2008.

Henken, Ted. "Condemned to Informality: Cuba's Experiments with Self-Employment during the Special Period (the Case of the Bed and Breakfasts)." *Cuban Studies* 33 (2002): 1–29.

Henken, Ted. "A Blogger's Polemic: Debating Independent Cuban Blogger Projects in a Polarized Political Context." In *Cuba in Transition*, vol. 11, 171–85. Washington, DC: Association for the Study of the Cuban Economy, 2011.

Hernández-Reguant, Ariana. "Copyrighting Che: Art and Authorship under Cuban Late Socialism." *Public Culture* 16, no. 1 (2004): 1–29.

Hernández, José M. "¿Fue Varela el primer revolucionario de Cuba?" *Cuban Studies* 28 (1998): 70–82.

Hernández, Rafael. *Mirar a Cuba: Ensayos sobre cultura y sociedad civil*. Havana: Editorial Letras Cubanas, 1999.

Hernández, Rafael, and Haroldo Dilla. "Political Culture and Popular Participation." In *The Cuban Revolution into the 1990s*, edited by Centro de Estudios sobre América, 31–46. Boulder, CO: Westview Press, 1992.

Hoffman, Bert. "Cuba, Civil Society within Socialism—and Its Limits." In *Modern Political Culture in the Caribbean*, edited by Holger Henke and Fred Reno, 302–21. St. Augustine, Trinidad and Tobago: University of the West Indies Press, 2003.

Holbraad, Martin. "Revolución o Muerte: Self-Sacrifice and the Ontology of the Cuban Revolution." *Ethnos: Journal of Anthropology* 79, no. 3 (2014): 365–87.

Holgado Fernández, Isabel. *¡No es fácil! Mujeres cubanas y la crisis revolucionaria.* Barcelona: Icaria Editorial, 2000.

Hooker, Juliet. *Race and the Politics of Solidarity.* Oxford: Oxford University Press, 2009.

Horowitz, Irving Louis. "Castro and the End of Ideology." In *Cuban Communism, 1959–1995*, edited by Irving Louis Horowitz, 861–64. New Brunswick, NJ: Transaction Publishers, 1995.

Howe, Linda. S. *Transgression and Conformity: Cuban Writers after the Revolution.* Madison: University of Wisconsin Press, 2004.

Huberman, Leo, and Paul Sweezy. *Cuba: Anatomy of a Revolution.* New York: Monthly Review Press, 1961.

Hunt, Christopher. *Waiting for Fidel.* Boston: Houghton Mifflin, 1998.

Ibarra Cuesta, Jorge. *Cuba: 1889–1958. Estructura y procesos sociales.* Havana: Editorial de Ciencias Sociales, 1995.

Ibarra Cuesta, Jorge. *Prologue to Revolution: Cuba, 1898–1958.* Boulder: Lynne Rienner, 1998.

"Inauguró Raúl tres cursos de la Escuela Nacional de Dirección de la Economía." *Granma*, March 4, 1976, 1.

"Inicia el Ministerio de Comunicaciones Seminario Nacional de planificación de la Economía." *Granma*, June 16, 1977.

James, Daniel. *Cuba: The First Soviet Satellite in the Americas.* New York: Avon, 1961.

Jatar-Hausmann, Ana Julia. *The Cuban Way: Capitalism, Communism and Confrontation.* West Hartford, CT: Kumarian Press, 1999.

Jenco, Leigh. "'What Does Heaven Ever Say?' A Methods-Centered Approach to Cross-Cultural Engagement." *American Political Science Review* 101 (2007): 741–55.

Kapcia, Antoni. *Cuba: Island of Dreams.* Oxford: Berg, 2000.

Karol, K. S. *Guerrillas in Power: The Course of the Cuban Revolution.* New York: Hill and Wang, 1970.

Kirk, John M. *José Martí: Mentor of the Cuban Nation.* Tampa: University of South Florida Press, 1983.

Kirk, John M., and Leonardo Padura Fuentes, eds. *Culture and the Cuban Revolution: Conversations in Havana.* Gainesville: University Press of Florida, 2001.

Kohan, Néstor. "*Pensamiento Crítico* y el debate por las ciencias sociales en el seno de la Revolución Cubana." In *Crítica y teoría en el pensamiento social latinoamericano*, edited by Fernanda Beigel, 389–437. Buenos Aires: CLACSO, 2006.

Kuhn, Thomas S. *The Structure of Scientific Revolutions.* Chicago: University of Chicago Press, 1964.

Lage Dávila, Carlos. *Enfrentamos el desafío: Entrevista concedida por el Secretario del Consejo de Ministros a Mario Vázquez Raña.* Havana: Editora Política, 1993.

Lage Dávila, Carlos. *Las estrategias ante la situación económica actual.* Havana: Editora Política, 1994.

Lechuga, Vivian, Denia García Ronda, and Rafael Hernández Rodríguez. *Último jueves: Los debates de Temas.* 4 vols. Havana: Ediciones ICAIC, 2004–10.

Leogrande, William M., and Julie M. Thomas. "Cuba's Quest for Economic Independence." *Journal of Latin American Studies* 34, no. 2 (2002): 325–63.

Linden, Ronald H. "Analogies and the Loss of Community: Cuba and East Europe in the 1990s." In *Cuba after the Cold War*, edited by Carmelo Mesa-Lago, 17–58. Pittsburgh: University of Pittsburgh Press, 1993.

Lobe, Jim. "Learn from Cuba, Says World Bank." Inter Press News Service Agency, April 30, 2001.

Lockwood, Lee. *Castro's Cuba, Cuba's Fidel*. Boulder: Westview Press, 1990.

López, Juan J. *Democracy Delayed: the Case of Castro's Cuba*. Baltimore: John Hopkins University Press, 2002.

Luciak, Ilja A. *Gender and Democracy in Cuba*. Gainesville: University Press of Florida, 2007.

Lumsden, Ian. *Machos, Maricones, and Gays: Cuba and Homosexuality*. Philadelphia: Temple University Press, 1996.

Lutgens, Sheryl L. "National Security, the State, and the Politics of U.S.-Cuba Educational Exchange." *Latin American Perspectives* 33, no. 5 (2006): 58–80.

Maceo, Antonio. "Al General José Lamothe." In *Antonio Maceo. Ideología política. Cartas y otros documentos*, 107–9. Havana: Editorial de Ciencias Sociales, 1998.

Maceo, Antonio. "A los cubanos de color." In *Ideología política: Cartas y otros documentos*, 112. Havana: Editorial de ciencias sociales, 1998.

Maceo, Antonio. "Proclama ¡Viva Cuba Independiente! (1879)." In *Ideología política: Cartas y otros documentos*, 106–7. Havana: Editorial de Ciencias Sociales, 1998.

Machado Rodríguez, Darío L. "Democracia, política e ideología: Una opinión después del V Congreso del Partido." *Cuba Socialista* 9 (1998): 48–61.

Machado Rodríguez, Darío L. *Cuba: Ideología revolucionaria*. Havana: Editora Política, 2000.

Mannheim, Karl. *Ideology and Utopia: An Introduction to the Sociology of Knowledge*. New York: Harcourt, 1936.

Mariátegui, José Carlos. *The Heroic and Creative Meaning of Socialism*. Edited by Michael Pearlman. Atlantic Highlands, NJ: Humanities Press, 1996.

Mariátegui, José Carlos. *Seven Interpretive Essays on Peruvian Reality*. Austin: University of Texas Press, 1971.

Marín-Dogan, Michelle. "Civil Society: The Cuban Debate." In *The Changing Dynamic of Cuban Civil Society*, edited by Antoni Kapcia and Alexander I. Gray, 40–64. Gainesville: University Press of Florida, 2008.

Marrero, Levi. *Cuba, economía y sociedad: Azucar, ilustración y conciencia (1762–1868)*. 15 vols. Vol. 1. Madrid: Editorial Playor, 1983.

Martí, José. "Bases del Partido Revolucionario Cubano (1892)." In *Pensamiento cubano, Siglo XIX*, edited by Isabel Monal and Olivia Miranda Francisco, 299–301. Havana: Editorial de Ciencias Sociales, 2002.

Martí, José. "Lectura en la Reunión de Emigrados Cubanos (1880)." In *Pensamiento cubano, Siglo XIX*, edited by Isabel Monal and Olivia Miranda Francisco, 267–89. Havana: Editorial del Ciencias Sociales, 2002.

Martí, José. "Our America." In *José Martí: Selected Writings*, edited and translated by Esther Allen, 288–95. New York: Penguin, 2002.

Martí, José. "Tributes to Karl Marx, Who Has Died." In *Jose Martí: Selected Writings,* edited and translated by Esther Allen, 130–39. New York: Penguin, 2002.
Marx, Karl. *Capital: A Critical Analysis of Capitalist Production.* New York: International Publishers, 1967.
Marx, Karl. *Critique of the Gotha Program.* New York: International Publishers, 1966.
Marx, Karl. "On the Jewish Question." In *The Marx-Engels Reader,* edited by Robert C. Tucker, 26–52. New York: W.W. Norton, 1972.
Marx, Karl. *The German Ideology.* New York: International Publishers, 1947.
Marx, Karl, and Friedrich Engels. "Manifesto of the Communist Party." In *The Marx-Engels Reader,* edited by Robert C. Tucker, 469–500. New York: W.W. Norton, 1967.
Matthews, Herbert L. *The Cuban Story.* New York: George Brazillier, 1961.
Matos, Huber. *Cómo llegó la noche.* Barcelona: TusQuets, 2004.
McFayden, Deirdre. "The Social Repercussions of the Crisis." *NACLA Report on the Americas* 29, no. 2 (1995): 20–22.
Medin, Tzvi. *Cuba: The Shaping of Revolutionary Consciousness.* Translated by Martha Grenzback. Boulder: Lynne Rienner, 1990.
Mena, Jesús. "Garantizarán la implantación y perfeccionamiento del SDPE en el MINCOM." *Granma,* June 4, 1981.
Mesa-Lago, Carmelo. *Cuba in the 1970s: Pragmatism and Institutionalization.* Albuquerque: University of New Mexico Press, 1974.
Mesa-Lago, Carmelo. "The Cuban Economy: Patterns of Continuity and Change." Paper presented at the Latin American Studies Association Annual Meeting, Miami, 2000.
Mesa-Lago, Carmelo. *Dialéctica de la Revolución Cubana: del idealismo carismático al pragmatismo institucional, Biblioteca cubana contemporánea.* Madrid: Playor, 1979.
Mesa-Lago, Carmelo. "On the Objectives and Objectivity of Cubanology: A Response to a Critic from Cuba." *Cuban Studies* 16, no. 1 (1986): 225–33.
Mesa-Lago, Carmelo. "Three Decades of Studies on the Cuban Revolution: Progress, Problems, and the Future." In *Cuban Studies since the Revolution,* edited by Damián Fernández, 9–49. Gainesville: University Press Florida, 1992.
Mills, C. Wright. *Listen Yankee: The Revolution in Cuba.* New York: McGraw-Hill, 1960.
Monal, Isabel, and Olivia Miranda Francisco. *Pensamiento cubano: Siglo XIX.* 2 vols. Vol. 1. Havana: Editorial de ciencias sociales, 2002.
Moore, Robin D. *Music and Revolution: Cultural Change in Socialist Cuba.* Berkeley: University of California Press, 2006.
Morales, Emilio, and Joseph L. Scarpaci. "Opening Up on Both Shorelines Helps Increase Remittances Sent to Cuba in 2011 by 20%." Havana Consulting Group, March 2012. Available at http://www.thehavanaconsultinggroup.com/.
"Muy atrasadas algunas tareas iniciales del balance de relaciones intersectoriales." *Granma,* April 6, 1981.
Navarro, Desiderio. "In Medias Res Republicas: On Intellectuals and Social Criticism in the Cuban Public Sphere." *Napantla: Views from South* 2, no. 2 (2001): 355–71.

Norniella, José. "Aprobado el reglamento general para la utilización del fondo para medidas socioculturales y construcción de viviendas." *Granma*, January 30, 1980.

Norniella, José. "A propósito del mercado paralelo (III): Quien trabaje más y mejor tiene derecho a recibir más de la sociedad." *Granma,* October 16, 1980.

Norniella, José. "Atrasadas la mitad de las empresas del país en la entrega de sus normas de consumo." *Granma*, June 4, 1981.

Norniella, José. "¿Cuántas empresas conocen las consecuencias que entrana el principio de la responsabilidad material por el incumplimiento de los planes?" *Granma,* October 14, 1978.

Norniella, José. "Cumplidas importantes tareas en materia de precios que han ido permitiendo al SDPE crear las bases para el establecimiento de un sistema de precios económicamente fundamentados." *Granma,* June 19, 1982.

Norniella, José. "Dejaron de aportar las empresas más de 48 millones de pesos al presupuesto estatal por concepto de trabajo voluntario." *Granma,* February 19, 1980.

Norniella, José. "Discuten en Sancti Spiritus los principales problemas que afectan el proceso de implantación." *Granma*, April 1, 1982.

Norniella, José. "El aspecto moral del premio tiene para mi un valor tan alto que no se puede pagar ni con todo el dinero del mundo." *Granma*, April 2, 1980.

Norniella, José. "El cálculo económico obliga a dirigentes y obreros de las empresas a proyectarse con nuevas concepciones en el trabajo." *Granma*, August 23, 1980.

Norniella, José. "El control de los inventarios en la construcción es un ejemplo positivo que todos debemos imitar." *Granma*, January 7, 1980.

Norniella, José. "El éxito del SDPE dependerá siempre de la participación consciente y activa de los trabajadores." *Granma*, July 10, 1978.

Norniella, José. "El mercado paralelo: El trabajo y solo el trabajo es la fuente y la base del consumo." *Granma*, October 14, 1980.

Norniella, José. "El premio." *Granma*, May 24, 1980.

Norniella, José. "El rescate de la disciplina estadística es el primer gran resultado inmediato logrado por el Balance de Relaciones Intersectoriales Estadistico (BRIE)." *Granma,* March 10, 1982.

Norniella, José. "Emite JUCEPLAN la Resolución 576 que establece el reglamento general para la utilización del Fondo de Medidas Socioculturales y Construcción de Viviendas." *Granma*, January 31, 1980.

Norniella, José. "Inercia y pasividad en materia arbitral son las características dominantes en las empresas agropecuarias." *Granma*, January 15, 1983, 2.

Norniella, José. "La auditoría es una función administrativa del Estado para prevenir a tiempo los errores indisciplinas." *Granma*, April 4, 1980.

Norniella, José. "La contabilidad en el socialismo (final): El contador y la implantación del Sistema de Dirección y Planificación de la Economía." *Granma*, August 6, 1976, 3.

Norniella, José. "La contabilidad en el socialismo (I): Su relación con la formación económico-social." *Granmma*, August 4, 1976, 4.

Norniella, José. "La contabilidad en el socialismo (II): La contabilidad y el Sistema de Dirección y Planificación de la Economía." *Granma*, August 5, 1976, 5.

Norniella, José. "La implementación del SDPE nos obligó a pensar distinto a como la hacíamos antes, a organizarnos de otra manera, a trabajar pensando en el costo." *Granma,* February 23, 1980.

Norniella, José. "La indisciplina estadística atenta directamente contra la normal coordinación que debe existir entre todos los subsistemas que conforman el SDPE." *Granma,* December 20, 1979.

Norniella, José. "Los estímulos económicos en el socialismo." *Granma*, March 12, 1980.

Norniella, José. "Pasó ayer el banco a créditos vencidos los saldos de los sobregiros en las cuentas de operaciones de las empresas." *Granma,* April 2, 1980.

Norniella, José. "Por cada model del SIEC utilizado para enviar enformacion estadistica, las empresas emiten 1,5 models no aprobados." *Granma,* December 18, 1979.

Norniella, José. "¿Qué nos enseñan las ferias de Bienes de Consumo?" *Granma*, August 27, 1981.

Norniella, José. "Se desarrolla y perfecciona la organización masiva de la enseñanza y entrenamiento de cuadros de dirección económica." *Granma,* June 4, 1981.

Oramas, Joaquin. "Terminó el primer curso para directores de empresas de Ciudad de la Habana." *Granma,* August 23, 1977.

Otero, Gerardo, and Janice O'Bryan. "Cuba in Transition? The Civil Sphere's Challenge to the Castro Regime." *Latin American Politics and Society* 44, no. 4 (Winter 2002): 29–57.

Pastor, Manuel, Jr., and Andrew Zimbalist. "Cuba's Economic Conundrum." *NACLA Report on the Americas*, September–October 1995, 7–12.

Pérez-Stable, Marifeli. *The Cuban Revolution: Origins, Course, and Legacy.* New York: Oxford University Press, 1993.

Pérez-Stable, Marifeli. "The Invisible Crisis: The Exhaustion of Politics in 1990s Cuba." In *Toward a New Cuba: Legacies of a Revolution*, edited by Miguel Angel Centeno and Mauricio Font, 25–38. Boulder: Lynne Rienner, 1997.

Pérez, Humberto. "Humberto Pérez en el Congreso de la ANEC Che: El más destacado economista de nuestro país después del triunfo de la revolución." *Bohemia* 71, no. 25 (June 22, 1979): 51–60.

Pérez, Louis A., Jr. *On Becoming Cuban: Identity, Nationality, and Culture.* Durham: University of North Carolina Press, 1999.

Pérez, Louis A., Jr. *Cuba: Between Reform and Revolution.* Edited by James A. Scobie. New York: Oxford University Press, 1988.

Pérez, Louis A., Jr. "History, Historiography, and Cuban Studies: Thirty Years Later." In *Cuban Studies since the Revolution*, edited by Damián J. Fernández, 53–78. Gainesville: University Press of Florida, 1992.

Pérez, Louis A., Jr., ed. *Slaves, Sugar, and Colonial Society: Travel Accounts of Cuba, 1801–1899.* Wilmington, DE: Scholarly Resources, 1992.

Pérez, Louis A., Jr. Review of *The Limits of Charisma: Cuba under Castro,* by Edward Gonzalez. *The Americas* 3, no. 3 (January 1976): 489.

Pérez Roque, Felipe. "Conferencia de prensa ofrecida por el canciller Felipe Pérez Roque con relación a los mercenarios al servicio del imperio que fueron juzga-

dos los días 3, 4,5 y 7 de abril." Havana: Versiones Taquigráficas, Consejo de Estado, 2003.
Pérez de la Riva, Juan. *Demografía de los culies chinos*. Havana: Pablo de la Torriente Editorial, 1996.
Poyo, Gerald E. *"With All, and for the Good of All": The Emergence of Popular Nationalism in the Cuban Communities of the United States, 1848–1898*. Durham: Duke University Press, 1989.
"Preguntas sobre películas." In *Polémicas culturales de los 60*, edited by Graziella Pogolotti, 145–48. Havana: Editorial Letras Cubanas, 2006.
"Qué película debemos ver? Las mejores." In *Polémicas culturales de los 60*, edited by Graziella Pogolotti, 149–51. Havana: Editorial Letras Cubanas, 2006.
Quintero Herencia, Juan Carlos. *Fulguración del espacio: Letras e imaginario institucional de la Revolución Cubana (1960–1971)*. Rosario: Beatriz Viterbo Editora, 2002.
Quiroga, José. *Cuban Palimpsests*. Minneapolis: University of Minnesota Press, 2005.
"Reorganizan la comisión de implantación del Nuevo Sistema de Dirección y Planificación de la Economía en Cienfuegos." *Granma*, June 7, 1977.
Rice, Donald E. *The Rhetorical Uses of the Authorizing Figure: Fidel Castro and José Martí*. New York: Praeger, 1992.
Rodríguez García, José Luis. *Crítica a nuestros críticos*. Havana: Editorial de Ciencias Sociales, 1988.
Rodríguez García, José Luis. "The So-Called Cubanology and Cuban Economic Development." *Cuban Studies* 16, no. 1 (1986): 211–20.
Rodríguez, Carlos Rafael. "José Martí." In *Letra Con Filo*, vol. 3, 215–24. Havana: Ediciones Unión, 1987.
Rodríguez, Carlos Rafael. "Nuestro Tiempo." In *Letra Con Filo*, vol. 3, 555–58. Havana: Ediciones Unión, 1987.
Ronning, C. Neale. *José Martí and the Émigré Colony in Key West: Leadership and State Formation*. New York: Praeger, 1990.
Rosenthal, Mona. *Inside the Revolution: Everyday Life in Socialist Cuba*. Ithaca: Cornell University Press, 1997.
Ryer, Paul. "Millennium's Past Cuba's Future?" *Public Culture* 12, no. 2 (2000): 499.
Saco, José Antonio. "Ideas sobre la incorporación de Cuba en los Estados Unidos (1848)." In *Contra la anexión: recopilación de sus papales, con prólogo y ultílogo de Fernando Ortíz*, edited by Fernando Ortíz, 95–111. Havana: Instituto Cubano del Libro, Editorial de Ciencias Sociales, 1974.
Saco, José Antonio. Párrafos del 'Paralelo entre la Isla de Cuba y algunas colonias inglesas' (1837)." In *Contra la anexión: recopiliación de sus papales, con prólogo y ultílogo de Fernando Ortíz,* edited by Fernando Ortíz, 77–79. Havana: Instituto Cubano del Libro, Editorial de Ciencias Sociales, 1974.
Saco, José Antonio. "Párrafos de la 'Replica a V. Vásquez Queipo en la polémica con J.A. Saco sobre el incremento de la población blanca en Cuba (1847)." In *Contra la anexión: recopilación de sus papales, con prólogo y ultílogo de Fernando Ortíz*,

edited by Fernando Ortíz, 81–86. Havana: Instituto Cubano del Libro, Editorial de Ciencias Sociales, 1974.

Saco, José Antonio. "Origen del movimiento anexionista en Cuba." In *Contra la anexión: recopiliación de sus papeles, con prólogo y ultílogo de Fernando Ortíz,* edited by Fernando Ortíz, 87–93. Havana: Instituto Cubano del Libro, Editorial de Ciencias Sociales, 1974.

Scott, James C. *Domination and the Arts of Resistance: Hidden Transcripts.* New Haven: Yale University Press, 1992.

Scott, Rebecca J. *Slave Emancipation in Cuba: The Transition to Free Labor, 1860–1899.* Princeton: Princeton University Press, 1985.

"Señalan incumplimientos y deficiencias en la aplicación del SDPE en la provincia Santiago de Cuba." *Granma*, December 25, 1979.

Shelton, Alex. "Preparase Cuba para adoptar formas superiores de organización del trabajo." *Granma*, March 17, 1976, 3.

Silverman, Bertram. "Man and Socialism in Cuba: The Great Debate." In *Man and Socialism in Cuba: The Great Debate*, edited by Bertram Silverman, 3–28. New York: Atheneum, 1971.

Smorkaloff, Pamela Maria. *Readers and Writers in Cuba: A Social History of Print Culture.* New York: Garland, 1997.

Smith, Adam. *An Inquiry into the Nature and Causes of the Wealth of Nations.* Chicago: University of Chicago Press, 1976.

Solaún, Mauricio. "On Political Change in Cuba: A Comparative Introduction." In *Cuba in Transition,* vol. 9, 173–77. Washington, DC: Association for the Study of the Cuban Economy, 1999.

Sousa Santos, Boaventura de. "Why Has Cuba Become a Difficult Problem for the Left?" *Latin American Perspectives* 36, no. 3 (2009): 43–53.

Suárez, Andrés. *Cuba: Castroism and Communism, 1959–1966.* Translated by Joel Carmichael and Ernst Halperin. Cambridge: MIT Press, 1967.

Suárez, Andrés. "Leadership, Ideology and the Political Party." In *Revolutionary Change in Cuba*, edited by Carmelo Mesa-Lago, 3–21. Pittsburgh: University of Pittsburgh Press, 1971.

Sweig, Julia. *Cuba: What Everyone Needs to Know.* Oxford: Oxford University Press, 2009.

Sznajder, Mario, and Luis Roniger. *Politics, Social Ethos and Identity in Contemporary Cuba.* Jerusalem: Harry S. Truman Research Institute for the Advancement of Peace, Hebrew University of Jerusalem, 2001.

Tablada, Carlos. *Economics and Politics in the Transition to Socialism.* New York: Pathfinder, 1989.

Tanuma, Sachiko. "Post-utopian Irony: Cuban Narratives during the 'Special Period' Decade." *PoLAR: Political and Legal Anthropology Review* 30, no. 1 (May 2007): 46–66.

Tesis y resoluciones: Primer congreso del Partido Comunista de Cuba. Havana: Editoral de ciencias sociales, 1978.

Thomas, Hugh. *Cuba; or The Pursuit of Freedom.* Updated ed. New York: Da Capo Press, 1998.

Thomas, Hugh. *The Cuban Revolution.* 2nd ed. New York: Harper and Row, 1971.

Thomas, Megan. *Orientalists, Propagandists, and Illustrados: Filipino Scholarship and the End of Spanish Colonialism.* Minneapolis: University of Minnesota Press, 2012.

Torres-Cuevas, Eduardo, and Oscar Loyola Vega. *Historia de Cuba 1492–1898: Formación y liberación de la nación.* Havana: Editorial Pueblo y Educación, 2001.

Trouillot, Michel-Rolph. *Silencing the Past: Power and the Production of History.* Boston: Beacon Press, 1995.

Unión de Periodistas de Cuba. 2004. Dos fuerzas negativas: El bloqueo y los llamados Independientes. www.cubaperiodistas.cu/libertaddeprensa/principio3.htm. Accessed August 13, 2004.

Valdés, Nelson P. "Estudios cubanos en los Estados Unidos." *Temas* 2 (1995): 5–10.

Valdés, Nelson P. "Ideological Roots of the Cuban Revolutionary Movement." Occasional Paper No. 15. Glasgow: Institute of Latin American Studies, University of Glasgow, 1975.

Valle, Sandra del. "Cine y Revolución: La política cultural del ICAIC en los sesenta." *Perfiles de la cultura Cubana*, January–February 2008.

Varela, Félix. "Consideraciones sobre el estado actual de la isla de Cuba." In *Pensamiento cubano, Siglo XIX*, edited by Isabel Monal and Olivia Miranda, 281–86. Havana: Editorial de Ciencias Sociales, 1824.

Vasquez, Miguel. "Cultural Integrity in Non-traditional Societies: Cuba Encounters the Global Market System." *Cultural Dynamics* 14 (2002): 185–204.

Warner, Michael. *Publics and Counterpublics.* New York: Zone Books, 2002.

Weinreb, Amelia Rosenberg. *Cuba in the Shadow of Change: Daily Life in the Twilight of the Revolution.* Gainesville: University Press of Florida, 2009.

Weppler-Grogan, Doreen. "Cultural Policy, the Visual Arts, and the Advance of the Cuban Revolution in the Aftermath of the Gray Years." *Cuban Studies* 41 (2010): 143–65.

Weyl, Nathaniel. *Red Star over Cuba: The Russian Assault on the Western Hemisphere.* New York: Devin-Adair, 1960.

Whitefield, Mimi, and Juan O. Tomayo. 1996. "Raul Castro's Attack on Intellectuals Stirs Backlash." Knight_Ridder News Service, www.hartford-hwp.com/archives/43b/197.html. Accessed September 2004.

Whitfield, Esther. *Cuban Currency: The Dollar and "Special Period" Fiction.* Minneapolis: University of Minnesota Press, 2008.

Yanes Quintero, Hernán. "Comment." *Cuban Studies* 13, no. 2 (1983): 112–17.

Yúdice, George. *The Expediency of Culture: Uses of Culture in the Global Era.* Durham: Duke University Press, 2003.

Yurchak, Alexei. "Soviet Hegemony of Form: Everything Was Forever, Until It Was No More." *Comparative Studies in Society and History* 45, no. 3 (2003): 480–510.

Zimbalist, Andrew. "Incentives and Planning in Cuba." *Latin American Research Review* 24, no. 1 (1989): 65–93.

Žižek, Slavoj. *First as Tragedy, Then as Farce.* New York: Verso, 2009.

Zurbano, Roberto. "El Rap Cubano: Can't Stop, Won't Stop the Movement!" In *Cuba in the Special Period: Culture and Ideology in the 1990s*, edited by Ariana Hernández-Reguant, 143–58. New York: Palgrave Macmillan, 2009.

Index

academic(s)
  Cuba based, 32, 123–24, 141, 143, 147, 217n4, 237n4 (*see also* Cuban intellectuals)
  exchange between U.S. and Cuba, 123–27, 238n20
  U.S. based, 32, 123–24
Acanda, Jorge, 19, 252n17
Accattone, 78
Acción nacional revolucionaria, 244n18
accounting, 98
Afro-Cuban culture, 64–65, 189, 250n106
Afro-Cuban religious organizations, 18
agrarian reform law (1959), 40, 41, 137
Agramonte, Ignacio, 45, 47–48, 51, 54, 58
agricultural cooperatives: Basic Units of Cooperative Production (UBPCs), 172
agricultural diversification, 91, 92
Aguirre, Mirta, 71, 74, 77, 83
Alias gardelito, 78
alienation, 77
Alonso, Aurelio, 81, 128, 131, 143, 150, 153–55, 206, 242n119
Althusser, Louis 14, 210. *See also* interpellation
Álvarez García, Alberto F., 136, 138, 240n61
amigoism, 119
Amnesty International, 95

anarchists, 41, 181
El ángel exterminador, 78
annexation, 49–52, 55, 96
Anónimo Consejo, 189
Aponte, José Antonio, 49, 53, 222n98
Arango, Arturo, 252n17
Arco Democrático Progresista, 206
Artaraz, Kepa, 81
Asociación Científica Autónoma y No Gubernamental, 127, 215n29
Autonomist Party, 56
Avance, 226n23
Azcuy, Hugo, 240n72

Balaguer, José R., 134, 144
Balance of Statistics on Intersectorial Relations (BRIE), 118
balsero crisis, 168
baseball, 205
Batista Zaldívar, Fulgencio, 30, 34, 38, 41, 61, 65, 91, 105, 164, 244n18
Bay of Pigs Invasion, 66
Bengelsdorf, Carrollee, 151, 247n65
Benjamin, Walter, 162, 163, 174, 191
Benvento, Sergio, 71, 74, 75
Black Cubans, 58, 64, 66
  effects of special period on, 175–76, 247n62, 247n64
black market, 93, 106, 176, 179
Blanco, Juan, 73
blockade, U.S., 7, 17

blogosphere, Cuban, 206, 252*n*21
Bohemia, 96, 105, 108
Boorstein, Edward, 91
bourgeois political economy, 11, 214*n*8
Brotherton, P. Sean, 20, 249*n*99
Budgetary Finance System (revolutionary ethics), 23, 88, 91–92, 109–13, 165. *See also* Guevara, Ernesto "Che"
Buena Fe, 189, 191
Buñuel, Luis, 78
Bureau for the Repression of Communist Activities (BRAC), 73

Cabrera Infante, Guillermo, 65
Caimán Barbudo, 81, 155
Campaign for Peace and Democracy, 154, 252*n*20
capitalism, 93–94, 99, 124, 127, 130, 136, 142, 160, 172, 187, 189, 205–6
capitalist enterprise (vs. socialist), 93, 100, 172
Carabalí, 189, 250*n*105
Carbonell, Walterio, 222*n*98
Carranza Valdés, Julio, 128, 131, 142, 148, 149, 242*n*120
Casa de las Américas, 64, 82
Casal, Lourdes, 247*n*65
Castillo, Arturo, 252*n*17
Castro, Fidel, 2, 5–6, 8, 36–43, 54, 71, 62, 64, 89, 110, 144, 149–51, 153, 161, 164–65, 176, 178, 193–94, 200, 225*n*21, 249*n*93
    analysis of SDPE, 118–19
    as representative of Cuban socialist ideology, 33, 36, 207
    and attack on Moncada Barracks, 38
    declaration of socialist nature of revolution, 66, 164
    "History will Absolve me," 38, 46
    and Marxism-Leninism, 34, 35, 37, 39, 42, 218*n*30
    on invasion of Czechoslovakia, 94–95
    opportunism of, 34, 35, 40, 220*n*53
    "Words to the Intellectuals," 22, 66–72, 75–76, 78–80, 83–84, 87, 132, 152, 154
Castro, Raul, 2, 139, 150–51
    on Cuban NGO's and civil society, 132, 133, 134, 138, 139, 141
    on glasnost, 240*n*56
    sixth party congress, 197, 251*n*11
Castroism, 34, 35
Catholic Church, 18
censorship, 9, 12, 67, 95
Center Félix Varela, 135
Center for Psychological Research, 135, 242*n*119
Center for Research and Development of Cuban Culture "Juan Marinello," 163
Center for Sociopolitical Studies and Public Opinion, 134
Center for the Study of America (Centro de Estudios sobre America or CEA), 18, 23, 122–26, 206, 213*n*7, 241*n*100
    academic production of, 127–32
    defense of, 138–50
    definition of political unity, 151–56
    members and their dispersal, 238*n*28, 240*n*58, 240*n*72, 242*n*119
    parallels to *Pensamiento Crítico*, 135–80
    Raul Castro's criticism of, 132–35
Center for the Study of the Cuban Economy (CEEC), 242*n*120
Central Committee of the Cuban Communist Party, 72, 127, 138
Central Planning Board (Junta Central de Planificación or JUCEPLAN), 92, 97, 105, 114
Céspedes, Carlos Manuel de, 45, 48, 52–54, 56, 163, 222*n*94
Chanan, Michael, 66, 67
CIMEX S.A., 194, 243*n*1
Cienfuegos, Camilo, 29 (*photo*)

Cine Cubano, 73
civil society, 15–21, 127, 136, 153, 204, 210, 214n21
   socialist civil society, 19, 24–25, 122, 136
   and Track II, 132
class, 13, 41, 58, 61
   and character of culture, 71, 74, 76, 77, 80
CNC. *See* National Council for Cuban Culture
Coatsworth, John H., 153
Cold War, 22, 34–35, 93
Commission for the Study and Classification of Film (CECP), 66
Committees for the Defense of the Revolution (CDRs), 86, 182, 214n18
communism, 6, 34–35, 39, 42, 53, 58, 65, 88–90, 97, 103, 106, 110-111, 113, 177, 192, 218n30
Communist Party of Cuba, 3, 8, 12, 46, 64, 89, 95, 97, 127–28, 132, 134–35, 169, 179, 213n5, 248n82. *See also* Partido Communista de Cuba (PCC)
comparative political theory, 15
Concilio Cubano, 18
Congresses of the Cuban Communist Party, 8
   first (1975), 89, 97, 109–10
   second (1980), 118–19
   third (1985), 89, 135
   fourth, 139, 200
   fifth (1995), 134
   sixth (2011), 194, 197, 200, 203
consciousness, 99, 100–101, 103, 116, 118–19
constitution of Cuba (1940), 35, 38
constitution of Cuba (1975), 103, 248n82
consumerism, 24, 157, 159, 176, 188, 209
Council for Mutual Economic Assistance (CMEA or COMECON), 92, 94, 166–67, 178, 231n18, 245n22.

   See also Soviet trading block
   effects of its disappearance on Cuba, 166–67, 178
Council of Ministers, Cuban, 178
counterpublic, 210, 253n34
Creole planters, 49–51, 58
Criterios, 136, 252n17
Cuadernos de Nuestra América (*CNA*), 128, 131, 135, 136, 140
Cuba Socialista, 46, 71, 74
Cuban Armed Forces (FAR), 64, 83
Cuban Democracy Act (Torricelli bill), 127. *See also* Track II
Cuban Foreign Investment Act. *See* Law-Decree 77
Cuban leadership, 12, 30, 42, 45, 71, 141, 169
Cuban peso (moneda nacional), 172, 180, 197
Cuban press, 90, 95, 96, 246n58
Cuban public, 71, 78, 80
Cuban Revolution, 18, 20, 23, 30, 73. *See also* institutionalization
   historiography of, 22–23, 48, 244n15
   as process, 5, 34, 39
   studies of, 3, 33–35
Cuban Revolutionary Party. *See* Partido Revolucionario Cubano (PRC)
Cuban Studies, 124–25
Cuban studies, 124–25, 136
Cuban Women's Federation. *See* FMC
Cubania, 10, 47, 59–60, 194
cubanologist and cubanology, 124–25, 132–33, 237n9
cuentapropista, 175, 197–99 (*photos*), 201. *See also* self-employment
culture, 71, 76
   popular, 187–88
   relationship to revolution, 64, 67, 76, 80
   Western European bourgeois, 69–70, 74
Czechoslovakia, Soviet invasion of (1968), 82–83, 93

Dalton, Roque, 82, 229*n*128
Delgado, Frank, 188, 250*n*104
democracy, 94, 128, 145, 206, 208
Depestre, Rene, 82
Desnoes, Edmundo, 82, 84, 86
dialectical image(s), 162–63, 168, 184
dialectical materialism, 74, 76. *See also* Marx, Karl
Diario de la Marina, 41, 226*n*23
Diáz Castañon, Maria del Pilar, 41
Diáz, Jesús, 154–55
Dilla, Haroldo, 19, 128–32, 142, 145–46, 148, 153–54, 170, 183, 237*n*2, 242*n*119
Directorio Revolucionario (DR), 71, 217*n*9. *See also* Revolutionary Directorate
discourse, 13
dissidents, 17–19, 21, 133, 180, 104, 206, 216*n*34, 220*n*60, 252*n*20
doble-moral (double morality), 12, 177
dogmatism, 74–75, 85, 143
La dolce vita, 78
dollar stores, 184
Domínguez, Jorge, 124–26, 129–30, 148
Dorticós, Osvaldo, 66, 225*n*21

Eagleton, Terry, 15
Eastern Europe, 7, 18, 127, 245*n*22
  market socialism, 91, 231*n*13
Eckstein, Susan, 100–101
Economía y Desarrollo, 101
economic accounting system (self-management), 91, 113
economic calculus, 23, 88, 91, 99–101, 109–13, 116, 118–19, 165. *See also* SDPE
economic determinism, 13
economic rationality, 91. *See also* economic accounting system
economic stimulus funds, 114, 117, 235*n*102
economy, 6
  centrally planned, 12, 16, 90

education, 37, 40, 70, 107, 172, 175–76, 182, 195, 201, 209, 218*n*30, 247*n*65
  free, 4, 7, 10, 63–64, 130, 156, 179–80, 182–83, 187, 249*n*98
  ideological, 84, 89, 104
elections, 13, 19, 128, 249*n*94
emulation, 114
Encuentro de la Cultura Cubana, 154
EPG&B, 189, 250*n*106
ethnography and fieldwork, 1, 18, 20, 213*n*1
equality, 90, 103–4, 159, 186
  abstract/political, 10, 103
  racial, 48, 52, 56, 59, 203
  socioeconomic, 10, 24, 48, 90, 93, 103, 121, 123, 130, 166, 205
escuelas del campo, 203
Espín, Vilma, 176
Estado de SATS, 207
exiles, Cuban, 45, 55–57

Fagan, Richard, 40
Family Code (1975), 175
Farber, Samuel, 207
farmers' markets, free, 172
Federation of Cuban Women (FMC), 135, 176, 240*n*60
Fernandes, Sujatha, 20, 251*n*109
Fernández Retamar, Roberto, 46, 82, 84, 86
Fellini, Federico, 78
Feuerbach, Ludwig, 77
fidelismo, 46
firm autonomy, 99–100, 110, 116–17, 119, 131
First Congress of Latin American Youth (1960). *See* Guevara, Ernesto "Che"
"Five heroes" (the Cuban five), 202, 203 (*photo*)
Flo, Juan J., 72, 75, 83
foreign investment in Cuba, 171–73, 246*n*53
foreign policy, Cuban, 139
Fornet, Abrosio, 82–86

Foucault, Michel, 13–14
Fraga, Jorge, 72, 76–77
Franqui, Carlos, 39, 65
free market, 16, 179, 191. *See also* market
freedom of expression, 3, 95, 122, 125, 138, 152, 190, 249n94
Freeden, Michael, 2–3, 15
Fuerzas Armadas Revolucionarias (FAR). *See* Cuban Armed Forces
functionaries, 117, 213n5
Fusco, Coco, 176, 247n68

La Gaceta de Cuba, 71–73
García Buchaca, Edith, 65–66, 71, 74, 76, 83
García Espinosa, Julio, 72–73, 77–78
gender, 82, 175, 203, 219n44, 246n59
Giuliano, Maurizio, 136–37, 240n64, 240n65, 240n78
global capital, 19, 93, 187
Gómez, Máximo, 45, 54–55
Gómez, Sara, 72
González, Elián, 202, 219n43
González Núñez, Gerardo, 136
Gramsci, Antonio, 11, 14, 19, 41–42, 180, 190, 219n50
Granma, 89, 96, 100, 104–6, 115–16, 119, 132, 167, 232n36
Great Debate (1962–65), 60, 91, 109, 166. *See also* Guevara, Ernesto "Che"
Gray Years (1971–76), 62, 82, 252n17. *See also* Quiquenio Gris
Guerra Chiquita, 56
Guevara, Alfredo, 72, 79, 80, 151, 227n46
Guevara, Ernesto "Che," 5, 6, 48 (*photo*), 61, 80, 108, 119, 160, 194. *See also* Great Debate (1962–65)
    on budgetary finance system, 23, 88, 91–92, 109–13, 165
    on economic calculus, 91, 101, 110–12
    Marxism of, 61, 64, 113, 130, 228n85
    new man, 93, 235n101
    on material incentives, 36, 91, 110–12
    on moral incentives, 36, 91

Guillén, Nicolas M., 72
Gutiérrez Alea, Tomás, 72, 77, 79, 81–82
Gutiérrez, Carlos Maria, 82
Gutiérrez, Luis, 128, 130

El Habanero, 50
Haitian Revolution (1789), 44, 56, 49. *See also* Trouillot, Michel-Rolph
hard currency, 159, 167, 171, 186, 249n96
Harnecker, Marta, 105
Hart, Armando, 66, 151
health care, 10, 20, 179–80, 182
Hearne, Adrian, 20
Hegel, Friedrich, 16, 19, 77
hegemony, 65–66, 180
Hernández, Rafael, 19, 126, 128, 136, 143, 153, 169, 206, 242n119, 252n17
Hernández-Reguant, Ariana, 19
hidden transcripts, 216n45
hip-hop, 189, 251n109
historical materialism, 77, 163
history, 22, 38, 44, 46, 162
    as progress, 162, 168, 191
Hobbes, Thomas, 53
Holbraad, Martin, 181
Holguín, 163, 165, 180
homosexuals, 83, 225n12
housing, 10, 114, 179, 249n98, 252n13
Hoy, 64, 71, 78–79
humanism, 190

idealism, 16, 76–77, 93, 120
    German philosophical tradition, 77, 86 (*see also* Hegel, Friedrich; Marx, Karl)
    opposed to pragmatism, 16, 88–89, 90, 93
ideological bias, 124, 126
ideological struggle, 132, 141–42, 145–47
ideology, 8–15, 30, 37, 42, 57, 62, 72, 74, 144, 197, 209
    as an object of study, 27–33
    and history, 11, 44
    instrumental use of, 22, 30, 60
    living, 1–2, 9–13, 159–60

ideology (*continued*)
  socialist, Cuban, 1–12, 16–18, 20–22, 24, 28, 30, 32–34, 36, 40, 42, 54, 56, 59, 61–63, 81, 89, 96, 98, 121, 159, 162, 166, 182–83, 186–87, 191–93, 196, 201–2, 204–5, 207–8
  imperialism, 46, 66, 72–74, 79, 82, 93–94, 127–28, 139, 218*n*21
  anti-imperialism, 44, 145, 183, 187
independence, Cuban, 22, 33, 48, 50, 56–57, 137, 173. *See also* Cuban Wars of Independence
industrialization, 91, 92
inequality, 179, 201, 224*n*8, 248*n*85
  racial, 59, 203
El Instituto Cubano de Arte e Industria Cinematográficos (ICAIC), 64–67, 69, 71, 72–76, 79–82
Instituto de filosofía, 237*n*2
institutionalization, 71, 83, 120
Integrated Revolutionary Organizations (ORI), 71
intellectuals, Cuban, 22–23, 48, 69, 75–76, 81–82, 85–86, 122, 146, 168–69, 202, 205, 250*n*100
  as revolutionary, 71, 85, 140
  on ideology, 27, 61
  on intellectual production, 62–63, 67
  view of civil society, 19, 219*n*49
interpellation, 14. *See also* Althusser, Louis

jinetero(a)s and *jineterismo*, 7, 174–77, 189, 243*n*5, 247*n*64, 247*n*65, 247*n*68
Juventud Rebelde, 81

Kapcia, Antonio, 59–60
Kirk, John, 46
Kohan, Néstor, 229*n*123

labor, 41, 93, 103, 173, 201, 222*n*222
  voluntary, 115–16, 181
Lage, Carlos, 144, 178, 200
Latin America, 58, 60–61, 81, 92, 125, 127, 131, 136, 139, 142, 168, 197

Latin American Perspectives, 128
Latin American Studies Association (LASA), 154, 217*n*4
Law-Decree 50 (Cuban Foreign Investment Act; 1982), 172. *See also* foreign investment
Law-Decree 77 (Cuban Foreign Investment Act; 1995) 172. *See also* foreign investment
Law-Decree 140 (legalization of U.S. dollars), 171. *See also* U.S. dollars
Law-Decree 141 (self-employment law), 171. *See also* self-employment
Law-Decree 142, 172. *See also* Basic Units of Cooperative Production
Law-Decree 171 (regulating private bed and breakfasts; 1997), 173
law of value, 102, 111–13, 117, 235*n*101
Lenin, V.I., 39, 44, 98, 165, 228*n*85
liberals, 208–9
  Cuban, 23, 41, 57, 62–63, 67, 85–86, 176, 225*n*21
liberalism, 4, 25, 52, 90, 130, 205, 208, 219*n*51
  conception of civil society, 19, 204
  pluralism, 124, 128
  subjectivity, 181
Literacy Campaign, 40, 219*n*44
llamamiento (the call), 135, 169
Locke, John, 208
Lockwood, Lee, 37
Lunes de Revolución, 64–66, 71

Maceo, Antonio, 44–45, 47, 48 (*photo*), 54–56
Machado, Dario L., 134, 138, 153
Magín, 135, 240*n*60
Maleconazo, 168, 249*n*93
Mannheim, Karl, 60
Mariátegui, José Carlos, 14, 228*n*85
market(s), 7, 11, 16, 19, 24, 50, 73, 88–89, 98, 101, 104, 112, 116–17, 130, 159, 173, 187, 204
  parallel, 23, 89, 103–7
  world, 94, 131

market mechanisms, 23, 89, 92–93, 98–99, 111, 132, 165–66, 171
marketization, 24, 157, 183
Martí, José, 54–59, 73, 193, 194 (slogans), 248n82
  in Cuban historiography, 45, 47
  and Marxism, 44–46, 58
  "Our America," 58
  Partido Revolucionario Cubano, 45, 56, 58
Martiano, 46, 203
Marx, Karl, 23, 35, 58, 72, 98, 108, 160, 165, 214n21, 228n85, 234n80
  Critique of the Gotha Program, 23, 103
  The Economic and Philosophic Manuscripts of 1844, 113
  The German Ideology, 86, 108, 234n79
  Manifesto of the Communist Party, 37, 234n80
  use in Cuban academic production, 146
Marxism and Marxist theory, 4–5, 11, 13, 30, 35, 39, 61, 70, 75–77, 81, 130, 136, 143, 237n2. *See also* Marxism-Leninism
  and Martí, 45–46, 58
  Latin American, 194
  and Cuban intellectuals, 61, 75–77, 81, 127, 135–36, 143, 145
Marxism-Leninism, 30, 33–34, 44, 71–78, 81, 87, 135
  of Fidel Castro, 34–35, 37, 46
material incentives, 23, 36, 92, 99, 106–7, 112, 166. *See also* Guevara, Ernesto "Che"
  and SDPE, 114, 115
materialism, 13, 76
Medin, Tzvi, 43–44
Memories of Underdevelopment, 82
Mesa-Lago, Carmelo, 125, 217n6
Military Intelligence Service (SIM), 73
Monal, Isabel, 53
Moncada barracks attack, 38, 165
monetary mercantile categories, 101, 120

Monreal, Pedro, 128, 130, 143, 149, 242n120
Moore, Robin, 20
moral incentives, 23, 36, 92, 110, 165, 166. *See also* Guevara, Ernesto "Che"
multiparty system, 128
Murúa, Lautaro, 78

National Association of Cuban Economists, 108
National Council for Culture (CNC), 64, 66, 69, 79
National Printing House, 64, 69
nationalism, Cuban, 33, 138, 159, 186, 194, 201, 244n15
  and cubanidad, 59
  inclusive, 1, 10, 6, 166
  in Martí, 56–57
  relationship to socialism, 34, 43–44
nationalization, 40, 92
Navarro, Desiderio, 19, 168, 205–6
neoliberalism, 142, 178, 190, 211, 215n28
New Association Act, 18
New Left Review, 82
nongovernmental organizations (NGOs), 16, 18–19, 122, 127, 132, 136, 215n28, 215n31, 216n32
Norniella, José, 96
Nuestro Tiempo, 227n46
nueva trova, 188

Obama, Barack, 209
Omni Zona Franca, 207
opinion polls, 13, 180
opositor (as term), 180–81. *See also* dissidents
opportunism, 35, 90, 124, 148
Organizaciones Revolucionarias Integradas (ORI). *See* Integrated Revolutionary Organizations
Organs of Popular Power (OPP), 100, 248n82

País, Frank, 244n18
Pact of Zanjon (1878), 55

Padilla, Herberto, 83, 155
Padura, Leonardo, 252*n*17
Partido Comunista de Cuba (PCC), 46, 65, 139. *See also* Communist Party, Cuban
Partido Socialista Popular (PSP), 34, 36, 46, 65, 71, 217*n*9
Partido Revolucionario Cubano (PRC), 45–46, 56–57. *See also* Martí, José
Pastors for Peace, 133
Pensamiento Crítico, 81–82, 134, 135–36, 151, 154–55, 240*n*58, 240*n*72
Pérez, Humberto, 81, 105–11, 113, 165
Pérez Jr., Louis, 40, 220*n*56
Pérez-Roque, Felipe, 256*n*9
período especial. *See* Special Period in Times of Peace
Platt Amendment (1901), 164
Plaza Carlos III, 157, 184, 185 (*photo*), 186, 193–94, 197, 200 (*photo*), 202, 205
P.M., 66, 79
political pluralism, 130, 148
popular participation, 129–31, 136, 169, 186, 207–8, 239*n*37
Popular Socialist Party (PSP). *See* Partido Socialista Popular
Poyo, Gerald, 57
pragmatism, 89, 93, 107, 109, 120, 211
  opposed to idealism, 16, 88, 96, 103, 120
Prensa Libre, 226*n*23
principle(s)
  as components of ideology, 1–2, 9–10, 12, 47
  of Cuban socialism, 24, 90, 97, 103, 105, 107–8, 122, 141, 148, 159, 194, 204
  market, 24, 88
profit criteria, 91–92, 101, 110
proletariat(n), 75, 77, 80
property, 104, 132
  forms of in Cuba, 7
  private, 7, 77, 100, 130, 166

post-Soviet Cuba, 157, 162. *See also* Special Period in Times of Peace
public sphere, 62, 159, 168, 207, 210, 252*n*17

Quiquenio Gris (1971–76), 62. *See also* Gray Years
Quintero Herencia, Juan Carlos, 68

race, 58, 82, 136
racism, 6, 8, 57, 59, 175, 188
Radio Martí, 45, 151
rap, 250*n*107. *See also* hip-hop
ration cards (*libretas*), 89, 103–6, 181, 203, 233*n*64
Reagan, Ronald, 45
Rectification Campaign of Ideological Errors and Negative Tendencies, 89, 119–20, 135, 166, 172, 230*n*3
Red Observatorio Crítico, 207
remittances, 7, 246*n*43
Reporters without Borders, 95–96
Revista Casa de las Américas, 64, 82
Revolución, 39, 64–66
"Revolution betrayed" thesis, 30–31, 36, 41–42, 45
Revolutionary Directorate, 217*n*9
revolutionary government (post-1959), 61–64
Revolutionary Offensive (1968), 83, 92–93, 166
rights, 14, 53, 130, 206
Roca, Blas, 72, 78–80, 83
Rodiles, Antonio G., 207. *See also* Estado de SATS
Rodríguez, Carlos Rafael, 46–48, 72
Rodríguez García, José Luis, 125
Rodríguez, Silvio, 192
Rosenthal, Mona, 180, 190
Rousseau, Jean-Jacques, 19, 53
Ryer, Paul, 161–62

Saco, José Antonio, 45, 47–49, 51–52, 55–57
sacrifice, 165–66, 181, 187, 193–94

salaries, 98, 107, 114, 172, 180
Sanchez, Yoani, 206
Santamaría, Abel, 163, 165
Sartre, Jean-Paul, 39–40
self determination, 145
self-employment, 92, 132, 137, 171–73, 197, 202–3, 246*n*45. *See also* cuentapropista; Law-Decree 141
self-interest, 93, 108
self-management system. *See* economic rationality
sexism, 175
slavery, 48–50, 52, 56–57, 221*n*77
   abolition of, 50–52, 56, 221*n*80
   slave uprisings, 49, 50
Smith, Adam, 108, 160, 234*n*81
social justice, 123, 131, 138
social security, 179
social services, 104, 132, 180, 182–83, 186–87
socialism, 1, 129, 145
   Cuban, 12, 59, 178–79, 183, 206 (*see also under* ideology)
socialist labor ethic, 159
socialist realism, 62, 65, 67, 75, 80
Solas, Humberto, 72
Soto, Lionel, 81
Sousa Santos, Boaventura de, 121
sovereignty, 121, 202
Soviet Union, 6, 18, 83, 164, 174, 177, 194, 248*n*82
   Cuba's relative autonomy from, 125
   invasion of Czechosovakia, 83, 94 (*see also* Czechoslovakia)
   model of economic planning, 88 (*see also* System of Management and Planning of the Economy)
   trading block, 6, 8, 131, 166–67, 179 (*see also* Council for Mutual Economic Assistance)
   view of Cuban socialism in 1960s, 36, 218*n*21
Spanish-American War, 164
Special Period in Times of Peace (Periodo especial en tiempos de paz), 6, 127–28, 157, 160–61, 174–75, 177–78, 184, 191, 200, 207, 213*n*4. *See also* post-Soviet Cuba
spheres, 1, 12, 17, 81, 159, 207, 208, 210, 211. *See also* public sphere
   academic, 21, 24, 81, 122, 205
   official, 63, 81
   popular, 21, 81
structural adjustment, 178
Suárez, Luis, 128, 134, 138
sugar, 92, 119
supply and demand, 98, 117
System of Management and Planning of the Economy (SDPE), 23, 88–90, 92, 96–98, 100, 102, 105, 110, 113–14, 118, 165–66, 232*n*36, 236*n*129

Tanumo, Sachuko, 177
teleology, 31, 244*n*15
Temas, 136, 182, 205–6
Ten Million Ton Sugar Drive, 92
Ten Years War, 54–57
Tiendas para la Recuperación de Divisas, 246*n*42. *See also* dollar stores
Todos Unidos, 18
totalitarian(ism), 13–14, 121, 155
tourism, 132, 171, 174, 179, 249*n*99
Track II, 127, 132, 135, 138. *See also* civil society; Cuban Democracy Act
Tropicola, 93, 184
Trouillot, Michel-Rolph, 44. *See also* Haitian Revolution
26th of July Movement, 34–36, 38–40, 62–65, 71, 85, 164, 227*n*46, 244*n*18

UMAP (Military Units to Assist Production), 82–83, 155
UNEAC (National Union of Cuban Writers and Artists), 71, 83, 151
unemployment, 224*n*8
Unión, 71
Union of Communist Youth (UJC), 181, 200

Union of Journalists of Cuba, 96
unions, 101, 131
United States
  as object of study, 127
  Civil War, 51
  relations with Cuba, 133
  role of ideology in, 25, 208
  threats to Cuba from, 121
U.S. dollar(s)
  access to, 7, 171, 174, 180, 197, 249*n*96
  legalization of, 157, 171–74, 243*n*1, 246*n*43. *See also* Law Decree 140
  replaced with pesos convertibles, 197, 249*n*96
  via remittances, 174
U.S. Embargo (blockade 1962–present), 119, 179
U.S. imperialism. *See* imperialism
U.S. State Department, 32, 217*n*4
unity, political, understanding of, 1, 120–23, 134, 138, 144, 148–49, 151–53, 159, 186, 205
  meaning of in 19th century debates, 54–58
  as socioeconomic equality, 43
University of Havana, 81, 101, 135, 181, 229*n*123, 240*n*58
urban gardens, 207
Uz, Félix de la, 81

Valdés, Nelson, 42
Valdés Paz, Juan, 128, 131, 143, 153, 242*n*119, 242*n*123, 243*n*130
vanguard, 85, 106
Varela, Carlos, 188, 250*n*102, 250*n*103
Varela, Félix, 47–50, 56–57
Varela Project, 182, 249*n*94
Verde Olivo, 64, 83, 224*n*2
voluntarism, 91, 194

wage differentials, 114, 246*n*57
Wars of Independence, 44–45, 163. *See also* Guerra Chiquita; Ten Years War
welfare state, 187
Western political thought, 15
Whitfield, Esther, 159
women, 16, 135–36, 162, 175–76, 219*n*44, 243*n*5, 246*n*59, 247*n*65
worker(s), 100–101, 131, 207
World Bank Development Indicators, 179
World Press Freedom Committee, 95, 231*n*27

Yanes, Hernán, 124–25, 237*n*16
Yurchak, Alexei, 177

Zimbalist, Andrew, 98, 99
Žižek, Slavoj, 209–10